DATE DUE

DEMCO 38-296

CONTEMPORARY MUSICIANS

ISSN 1044-2197

CONTEMPORARY MUSICIANS

PROFILES OF THE PEOPLE IN MUSIC

MICHAEL L. LaBLANC,
Editor

VOLUME 3

Includes Cumulated Indexes

 **Gale Research Inc.** · *DETROIT* · *NEW YORK* · *LONDON*

STAFF

Michael L. LaBlanc, *Editor*

Stephen Advokat, Shelly Andrews, Victoria France Charabati, Laurie Collier, Carleton Copeland,
Robert Dupuis, Christine Ferran, Joan Goldsworthy, Gary Graff, Motoko Fujishiro Huthwaite,
Anne Janette Johnson, Kyle Kevorkian, Jeanne M. Lesinski, Meg Mac Donald, Greg Mazurkiewicz,
Louise Mooney, Robert Nagel, Nancy Pear, Jon Saari, Calen D. Stone, Elizabeth Thomas,
and Denise Wiloch, *Contributing Editors*

Peter M. Gareffa, *Senior Editor*

Jeanne Gough, *Permissions Manager*
Patricia A. Seefelt, *Permissions Supervisor (Pictures)*
Margaret A. Chamberlain, *Permissions Associate*
Pamela A. Hayes and Lillian Quickley, *Permissions Assistants*

Mary Beth Trimper, *Production Manager*
Marilyn Jackman, *External Production Assistant*
Arthur Chartow, *Art Director*
Cynthia Baldwin, *Graphic Designer*
C.J. Jonik, *Keyliner*

Laura Bryant, *Production Supervisor*
Louise Gagné, *Internal Production Associate*

Special thanks to the Biography Division Research staff

Cover Illustration: *John Kleber*

Copyright © 1990
Gale Research Inc.
835 Penobscot Bldg.
Detroit, MI 48226-4094

Library of Congress Catalog Card Number 89-7123
ISBN 0-8103-2213-7
ISSN 1044-2197

Printed in the United States of America
Published simultaneously in the United Kingdom by Gale Research
International Limited (An affiliated company of Gale Research Inc.)

Computerized photocomposition by
Roberts/Churcher
Derby Line, Vermont

Contents

Introduction   ix

Photo Credits   xi

Cumulative Subject Index   251

Cumulative Musicians Index   259

Introduction

Fills the Information Gap on Today's Musicians

Contemporary Musicians profiles the colorful personalities in the music industry who create or influence the music we hear today. Prior to *Contemporary Musicians*, no quality reference series provided comprehensive information on such a wide range of artists despite keen and ongoing public interest. To find biographical and critical coverage, an information seeker had little choice but to wade through the offerings of the popular press, scan television "infotainment" programs, and search for the occasional published biography or expose. *Contemporary Musicians* is designed to serve that information seeker, providing in one ongoing source in-depth coverage of the important figures on the modern music scene in a format that is both informative and entertaining. Students, researchers, and casual browsers alike can use *Contemporary Musicians* to fill their needs for personal information about the artists, find a selected discography of the musician's recordings, and read an insightful essay offering biographical and critical information.

Provides Broad Coverage

Single-volume biographical sources on musicians are limited in scope, focusing on a handful of performers from a specific musical genre or era. In contrast, *Contemporary Musicians* offers researchers and music devotees a comprehensive, informative, and entertaining alternative. *Contemporary Musicians* is published twice yearly, with each volume providing information on 80 to 100 musical artists from all the genres that form the broad spectrum of contemporary music—pop, rock, jazz, blues, country, new wave, New Age, blues, folk, rhythm and blues, gospel, bluegrass, and reggae, to name a few, as well as selected classical artists who have achieved "crossover" success with the general public. *Contemporary Musicians* will occasionally include profiles of influential nonperforming members of the music industry, including producers, promoters, and record company executives.

Includes Popular Features

In *Contemporary Musicians* you'll find popular features that users value:

- **Easy-to-locate data sections**—Vital personal statistics, chronological career summaries, listings of major awards, and mailing addresses, when available, are prominently displayed in a clearly marked box on the second page of each entry.

- **Biographical/critical essays**—Colorful and informative essays trace each personality's personal and professional life, offer representative examples of critical response to each artist's work, and provide entertaining personal sidelights.

- **Selected discographies**—Each entry provides a comprehensive listing of the artist's major recorded works.

- **Photographs**—Most entries include portraits of the artists.

- **Sources for additional information**—This invaluable feature directs the user to selected books, magazines, and newspapers where more information on listees can be obtained.

Helpful Indexes Make It Easy to Find the Information You Need

Contemporary Musicians features a Musicians Index, listing names of individual performers and musical groups, and a Subject Index that provides the user with a breakdown by primary musical instruments played and by musical genre.

We Welcome Your Suggestions

The editors welcome your comments and suggestions for enhancing and improving *Contemporary Musicians*. If you would like to suggest musicians or composers to be covered in the future, please submit these names to the editors. Mail comments or suggestions to:

The Editor
Contemporary Musicians
Gale Research Inc.
835 Penobscot Bldg.
Detroit, MI 48226-4094
Phone : (800) 521-0707
Fax: (313) 961-6241

Photo Credits

Permission to reproduce photographs appearing in *Contemporary Musicians*, Volume 3, was received from the following sources:

AP/Wide World Photos: pp. 1, 3, 6, 11, 13, 22, 32, 35, 39, 41, 44, 46, 51, 53, 56, 59, 61, 64, 67, 71, 74, 77, 80, 85, 87, 92, 95, 100, 108, 111, 113, 117, 119, 121, 127, 129, 133, 136, 138, 142, 145, 147, 149, 152, 162, 165, 167, 170, 172, 175, 177, 179, 182, 188, 190, 199, 203, 206, 208, 210, 217, 219, 221, 225, 233, 236, 238, 241, 248; **© 1989 Susan Plummer:** pp. 16, 18; **UPI/Bettmann Newsphotos:** pp. 25, 82, 124, 155; **The Bettmann Archive:** p. 28; **© Tim Bauer/Retna Ltd.:** p. 90; **Courtesy of the Country Music Foundation, Inc.:** pp. 103, 192; **Courtesy of Warner Brothers Records:** p. 158; **Courtesy of Columbia Artists Management Inc.:** p. 185; **© Tannen Baum/Sygma:** p. 195; **Reuters/Bettmann Newsphotos:** p. 245.

CONTEMPORARY MUSICIANS

Paula Abdul

Singer, dancer, choreographer

A multi-faceted performer, Paula Abdul has made a name for herself as a dancer, choreographer, and vocalist. She is one of the most sought-after choreographers in Hollywood, demanded by entertainers of all kinds, and her 1988 debut album, *Forever Your Girl,* launched her career as a popular vocalist.

Born on June 19, 1962, Paula is the second daughter of Harry and Lorraine Abdul. Paula's father, of Syrian and Brazilian extraction, was a livestock dealer, and her mother, a Jewish French-Canadian, worked at the Hollywood film studios and was for many years an assistant to director Billy Wilder. Paula and her sister Wendy, seven years her senior, grew up in North Hollywood in a middle-class area known as the Condos. Paula started dancing at age seven, about the same time that her parents divorced. Soon she was spending her summers performing with Young Americans, a traveling theatrical musical group. At age ten she studied tap and jazz dancing and won a scholarship to study with Joe Tramaine and the Bella Lewitzky Company.

Abdul was influenced by the musical tastes of her sister, who introduced her to the music of such singers as Joni Mitchell, Stevie Wonder, Carole King, and Iron Butterfly. Abdul started singing while in her teens and participated in many activities during her years at Van Nuys High School, which had been attended by such celebrities as Marilyn Monroe and Robert Redford. Abdul was head cheerleader, class president, a flutist in the orchestra, and a member of the science team.

In 1980, Abdul beat out hundreds of others for a job with the Laker Girls, the Los Angeles Lakers basketball team's professional cheerleading squad. In the early 1980s, Abdul was also a student at Cal State Northridge, where she studied radio and television sportscasting. But what had started as just fun became a job that lasted six years. After her first year with the Laker Girls, Abdul was choreographing the routines, in which she emphasized dancing and de-emphasized the gymnastics of cheerleading. Abdul maintains that she did some of her best choreography while with the Laker Girls.

Because there are many people from the entertainment business in the stands at Lakers games, Abdul's work with the Laker Girls was an advertisement for her choreographic skills. In 1984, after seeing her at a Lakers game, the Jacksons asked Abdul to choreograph a routine for the cut "Torture" from their *Victory* album. Scared and unsure of herself, Abdul nevertheless jumped at the opportunity. "My only problem was how to tell the Jacksons how to dance," she told Dennis Hunt of the *Los Angeles Times.* "Imagine me telling *them* what routines to do." She then worked as a private

Full name, Paula Julie Abdul; born June 19, 1963, in Los Angeles, Calif.; daughter of Harry (a livestock dealer) and Lorraine (a concert pianist and in the motion picture industry) Abdul. *Education:* Studied tap and jazz dancing with Joe Tramine and the Bella Lewitzky Company; attended California State University, Northridge, c. 1981-82.

Member of and choreographer for the Laker Girls (cheerleading squad of Los Angeles Lakers professional basketball team), 1982-88; choreographer of dance routines for music videos for the Jacksons ("Torture"), 1984, Janet Jackson ("Nasty," "Control," "When I Think of You," and "What Have You Done for Me Lately?"), 1986, ZZ Top ("Velcro Fly"), 1986, and Steve Winwood ("Roll With It"), 1988; for motion pictures, including *The Running Man,* 1987, *Coming to America,* 1988, *The Karate Kide, Part III,* 1989, and *She's Out of Control,* 1989; and for television, including *The Tracy Ullman Show,* 1987-89; recording artist 1988—.

Awards: Winner of *Soul Train* award; American Video Arts Award for choreographer of the year, 1987, from National Academy of Video Arts and Sciences; Emmy Award for best choreography, 1988-89, for *The Tracy Ullman Show;* MTV awards for best female video, best dance video, best choreography in a video, and best editing in a video, all 1989, all for video song "Straight Up."

Addresses: *Office*—5455 Wilshire Blvd., Los Angeles, CA 90036. *Publicist*—Solters/Roskin/Friedman, Inc., 45 West 34th Street, New York, NY 10001.

dance trainer for Janet Jackson, with whom she became a close friend. Abdul staged Jackson's hit "What Have You Done for Me Lately" and several follow-up videos.

Following her work with the Jackson's, Abdul was flooded with job offers, becoming so busy that she was forced to quit the Laker Girls. Abdul has choreographed commercials for diverse products and videos for such groups as ZZ Top, Duran Duran, and the Pointer Sisters. On the motion picture scene, she has coached the movements of Eddie Murphy and Arsenio Hall in *Coming to America,* and Arnold Schwarzenegger in *The Running Man,* among others.

In 1989 the multi-talented Abdul surprised the music industry with her funky and personable debut album, *Forever Your Girl,* which rose to multi-platinum status with the top hits "Straight Up," "Cold Hearted," and the title song. Abdul followed the album with a series of eye-catching videos that showcase her choreography and helped fuel the album's multi-million dollar sales. Despite the record's apparent success, Abdul realizes her technical limitations as a singer. In an effort to improve her voice she works with a vocal coach in a rigorous training program.

For her striking and innovative work as a choreographer, Abdul has won critical recognition: Soul Train Award, National Academy of Video Arts and Sciences Award, an Emmy for her choreography on the *Tracey Ullman Show,* and MTV awards for best female video, best choreography, best dance video, and best editing.

Selected discography

Forever Your Girl (includes "Straight Up," "The Way That You Love Me," "Knocked Out," "Opposites Attract," "State of Attraction," "I Need You," "Forever Your Girl," "Next To You," "Cold Hearted," and "One or the Other"), Virgin Records, 1988.

Sources

DanceMagazine, April, 1988.
Los Angeles Times, February 12, 1989.
Providence Journal Bulletin, July 30, 1989; September, 1989.
Rolling Stone, November 30, 1989.
Us, December 11, 1989.

—*Jeanne M. Lesinski*

Will
Ackerman

Songwriter, guitarist, record company executive

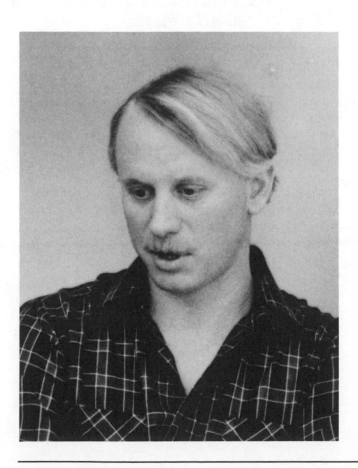

Will Ackerman planned to be a guitar-playing construction worker. Windham Hill Records, his iconoclastic record production company, was to be merely a lark; a hobby. He liked to play soft jazz in the evenings, and when his friends started asking him to record the music so they could hear it often, Windham Hill was started as a way to get them off his back. But before long, Ackerman discovered that his melodic tunes appealed to a Yuppie market that was weaned on the Beatles, the Moody Blues, and Donovan. It was a market that was being ignored by the major record labels. In fact, that market turned out to be so large that by 1986 Windham Hill, Ackerman's lark, had grossed more than $24 million.

To reach such a height seemed impossible back in 1975, when Ackerman was building houses in Palo Alto, California. His friends were starting to become bothersome, always coming over in the evening with tape recorders, recording his music so they could play it at home. The music itself was hard to define: soft rock, soft jazz, folk. He played alone—no accompaniment—on his steel guitar. After a while Ackerman thought he had finally come upon a solution to the problem. He asked his friends to chip in $5 each so he could cut a record and make a copy for each of them. Sixty friends kicked in the money. That was the beginning of Windham Hill, named after a Vermont inn where Ackerman spent several summers when he was a child.

Ackerman was born in Germany in 1949 and brought to the United States as a youth by his adoptive parents, a Stanford University English professor and his wife. Ackerman was raised in New England and California. He was a below-average student at Northfield-Mount Herman School, where he did particularly poorly in mathematics. And his college grades at Stanford University were not much better. He even managed to fail a course in his native language, German. In the summers he landed a minimum wage job as a carpenter. With only one English course to go before graduation (ironically, one taught by his father), Ackerman dropped out of college and concentrated on his two loves, building small music studios for independent record labels and playing his guitar. Even after his friends urged him to record some of his music, and he found that there was a nice cottage industry for his work, Ackerman could not decide between carpentry and music.

He cut 500 copies of his first album, *The Search for the Turtle's Navel*. His friends each got a copy, and the rest were distributed to a bookstore run by Anne Robinson, who would later become his wife. "Will and I did not get into this business to make money," Robinson told *Republic* magazine. "We believed that somewhere there were people who would have the same feelings for music that we did." Ackerman agreed in *Esquire:* "We had no intention of being commercial. Solo guitar was hardly tearing up the charts. And we weren't doing it for the money. Annie was running a bookstore and I was framing houses. We did our records purely out of a desire to make something well."

For the next four years Ackerman and Robinson worked their regular jobs during the day and nurtured Windham Hill Records by night. A desk in the corner of their house was their office; their garage became the warehouse, overflowing with records and jackets and shipping crates. "We did not advertise," Robinson told *Republic*. "We didn't have the money to advertise. We built up a very loyal following by having a mailing list, and we knew everybody on the mailing list because we wrote to them and talked to them on the telephone." Money was so tight that when orders came in Ackerman and Robinson glued the photos on the record jackets themselves. A friend squeezed ten records from them and sent them to radio stations. Robinson thought that was waste, but those records were to become the springboard that catapulted Windham Hill to success. In 1977 Ackerman cut another album, *It Takes a Year*. His records were being played on radio stations, and more importantly, people were asking stations about the music. By 1978 Ackerman was getting airplay in Massachusetts, New Hampshire, Vermont, and Colorado. By their fourth year it became clear to Ackerman and Robinson that they would have to quit their jobs and concentrate on the new record label.

Although critics and fans alike have a difficult time classifying the music, one thing is clear: Ackerman developed a sound that appealed to a large record-buying audience that had outgrown the current rock scene but found itself with no place else to turn. "They [record companies] ceased to pay attention to the age group which was, historically, a tremendous record-buying group, and, secondarily, a group for which music was almost a religious entity," Ackerman told *Republic*. "Music was a terribly important part of life to my generation and suddenly nothing was being made for us."

By 1980 Windham Hill had gotten too large for Ackerman and Robinson to handle alone. They signed a distribution deal with Pickwick, an independent company unaffiliated with any record label, that allowed Ackerman to retain full control of his music and records. That same year Ackerman signed George Winston, a Montana-born delivery man who had been dogging him with suggestions for artists for Windham Hill. Although Ackerman didn't like Winston's suggestions, he

---

Ackerman still looks more the part of a California construction worker than a record executive.

---

liked Winston. Winston has since recorded *Autumn*, one of Windham Hill's most successful albums. By 1982, Winston's *Winter into Spring* had climbed to the seventh spot on the jazz charts, the company had grossed $5 million, and Windham Hill had signed its first band, Shadowfax.

While other record companies promoted their artists, Windham Hill customers were coming into record stores to buy the Windham Hill label. It didn't seem to matter who the artist was. Followers had come to expect and trust that Windham Hill would provide a certain sound they knew they would enjoy. Whatever the allure, it wasn't enough to keep Pickwick afloat; the independent record company went out of business in 1983. But by then, Windham Hill had caught the attention of the nation's largest record companies. It took nine months to finalize a new contract, but Ackerman eventually signed with A&M Records, a company founded by Herb Alpert and Jerry Moss. Under their new agreement, Windham Hill could manufacture whatever records it wanted, and A&M received no company stock. Windham Hill could charge whatever it wanted for its records and could launch whatever new labels it wanted. It could also retain the Ma & Pa bookstores, holistic medicine, herbal tea, and health food stores that helped finance the fledgling record company. In effect, Ackerman got a distribution deal with no strings attached.

Since then Windham Hill has branched out. Open Air Records is to lyrics what Windham Hill is to instrumentals. And another offshoot, Magenta Records, specializes in jazz. The company produces only about a dozen albums a year. Yet customers come in asking not for the albums by artist but for the latest Windham Hill recording. By 1985 sales exceeded $20 million, and Winston's *Autumn* has gone platinum, selling over one million copies. "What Windham Hill has done is amazing," Stephen Traiman, vice-president and executive director of the Recording Industry Association of America, told the *Wall Street Journal.* "You have got to remember that jazz albums are only 4 percent of the retail market." Added Kurt Loder, senior editor of *Rolling Stone* magazine, "There's nothing else like Windham Hill. Their popularity is due to a reaction against loud music." Indeed, they are so popular that the company spends less than half of 1 percent of its net revenue on promotion, compared to about 20 percent spent by other record companies.

Ackerman still looks more the part of a California construction worker than a record executive. And despite the laid-back nature of his music, his life seems to have acquired some of the frenetic trappings of West Coast success. He tools around in a Mercedes, his blood pressure has risen to 190 over 120, and he and Anne Robinson have since divorced. (They remain friends, and she still runs the office.) He scuba dives, backpacks, plays hockey, enjoys wine tastings, and is a fervent fan of the San Francisco 49ers.

He has built himself a retreat on 79 acres in Windham County, Vermont. And he attributes Windham Hill's success and his own to an axiom that seems to mark the Sixties generation: Do your own thing. "We've gotten here because we've never compromised," Ackerman told *Republic* magazine. "We've done exactly what we wanted. If it didn't fly, it wouldn't have mat-

tered. We would have gone on being a hobby company. I would have been pounding nails and making a good living and there would have been good wine on the table. We became what we are because we are different, we are unique, and we care about what we're doing. Why would we ever compromise?"

Selected discography

LPs; Released by Windham Hill

The Search for the Turtle's Navel, 1976.
It Takes a Year, 1977.
Childhood and Memory.
Passage.
Past Light.
Conferring with the Moon: Pieces for Guitar, 1986.
(With Philip Aaberg, Michael Manring, and others) *Imaginary Roads,* 1989.

Sources

Chatanooga Times, September 12, 1986.
down beat, October 1979.
Esquire, April 1984; December 1984.
Gentlemen's Quarterly, April 1984.
Honolulu Advertizer, April 1, 1987.
Los Angeles Times, January 1, 1985.
New York City Tribune, September 4, 1986.
New York Times, May 4, 1986.
Oakland Tribune, June 1986.
Republic, May 1985.
Rolling Stone, March 17, 1983; December 18, 1986.
Time, March 1, 1985.
Variety, February 8, 1984.
Wall Street Journal, December 13, 1983.

—*Stephen Advokat*

Aerosmith

Rock band

For years rock critics dismissed Aerosmith as little more than a tasteless imitation of the Yardbirds or the Rolling Stones, but that didn't keep fans from making the relentlessly hard-rocking group one of the most popular acts of the 1970s. Neither did it deter a younger generation of rockers from co-opting Aerosmith's style to create some of the most popular bands of the 1980s. "What the critics don't know, the little boys understand," admitted Deborah Frost in *Rolling Stone*. "Aerosmith is probably the most influential hard-rock band of the Seventies. Joe Perry's sting and stance and Steven Tyler's scarfs and squawk have provided role models and bad attitudes for Bon Jovi, Cinderella, Ratt, Motley Crue, and every band being signed out of L.A. today."

Aerosmith was formed in 1970 around the nucleus of guitarist Joe Perry, vocalist Steve Tyler, and bassist Tom Hamilton. The three had become acquainted during their families' summer vacations in Lake Sunapee, New Hampshire. The following year they filled out their lineup with rhythm guitar player Brad Whitford and

For the Record. . .

Band formed in 1970 in Boston; original members were **Steve Tyler** (real name, Tallarico; born March 26, 1948, in Yonkers, New York), lead vocals; **Joe Perry** (born September 10, 1950, in Boston, Mass.), lead guitar; **Brad Whitford** (born February 23, 1952, in Mass.), rhythm guitar; **Tom Hamilton** (born December 31, 1951, in Colorado Springs, Colo.) bass; and **Joey Kramer** (born June 21, 1950, in New York, New York), drums.

Addresses: c/o Collins/Barasso Mgmt., 215 1st St., Cambridge, Mass., 02142.

drummer Joey Kramer and began playing in the Boston area. Often their only payment was the publicity they received, but their hard work soon won them a loyal local following. Their next goal was a national audience. Once again, they earned it "the hard way—making endless cross-country forays opening for anyone they could, because radio in most parts of the country wouldn't touch their raunched-out sound," noted Johnny Angel in the Boston *Phoenix.*

By 1972 their raw, loud, high-voltage sound had caught the ear of Columbia Records executive Clive Davis, who offered them a contract. *Aerosmith* and *Get Your Wings,* the group's first two LPs, sold modestly. Their third album, *Toys in the Attic,* was their breakthrough. According to Phil Hardy and Dave Laing in their *Encyclopedia of Rock,* it represented "the perfect distillation of the Aerosmith sound—a muscular but surprisingly agile rhythm section, with the twin guitars howling and snapping around Tyler's vocal lines." *Toys in the Attic* stayed on the charts for almost two years, eventually selling more than 4 million copies. *Rocks* followed the formula of *Toys in the Attic* and was nearly as successful. By 1978, Aerosmith was the undisputed leader of arena-rock bands.

The years of constant touring had taken Aerosmith to the top. Unfortunately, they'd also led to drug abuse of legendary proportions and the development of deep personal animosities among band members. Perry later described that period to *People* magazine contributor Steve Dougherty: "In the late '70s it just stopped being fun. It was like, 'I can't wait to finish this song so I can get backstage and do some blow,' or, 'Jeez, I gotta get through this solo so I can get back to my roadie and have a pop,'. . .We were addicted." Tyler remembered: "I was a garbage. . . . Heroin, coke, valium, anything that anyone came near me with." Aerosmith's vitality

began to fade under the strain. *Audio* magazine accused them of staleness in a review of their seventh album, *A Night in the Ruts:* "Once success struck there wasn't far for them to go—there's no real good instrumental virtuoso in Aerosmith, no active creative intelligence, and no visionary philosophy. It seems this group is determined to make themselves nothing more than a minor footnote in the book of rock 'n' roll, an afterthought to heavy metal, and the cornerstone that true mediocrity is judged by."

Shortly after A *Night in the Ruts* was completed, Joe Perry walked out on Aerosmith to form his own group, the Joe Perry Project. Brad Whitford soon followed suit. Aerosmith labored on, replacing Perry with Jim Crespo and Whitford with Rick Dufay but their popularity was plunging. Then in 1981 Tyler was seriously injured in a motorcycle accident. He told *People* he realized then that his group was about to hit bottom: "I lay there in the hospital crying and flipping out, knowing some other group was going to step into our space. Through the

> *"The raw, dirty edges of the Aerosmith of old slash through the power schmaltz. . . . The band has never sounded better or more charged."*

stupor of my medication, I pictured a spotlight. We walked out of it." His vision was prophetic. Aerosmith was inactive for the next few years.

Finally, in 1984, Tyler and Perry made peace with each other and agreed to try putting the band back together. With no record contract and no album out, they began touring. At the same time, band members were beginning to renounce the drugs and alcohol that dominated their lives. Tyler went through four different rehabilitation programs; Perry even tried a complete blood transfusion in an attempt to rid himself of his addictions, but eventually had to submit to conventional rehabilitation The reformed group won a contract with Geffen Records, but only after auditioning for the company.

Their first reunion album, *Done with Mirrors,* "sported the band's most powerful playing ever," according to Johnny Angel, but other critics were skeptical about a sober Aerosmith. A *Stereo Review* writer admitted that the band's playing was tighter than ever before, but suggested that the band's drunken antics had supplied the greater part of their charm. "A mediocre Aerosmith concert was two hours of imitation Stones," he wrote. "A great Aerosmith concert was a two-minute sound check punctuated by Steve Tyler hurling a bottle of Jack Daniels' against Perry's amplifier, followed by ten minutes of pugilism, after which the band would stumble off-stage." Sales of *Done with Mirrors* were flat, too, indicating that Aerosmith's once-loyal audience had come to doubt them.

A shot of much-needed publicity came in 1986, courtesy of rap group Run-D.M.C. They remade Aerosmith's 1976 hit "Walk This Way" and featured Tyler and Perry in the accompanying video. The cover was a tremendous hit, and a generation of young MTV viewers was suddenly interested in Aerosmith. Their 1987 release, *Permanent Vacation,* sold more than 2 million copies and spawned a Top-20 hit, "Dude (Looks Like a Lady)." It even drew positive comments from music reviewers. Deborah Frost criticized *Permanent Vacation* as overproduced, but praised the band in *Rolling Stone:* "[Aerosmith] has never worked with people so determined to turn it into Bon Jovi, Heart, or Starship. The good news is that it can't be done. . . . The raw, dirty edges of the Aerosmith of old slash through the power schmaltz. . . . The band has never sounded better or more charged."

Aerosmith continued to build up their newfound audience by touring with many of the groups they'd inspired, such as Dokken, Guns n' Roses, and Poison. According to Johnny Angel, working with younger musicians has revitalized Aerosmith, allowing them to create their best music to date on the album "If the child is partly father to the man, then Guns n' Roses are partly the sire of Aerosmith's new *Pump.* The band sounds reborn, though definitely not born again, on this album. It's as if last year's tour with Axle Rose and Company had reminded Aerosmith that folks want the raunch again. . . .*[Pump]* accomplishes what Aerosmith's many imitators, from Ratt to Motley Crue to Dangerous Toys

and Tora-Tora, could never do: swing rather than hammer. This is what has made Aerosmith so enduring."

Selected discography

Aerosmith, Columbia, 1973.
Get Your Wings, Columbia, 1974.
Toys in the Attic, Columbia, 1975.
Rocks, Columbia, 1976.
Pure Gold, Columbia, 1976.
Draw the Line, Columbia, 1977.
Live Bootleg, Columbia, 1978.
A Night in the Ruts, Columbia, 1979.
Greatest Hits, Columbia, 1980.
Rock in a Hard Place, Columbia, 1982.
Done with Mirrors, Geffen, 1986.
Classics Live, Columbia, 1986.
Permanent Vacation, Geffen, 1987.
Gems, Columbia, 1989.
Pump, Geffen, 1989.

Sources

Books

Hardy, Phil and Dave Laing, *Encyclopedia of Rock,* Macdonald, 1987.

Periodicals

Audio, April, 1980.
People, January 21, 1980, October 19, 1987, February 22, 1988.
Phoenix (Boston), September, 1989.
Rolling Stone, October 22, 1987.
Stereo Review, April, 1986.

—*Joan Goldsworthy*

Beaver Brown Band

Rock group

From their roots in the nightclubs of Rhode Island, John Cafferty and the Beaver Brown Band have attracted an audience nationwide. Cafferty's songs range from soul to rock and role—he blends the elements of a sixties sound with those of eighties rock 'n' roll and brings them on stage with aplomb.

Although Cafferty had been playing the guitar since he was thirteen, he did not plan to become a professional musician. He wanted to be a lifeguard, and as he became more practical he decided to study art. When he started college, he and other musicians he had known since high school formed Beaver Brown, as the band was then known: saxophonist Michael Antunes, keyboardist Robert Cotoia, guitarist Gary Gramolini, bassist Pat Lupo, and drummer Kenny Jo Silva.

They made a reputation for themselves locally as a good roadhouse band. Hoping to get local airplay, the band cut a single on Coastline Records called "Wild Summer Nights," with "Tender Nights" on the flip side. The record did get played by major stations in the East and helped to make the band popular on the circuit from Virginia in the south, north to Boston. But a major record deal did not follow, which Cafferty attributes to the non-commerciality of the band's sound and the slump in the record business in the late 1970s.

The Beaver Brown Band has often billed itself as a working-class band—every week the band would try to earn a week's wages for playing music. And they did not lack interested listeners. One listener in particular changed the course of the band's career. Kenny Vance heard the band perform at a bar in Greenwich Village and remembered it four years later when he was hired as the music producer for the film *Eddie and the Cruisers,* a low-budget film about a fictional rock band. The band members found it exciting to work in a movie studio, though it was difficult to watch their music being lip-synched by actors. When *Eddie and the Cruisers* was released in September of 1983 it flopped, but when it was later shown on HBO (Home Box Office cable television), it was a hit and the Beaver Brown Band bounded into prominence. The soundtrack sold almost two million copies in only six months. It was a top ten album on record charts and the single "On the Dark Side" reached the number one spot on *Billboard's* "Top Rock Charts." And as often happens, the top single engendered a video that was number one on MTV for a number of weeks.

The exposure allowed the band to cut an album of its own material with Scotti Brothers—*Tough All Over.* Cafferty often focuses on the vicissitudes of blue-collar Americans, and this album is no exception. It includes the vignettes "Dixieland," a gospel-sounding song about Frost Belt refugees in the South, "Small Town Girl," a love song, and "Crystal Blue," a heartbreak ballad with a Tex-Mex influence, as well as the rock and roll tune "Voice of America." Two of the songs became Top 20 hits: "Tough All Over" and "C.I.T.Y."

Cafferty likes songs that tell stories, and in writing the twelve that make up *Roadhouse,* he tried to capture the emotions of everyday life. "I guess I was thinking a lot about our story and how we started out. I was thinking a lot about winning and losing and putting yourself on the line and taking risks." Penned over three years, the songs on *Roadhouse* seem to symbolize the struggles the band has had to succeed. "Bound For Glory" is about a man full of optimism, "Victory Dance" about being on the sidelines waiting for that golden opportunity, "Song and Dance" about repeatedly hitting dead ends but always trying again. On the album's second side "Penetration," "Wishing Well," and "Customary Thing" trace a path toward emotional commitment. The final cut, "Road I'm Running," seems to sum up all that precede it. The character confronts all that has happened in his life and decides that life if worth living, "Wherever it leads, I'll follow this road I'm running."

Some critics of John Cafferty and the Beaver Brown have called the act a clone of Bruce Springsteen,

For the Record. . .

Full name of group, John Cafferty and the Beaver Brown Band; formed as Beaver Brown in Rhode Island by guitarist, vocalist, and songwriter **John Cafferty** during mid-1970s; members also include saxophonist **Michael Antunes**; keyboardist **Robert Cotoia**; guitarist **Gary Gramolini**; bass guitarist **Pat Lupo**; and drummer **Kenny Jo Silva**; performed in East Coast Clubs during late 1970s and early 1980s; performed music for motion picture soundtracks of *Eddie and the Cruisers,* 1983, and *Eddie and the Cruisers II,* 1989.

Addresses: *Fan club*—Beaver Brown Fan Club, P.O. Box 3999, Centerdale, RI 02911-0199. *Publicist*—Epic Media Relations, 51 West 52nd Street, New York, NY 10019.

though the band had a sound similar to that of "The Boss" before Springsteen was nationally known. Cafferty attributes these similarities largely to similar musical experiences. "I think that with a lot of the bands in the Northeast, there seems to be an influence of the early rhythm and blues from the fifties and sixties, probably because a lot of that music came out of the New York area and we were close enough to pick up the New York stations," he told *Gavin Report* writer Ron Fell. But Cafferty also admits that in the songwriter arena he was definitely influenced by Springsteen, who he says "has given us a lot of advice and encouragement over the years, especially with me as a songwriter. When I first started writing songs," Cafferty told Fell, "I had a lot of questions about how to become a better writer, and he was always a great writer and he took the time to help. We'd just talk about our favorite records and what was a good song and why."

Like many popular singers of the eighties, Cafferty put

his talent to work to aid charitable causes. He and the band put on a special benefit concert for high school students to put across an anti-drug message and performed at the United Nations for the CARE/Sport Aid global run to raise money for the world's sick, hungry, and homeless children.

In an era of motion picture sequels, it is no surprize that *Eddie and the Cruisers II: Eddie Lives* was released, in the summer of 1989. The movie was panned by critics and the soundtrack did not repeat the success of *Eddie and the Cruisers.*

Selected discography

Eddie and the Cruisers (movie soundtrack), Scotti Brothers/CBS, 1983.
Tough All Over, Scotti Brothers/CBS, 1985.
Roadhouse, Scotti Brothers/CBS, 1988.
Eddie and the Cruisers II (movie soundtrack), Scotti Brothers/CBS, 1989.

Sources

Cash Box, July 20, 1985.
The Gavin Report, May 17, 1985.
Orlando Sentinel, July 23, 1988.
Plain Dealer, October 22, 1984; May 30, 1988.
Providence Journal-Bulletin, December 29, 1986; October 27, 1989.
ROCK Magazine, February, 1985.
San Antonio Express-News, July 30, 1988.
Tulsa Tribune, August 9, 1985.
Tyler Courier-Times, July 22, 1988.

—*Jeanne M. Lesinski*

The Bee Gees

Pop/rock, disco group

From lyrical ballads to falsetto-sung disco hits and beyond, the Bee Gees have always displayed a unique style of elaborate harmony and melodic structure. Despite a career setback due more in part to a perceived disco lifestyle and flavor precipitated by the media than to actual musical direction, the group perseveres, reminding listeners that long before there was *Saturday Night Fever,* there was a group comprised of three talented brothers once hailed by Robert Stigwood as "the new Beatles."

Popularly believed to have hailed from Australia, the Bee Gees were actually born in England; Barry (born Douglas) on the Isle of Man in 1947, and the twins, Maurice and Robin, in Manchester in 1949. The brothers began performing as the Blue Cats at an early age, continuing their musical act when the family emigrated to Australia in 1958. After debuting on Brisbane's ABC-TV channel, the Gibbs won their own weekly TV series and the "Bee Gees" quickly became the favorite group of Australia's teens and preteens. Their first single, "Three Kisses of Love," was released by Festival Records in 1963 and made the top 20 in Australia, to be followed by a number of hit singles over the next few years. Returning to England in 1967, the group signed with Robert Stigwood of NEMS, adding drummer Colin Peterson to their group and having a sell-out debut at the Saville Theatre in London.

The group's first LP released in the United States, *The Bee Gees First,* followed the successful singles "Spicks and Specks" and "New York Mining Disaster—1941" in 1967. As their record sales increased, the group toured extensively in Europe and the United States, promoting a series of hit songs such as the melodic "I Started a Joke" and one of their best sellers, "Words." In 1969, after their concept album *Odessa* went almost unnoticed, Robin Gibb parted company with his brothers for a brief solo career, rejoining them in 1970 for the hit single "Lonely Days." The following year found them touring again, promoting a new album and enjoying their number-one hit on the U.S. charts, "How Can You Mend a Broken Heart."

The next two years were modest ones, with little changing in the group's focus until they began to use a rhythm-and-blues sound that would soon lead to the disco sound the group became associated with in the mid-1970s. "But we weren't after disco," Maurice pointed out in a 1989 interview in the *Detroit Free Press.* "We were into this new kind of music out of New York, real tough and sensual grooves. Disco to us was K.C. & the Sunshine Band; light dance is what we called it." No matter what they called it, after the *Main Course* album in 1975 and popular disco-styled hits "Jive Talkin'" and "Nights on Broadway," the group was consistently on the charts, ascending to an even higher level of popularity after their involvement in the *Saturday Night Fever* film and soundtrack album in 1977. Produced in only two weeks, the album featured what would become some of the Bee Gees' biggest hits—including "Night Fever," "How Deep Is Your Love," "Stayin' Alive," and, for Yvonne Elliman, "If I Can't Have You." Said John Rockwell in the *New York Times,* the Gibbs' sound was "both telling and instantly identifiable amidst the other disco pap one encounters on the radio." The group was to follow their success in 1979 with another chart-topping disco-style album, *Spirits Having Flown*.

Though the group's participation in *Fever* was casual, the immediate success of the album, which sold over 40 million copies, linked the Bee Gees directly to the disco sound and the white suit, gold chain image created by the film. This image would prove more difficult to shake after ten years than their participation with Peter Frampton in 1978 in the ill-conceived and -received movie version of *Sgt. Pepper's Lonely Hearts Club Band.* Said Barry, "I think what people *don't* like is the whole disco syndrome, which is more about style and not about the music. A lot of people tend to have forgotten that there's more to us than that stuff. We were probably on our fourth platinum album by the time the 'Fever' thing came along."

After spending much of the 1980s producing artists such as Dionne Warwick, Barbra Streisand, and Diana Ross, the Bee Gees reemerged in 1987 with the album *E.S.P.,* which sold three million copies in Europe but failed in the United States. In 1988, promoting a new album (*One*) and rereleasing the single "You Win Again" from *E.S.P.,* the group began touring the U.S., battling what remained of their disco image. According to Barry, "We want to re-establish ourselves on the forefront of American music, where we at least believe we have a place. We want to erase the illusion of 'Saturday Night Fever' and the effect it's had on us. We're going to stay active, stay as visible as possible . . . as long as there are people out there who like what we do."

Selected discography

First, Atco, 1967.
Horizontal, Atco, 1968, Polydor, 1987.
Idea, Atco, 1968, Polydor, 1987.
Rare, Precious and Beautiful, Atco, 1968.
Best, Atco, 1969, RSO, 1987.
Odessa (double album), Atco, 1969.
Odessa (condensed), 1969.
Rare, Precious and Beautiful, Vol 2, Atco, 1970.
Cucumber Castle, Atco, 1970.
Two Years On, Atco, 1970, RSO, 1989.
Melody (soundtrack), Atco, 1971.
Trafalgar, Atco, 1971, RSO, 1989.
To Whom It May Concern, Atco, 1972.
Life in a Tin Can, RSO, 1973.
Best, Vol. 2, RSO, 1973, reissued, 1987.
Mister Natural, RSO, 1974.
Main Course, RSO, 1975, Polydor, 1988.
Children of the World, RSO, 1976, reissued, 1989.
Gold, Vol. 1, RSO, 1976.
Here at Last . . . Live (double album), RSO, 1977.
Saturday Night Fever (soundtrack), RSO, 1977.
Sgt. Pepper's Lonely Hearts Club Band (soundtrack; double album), RSO, 1978.
Spirits Having Flown, RSO, 1979, reissued, 1989.
Greatest Hits (double album), RSO, 1979.
Livin' Eyes, RSO, 1982.
E.S.P., Warner Bros., 1988.
One, Warner Bros., 1989.

Sources

Books

Anderson, Christopher P., *The New Book of People,* Perigee, 1986.
Nite, Norm N., and Ralph M. Newman, *Rock On: The Illustrated Encyclopedia of Rock 'N' Roll,* Volume II, Crowell, 1978.
Stambler, Irwin, *The Encyclopedia of Pop, Rock, and Soul,* St. Martin's, 1984.

Periodicals

Detroit Free Press, July 30, 1989.
People, August 7, 1989.

—Meg Mac Donald

The Blues Brothers

Blues duo

The Blues Brothers began as a novelty musical act formed by famed comedians Dan Aykroyd and John Belushi to warm up audiences of the television show "Saturday Night Live," but the duo's brand of rhythm and blues proved so popular that their debut album, *Briefcase Full of Blues,* went double-platinum, selling over 2.8 million copies. Elwood and Joliet Jake Blues—as Aykroyd and Belushi respectively called their alter egos in matching dark suits, skinny ties, dark glasses, and fedoras—went on to make other successful albums and starred in the popular 1980 film *The Blues Brothers.* The act came to an end with Belushi's death in 1982.

Aykroyd and Belushi came from very different backgrounds. Aykroyd was born in Ottawa, Ontario, Canada, and had once been on his way to becoming a priest before he was kicked out of the seminary. Belushi was born and raised in Wheaton, Illinois, a suburb of Chicago; in his youth he was undecided whether to pursue a show-business career or concentrate on football (his talents at the latter would have paid his way through

For the Record. . .

Blues Brothers formed, 1978; appeared on television program "Saturday Night Live"; featured in film *The Blues Brothers,* 1980; recording artists and concert performers, 1978-82.

Dan Aykroyd (Elwood Blues), full name Daniel Edward Aykroyd; born July 1, 1952, in Ottawa, Ontario, Canada (came to United States, 1974; naturalized citizen); son of Samuel Cuthbert Peter Hugh (a Canadian government official) and Lorraine Gougeon Aykroyd; married Donna Dixon (an actress), April 29, 1983. *Education:* Attended Carleton University.

John Belushi (Joliet Jake Blues); born January 24, 1949, in Wheaton, Illinois; died of a suspected drug overdose March 5, 1982, in Los Angeles, California (buried in Martha's Vineyard, Massachusetts); son of Adam (a restaurant owner) and Agnes (a cashier) Belushi; married Judy Jacklin (a writer), December 31, 1976. *Education:* Attended University of Wisconsin at Whitewater, c. 1967-68; earned associate's degree, College of DuPage, 1970; attended University of Illinois, Circle campus.

Addresses: *Dan Aykroyd*—8955 Beverly Blvd., Los Angeles, CA 90048.

college). Neither had much in the way of formal musical training in his youth, but Aykroyd became a proficient harmonica player, and Belushi served as the drummer in a band called the Ravins when he was in high school. Belushi also made quite an impression on comedy critics with his famed imitation of rock star Joe Cocker, which he performed during his days with the Second City comedy troupe in Chicago and in the National Lampoon musical stage spoof "Lemmings."

The two future blues musicians met when Belushi went to check out the Toronto version of Second City, in which Aykroyd was one of the most promising players. They quickly became friends, and in 1975 they both found themselves cast members of the ground-breaking television comedy show "Saturday Night Live." Though at first they stood in the shadow of the popular comedian Chevy Chase, after Chase left the show Aykroyd and Belushi came into their own with routines like the Coneheads and various Samurai warrior interpretations, respectively.

Meanwhile, Aykroyd had introduced Belushi to the blues, a music genre with which he had long been enamored, and Belushi came to share his enthusiasm. A prototype—of sorts—of the Blues Brothers act was first seen on "Saturday Night Live" on January 17, 1976. According to Bob Woodward in his biography of Belushi, *Wired: The Short Life and Fast Times of John Belushi,* the pair asked "Saturday Night" producer Lorne Michaels if they could do a blues number on that show. Michaels preferred that they do a bee skit—another of the program's recurring sketches, and one that Belushi despised—so a compromise was reached. Woodward describes the result: "Danny wore a fedora with antennae and sunglasses, and John dressed in his bee costume and wire-rimmed glasses. Danny played the harmonica while John sang, 'I'm a King Bee,' interrupting the song to do full body flips, landing flat on his back once. He started out singing the blues but slipped gradually into his Joe Cocker voice; it was a big hit with the audience, clearly not because they were talented musicians but because Belushi hurled himself into the part with such vehemence."

Later, in the costumes that would become the Blues Brothers' standard look, Aykroyd and Belushi warmed up the "Saturday Night" live audience before most of the shows. By that time they had invented personas and life histories for the Blues Brothers: their names were Elwood and Joliet Jake, they'd spent the earliest part of their lives in a Catholic orphanage before being adopted by black parents in Calumet City, Illinois, and they'd been playing Chicago area clubs since the age of eight. Elwood had spent time in the industrial diamond trade and washed windows; Jake had *done* time for armed robbery at Joliet Prison—hence the nickname. Eventually, they made their debut on "Saturday Night Live." On April 22, 1978, Aykroyd and Belushi performed "Hey, Bartender" and "I Don't Know." As Woodward reports, "the audience loved the performance, but it seemed perplexed. . . .Was it a joke? Aykroyd played a mean [harmonica], and Belushi—even though he had a lousy voice—put his heart and soul into singing, and that was the power of the blues. But they were two of the hottest comedians in the country. This couldn't be serious."

But Aykroyd and Belushi enjoyed their new alter egos and the response they generated so much that they got their agent to set up a recording contract and a series of concert dates. On September 9, 1978, they did their first show, opening for comic Steve Martin at the Universal Amphitheater in Los Angeles, California. They also performed over the next eight nights, and during these appearances recorded their live debut album, *Briefcase Full of Blues,* on Atlantic. *Briefcase* was an almost instant success, quickly reaching platinum and then double-platinum status, aided by hit singles like the remakes of "Soul Man," "Rubber Biscuit," and "Almost." Though the Blues Brothers were a tremendous success with fans, critics gave them mixed reviews.

Some complained that Aykroyd and Belushi, as whites, were delivering a poor, exploitative substitute for the work of real blues musicians, predominantly black. But black soul singer James Brown told *Rolling Stone* reporter Abe Peck that he thought the Blues Brothers had "heart and soul." Many, like rock musician Jerry Garcia of the Grateful Dead, took the middle ground. "Too good to be a parody, and not good enough to be good for what it was," he explained to Peck.

Nevertheless, in 1980 the Blues Brothers decided to translate their success to the big screen. The motion picture, aptly titled *The Blues Brothers,* was primarily written by Aykroyd and, like the Brothers' music, was a popular favorite but did not fare as well with the critics. Its simple plot involved Elwood and Jake rounding up their old band—a group of talented, legitimate musicians whom Aykroyd and Belushi had recruited to back them up during their concerts—to play for the financial benefit of the Catholic orphanage where they had spent their childhood. The movie served as a framework for the musical talents of not only the Blues Brothers, but legitimate legends like Cab Calloway, Ray Charles, and Aretha Franklin. The soundtrack album produced another hit for the duo, "Gimme Some Lovin'," and also resulted in a nationwide concert tour. The Blues Brothers released a third album, *Made in America,* later the same year, Aykroyd planned a film sequel, and the duo came out with a *Best of the Blues Brothers* album in 1981.

Belushi did not exactly lose interest in his alter ego, but he later became more attracted to punk music and actively promoted a band called Fear. Though Aykroyd told *People* that his partner was not a regular drug user,

Belushi died of a suspected overdose of cocaine and heroin on March 5, 1982, putting an end to the Blues Brothers.

Selected discography

Albums on Atlantic Records

Briefcase Full of Blues (includes "Soul Man," "Rubber Biscuit," and "Almost"), 1978.
The Blues Brothers (includes "Gimme Some Lovin'"), 1980.
Made in America (includes "Who's Making Love"), 1980.
Best of the Blues Brothers, 1981.

Sources

Books

Woodward, Bob, *Wired: The Short Life and Fast Times of John Belushi,* Simon & Schuster, 1984.

Periodicals

People, July 19, 1982.
Rolling Stone, November 2, 1978; February 22, 1979; August 7, 1980.

—Elizabeth Thomas

BoDeans

Rock group

Music critics generally agreed that the first BoDeans album, *Love & Hope & Sex & Dread* was a fine piece of work. There was little consensus on what to call the group's unique brand of rock, however: it was variously referred to as cowpunk, rockabilly, roots-rock, revivalist rock, and as a synthesis of the Rolling Stones and the Everly Brothers. Band member Sammy Llanas made more modest claims for the group, telling *Cosmopolitan* columnist Michael Segell, "I'd describe us as a band that writes a lot of good songs in different styles and plays most of them pretty well. . . . Our biggest influence was midsixties radio when it was wide open—you'd hear everything from Sonny and Cher to the Beatles, Stones, Motown, Petula Clark, and all the junk singles that came and went real fast. I loved that diversity. It all worked together because they were all good songs. That's what we're trying to do."

Although they're frequently referred to as a "Tex-Mex" group, their sound evolved in their hometown of Waukesha, Wisconsin. Front men Kurt Newmann and Sammy Llanas met in high school there during 1977. Newmann taught Llanas to play guitar, while Llanas—

For the Record. . .

Band formed in 1984, in Waukesha, Wis. Original members include **Kurt Newmann,** electric guitar; **Sammy Llanas,** acoustic guitar; **Bob Griffin,** bass; **Guy Hoffman,** drums (Hoffman has left the group).

Addresses: *Record company*—c/o Slash/Warner Records, 3300 Warner Blvd.,Burbank, CA 91510.

who has "one of the wildest vocal tones in the business . . . like a Munchkin on a dirt bike," according to *Time's* Jay Cocks—gave Newmann tips on singing. They worked together in several local bands before deciding to strike out as a rocking guitar duo, featuring Newmann on electric and Llana on acoustics. In this format, they developed what *Rolling Stone* contributor Anthony DeCurtis called "their distinctively skewed harmonies, which evolved from Newmann's warm Midwestern drawl and Llanas's eccentric treble rasp."

The guitarists eventually made it to the big time of nearby Milwaukee, where they met drummer Guy Hoffman. They liked what he added to their sound in jam sessions, and decided to create a new group including Hoffman and bassist Bob Griffin, a friend from high school. BoDeans—named after the Jethro Bodine character in *The Beverly Hillbillies*—were born. Newmann became "Beau BoDean" for stage purposes, and the other band members also adopted the BoDean surname. The new band didn't have much of a following at first, even in Waukesha. Llanas described L. T. Lyles, a local bar where many of the band's early gigs were played, to Cocks: "There was a bar in one room and a connecting room with a couple of pool tables. . . . Sometimes there'd be a couple of guys shooting a game, but usually we played to nobody." Llanas said he didn't feel stifled by the sleepy, small-town atmosphere, however. He told Segell: "You've got to be from somewhere. . . . I'm just as happy it's Waukesha. In the Midwest, there weren't a lot of crazy music trends going on like on the coasts. So we had a lot of time and freedom to develop our own style."

Newmann expressed a different point of view. "I think the only advantage to a small town," he told DeCurtis, "is that it's so boring that you have to do something dramatic if you're going to get out." The BoDeans' bid to get out of Waukesha began when they cut some demo tapes of their material and sent them to record companies. One found its way to veteran producer T-Bone Burnett, who had helped launch Los Lobos on the national scene. He liked what he heard. Besides arranging a contract for BoDeans with Slash Records, he produced *Love & Hope & Sex & Dreams,* which Segell

called "an incandescent debut" for the group. *Love & Hope & Sex & Dreams* wasn't a runaway hit, but it sold a respectable 100,000 copies. More importantly, it drew glowing reviews from national music critics, who found it richly textured and full of innovative musical references. *Stereo Review* called the album a subtle, savvy, and intelligent interweaving of country, folk, and root-level rock-and-roll, wrapped in a cloak of cool." The reviewer noted that the band's music resonated with echoes of Bob Dylan, Elvis Presley, and the Beatles, but emphasized, "the important thing is that BoDeans don't just surgically graft this stuff together; it all comes out of some higher sensibility and synthesis of style."

Rolling Stone's Jimmy Guterman concurred that BoDeans are a highly creative group. "[Llanas and Newmann] write tight, snappy pop songs that acknowledge tradition and then expand on it—this is no mere revivalism or wistful nostalgia." Guterman pessimistically concluded that putting out creative music would not assure BoDeans of popular success, however, for "despite the reams written about getting back to basics, most radio music is constructed around a synthesizer and a drum machine. . . . This album's strongest tracks . . . are so stark and unfussy that they'd seem out of place between synth moaners in vapid radio formats." Indeed, the band's follow-up album, *Outside Looking In,* received little airplay, although Segell declared that it "brims with real life: songs of innocence and experience, exhilaration and melancholy, given flight by exquisite harmonies." BoDeans themselves seem philosophical about falling short of superstardom, at least for now. Llanas told Segell: "We started the band with the idea of taking small steps. . . . We just want to keep growing musically. We don't want it to move too fast or to get weird. We don't want anybody freaking out. The bottom line of this band is friendship."

Selected discography

Love & Hope & Sex & Dreams, Slash, 1986.
Outside Looking In, Slash, 1988.
Home, Slash, 1989.

Sources

Cosmopolitan, December, 1987.
High Fidelity, September, 1986.
People, June 16, 1986.
Rolling Stone, July 3, 1986; September 11, 1986.
Stereo Review, August, 1986.
Time, June 9, 1986.

—*Joan Goldsworthy*

Edie Brickell

Singer, songwriter

Edie Brickell and New Bohemians can claim one of the decade's most remarkable pop-rock success stories. In their early days in Dallas's downtown art scene, they attracted a faithful core of local fans. That was 1985; one year later, word of their music had reached a few record-label talent scouts, and the group landed a deal. Then came *Shooting Rubberbands at the Stars,* the debut album that, within months of its 1988 release, moved quickly up the charts into multi-platinum territory. "I liken our success to Jiffy Pop popcorn," Brickell, the lead singer, told *Rolling Stone.* "All of a sudden there's just a rise to fame. *Poof.* And we're transformed into . . . *something else."* Coming up with a more appropriate metaphor, she added, "We shot rubber bands at the stars, and they hit."

New Bohemians include guitarist Kenny Withrow, bass player Brad Houser, drummer Matt Chamberlain, rhythm guitarist Wes Burt-Martin, percussionist John Bush, and Brickell, who strums an acoustic guitar and blows a blues harp in addition to singing. Straddling the line between accessibility and artiness, their songs alternately explore various genres—funk, disco, reggae, neo-rockabilly, psychedelia—while sticking to a catchy, hard-driving folk-pop base. The signature of their style comes from Brickell. Through her voice, which can be wispy and carefree, yet full of innuendo, she has the rare ability to evoke naivety and sensuality in a single phrase. She tends to sing around notes: like a bee hovering over a flower but alighting only briefly, she'll swoop up to a pitch or slide off it without meeting it head-on. It's a style that's loose-limbed and laid-back, tending to showcase her delivery of a melody more than the melody itself. And, like her neo-hippie looks— long flowing hair topped with a beret, faded jeans tucked into cowboy boots—it's a style that embodies the band's bohemian spirit.

Brickell first captivated listeners with "What I Am," the debut single of *Shooting Rubberbands,* which concludes with the disarming refrain "Choke me in the shallow water / before I get too deep." While some took the song as a kind of anthem for the Reagan era—a celebration of surface over depth—Brickell was actually expressing a philosophy of her own. "Spirituality, beliefs, the whole picture—I don't think you can make anybody see things the way you see them," she explained in *Spin.* "I'd rather die than be thrown into some heavy conversation." Instead, she uses her songs to philosophize—but subtly, often presenting her ideas in simple and poetic images. Most of her songs delve into the quirks and contradictions in human relationships, details that she gleans through continual observation. "I've never been that active socially but I've always watched people," she said in a publicity release written by Geffen Records. "I like to second-guess their thoughts and create songs about what I think's going on in their lives." She elaborated in *East Coast Rocker:* "I write about impressions I get from everybody, the way I see people think, the problems friends come to me with. It's usually the same things: 'She did this,' 'He broke my heart,' 'I want to be alone.' I take those things and roll them into one line or expression to hold it together, and get a universal feeling in a simple way."

Born in 1966 in Oak Cliff, a working-class suburb of Dallas, Edie had an unorthodox childhood. Her parents divorced when she was three, and spending time with her father, a professional bowler, meant hanging out in bowling alleys. Mostly, though, she was raised by her mother, a receptionist. "Money was short and we moved every year, all over Dallas," Brickell told *People.* "It was like *One Day at a Time*—crazy, and a whole lot of fun." Then as now, she was free-spirited and whimsical. "I always sang around the house," she told *East Coast Rocker,* "made up little songs on the guitar, my sparse picking. Music was a hobby then. I always wanted to play, but I was too chicken and I didn't know any musicians. I got my first guitar when I was in fifth grade, and I got to a certain point of basic chords and stuff." On the radio she'd listen to country and blues musicians. From her mother, who she recalls would get up early before work to dance to records by Al Green and Ike and Tina Turner, she inherited a love for soul music; such singers as Irma Thomas, Otis Redding, and Aretha Franklin became her idols.

During her teens, while driving around Dallas's suburbs in a Volkswagen bug (since replaced by a pickup truck), Brickell would listen to XTC, the Psychedelic Furs, and David Bowie. She attended Arts Magnet High School, an arts-oriented school, where her focus on the visual arts, combined with her striking shyness, kept her from hooking up with the music crowd. After graduating, she enrolled at Dallas's Southern Methodist University as an art major, waiting tables to help pay tuition, but left after three semesters. "I felt awful going there, because all the kids there were such dedicated artists, and I was just going along with it," she told *Spin.* "I realized that I was insulting them by calling myself an artist. They wanted to draw everything, and I didn't. My passion was writing songs."

Yet, as she confessed in *Spin,* "I never gave much thought to the idea of being a singer. It was like some faraway fantasy. I was way too chicken to try it." One night during her art-school days, she cast aside her fear. "A good friend of mine took me to a bar to see some friends of hers who were in a band. It was New Bohemians, though they were like a ska band, nothing like now. This was in mid-'85. My friend bought me a shot of Jack Daniels and I'd never drank whiskey before, so I got out of it in about 10 seconds. It was like a shot of bravery, so I asked the guys if I could sing one with them. They started playing some jazzy sort of jam and I improvised the lyrics. It was the greatest rush singing on stage with a band and I knew right there that it was what I wanted to do. I sang with the band the next week and afterwards they asked me to join." Faced with the choice of continuing school or dropping out to be a rock singer, she chose the latter. (In a *Rolling Stone* interview, Brickell noted that part of the story had been blown out of proportion. "It was frustration that got me to do it, not Jack Daniels," she clarified. "The Jack Daniels just said, 'Go for it, stop being such a chicken.'")

"For about a year and a half we were able to make enough money on weekends to survive during the week," Brickell recalled in *Spin.* "We were playing teeny-weeny clubs in Dallas, playing all originals. We were lucky enough to be part of the original live music club scene." The scene was Deep Ellum, a former red-light district east of downtown Dallas that was becoming a thriving artists' community. Though it was the mid-eighties, a 1960s spirit was in full bloom. Musicians lived there in warehouses, drugs were in wide supply and demand, and the music, which ranged from punk to rock to the avant-garde, was played in the open-ended jamming style of the Grateful Dead. New Bohemians had come to the proverbial right place at the right time. "It was all weirdos, mostly under 20 or 21," recalled Brent Butterworth, a former Dallas scene maker, in *Spin.* "It was the first arty thing that ever happened in Dallas. If Deep Ellum hadn't happened, New Bohemians wouldn't have had a place to play."

In mid-1986 New Bohemians put out a demo tape that

sold well locally and drew a wide audience for their Dallas gigs. Yet they were becoming increasingly anxious to expand their turf—especially Brickell, who resolved to quit the band if they didn't have a record deal by November. Her worries were needless. In November, a representative of Geffen Records flew to Dallas, saw one show, and offered them a record deal. (The rep had been tipped off to New Bohemians by an MCA scout, who liked the band but couldn't convince her label that they were marketable.) A year later they were paired with producer Pat Moran, whose credits included working with Robert Plant, and flown to Wales (Brickell's first time out of Texas) to record. The sessions were not without problems. When Geffen and Moran began making changes in both song material and band personnel, tensions developed within the group—mostly between the other band members and Edie, who, anxious to get the record done, sided with the label. The rift was exacerbated by Geffen, who changed the group's name from New Bohemians to Edie Brickell and New Bohemians. ("We were told that the band was breaking up," explained Geffen executive Tom Zutaut to *Rolling Stone,* "and we wanted to

---

Edie Brickell has retained the girl-next-door folkiness that drew her early listeners in.

---

protect our huge investment.") But tensions dissolved with the completion of the album; as for the name issue, the band is unanimously pushing to resume its original name with its next release.

During the now-classic first encounter between Edie and New Bohemians, the singer revealed her uncanny ability to pick lyrics and melody out of the air. Since then, improvisation has become both an ends and a means for the band: not only does it define much of their live act, but as with *Shooting Rubberbands,* it also provides their basic approach to songwriting. "A lot of the time, we don't have any ideas at all and start with a really silly image, like biscuits or paper plates, to see how it goes," Brickell told the *New York Times.* "When we come up with a melody we all like, we blend it all together and somehow a song naturally arrives." Yet her fascination with wordplay began long before she met New Bohemians. "I've always liked words," she told Geffen. "I'd write little things on pieces of paper and put them in drawers. Strange thoughts would run through my head. So I started putting them in songs and brought them to the band."

In the band's early days, Brickell was far from self-assured. While other pop singers tend to bop around onstage, dancing or clapping or shaking a tambourine, she would bend down to pick lint off the floor. "Edie was excruciatingly self-conscious on stage," commented Tom Marstaud, a Dallas writer, in *Spin.* "She would keep her eyes down and fumble with her hands. . . . You really winced at how uncomfortable she looked." Gradually she overcame her shyness. But as several writers have observed, she has retained the girl-next-door folksiness that drew her early listeners in; for instance, she still spends time between sets mixing with the audience. "Spacey as she occasionally seems, Brickell seductively exudes down-to-earth normalcy— no small virtue in a pop singer," wrote Chris Willman in the *Los Angeles Times.* In *Spin,* Marstaud offered a corroborating anecdote: "One night she had the flu, so she laid out a quilt on the stage, wrapped herself in a comforter and sang from a prone position. If anyone else did that you'd just roll your eyes, but with Edie it came off completely unaffected."

Aside from music, Brickell is passionate about playing football and baseball, trampolining, drawing (the illustrations on *Shooting Rubberbands* are hers), walking at night, and driving around in her pickup truck. Yet when free time is limited, as it has become, her first concern is for solitude; as she told *Spin,* "I need to be alone to get my head together, to feel like an individual." That she, a private, basically introverted person, should become a national star is a source of bemusement to her. "I think it's really ironic that I'm doing what I'm doing," she told *Rolling Stone.* "But that's one of the reasons I'm doing it: because really, I didn't want to live a boring life. I wanted a challenge, and this really is." In the *New York Times,* she added, "Though it meant I had to choose between going to school or devoting time to a band— and everyone was against my joining a band—I couldn't risk blowing what I really wanted to do." And what does she want to do, now that she's shot a few rubber bands? "I want to write songs that make people feel good and escape and lose themselves in it," she told *Musician.* "When I'm driving on a great day with the windows rolled down, I want to hear something that accentuates it, that makes that mood blow over the top. . . . So that's what I want to present to people."

Selected discography

With New Bohemians

The Sound of Deep Ellum (compilation LP of local bands), 1987. *Shooting Rubberbands at the Stars* (includes "What I Am," "Little Miss S.," "Air of December," "The Wheel," "Love Like We Do,"

"Circle," "Beat the Time," "She," "Nothing," "Now," and "Keep Coming Back"), Geffen, 1988.

Sources

East Coast Rocker, February 8, 1989.
Elle, April, 1989.
In Fashion, February, 1989.
Los Angeles Times, December 7, 1988.
Musician, December, 1988.
New York Times, November 18, 1988; November 21, 1988.
People, September 12, 1988; October 24, 1988.
Spin, March, 1989.
Rolling Stone, May 4, 1989.
Variety, December 7, 1988.

—*Kyle Kevorkian*

Jackson Browne

Singer, songwriter, guitarist, pianist

Like Bob Dylan, whose music inspired many during the sixties, Jackson Browne is a song poet, and one of the most prolific of the 1970s. His early music dealt with themes of love and innocence; later songs with humanitarian and political concerns, often interspersed with a recurring, ominous apocalyptic theme. Though much of his early success was attributed to his gift as a composer, Browne was later to score major hits as a performer as well. Said David Spiwack in *Crawdaddy,* Browne's songs "consistently express moods and emotions many of us have felt but couldn't conjure up the words to describe."

Born in Heidelberg, West Germany, on October 9, 1948 (some sources say 1950), Browne was raised in Los Angeles, California, where he studied various musical instruments in his early years. By his late teens he was a proficient guitarist and pianist and an active member in the early efforts of the Nitty Gritty Dirt Band. Too shy to perform his own work at first, Browne gained a reputation as a songwriter, his work showcased by performers such as the Byrds, Linda Ronstadt, and folksinger Tom Rush. His solo career began to take off late in 1969 when he opened for Linda Ronstadt at a Los Angeles club.

The following year Browne shed his stage-shyness and gained experience and publicity touring as Laura Nyro's opening act, and in 1972 his spare, self-titled debut album arrived, featuring the successful singles "Doctor My Eyes" and "Rock Me on the Water." According to *Melody Maker,* the album established Brown "not just as a versatile songwriter but as an artist of major stature." His second album, *For Everyman,* boasted a fuller instrumental and vocal sound and included Browne's version of "Take It Easy," an enormous Eagles hit he had co-penned with Eagle Glenn Frey.

Late for the Sky, released in 1974, was perhaps Browne's most poignant and penetrating album. As a composer, he was recognized for the raw, honest emotion displayed in what were otherwise unremarkable, even repetitous melodies. Nevertheless, according to *Rolling Stone,* the album was Browne's "most mature, conceptually unified work to date." It was also his first certified gold album. Following suit was Browne's next effort, *The Pretender.* In progress at the time of his wife's suicide, the album displays the composer's sense of loss, revealing and reconciling him with his grief in intense and disturbing vocals on such songs as "Sleep's Dark and Silent Gate" as well as both the title track and the hit "Here Come Those Tears Again."

Browne's next project was a clear departure from anything he'd done previously. *Running on Empty* featured all new material, much of which was written by or with others. Recorded entirely "on the road"—on stage, in

For the Record. . .

Full name, Clyde Jackson Browne; born October 9, 1948, in Heidelberg, West Germany; son of Clyde Jack (a printer, musician, and teacher) and Beatrice Amanda (a teacher; maiden name, Dahl) Browne; married Phyllis Major, December 1975 (died, March 25, 1976); married Lynne Sweeney, January 17, 1981 (divorced); children (first marriage) Ethan Zane; (second marriage) Ryan Daniel.

Member of Nitty Gritty Dirt Band, 1966; solo performer, 1966—; staff writer at Nina Music (music publishing branch of Elektra Records), 1966-69; recording debut as guitarist on *Chelsea Girl*, by Nico, 1967; opening act for Laura Nyro, 1970; solo recording debut, 1972; producer of recordings, including Warren Zevon's *Warren Zevon* (1976) and *Excitable Boy* (1977), and co-producer of David Lindley's *El Rayo X* (1981). Co-founder of Musicians United for Safe Energy (MUSE), 1979.

Awards: Gold record awards for *Late for the Sky*, 1974, and *The Pretender*, 1976; platinum record award for *Running on Empty*, 1977.

Addresses: *Office*—c/o Creative Artists Agency, 1888 Century Park East, Suite 1400, Los Angeles, CA 90067.

dressing rooms, on the tour bus—*Running on Empty* was Browne's best-selling album to date and was named favorite album of 1978 in the Second Annual Rock Radio Awards. Browne himself was named favorite male singer as well as favorite singer/songwriter. Said Steve Simels in *Stereo Review, Running on Empty* contains "the work of an artist newly matured and unafraid to take risks."

Simel's claim was strengthened when Browne took a deliberate stand against nuclear power in 1979 and co-founded Musicians United for Safe Energy (MUSE). Browne also helped back and organize the impressive NO NUKES five-day benefit concert, album package, and film to aid the antinuclear cause, a project that took him out of the studio for a year. His next solo project was the 1980 album *Hold Out*, which continued on the rock and roll track he'd laid on *Running on Empty*, with simpler melodies and lyrics bringing Browne mixed reviews. *Rolling Stone* noted that "the music represents a real advance" yet complained that "lyrically, *Hold Out* is probably the weakest record [Browne has] ever made." Despite the varying critiques, the album yielded several hits, including "Boulevard" and "That Girl Could Sing."

If *Hold Out* was indeed weak, the same could not be said of Browne's seventh album, *Lawyers in Love* (1983), which met with critical acclaim. Again, Browne passed over highly personal, autobiographical material in favor of broader views of comtemporary life. In his *Time* review of the album, Jay Cocks summed it up well, saying, "Browne's music pulses with a feeling of renewal and new possibilities . . . he is writing some of the best songs west of the Rockies."

Embracing the political arena, Browne moved farther from his poetic origins in 1986 with *Lives in the Balance*, concentrating on terser melodies and concise phrasing. Like *Hold Out*, the album received mixed reviews, hailed as both bold and tepid. "For America" came under fire from one critic for having "a chorus guaranteed to make you wince," yet another called it "a prayer and a love song, which damns 'a generation's blank stare.'" Having spent much of the preceding two years visiting Nicaragua, Browne focused, not surprisingly,

---

Too shy to perform his own work at first, Browne gained a reputation as a songwriter, his work showcased by performers such as the Byrds, Linda Ronstadt, and folksinger Tom Rush.

---

primarily on Latin America and its conflicts with the U.S. Government, exemplified by the songs "Lives in the Balance" and "Soldier of Plenty." According to *Rolling Stone*, Browne's "new-found ability to link the personal to the political breathes life into these songs and prevents them from becoming too didactic." The music itself is considered "terse and memorable," with even love songs like "In the Shape of a Heart" seeming more mature than ever before.

Browne is issue-conscious again on the *World in Motion* album. Instead of politics, though, Browne aims at "universal truths bound together by a highly personal focus." He sings of moral and legal violations ("How Long" and "The Word Justice"), of pride and hope ("I Am a Patriot"), of revenge (in the chilling Hispanic ballad "My Personal Revenge"), and of enduring love and the potential for change ("Anything Can Happen"). As difficult as it is to successfully deliver "good-conscience pop," Browne maintains his ground. If, as in

"Anything Can Happen," love is possible in this world, amid strife and pain, Browne reasons, then anything can be accomplished. *Rolling Stone* said it succinctly in commenting that *World in Motion* (and perhaps Browne overall) "gets your attention by getting under your skin."

Selected discography

Jackson Browne, Asylum, 1972.
For Everyman, Asylum, 1973.
Late for the Sky, Asylum, 1974.
The Pretender, Asylum, 1976.
Running on Empty, Asylum, 1977.
Hold Out, Asylum, 1980.
Lawyers in Love, Asylum, 1983.
Lives in the Balance, Asylum, 1986.
World in Motion, Elektra, 1989.

Sources

Crawdaddy, January, 1975.
down beat, July, 1985.
High Fidelity, November, 1983; July, 1986.
Los Angeles Times, February 22, 1986.
Melody Maker, March 25, 1972.
Musician, May, 1986; June, 1986.
New York Times, July 31, 1983; August 4, 1983.
People, October 5, 1981; September 12, 1983; April 7, 1986.
Rolling Stone, March 2, 1972; November 7, 1974; December 16, 1976; January 27, 1977; March 9, 1978; October 19, 1978; November 5, 1979; August 7, 1980; September 4, 1980; July 22, 1982; September 15, 1983; September 29, 1983; April 10, 1986; April 24, 1986; July 3, 1986; November 5-December 10, 1987; January 14, 1978; January 29, 1987; July 13-27, 1989.
Stereo Review, June, 1986.
Time, September 12, 1983; March 10, 1986.

—*Meg Mac Donald*

Benny Carter

Jazz saxophonist

"I can only do what I know," stated Benny Carter in a 1989 interview on Marian McPartland's "Piano Jazz," a National Public Radio syndicated program. Taken at face value, Carter's statement leads to the conclusion that he can do virtually anything in the diverse world of music. Dating back to the mid-1920s, Carter has successfully combined the following roles: alto saxophonist; trumpeter; band leader; pianist; clarinetist; trombonist; vocalist; arranger and composer for big swing bands; composer for Hollywood film scores; film actor; composer and arranger for many top vocalists; composer of scores for television series and programs; composer of popular songs; teacher; lecturer; State Department representative. As he approached his eighty-second birthday, Carter was still vitally active in several of these callings.

With Johnny Hodges and Charlie Parker, Carter set the standard for jazz alto saxophonists of all styles. His trumpet and clarinet work has drawn raves from critics and fellow players. As an arranger early in the Swing Era, Carter led the breakthrough that blended jazz solos with ensemble playing in a manner that freed big bands to really swing. His writing for films and television likewise paved the way for acceptance by media moguls and the paying public of newer, jazz-oriented sounds. And, although his bands of whatever size never achieved commercial success, two generations of chosen musicians cherish the time spent playing in one of the bands led by Benny Carter.

Born in the tough San Juan Hill section of New York, Carter began taking piano lessons from his mother and an older sister. When a cornet couldn't be mastered in a few days, he traded it in for a C-melody saxophone which was soon replaced by an alto at the urging of his first leader. Carter remembers that his first professional job, with the legendary pianist Willie "The Lion" Smith's trio, brought out that leader's "iron-fist-in-a-velvet-glove" quality. When, in 1925, Carter joined Horace Henderson who was leading Wilberforce (Ohio) University's "Collegians," he considered himself, at age eighteen, a professional musician. Extremely curious and largely self-taught, Benny Carter had already begun acquiring some of the musical tools that would foster his astounding versatility. Upon returning to New York in 1926, he played with a variety of bands including those of Horace's better-known brother, Fletcher Henderson, Chick Webb, Duke Ellington, and Charlie Johnson, with whom he probably made his 1927 recording debut.

Carter's interest in arranging burgeoned while playing with Fletcher Henderson and Johnson, whose band recorded what is Carter's first confirmed arrangement, "Charleston Is the Best Dance of All," in 1928. After

For the Record...

Full name Bennett Lester "Benny" Carter; born August 8, 1907, in New York City; son of Norrell (a postal clerk and longshoreman) and Sadie (Bennett) Carter; married Rosa Lee Jackson, 1925 (marriage ended); married Margaret Johnson, 1956 (marriage ended); married Hilma Ollila Arons.

Sideman in Wilberforce University's "Collegians," 1925-26; Sideman with bands of Fletcher Henderson, Charlie Johnson, Duke Ellington, Chick Webb, McKinney's Cotten Pickers, 1926-33; Arranger/composer for Benny Goodman, Count Basie and others, 1927-88; Arranger/composer for big swing bands, Hollywood films, and television programs, 1927-89; Leader of orchestras and small bands, 1928-86; Staff arranger, British Broadcasting Corp., London, 1936-37; Arranger for vocalists Louis Armstrong, Ray Charles, Ella Fitzgerald, and Carmen McRae, 1955-75; Visiting artist/lecturer/professor, 1970s; Conductor for Concert and Lecture Tour of the Middle East, U.S. State Department, 1975.

Awards: Grammy Award for arrangement of "Busted," by Ray Charles, 1963; Award from Academie du Disque, France, for *The King*, 1976; Received Golden Score Award from American Society of Music Arrangers, 1980.

Addresses: *Residence*—8321 Skyline Drive, Los Angeles, Calif. 90046. *Record company*—c/o Concord Jazz, Inc., Box 845, 2888 Willow Pass Rd., Concord, Calif. 94522.

is's band for about eight months in Paris, then became a staff arranger for the British Broadcasting Corporation in London, which he used as a home base for successful tours throughout Europe before returning to New York in 1938. With a new big band he took up residence at the Savoy Ballroom for nearly three years, with intermittent tours both locally and out of town, following which he worked with smaller groups. One of these groups included the young trumpeter, Dizzy Gillespie. Other musicians in Carter's groups from the late 1930s to the mid-1940s included trumpeter-arranger Neal Hefti, drummers Kenny Clarke and Max Roach, trombonists J. J. Johnson and Al Grey, saxophonists Dexter Gordon and Lucky Thompson, and trumpeter Miles Davis, all of whom became leading voices when the Bebop movement elbowed its way to prominence.

Beginning in about 1946, Carter settled in Hollywood, where in 1943 he had written and arranged music for the film, *Stormy Weather*. Work on other films soon followed, including: *The Gang's All Here*, *Thousands*

> *Benny Carter led the breakthrough that blended jazz solos with ensemble playing in a manner that freed big bands to really swing.*

Cheer, *Love Happy*, *The Gene Krupa Story*, *The Five Pennies*, *A View from Pompey's Head*, and *The Snows of Kilimanjaro*. In the latter two Carter performed acting roles as well. Dating to 1958, television scoring commanded most of Carter's attention as he produced music for series such as "M Squad," "It Takes a Thief," "Bob Hope Presents," "The Chrysler Theater," and the Alfred Hitchcock series. Concurrently, he wrote arrangements and sometimes conducted for several vocalists, including Ray Charles, Peggy Lee, Ella Fitzgerald, and Carmen McRae. Carter also used his considerable influence to help bring about the 1953 merging of the segregated black and white musicians' unions into an integrated Local 47.

Of Carter's solo playing Whitney Balliett wrote in the *New Yorker*: "To be sure, Carter was the most admired alto saxophonist of the thirties, but that was hardly surprising. Johnny Hodges didn't draw himself to his full height until 1940. . . . [Carter's 1976] alto-saxophone playing has grown even statelier. The joyous declamatory tone has broadened, and the melodic

leading different versions of his own band, his next move was to join the popular McKinney's Cotton Pickers in Detroit, replacing Don Redman in 1931 as music director. Gunther Schuller, in his first volume on the history of jazz, *Early Jazz*, describes how Carter was instrumental in freeing up arrangements: "Carter obviously has found the long-sought-after solution for making a section swing: the answer lay in syncopation. . . . Once the [soloist] could detach himself from explicitly stating the four beats and thus get 'inside' the beats a vast field of rhythmic emancipation lay ahead." He was encouraged (and sometimes coached) by trumpeter Doc Cheatham to apply his obvious gifts to the trumpet. By the time of his 1933 recordings with the Chocolate Dandies, Carter's prowess on alto, trumpet, and clarinet was acknowledged throughout the music business, as was his talent as a writer and arranger. During this period, fellow musicians were constantly amazed as Carter revealed the layers of his talent.

Pressed by economics, Carter disbanded in 1934, leaving for Europe in 1935. He played with Willie Lew-

lines have become longer and more complex." In his 1989 second volume on the history of jazz, *The Swing Era*, Gunther Schuller describes Carter's 1930 clarinet work (on "Dee Blues"): "Carter's clarinet solos—enclosing the performance at either end like the covers of a book—are quite extraordinary. His tone is full and firm with a hue much like that of an A clarinet, and with a slightly edgy thrust in the middle and upper range, taking on the color of both a trumpet and an alto saxophone. In this manner Carter was almost able to match the awesome majesty of [Coleman] Hawkins in his brief sweeping 'gliding' solo. Creatively both clarinet solos are superior examples of Carter's effortless control of ideas, his always cogent sense of direction." Though he has played the trumpet only sporadically through the years, several beautiful records attest to Carter's mastery of that instrument, including "Once upon a Time," "Stardust," and "I Surrender Dear," which became a Carter showpiece. The sustained demand for Carter as a writer-arranger speaks to his standing in these disciplines.

The absence of commercial acceptance of Carter's various large and small bands has caused many musicians and critics to wonder just what is required to achieve this kind of success. While Carter has continued to assimilate and originate new concepts and fresh sounds, he has never sacrificed musicianship for faddish effects. Some have argued that Carter's extravagant versatility in itself is a problem in that the listening public finds difficulty in attaching a label, a positive identity, to Carter. Others have claimed that the great Carter facility that allows all his feats to seem so polished and effortless appears to rob his playing and writing of passion. In his 1989 book, Schuller concludes his discussion of Carter in this way: "As one hears the late [most recent] Benny Carter and hears the tremendous authority—and yes, even passion—with which he discharges a wide range of assignments, one is tempted to conclude that Benny Carter, the restless ever-searching seeker, has finally found his rightful place (or two) in the sun. His playing as well as his composing and arranging now have a conviction, an inevitableness, and above all a reaching out to an audience, whatever audience or audiences—and there are several—in a way that he somehow could never attain earlier."

Selected discography

The Chocolate Dandies, Parlophone, 1930.
Benny Carter—1933, Prestige, 1933.
Spike Hughes & His All-American Orchestra, London/Ace of Clubs, 1933.

Benny Carter and His Orchestra: 1940-41, RCA Victor (France), 1940-41.
Benny Carter, Big Band Bounce, Capitol, c. 1945.
(With Coleman Hawkins) *Further Definitions*, Impulse/MCA, 1962.
Additions to Further Definitions, Impulse, 1966.
(With Dizzy Gillespie) *The King*, Pablo, 1976.
(With the Count Basie Orchestra) *Basie Jam #2 and #3*, Pablo, 1976.
Benny Carter All Stars (in Tokyo), Pablo, 1977.
A Gentleman and His Music, Concord, 1986.
Only Trust Your Heart, 1989.

Sources

Books

Berger, Morroe, *Benny Carter, A Life in American Music*, Volumes I and II, Scarecrow Press and the Institute of Jazz Studies, Rutgers University, 1982.
Biographical Dictionary of Afro-American and African Musicians, Greenwood Press, 1982.
Biographical Dictionary of Jazz, Prentice Hall, 1982.
Case, Brian, and Stan Britt, *The Illustrated Encyclopedia of Jazz*, Salamander Books, Ltd., 1978.
Chilton, John, *Who's Who of Jazz*, Time-Life Records, 1978.
The Complete Encyclopedia of Popular Music and Jazz, 1900-1950, Arlington House, 1974.
Feather, Leonard, *The New Edition of The Encyclopedia of Jazz*, Bonanza Books, 1960.
Gitler, Ira, *Swing to Bop*, Oxford University Press, 1985.
New Grove Dictionary of American Music, Macmillan, 1986.
Rust, Brian, *Jazz Records 1897-1942*, 5th revised and enlarged edition, Volume 1, Storyville Publications, 1982.
Schuller, Gunther, *Early Jazz*, Oxford University Press, 1968.
Schuller, Gunther, *The Swing Era*, Oxford University Press, 1989.
Shaw, Arnold, *The Street That Never Slept*, Coward, McCann & Geoghegan, 1971.
Simon, George T., *The Big Bands*, revised and enlarged edition, Collier, 1974.

Periodicals

New Yorker, July 5, 1976.
New York Times, June 5, 1986.
Village Voice, May 11, 1982.

—Robert Dupuis

The Carter Family

Folk/country performers

Family groups have always been a staple of popular music in America, but none has blazed a more influential trail than the Carter Family of Maces Springs, Virginia. The Carters—A. P., his wife Sara, and his sister-in-law Maybelle—brought their Blue Ridge mountain ballads to nationwide audiences during the Great Depression, creating a rich trove of folk songs that are sung and performed to this day. According to John Atkins in *Stars of Country Music,* the Carters' style and repertoire "provide much of the nucleus of that branch of country music which has always remained apart from the well-defined patterns of commercial success determined by Nashville, Tennessee."

Each of the 300-odd songs the Carter Family recorded bears the distinctive Carter mark. Only a scant few cater to popular trends. Unlike their exact contemporary, Jimmie Rodgers, the Carters rarely experimented with nontraditional arrangements or backup bands. In *Country Music U.S.A.,* Bill C. Malone notes that, save for a marked improvement in instrumental technique over time, the Carter recordings "never varied substantially in . . . sixteen years." Malone suggests that the group achieved national stardom because the Carters "sang of an America that was gradually disappearing, an America whose values had seemed inextricably interrelated with rural or small-town life. That America had been fading since before the Carters were children, though its vision may have burned brighter in the South and Midwest than anywhere else in the nation. Songs about wandering boys, abandoned mothers, dying orphans, and forsaken lovers had a special poignancy for people who saw the stable world of their parents disintegrating around them. The paeans to the 'Homestead on the Farm,' the 'Little Village Church Yard,' or 'The Little Poplar Log House' became increasingly meaningful as such nostalgic symbols of rural innocence and security receded farther and farther into memory." That same nostalgia became the focal point of the folk renaissance of the early 1960s, so it is not surprising that the living members of the Carter Family enjoyed an unprecedented comeback at that time.

The Carter Family was founded by Alvin Pleasant Delaney Carter, better known as A. P. He was born in Maces Springs, Virginia, a small town near the Tennessee border, and was one of nine children of deeply religious parents. Growing up, A. P. was encouraged to sing in church quartets with other members of his family, but he was dissuaded from learning to play the fiddle because of the temptation to play "sinful" dance tunes. In 1915, A. P. met and married Sara Dougherty, a native of the nearby town of Copper Creek. The lively Sara was proficient on the banjo, guitar, and autoharp, and she had been performing locally with her equally talented cousin, Maybelle Addington. Sara returned to Maces

Springs with A. P., and they formed a duo that was soon much in demand in the region. In the early 1920s they were actually offered a recording contract by Brunswick Records, but since the company wanted square-dance fiddle tunes, A. P. turned down the deal. In 1926 Maybelle Addington married A. P.'s brother Ezra, they settled in Maces Springs, and she became the third Carter Family member. Atkins writes: "Soon the trio began to unite their musical talents into a firmly knit group, with Sara singing lead, Maybelle alto harmony, and A. P. bass."

In 1927 the Carters were one of a number of local groups who travelled to Bristol, Virginia, to audition for Victor Records. During the same week that Jimmie Rodgers cut his first songs for Victor, the Carters were offered fifty dollars per song for six tunes by record executive Ralph Peer. Having concluded the session, the Carters returned to their farms and young children in Maces Springs. Months later, they were surprised to find that their first recordings had sold quite well indeed. Early in 1928, Peer invited the group to the Victor

studios in Camden, New Jersey, for a whole series of recording sessions. Quite magnanimously, Peer raised the Carters' take to seventy-five dollars per song. These Victor recordings on 78 RPM were almost all best-sellers, especially "Wildwood Flower," released in May 1928. A tale of lost love that highlights Maybelle's melody-and-rhythm guitar picking, "Wildwood Flower" was one of the first country songs heard outside the South.

The Carters quickly found themselves in demand for radio and live appearances. They answered the demand for new material by scouring the Blue Ridge communities of Virginia and Tennessee for family songs and rhymes that could be put to music. A. P. led these "song-hunting" trips, and Sara and Maybelle arranged the music to suit the group. Scholars feel that A. P. Carter wrote only a few of the songs the family performed, even though he is listed as the songwriter in almost every case. "Carter's motivation for collecting songs was not to preserve them in print," writes Atkins, ". . . but purely to provide a source of original material—in terms of what was on phonograph records—for his group to record. The end product, however, . . . [had] the effect of preserving the songs for future generations. A. P. Carter thus firmly deserves a place in the annals of the collectors as well as the entertainers." Indeed, no rural family ever complained when the famous Carters recorded a cherished local song, and it is likely that this rich legacy of music might have been lost forever had the Carters not mined it so thoroughly.

The Carter Family oeuvre consists almost exclusively of Anglo-Saxon and Scotts-Irish traditional music, but the works were adapted from their traditional forms. "In addition to furnishing a rich legacy of songs for American folk and country music," writes Atkins, "the Carters introduced a new stylistic and rhythmic content to the music, and it was perhaps this that was to prove their greatest legacy. Based on Maybelle's guitar styling in such songs as 'Wildwood Flower' and 'Engine 143,' where she played melody on the bass strings while maintaining the rhythm with chords on the treble strings, the Carters offered a rhythm which was new to country music and even newer to the songs they performed." It can certainly be argued that the Carter Family's greatest contribution to modern American music is Maybelle's "Carter lick," a style that elevated the guitar from merely an accompanying instrument to one that might take the lead itself.

Even though A. P. and Sara Carter divorced in 1933, the Carter Family continued to perform together into the early years of World War II. As their children grew, they too were incorporated into the live and radio performances, especially Maybelle's daughters, Helen, Anita, and June. They switched to Decca Records in 1936 and were one of the few groups to be awarded royalties rather than flat fees per recording. In the latter half of the 1930s the family could be heard regularly on several high-wattage radio stations on the Texas-Mexico border. Despite obvious personal differences, the Carters maintained a singular air of professionalism in the studio and onstage. Most of their songs were recorded in a single take, having been practiced extensively beforehand, and their live shows exhibited nothing but amiability. The group finally disbanded in 1943, when A. P. and Sara chose to retire.

Undaunted by the loss of her original partners, Maybelle took her daughters and formed another group, the Carter Sisters and Mother Maybelle. Before long the new band was more in demand than the original, making regular appearances at the Grand Ole Opry and touring with other country stars. A. P. and Sara tried a comeback in 1952, adding their children Joe and Janette to their band. They did not receive much atten-

---

> The Carter Family's sound "was a mournful, American-gothic kind of gospel harmony that epitomized and reinforced the South's verities of church and home."

---

tion, so in 1956 they again retired. Sara moved to California and A. P. returned to Maces Springs, where he died in 1960.

With the resurgence of interest in folk music during the 1960s, Maybelle finally won the acclaim that her half-century career deserved. She became a perennial favorite at the Newport Folk Festival and even reunited with Sara for a 1967 album, *An Historic Reunion.* Throughout the 1960s Maybelle also toured with her daughters as part of Johnny Cash's travelling show. Her daughter June married Cash in 1967.

Maybelle Carter died of respiratory failure in October 1978. In a *Rolling Stone* eulogy, Chet Flippo maintained that "Mother Maybelle," through her playing and singing, "helped define the direction of country music: her unique guitar style revolutionized country instrumentation and influenced performers from Woody Guthrie to Joan Baez and Bob Dylan. . . . [The Carter Family's] sound, dominated by Maybelle's guitar, was a mourn-

ful, American-gothic kind of gospel harmony that epitomized and reinforced the South's verities of church and home." Sara Carter died in California in 1979, so far from the fame she had once enjoyed that few newspapers noticed her passing.

Atkins concludes: "Today the Carter Family's music enjoys a wider audience than ever before. Their music and style have survived analysis; their lives, both public and private, have been laid bare for all to see. But even before these words and many other similar treatises were written, it has always been there for inspection and analysis, because *everything* the Carter family ever did, *everything* they ever were is captured on the wonderful legacy of recordings they have willed to the world at large, and to country music for all time."

Selected discography

The Famous Carter Family, Columbia, 1961.
The Original and Great Carter Family, RCA, 1961.
'Mid the Green Fields of Virginia, RCA, 1963.
An Historic Reunion, Columbia, 1967.
Wildwood Flower, RCA, 1988.
Best of the Carter Family, Columbia.
Favourite Family Songs, Liverty.
Happiest Days of All, RCA.
More Golden Gems from the Original Carter Family, RCA.
My Old Cottage Home, RCA.
Keep on the Sunny Side, Columbia.
Travelin' Minstrel Band, Columbia.
Three Generations of the Carter Family, Columbia.
A. P. Carter's Clinch Mountain Ballads, Pine Mountain.
The Carter Family on Border Radio, John Edwards Memorial Foundation.
Country Sounds of the Original Carter Family, Harmony.
Home among the Hills, Harmony.
More Favorites by the Carter Family, Decca.
A Selection of Favorites by the Carter Family, Decca.
Will the Circle Be Unbroken? United Artists.

Sources

Books

Malone, Bill C., *Country Music U.S.A.,* revised edition, University of Texas Press, 1985.
Malone, Bill C. and Judith McCulloh, *Stars of Country Music,* University of Illinois Press, 1975.

Shestack, Melvin, *The Country Music Encyclopedia,* Crowell, 1974.

Periodicals

Rolling Stone, December 14, 1978.

—*Anne Janette Johnson*

Chicago

Pop/rock, jazz group

With distinctly midwestern roots and a distinctive big-band sound, Chicago took the pop music world by surprise in the 1970s with their jazzy, full instrumental arrangements. Though they were often compared with another big-band-sounding pop group, Blood, Sweat and Tears, member Robert Lamm points out one of their differences by saying, "Our roots are basically rock, but we can and do play jazz; Blood, Sweat and Tears is basically a jazz-rooted combo that can play a lot of rock."

Originally called the Big Thing, a phrase Lamm said "Mafia types" used to describe the band's unique music, the group later changed their name to Chicago Transit Authority, then, after their first album, simply Chicago. The musical diversity in the group was astounding from the beginning, with only two of the original six members (Robert Lamm, James Pankow, Danny Seraphine, Terry Kath, Walt Parazaider, and Lee Loughnane, with the addition of Peter Cetera in the late sixties, and, in 1974, percussionist Laudir De Oliverira) being self-taught, and the rest having considerable

formal training. The group boasted competent musicians not only on drums or guitar, but also on clarinet, trumpet, trombone, and piano. The group's impressive blend of jazz and rock elements and improvisational energy attracted a varied audience.

Before gaining national popularity, the band played at a number of rock clubs in the Los Angeles Sunset Strip district, eventually receiving a small following and favorable reviews from underground papers. They stepped into the spotlight with *Chicago Transit Authority* in 1969, an album that slowly made its way onto the charts to stay there well into 1971. Lamm's pop ballad "Does Anybody Really Know What Time It Is," became a hit single in 1969 and remains one of the group's most popular songs. A series of hit singles, including "Make Me Smile" and the curiously titled "25 or 6 to 4" followed the release of the group's second album, *Chicago,* in 1970. The disc also contained one of the first of many unusual tracks, a six-movement rock composition entitled "Ballet for a Girl in Buchannon."

More orchestral work was to follow in the band's third LP (a two-record set) with multiple-movement suites "Hour in the Shower" and the entire-side-long "Travel Suite." Another two-record set came in the form of a live album, *Chicago at Carnegie Hall,* released in 1971. According to *Rolling Stone,* the latter was "probably the worst live album in history." Released against Chicago's wishes, the band blamed their sloppy performance on the constant interference of the record's producer on stage. Said Pankow, "The horns on that record sound like kazoos. . . . How can you play? Every two seconds a curve was being thrown to everyone onstage." Nevertheless, the set rose swiftly into the top ten.

Subsequent albums were released almost every year, with two released in a single year on more than one occasion, and all were certified gold. Top-selling singles rose out of almost every album and included such songs as "Saturday in the Park" in 1972 and "Feelin' Stronger Everyday" in 1973. The group was immensely popular in concert as well, including a number of college and university campuses among as many as 200 concerts a year. The group also traveled to Europe and were extremely well-received in Scandinavia, belying any suggestion that their brand of jazzy pop

> *Chicago took the pop music world by surprise in the 1970s with their jazzy, full instrumental arrangements.*

was only a U.S. phenomenon. Their 1976 *Chicago X* album garnered three Grammys, with the single "If You Leave Me Now" recognized for both best arrangement and best pop vocal performance by a duo or group for the year.

Despite the overwhelming success enjoyed by the band, *Rock Who's Who* maintains they were "a big-band rock group that initially utilized jazz-style improvisations," later degenerating into "a pop group of huge popularity, issuing album after album of formulaic, predictable, middle-of-the-road fare." Again, the group members found fault with their producer and what they interpreted as a lack of enthusiasm. "It took so long to do things" Parazaider told *Rolling Stone.* "That's when it becomes like a factory gig, then you're just pumping it out." The band began coproducing their albums, then, finally, began coming in after-hours to record alone. "With [producer] Jimmy [Guercio] everything had to be technically correct," adds Seraphine. "Sometimes he would lose some of the magic because he was so meticulous." Eventually, toward the later seventies, the group's popularity seemed to fade, their vitality weakened by the tragic death of Terry Kath in 1978 and their previous cessation of ties to longtime producer/manager Guercio. This low point was not to last long.

Finding new confidence and enthusiasm in guitarist Donnie Dacus and co-producer Phil Ramone, the band turned out one of their finest albums, *Hot Streets,* in 1978. Instead of perfection, Ramone emphasized the group's natural sound, drawing on the excitement of an essentially "live" recording. Strong tracks from the album included the Bee Gees-backed "Little Miss Loving" and the chart-topping "Alive Again," which *People* described as exploding "with an awesome blend of power and finesse." Addressing the long-standing problem of the band having a recognizable "logo" but not "ego," the members were photographed on their album's cover for the first time. Newly focused and pushing foward as professional musicians concerned with the vitality of their music and its potential impact on future generations, the group did indeed appear to be "alive again."

After the release of *Chicago 17,* however, longtime member Peter Cetera left the group to pursue a solo career. His departure appeared to have little effect on the group, whose "corporate, or maybe it's municipal, kind of sound" (as reproduced on *Chicago 18*) remained unchanged. Still, *People* noted the album included a remake of the early hit "25 or 6 to 4," suggesting a certain desperation for hits that would lead them to "resuscitate its old ones." Despite such criticism, though, the LP found favor as "basic, hard-core Chicago, which history has shown to be a lot of people's kind of music."

Selected discography

As Chicago Transit Authority

Chicago Transit Authority, Columbia, 1969, reissued, 1989.

As Chicago

Chicago, Columbia, 1970.
Chicago III, Columbia, 1971.
Live at Carnegie Hall, Columbia, 1971.
Chicago V, Columbia, 1972.
Chicago VI, Columbia, 1973.
Chicago VII, Columbia, 1974.
Chicago VIII, Columbia, 1975.
Chicago IX—Chicago's Greatest Hits, Columbia, 1975.
Chicago X, Columbia, 1976.
Chicago XI, Columbia, 1977.
Hot Streets, Columbia, 1978.
Chicago XIII, Columbia, 1979.
Chicago XIV, Columbia, 1980.
Chicago's Greatest Hits, Vol 2, Columbia, 1981.
Chicago XVI, Full Moon, 1984.
Chicago 17, Full Moon, 1984.
Chicago 18, Warner Bros., 1986.
Chicago 19, Reprise, 1988.

Sources

Books

Helander, Brock, *Rock Who's Who,* Schirmer, 1982.
Nite, Norm N., *Rock On,* Volume 2, Harper, 1984.
Stambler, Irwin, *Encyclopedia of Pop, Rock, and Soul,* St. Martin's, 1977.

Periodicals

People, October 16, 1978; November 17, 1986; February 2, 1987.
Rolling Stone, December 14, 1978.
Time, June 2, 1975.

—*Meg Mac Donald*

Stanley Clarke

Bassist, composer, producer

"I don't feel I should have to make music to satisfy anyone," Stanley Clarke told a *Rolling Stone* interviewer. "But I do feel that one of an artist's fundamental duties is to create work other people can relate to. I'd be a fool to do something nobody else was going to understand." Thus jazz bassist Clarke creates music that a wide variety of record buyers and concert-goers are able to relate to and appreciate.

Born in Philadelphia in 1951, Clarke began his study of music at age ten on the accordion. He played the violin next, then cello, but soon settled on the bass. "The bass was tall and I was tall; it was similar to a violin and a cello, which was the direction I was taking anyway, so I started playing the bass," Clarke said in an interview for the book *Jazz-Rock Fusion: The People, the Music,* by Julie Coryell and Laura Friedman. Clarke's early training was in classical music. He studied music formally at the Philadelphia Musical Academy.

He began his jazz career in 1970 with the Horace Silver Band. In 1971 he joined Joe Henderson and later worked with the Stan Getz Band. While with Getz, Clarke met pianist Chick Corea, who also was a member of the band. In 1972 Corea formed his own group, taking Clarke along with him. The acoustic jazz group called Return to Forever "was a very energetic band," noted Mark Gridley in *Jazz Styles,* "whose flashy technical feats impressed musician and nonmusician alike." Corea then formed an electric Return to Forever, retaining Clarke, who switched to electric bass, and adding guitarist Al Di Meola and drummer Lenny White. The group was influenced by rock and was one of the forerunners of what was dubbed "jazz-rock fusion" music, combining the melodies and intricacies of jazz with the drive and power of rock. The band became increasingly popular until it broke up in 1976 and each member moved on to solo and other projects.

Clarke had begun releasing solo albums while still with Return to Forever, and in 1976 he formed his own group. The Stanley Clarke Group has had various members over the years and continues to tour and record in between Clarke's other activities. In his solo efforts and with his own band, Clarke has explored and combined many diverse musical influences. As he told *down beat,* his music "has a lot of elements in it—rock and roll, jazz, r&b, funk, classical, Latin, African."

In sessions outside his group, Clarke has worked with rock musicians as well as other jazz musicians. In 1979 he toured with Rolling Stones members Keith Richard and Ron Wood in what was called the New Barbarians tour. In 1980 Clarke teamed with jazz pianist George Duke as the Clarke/Duke Project and had a hit with the song "Sweet Baby." And in 1981 he played on Paul McCartney's album *Tug of War.*

For the Record. . .

Full name, Stanley Marvin Clarke; born June 31, 1951, in Philadelphia, Pa.; son of Marvin and Blanche (Bundy) Clarke; married Carolyn Helene Reese, November 29, 1974; children: Christopher Ivanhoe. *Education:* Attended Philadelphia Music Academy. *Religion:* Scientology.

Musician, composer, record producer. Member of Horace Silver Band, 1970, Joe Henderson Band, 1971, Stan Getz Band 1971-72, and Return to Forever, 1972-76; leader of Stanley Clarke Group, 1976—; member of Clarke/Duke Project, 1980—.

Awards: Selected bassist of the year, 1973, electric bassist of the year 1974, 1975, and 1976, in the *down beat* International Readers' Poll; selected bassist of the year, 1976, 1977, 1978, 1979, and 1980, in the *Playboy* Readers' Poll; selected jazz artist of the year, 1977, in *Rolling Stone* Music Critics' Poll; named to *Guitar Player* Gallery of Greats, 1980.

Addresses: *Office*—8817 Rangely Ave., Los Angeles, CA 90048.

Clarke's talents are not limited to playing bass. He has composed a number of songs and has sung on records by Return to Forever and his own group. He has also produced albums for both himself and for other artists, including guitarist Roy Buchanan and singers Dee Dee Bridgewater and Flora Purim. He wrote a magazine column on bass playing for a while, and he has plans to write a multiple-volume work on the bass. Clarke told *down beat,* "I'm writing a book on acoustic bass, maybe three or four volumes. It's going to be the full thing—everything that anyone would want to know about the acoustic bass."

Clarke had already earned a reputation as an accomplished jazz bassist even before joining Return to Forever. But "during his tenure as bassist for Return to Forever, Clarke established himself as one of the most prodigious instrumentalists in modern music: an exceptionally nimble, resourceful electric and acoustic bassist," says Mikal Gilmore of *Rolling Stone.* Joachim Berendt in *The Jazz Book: From New Orleans to Rock and Free Jazz* describes Clarke's talents by comparing him to two other noted bassists: "Stanley Clarke combines [Miroslav] Vitous's fluidity with Oscar Pettiford's 'soul.'"

Clarke's distinctive style of play rejects the usual background rhythm role of bass players and moves the bass right to the forefront of his music. Says Clarke in the book *Jazz-Rock Fusion,* "Years ago there was a fixed idea that bass players played background, and bass players have this particular theme—kind of subdued, numb, almost looking numb, and just to make a long story short, I wasn't going for any of that." Clarke's trademark on electric bass is a metallic sound. He also imparts some twist on the strings, what Chuck Carman of *down beat* describes as putting "English" on them. Clarke concurs: "I found from plucking the strings in various ways that just the slightest movement can change your whole sound . . . English is a great word. I just use English of various types on the strings."

His solos are known for some very fast runs. Regarding his approach to soloing, he told *Guitar Player* magazine: "On electric bass, I use any finger, even my thumbs—anything!. . . I pluck mainly with three fingers. I have certain patterns that I can only play with four fingers. Sometimes when I get to those real fast runs that just fly, they'll be a fourth finger in there to help play it." Clarke's energetic style was influenced by the techniques of Scott LaFaro, bassist for Bill Evans. According to Mark Gridley in *Jazz Styles,* LaFaro created a modern style that made the bass not just a timekeeper but a melodic instrument. Young jazz bassists, including Clarke, who were influenced by LaFaro "interacted with pianists and drummers in an imaginative and highly active manner." Clarke himself told *Rolling Stone:* "I've always been more drawn to melodic than rhythmic playing . . . I had all these melodies running around in my head, all this knowledge of classical music I was trying to apply to r&b and jazz, and I decided it would be a loss in personal integrity just to be a timekeeper in the background, going *plunk plunk thwack thwack.*"

Although Clarke has a reputation as a very fine musician, his move from pure jazz to jazz-rock fusion upset some jazz critics. His later projects with rock musicians, such as the New Barbarians tour, and the introduction of pop and rock themes into his music, have served to tarnish his image among some jazz "purists." Mikal Gilmore says that in recent years "Clarke has seemed to temper his talent, opting instead to play fairly prosaic, overbusy variations of rhythm & blues and even heavy-metal music." Gilmore is especially critical of Clarke's collaboration with George Duke. He states that the music of the Clarke/Duke Project is "pointedly devoid of the sort of compositional or improvisatory prowess that earned either musician his standing in the first place." Some other critics echo Gilmore's sentiments. In a review of a Sonny Rollins album on which both Clarke and Duke played, Chris Albertson of *Stereo Review* sniffed, "Pianist George Duke and bassist Stanley Clarke, men of great jazz potential who were bitten by the chart bug before they could show us more than the tip of their talent, here prove that they have spent too much time in fusionland."

Charges of commercialism, of "going Hollywood" have been especially biting. Don Heckman, in a *High Fidelity* review of the Clarke-produced Maynard Ferguson album *Hollywood,* quipped that "the title certainly tells you what to expect. But if there are any doubts, note that the album was 'produced and directed' by Stanley Clarke. . . . Jazz? Forget it." Clarke acknowledges the criticism he has received but is determined not to let it change him. Asked in *down beat* whether he knows any musicians who changed because of press criticism, Clarke responded: "I've seen guys do that, and I've seen them go right down the drain, too. That's one thing that an artist can't do—if any creative person starts listening to other people, he goes down." Clarke's penchant for exploring a number of different musical paths, he realizes, has led to much of the criticism. But as Clarke observed in *down beat,* "It would get boring for me if I just did one thing and played just one type of music for the rest of my life. I don't think I could take it."

Stanley Clarke believes in making an emotional impact with his music, to touch his audience.

And Clarke told *Rolling Stone,* "I know it upsets some people, but I could never be a conservative jazz musician."

And at least one critic has revised his opinion of Clarke. In a *Stereo Review* article, Chris Albertson remarked: "I used to think of Stanley Clarke as one of the defectors, a jazz man drawn away from his art by the waving of the green. Now I am inclined to think that I did Clarke an injustice."

Clarke presents himself, both off and on the stage, in an engaging manner. "Stanley Clarke struck me as a person who nobody could help but like," Carman wrote in *down beat.* "His expression was either a friendly smile or a more intent look as he listened to questions. Several times during the course of the interview he shied away from 'naming names,' when it might conceivably reflect adversely upon someone." In reviewing a 1983 reunion tour of Return to Forever, Bill Milkowski of *down beat* said, "Clarke remains the same crowdpleaser he always was, an engaging presence with a flashing

smile, playing up the rock theatrics during his explosive solos."

Clarke believes in making an emotional impact with his music, to touch his audience. To *down beat* he said, "I have an intention, regardless of what anyone thinks, to have my music reach out to someone. . . . I'm trying to get across good feelings." All in all, Clarke says that his goal is not to bore anyone. As he told Carman, "It's a nice goal to have. It keeps you busy."

Selected discography

Solo LPs

Stanley Clarke, Columbia, 1974.
Journey to Love, Columbia, 1975.
School Days, Columbia, 1976.
Modern Man, Columbia, 1978.
I Wanna Play for You, Columbia, 1979.
Rock, Pebbles, and Sand, Epic, 1980.
Let Me Know You, Epic, 1982.
Time Exposure, Epic, 1984.
Find Out!, Epic, 1985.
If This Bass Could Only Talk, Portrait, 1988.

With Chick Corea and group Return to Forever

Return to Forever, ECM, 1972.
Hymn to the 7th Galaxy, Polydor, 1973.
Light as a Feather, Polydor, 1973.
Where Have I Known You Before?, Polydor, 1974.
Children of Forever, Polydor, 1974.
No Mystery, Polydor, 1975.
Romantic Warrior, Columbia, 1976.
Music Magic, Columbia, 1977.
The Best of Return to Forever, Columbia, 1980.
Midnight Magic, Columbia.

Other

The Clarke/Duke Project (with George Duke), Epic, 1981.
The Clarke/Duke Project II (with Duke), Epic, 1983.
Hideaway (with George Howard, Herbie Hancock, Stanley Jordan, Stewart Copeland, Angela Bofill, Larry Graham, and others), Epic, 1986.

Also has played on record albums by a number of other artists, including Carlos Santana, Aretha Franklin, Quincy Jones, Paul McCartney, Sonny Rollins, and Chaka Khan.

Sources

Books

Berendt, Joachim, *The Jazz Book: From New Orleans to Rock and Free Jazz,* translation by Dan Morgenstern, Barbara Bredigkeit, and Helmut Bredigkeit, Lawrence Hill & Co., 1975.

Coryell, Julie, and Laura Friedman, *Jazz-Rock Fusion: The People, The Music,* Dell, 1978.

Gridley, Mark C., *Jazz Styles,* Prentice-Hall, 1978.

The Rolling Stone Encyclopedia of Rock & Roll, Rolling Stone Press, 1983.

Periodicals

down beat, March 24, 1977; July 13, 1978; July 1983.

Guitar Player, August 1981.

High Fidelity, July 1982.

People, December 1, 1975.

Rolling Stone, June 11, 1981.

Stereo Review, April 1981; May 1982; December 1982; January 1983.

—Greg Mazurkiewicz

Leonard Cohen

Singer, songwriter, guitarist

Multi-talented folksinger-songwriter Leonard Cohen was already a well-respected Canadian poet and novelist when he began penning tunes for folk star Judy Collins. Shortly afterwards, he started recording and performing his own lyrics and melodies successfully, though he is perhaps best known through the vocalizations of Collins and other singers, including Joe Cocker and Jennifer Warnes. Responsible for folk classics such as "Sisters of Mercy" and "Bird on a Wire," Cohen, with what critic David Browne labeled as his "sardonic verse and brooding demeanor," has influenced many late 1980s singer-songwriters, including Suzanne Vega, in addition to continuing his own career with the 1988 album *I'm Your Man.*

Cohen was born September 21, 1934, in Montreal, Quebec, Canada. Music was not his first love; rather, he began writing poetry and fiction as a teenager. But he had a friend whose father played guitar and sang folk songs to the boys; this man taught Cohen to play the instrument. Also, while the young writer worked towards a degree at McGill University, he played in an amateur country band called the Buckskin Boys. After he graduated from college, his first volume of poetry, *Let Us Compare Mythologies,* was published. Within a few years Cohen's verses had received wide critical acclaim, both in his native land and in the United States. He traveled both countries giving poetry readings during the late 1950s, and at these readings he was often accompanied by a musician who played while Cohen read. This reawakened the poet's interest in music, and he began playing the guitar and singing again for groups of friends.

By 1966 Cohen had published three more volumes of poetry and two novels, *The Favorite Game* and *Beautiful Losers.* Both eventually became best-sellers, with *The Favorite Game* achieving something of a cult following. But 1966 was the year that Cohen would begin focusing on his music. While doing a poetry reading in New York City, he was approached by the Columbia Broadcasting System which wanted him to appear in a television program based on his readings. They also wanted musical interludes. At the same time, Cohen went to see Judy Collins in concert; her performance inspired him to begin writing his own folk songs.

Collins liked his compositions, and she included two of them—"Suzanne" and "Dress Rehearsal Rag"—on her 1967 album *In My Life.* Other artists began to use Cohen's songs, and his friends persuaded him to begin performing them himself. Cohen did so, and his act met with warm receptions at the Newport Folk Festival, the Rheingold Music Festival, and Montreal's Expo '67. He also landed a recording contract with Columbia Records, and released his debut album, *Songs of Leonard*

Cohen, very late in 1967. Well received by most critics, it was later used as the soundtrack for the film *McCabe and Mrs. Miller.* In addition to his own version of "Suzanne," the album included the Cohen trademark songs "Hey, That's No Way to Say Goodbye" and "Sisters of Mercy."

Cohen followed his debut effort with *Songs from a Room* in 1969; it featured what is perhaps Cohen's best-known song, "Bird on the Wire." A long string of critically successful albums ensued; one of the most popular was 1971's *Songs of Love and Hate.* Throughout the 1970s Cohen composed and released several songs that have become folk standards, including "Joan of Arc," "Famous Blue Raincoat," "Story of Isaac," "Tonight Will Be Fine," and "Please Don't Pass Me By."

In the later 1970s, Cohen left Columbia Records to work at Warner Brothers with famed rock producer-composer Phil Spector. Despite the two men's widely different styles, they produced an album which combined Cohen's words and Spector's music, 1977's *Death of a Ladies' Man.* Critical response was mixed, and ranged from execration to exaltation; the effort was extremely popular with fans in Europe but did not sell well in the United States. Two years later, Cohen went back to Columbia to release *Recent Songs.* On several tracks he sang duets with singer Jennifer Warnes, who also released an album of her versions of several Cohen standards, *Famous Blue Raincoat.*

For the next nine years, Cohen did not record on any major labels, though he did release an album in 1984 called *Various Positions,* which Browne described as centering on "Judeo-Christian imagery." In 1988, however, *I'm Your Man* came out on Columbia. Cohen's always deadpan delivery is "now so low it sounds as if it were about to fall off the record," Browne quipped, but the *Rolling Stone* reviewer went on to praise several cuts on the album, including the title track, "First We Take Manhattan," "Ain't No Cure for Love," "Tower of Song," and "Everybody Knows." Though he labeled *I'm Your Man* as "the first Cohen album that can be listened to during the daylight hours," Browne concluded that because of the singer's insightful social commentary, "there's still absolutely nothing comforting about having Leonard Cohen around."

Selected discography

Albums; released by Columbia except as indicated

Songs of Leonard Cohen (includes "Suzanne," "Hey, That's No Way to Say Goodbye," and "Sisters of Mercy"), 1967.
Songs from a Room (includes "Bird on a Wire" and "You Know Who I Am"), 1969.
Songs of Love and Hate (includes "Joan of Arc," "Famous Blue Raincoat," and "Dress Rehearsal Rag"), 1971.
Live Songs (includes "Story of Isaac," "Nancy," "Tonight Will Be Fine," "Queen Victoria," "Please Don't Pass Me By," and "Passin' Thru"), 1973.
New Skin for the Old Ceremony, 1974.
Death of a Ladies' Man, Warner Brothers, 1977.
Recent Songs, 1979.
I'm Your Man (includes "I'm Your Man," "First We Take Manhattan," "Ain't No Cure for Love," "Everybody Knows," "Tower of Song," and "I Can't Forget"), 1988.

Also recorded *Various Positions* in 1984.

Sources

Chatelaine, October, 1985; September, 1988.
Rolling Stone, June 16, 1988.
Saturday Night, October, 1988.

—*Elizabeth Thomas*

Nat King Cole

Singer, songwriter, pianist

N at King Cole was one of the most popular performers in the history of the music business. From the early 1940s with his jazz combo, the King Cole Trio, through his later solo career, he was responsible for numerous hit records, including pop and ballad classics such as "Sweet Lorraine," "Nature Boy," "The Christmas Song," "Ramblin' Rose," and "Mona Lisa." Cole was one of the first recording artists to sign with Capitol Records, and was that company's most dependable talent for many years. Perhaps because of his enormous success with both black and white music fans, in 1957 he became the first black man to host a variety show on national television. Cole also appeared in motion pictures; his best remembered film performance, as a strolling balladeer in *Cat Ballou*, was completed a few months before his death in 1965.

Born Nathaniel Adams Coles on March 17, 1919, in Montgomery, Alabama, to a Baptist minister and his wife, Cole moved with his family to Chicago, Illinois, as a young child. Soon afterwards, at the age of four, he gave his first public performance, singing "Yes, We Have No Bananas" in a talent contest. Despite the fact that his older brother Edward had to push him onstage, young Nat won a turkey.

Cole's mother, Perlina, taught him to play the piano in the hopes that he would someday become a classic pianist. According to Maria Cole, the singer's second wife, in her book, *Nat King Cole: An Intimate Biography*, his musical talents were quickly put to practical, if not classical, use. In kindergarten, he played piano for the teacher as musical accompaniment to classroom games. By the time Cole was eleven, he and his sister shared the piano duties of their father's ministry at the True Light Baptist Church. But when he was sixteen, his interests turned to jazz, and he formed his own group, the Royal Dukes. They played for small change, or, as Maria Cole recounted, "when they couldn't get cash, often settled for hot dogs and hamburgers." Nat did not sing, because the other members of the group did not like his voice. Shortly afterwards, however, Cole left the Dukes to join the group his brother had formed, the Rogues of Rhythm.

The Rogues eventually joined the cast of "Shuffle Along," a black musical revue. While Cole was serving as the revue's pianist, he became acquainted with Nadine Robinson, one of its dancers. As the show was en route to California, Robinson became Cole's first wife, but "Shuffle Along" closed when it got to Long Beach, leaving Cole unemployed. He began playing piano in Los Angeles area bars to support himself. In one of these bars, Cole was discovered by another club owner, Bob Lewis, who urged Cole to form a small backup group and drop the *s* from his surname. Lewis wanted the more traditional quartet, but Cole could only find two other suitable musicians—thus, with the help of Wesley Prince on bass and Oscar Moore on guitar, the Nat Cole Swingsters Three began their first steady job in Lewis's club.

The group, quickly renamed by Lewis as the Nat King Cole Trio, was at first strictly instrumental. A traditional story says Cole was first led to use his voice professionally because of a persistent, drunken customer who kept demanding that he sing "Sweet Lorraine." More accurately, according to Maria Cole, the pianist began to sing a little to break the monotony of solid instrumental numbers. Though the Trio soon acquired renown in the Los Angeles area, a nationwide tour was not particularly successful.

But when Glenn Wallichs got together with songwriter Johnny Mercer and producer Buddy DeSylva to form Capitol Records in 1942, he remembered meeting Cole and his band, and decided to sign them to a record contract. By 1943 the Trio had recorded its first hit, "Straighten Up and Fly Right." A few years later, when Cole met his second wife, the former Maria Ellington, he was already well-known throughout the United States due to recordings like "Sweet Lorraine," "It's Only a

Paper Moon," and "Get Your Kicks on Route 66." In 1948, when his divorce became final and he married Maria, "Nature Boy," a song he recorded the previous year, became a tremendous hit and transformed Cole into a household name.

As time went on, Cole realized that he was having far more hit records when he sang solo ballads backed by a big band than when he played and sang jazz with the trio. In 1951, a year after he released what is perhaps his most famous song, "Mona Lisa," he left the trio and ceased playing the piano on his records. Even so, Cole is still recognized, in the words of critic Terry Teachout in *High Fidelity,* as "an extraordinarily gifted jazz pianist." The decision proved a turning point in the singer's career, and many gold records, featuring what Teachout described as Cole's "dark, grainy baritone," followed. "Unforgettable," "Ballerina," "When You're Smiling," and "Those Lazy, Hazy, Crazy Days of Summer" are a few of the hits that helped make Cole a favorite of music fans in the United States and worldwide. As Maria Cole explained, "Nat's impeccable taste and vocal styling . . . established him not only as one of the leading crooners of the day, but also as one of the best song salesmen in the business. He could take the most unlikely lyric and transform it to a hum or whistle on everybody's lips." She quoted Wallichs as once saying: "'All the publishers offer [Capitol] a tune for him first, because they know if Cole sings it, they have an eighty to twenty chance of having a hit.'"

In late 1964, while still experiencing much success as a concert performer and recording artist, Cole developed a severe cough and searing chest pains. A smoker, he was diagnosed with a fast-growing, cancerous tumor of the lung. Cole checked into a Santa Monica hospital in December; he died on February 15, 1965. Besides remaining popular through the legacy of his many recordings, Cole served as an influence for other pop balladeers, including Johnny Mathis, and Cole's own daughter, Natalie.

Selected discography

Singles on Capitol

"Straighten Up and Fly Right," 1943.
"Sweet Lorraine," 1943.
"Embraceable You," 1943.
"It's Only a Paper Moon," 1943.
"Body and Soul," 1944.
"What Is This Thing Called Love?" 1944.
"There, I've Said It Again," 1944.
"Stormy Weather," 1945.
"You're Nobody 'Til Somebody Loves You," 1945.

"Don't Blame Me," 1945.
"Sweet Georgia Brown," 1945.
"I'm in the Mood for Love," 1946.
"Get Your Kicks on Route 66," 1946.
"What Can I Say, Dear, After I Say I'm Sorry?" 1946.
"The Christmas Song," 1946.
"(I Love You) For Sentimental Reasons," 1946.
"In the Cool of the Evening," 1946.
"Smoke Gets in Your Eyes," 1946.
"You're the Cream in My Coffee," 1946.
"Honeysuckle Rose," 1947.
"Makin' Whoopee," 1947.
"Too Marvelous for Words," 1947.
"How High the Moon," 1947.
"Three Little Words," 1947.
"Nature Boy," 1947.
"Dream a Little Dream of Me," 1947.
"Then I'll Be Tired of You," 1947.
"Two Front Teeth," 1949.
"My Baby Just Cares for Me," 1949.
"I Almost Lost My Mind," 1950.
"Mona Lisa," 1950.
"Frosty the Snow Man," 1950.
"Red Sails in the Sunset," 1951.
"Too Young," 1951.
"Unforgettable," 1951.
"Walkin' My Baby Back Home," 1951.
"You Stepped Out of a Dream," 1952.
"Polka Dots and Moonbeams," 1952.
"Somebody Loves Me," 1952.
"Laura," 1952.
"Lover Come Back to Me," 1953.
"Tenderly," 1953.
"Almost Like Being in Love," 1953.
"Darling, Je Vous Aime Beaucoup," 1953.
"Smile," 1954.
"Tea for Two," 1955.
"Breezin' Along With the Breeze," 1955.
"Taking a Chance on Love," 1955.
"Don't Blame Me," 1955.
"Just One of Those Things," 1955.
"I Want to Be Happy," 1955.
"You Can Depend on Me," 1956.
"Ballerina," 1956.
"Caravan," 1956.
"When I Grow Too Old to Dream," 1956.
"Tangerine," 1956.
"Stardust," 1956.
"It's All in the Game," 1956.
"When I Fall in Love," 1956.
"Ain't Misbehavin'," 1956.
"When Sunny Gets Blue," 1956.
"Blue Moon," 1957.
"Don't Get Around Much Anymore," 1957.
"Who's Sorry Now?" 1957.

"Once in a While," 1957.
"The Party's Over," 1957.
"I Understand," 1957.
"An Affair to Remember," 1957.
"Fascination," 1957.
"Maria Elena," 1958.
"The More I See You," 1958.
"I Found a Million Dollar Baby," 1958.
"The Very Thought of You," 1958.
"Impossible," 1958.
"Mood Indigo," 1958.
"Lorelei," 1958.
"Only Forever," 1960.
"I Remember You," 1960.
"Capuccina," 1961.
"Cold, Cold Heart," 1961.
"September Song," 1961.
"Ramblin' Rose," 1962.
"Those Lazy, Hazy, Crazy Days of Summer," 1963.
"I've Grown Accustomed to Her Face," 1963.
"I Could Have Danced All Night," 1963.
"On the Street Where You Live," 1963.
"People," 1964.
"You're My Everything," 1964.
"More," 1964.
"My Kind of Girl," 1964.
"The Girl From Ipanema," 1964.
(With Stubby Kay) "The Ballad of Cat Ballou," 1964.
"They Can't Make Her Cry," 1964.

LPs

King Cole Trio, Trio Days, Capitol.
Anatomy of a Jam Session, Black Lion.
The Genius of Lester Young, Verve.
Jazz at the Philharmonic, 1944-46, Verve.
Cole Español, Capitol.
Cole Español (And More), Vol. 2, Capitol, 1987.
The Complete After Midnight Sessions, Capitol, 1988.

Sources

Books

Cole, Maria, with Louie Robinson, *Nat King Cole: An Intimate Biography,* Morrow, 1971.

Periodicals

High Fidelity, June, 1988.
Jet, August 18, 1986, March 20, 1989.
People, May 1, 1989.

—*Elizabeth Thomas*

Jim Croce

Singer, songwriter, guitarist

Gentle love songs and humorous character songs are the legacy of Jim Croce, whose tragic death occurred just before the release of what would become a top-selling album. His music, like his stage manner, was accessible and warm—the common man singing of the commonplace in such a way as to make it all new for his audience. According to *Time,* Croce was "a lean, needling, fun-poking man in work boots and work shirts . . . He took a mad kind of joy in the commonplace, and tomorrow was always the best of all possible times."

Born in Philadelphia on January 10, 1943 (some sources say 1942), Croce began playing the accordion at the age of six. Later, he purchased a 12-string guitar and learned to play it while attending Villanova University, where he earned a degree in psychology in 1965. It was also in college that he became emcee on the school radio station, hosting a three-hour blues and folk show. His early musical attempts, including coffeehouse performances and the recording of an album with his wife, Ingrid, proved less than profitable. By 1970, after settling on an old farm in Lyndell, Pennsylvania, Croce's financial situation became so difficult he was forced to pawn off his guitars and go back into the construction business, doing only occasional studio work for commercials. Despite the fact that his musical talent was being used mostly for "background 'oohs' and 'aahs,'" Croce remained optimistic: "I kept thinking, maybe tomorrow I'll sing some words."

Driving trucks gave Croce time alone to think, and out of those hours came a number of songs, many of which would later become hits. Traveling the country again, Croce played at coffeehouses and on college campuses, where his slightly nasal tenor voice delivered a series of well-received songs, most of which featured tight melodies and combined folk, blues, and pop styles. It was just such a trip he was making on September 20, 1973, when his chartered plane crashed in Natchitoches, Louisiana.

In the wake of his death, his first solo LP, *You Don't Mess around with Jim,* rapidly tripled its sales, selling over one million copies by February 1974, and reached the number one slot on *Billboard*'s chart of best-selling LP's in the same month. The album yielded two hit singles: the title track, featuring one of the humorous Croce "characters" ("You don't step on Superman's cape / You don't spit into the wind / You don't pull the mask off the ole' Lone Ranger / And you don't mess around with Jim"); and "Operator (That's Not the Way It Feels)." Also included on the album was "Time in a Bottle," which featured the kind of sensitive lyrics and melody that only hinted at Croce's great potential as a

Born January 10, c. 1943, in Philadelphia, Pennsylvania; died in a plane crash September 20, 1973, in Natchitoches, Louisiana; married wife Ingrid, 1966; one son, Adrian. *Education:* Bachelor's degree in psychology, Villanova University, 1965.

Awards: Croce earned gold records for *You Don't Mess around with Jim, Life and Times, I Got a Name,* and *Photographs and Memories.*

composer. Issued as a single in 1973, it too achieved hit status.

I Got a Name, recorded just a week before Croce's death, was released posthumously and yielded three hit singles: the oft-covered ballad "I Got a Name" in 1973; and in 1974, "I'll Have To Say I Love You in a Song" and "Working at the Carwash Blues." The album joined *You Don't Mess around with Jim* on the charts early in 1974, occupying the number two slot, while *Life and Times* (featuring the well-loved "Bad, Bad Leroy Brown," who was "Badder than ole' King Kong / And meaner than a junkyard dog") occupied the twenty-second spot. All three albums were certified gold during 1973, as was *Photographs and Memories,* released in 1974.

Commented *Time* magazine in 1974, "Croce had the gift to sing evocatively about a genuine slice of life: the young working class of Middle America." Sadly, his songs of hope and of tomorrow's possibilities surged into popularity only after his last recordings had been made. The haunting top-selling ballad "Time in a Bottle" explains the ultimate irony of Croce's late-arriving success: "There never seems to be enough time to do the things you want to do once you find them. . ."

Selected discography

You Don't Mess around with Jim, ABC (later on Lifesong), June 1972.
Life and Times, ABC (Lifesong), February 1973.
I Got a Name, ABC (Lifesong), November 1973.
Photographs and Memories: Greatest Hits, ABC (Lifesong), September 1974.
The Faces I've Been, Lifesong, October 1975.
Time in a Bottle: Greatest Love Songs, Lifesong, February 1977.
Bad, Bad Leroy Brown: Greatest Character Songs, Lifesong, October 1978.

Sources

Books

Nite, Norm N., *Rock On,* Vol. 2, Harper & Row, 1978.
Stambler, Irwin, *Encyclopedia of Pop, Rock, and Soul,* St. Martin's Press, 1974.

Periodicals

Time, February 11, 1974.

—Meg Mac Donald

David Crosby

Singer, songwriter, guitarist

David Crosby's musical career has been a long and productive one, despite repeated interruptions due to his much-publicized troubles with drugs and the law. Crosby first sang professionally with his brother, Ethan, in a folksinging duo. They played small clubs and coffeehouses around Los Angeles for a time before David hit the road as a solo act. For a few years he led a vagabond existence, barely eking out a living. Things changed drastically after he joined forces with another folkie, Roger McGuinn, and began experimenting with electronic amplification. By the summer of 1964, they had induced Gene Clarke, Chris Hillman, and Mike Clark to join them in a new group called the Byrds.

After several months of rehearsing, the Byrds released their first single in May 1965. "Mr. Tambourine Man" (a remake of the Bob Dylan song) went straight to the top of the pop charts. The group followed it up with another Dylan composition, "All I Really Want to Do," and Pete Seeger's adaptation of Ecclesiastes, "Turn! Turn! Turn!" In one year the Byrds became so popular that they were considered a serious threat to the Beatles, whose appearance they sought to imitate. Their success in blending folk music with an electric sound gave rise to a host of imitators and created a new category of popular music known as "folk rock." Crosby's fine harmony singing, rhythm guitar playing, and songwriting were crucial to the Byrds' first four albums, but in 1968 he was thrown out of the group after losing a power struggle within it.

Crosby used his settlement money from the Byrds to buy a yacht and spent several months relaxing in Florida. There he met Joni Mitchell, who had not yet recorded her first album. Crosby took a deep interest in her career, introducing her to key figures in the industry and helping her to produce her first record. The two were working on that project when Mitchell introduced Crosby to Neil Young and Stephen Stills of Buffalo Springfield. That group was about to break up, and the three men toyed with the idea of playing together professionally. Young had other commitments to see to first, but Crosby and Stills recruited former Hollies member Graham Nash and in 1969 recorded *Crosby, Stills and Nash,* which was a top seller for more than two years. Phil Hardy wrote in his *Encyclopedia of Rock:* "[The album] featured Stills' desperate love songs, Nash's gentler celebrations of 'peace and love' consciousness, and Crosby's mixture of romanticism and angry politics—all smoothed into a soft electric/acoustic music topped off by dazzling virtuoso singing."

Soon Neil Young had joined the trio, and Crosby, Stills, Nash and Young played their second live performance before 500,000 people at the Woodstock Festival in August 1969. Young's presence added a harder edge to their sound that boosted their popularity still further. By the time the first CSNY album, *Deja Vu,* had been released, two million advance orders had accumulated for it. Hardy commented: "The level of musicianship displayed on the album was reflected in their stage shows through late 1969 and 1970. The concerts contained an acoustic half in which the four of them sang solo and together, and an electric half of rock-n-roll in which. . .Crosby's rhythm guitar laid down the base for Stills and Young to engage in ferocious electric guitar duelling."

CSNY was short-lived, however. In 1970 they broke up, in part because each wanted to pursue directions of his own, and also because personal differences were constantly flaring up between them. They reunited briefly in 1974 for a United States tour, but Young insisted on traveling separately and the reunion was cut short. Crosby, Stills and Nash regrouped in various combinations for the next few years. They released *CSN* in 1977 and *Daylight Again* in 1982. Crosby also recorded four albums with Nash. His career was beginning to suffer from his escalating drug abuse, however, and he performed less and less frequently. By the mid-1980s he was freebasing cocaine daily, was addicted to heroin, and had been arrested repeatedly on drug and weapons charges. After several probations violations, he was sentenced to serve time in Texas State Penitentiary, where he underwent a complete detoxification. He was granted an early release in 1986. Since then, he

has performed in concert as a solo artist, in duet with Graham Nash, and with CSN and CSNY.

Discussing his addictions in *People,* Crosby stated: "Most people who go as far as I did with drugs are dead. Hard drugs will hook anyone. I don't care who you are. It's not a matter of personality. Do them and it's a matter of time before you are addicted. You can give me any rationalization you want. I know better. I have a Ph.D. in drugs. Fool with them and you'll get strung out. Then there are about four ways it can go: You can go crazy; you can go to prison; you can die; or you can kick. That's it. Anything else anybody says is bull."

Selected discography

LPs; with the Byrds

Mr. Tambourine Man, Columbia, 1965.
Turn! Turn! Turn!, Columbia, 1966.
Fifth Dimension, Columbia, 1966.
Younger than Yesterday, Columbia, 1967.
Greatest Hits, Columbia, 1967.
The Byrds, Asylum, 1973.
History of the Byrds, Columbia, 1973.
The Byrds Play Dylan, Columbia, 1980.
Never Before, Re-Flyte, 1988.

LPs; with Graham Nash

Crosby and Nash, Atlantic, 1972.
Wind on the Water, ABC, 1975.
Whistle Down the Wire, ABC, 1976.
Live, ABC, 1977.
Best of Crosby and Nash, ABC, 1977.

LPs; with Crosby, Stills and Nash

Crosby, Stills and Nash, Atlantic, 1969.
CSN, Atlantic, 1977.
Replay, Atlantic, 1980.
Daylight Again, Atlantic, 1982.
Allies, Atlantic, 1983.

LPs; with Crosby, Stills, Nash and Young

Deja Vu, Atlantic, 1970.
Four-Way Street, Atlantic, 1972.
So Far, Atlantic, 1974.
American Dream, Atlantic, 1989.

Solo LPs

If I Could Only Remember My Name, Atlantic, 1971.
Oh Yes I Can, A&M, 1988.

Sources

Books

Crosby, David and Carl Gottlieb, *Long Time Gone*, Doubleday, 1988.
Jahn, Mike, *Rock: From Elvis Presley to Rock and Roll*, Rolling Stone Press, 1976.

Laing, Dave, and Phil Hardy, *Encyclopedia of Rock*, McDonald, 1987.
Miller, Jim, ed., *Rolling Stone Encyclopedia of Rock and Roll*, Rolling Stone Press, 1983.

Periodicals

People, September 8, 1986; April 27, 1987.
Rolling Stone, January 12, 1989.
Stereo Review, June, 1988.
Time, March 11, 1985; November 4, 1985; August 11, 1986.

—*Joan Goldsworthy*

The Cure

Rock group

The Cure is a critically acclaimed British rock band with an uncompromising message of despair, frustration, and futility. Called "the masters of mope rock," members of the Cure have attracted an international cult following for their post-punk, angst-ridden music; after years as an "underground sensation," a 1989 tour saw the group playing its first stadium venues in America. The band is led by Robert Smith, a songwriter-singer who uses music to exorcise his personal existential demons. *Rolling Stone* contributor Michael Azerrad describes the enigmatic Smith as "a virtual messiah of melancholy, a guru of gloom. . . . Though Smith can write a catchy tune when he wants to, the Cure makes unlikely stadium pop—the sound relies on subtle seduction and the lyrics are profoundly self-absorbed."

Indeed, Cure albums offer few chances to tap toes or clap to the beat. The music is challenging, and it demands sober consideration, especially from live audiences. "If self-indulgence is one of the chief themes," writes Mark Peel in *Stereo Review,* "it is also one of its virtues. After all, ideas are what Smith is indulging in. . . . They may be disturbing, even distasteful ideas, but their savage eloquence makes . . . an intense and unforgettable listening experience." Azerrad suggests that the Cure "makes music that is therapeutic, a musical catharsis for Smith, the band and its fans."

The Cure established a presence in America in 1986, with the album *Standing on a Beach.* By that time Smith and his partners had been making music for more than ten years. A working-class youth who grew up in the dismal suburb of Crawley, Sussex, Smith found himself constantly at odds with his surroundings. Before he gravitated to music he suffered through difficulties with schoolteachers and with the law. "I find authority very difficult to deal with," he told *Seventeen* magazine. "I couldn't accept having to be responsible to someone, having to explain my actions." At fifteen Smith formed his first band, with friends Laurence Tolhurst and Brian Dempsey. They called themselves the Cure, Smith said, because "there was a lot of negativity around at the time: the no-future brigade. Rather than just give in to it, we thought it better to try and change things—first music and then everything around us. We were an *alternative.* That's always been my attitude, to be seen as apart from the mainstream."

Rather than borrowing from the punk movement, then, the Cure was in it from the start. Smith loved the freedom that punk music offered, both lyrically and melodically. Between its 1978 debut album and the subsequent issues *Boys Don't Cry, Seventeen Seconds,* and *Faith,* the Cure "went from being a sprightly pop band to being downbeat moodists, with songs such as 'The Funeral Party' and 'The Drowning Man' exuding a dark radiance," to quote Azerrad. The band members also cultivated a punk look, with stiffly coiffed haircuts, red lipstick, and black clothing. Smith's intense morbidity reached a nadir with the album *Pornography,* a work that mentions death in almost every song. "Everything I do has the tinge of the finite, of my own demise," Smith told *Rolling Stone.* "At some point you either accept death or you just keep pushing it back as you get older and older. I've accepted it."

The Cure's membership has changed little over the years. Dempsey left the group in the early 1980s, and Boris Williams, Porl Thompson, Roger O'Donnell, and Simon Gallup joined. Occasionally one or another member will take a sabbatical, and Smith often threatens to disband the group—largely to fight complacency. O'Donnell told *Rolling Stone:* "Robert likes to [talk about breaking up], he likes to keep us nervous. But of all people, I think Robert doesn't like change. Then again, he doesn't like things to be settled, either—it's a very difficult contradiction."

The Cure was quite well established in Europe by 1986, when *Standing on a Beach* was released in America. Actually a compilation of proven singles, *Standing on a Beach* became a favorite of campus radio stations. That work was followed by a more mainstream album, *Kiss Me, Kiss Me, Kiss Me,* which catapulted the Cure

For the Record. . .

Original members included **Robert Smith** (vocals, songwriting), born April 21, 1959, in England; **Laurence Tolhurst** (keyboards), and **Michael Dempsey** (bass). Other members include **Simon Gallup** (drums, bass), **Porl Thompson** (keyboards, guitar), **Boris Williams** (drums), and **Roger O'Donnell** (keyboards).

Band formed, 1976, in Crawley, Sussex, England. Signed with Fiction Records, 1978, recorded first album in Great Britain, 1978. Released first album in America, *Boys Don't Cry,* 1980; toured America in 1987 and 1989.

Addresses: *Record company*—Elektra Records, 75 Rockefeller Plaza, New York, NY 10019.

into not-particularly-desired notoriety. Although the songs on *Kiss Me, Kiss Me, Kiss Me* are more catchy, they do not suggest any thematic compromise. Peel calls the work "bold, self-indulgent, outrageous, and unsettling—sure signs of a rock visionary at work."

Kiss Me, Kiss Me, Kiss Me was the Cure's first best-selling album in America. It eventually sold two million copies worldwide and stayed on the Billboard Top One Hundred charts for over a year. The album *Disintegration,* released in 1989, did even better, placing two songs, "Fascination Street" and "Love Song," on the Top Forty charts. Despite this success (or perhaps because of it), Smith has threatened once again to leave the Cure. "It was never our intention to become big at this," he told the *Philadelphia Inquirer.* "The whole point was to enjoy what we were doing at the time. Most bands that reach our position have a retinue of people trying to keep them propped up so that the money keeps rolling in. We don't have that."

According to Azerrad, the Cure's albums "have always been suffused with what can only be termed the Dread—an all-encompassing sense of futility." Harsh, mocking, and energetic, the music of the Cure is intended to make listeners uncomfortable, to make them question any complacent acceptance of happiness, morality, or hope. Smith says that he hopes his work proves that one can descend to the depths and come back again, "that something can come out of nothing." He told *Rolling Stone:* "Knowing that everything's futile but still fighting, still raging against the dying of the light—that's what motivates me all the time."

Selected discography

Boys Don't Cry, 1980.
Seventeen Seconds, c. 1981.
Faith, c. 1983.
Pornography, c. 1984.
The Top, 1984.
Head on the Door, Elektra, 1985.
Standing on a Beach: The Singles, Elektra, 1986.
Kiss Me, Kiss Me, Kiss Me, Elektra, 1987.
Disintegration, Elektra, 1989.

Sources

Philadelphia Inquirer, August 22, 1989.
Rolling Stone, July 17-31, 1986; June 4, 1987; September 7, 1989.
Seventeen, April, 1987.
Stereo Review, October, 1987.

—Anne Janette Johnson

Tim Curry

Musical stage, screen performer

"There has never been enough of Tim Curry on-screen," famed film critic Pauline Kael asserted in the *New Yorker*. Possibly this is due to the varied nature of his career and talents. Curry is perhaps best known for his role in both the stage and film versions of the musical *The Rocky Horror Show*, in which he sang the memorable themes "Sweet Transvestite" and "I Can Make You a Man." But he also released rock albums, and starred in many other stage shows, including a stint in the title role of *Amadeus*. And despite Kael's words, Curry has done much film work, including the fantasy film *Legend,* and the comedy *Pass the Ammo.*

Curry grew up in southern England, where his father served as a Methodist chaplain for the British Navy. During his early school years he developed an interest in singing and acting, and he continued to pursue these activities when he attended the University of Birmingham. While in college, Curry sang with a swing band. He made his stage debut, however, in the London, England, production of the musical *Hair.*

"I like risky parts," Curry told a *People* interviewer, "abrasive characters the audience won't necessarily like." "Risky" is as apt a description as any of Curry's most famous screen role, Dr. Frank N. Furter, in the 1975 rock musical cult film *Rocky Horror Picture Show.* Furter is a kind of transvestite Frankenstein, working on a muscular male monster to service his sexual needs. Not content with this, however, he seduces both units of a young, somewhat nerdish couple stranded by a storm at his spooky mansion. *Rocky Horror*'s soundtrack album also proved a popular favorite and brought Curry's voice into the homes of many young music fans.

After *Rocky Horror* brought him to the public attention, Curry put much effort into making a career for himself as a rock musician. He told *People* that he "turned down a lot of roles to make time to record and tour." His albums include *Read My Lips* and *Fearless,* and he scored a hit single with "I Do the Rock" in 1979. But after 1981 Curry returned his concentration to stage and film. In that year he was cast in the British National Theatre version of the Broadway play about the life of composer Wolfgang Amadeus Mozart, *Amadeus.* The role was not as far a cry from Frank N. Furter as one might think; playwright Peter Schaffer expanded on historical sources that portrayed Mozart as somewhat immature. In the play, Curry explained to *People,* "I [went] from being an insufferable boor to a truly tragic figure." Schaffer hailed Curry's performance as "seamless," according to *People.* The singer/actor's other stage credits include the operatic version of playwright William Shakespeare's *A Midsummer Night's Dream,* and *Travesties.*

For the Record. . .

Born c. 1947; son of a Methodist chaplain in the British Navy; raised in England. *Education:* Graduated from University of Birmingham.

Singer, actor; released a few rock albums, 1978-81. Appeared in stage musicals and plays including *Hair, The Rocky Horror Show, Amadeus, Travesties,* and *A Midsummer Night's Dream* (opera). Appeared in films including *Rocky Horror Picture Show, Legend, Pass the Ammo, Times Square, Annie,* and *The Ploughman's Lunch.* Appeared in the BBC television miniseries, "The Life of Shakespeare." Provided voice for the animated film *Abel's Island.*

Addresses: c/o Cameron-Hayward & Company, 3 Lord Napier Pl., London W6, England.

As for Curry's motion picture career, one of his biggest successes since *Rocky Horror* was the 1986 film *Legend.* Though *Legend* proved a big box office draw, it was not a critical favorite. Nevertheless, *Time* reviewer Richard Corliss had praise for Curry's appearance as the film's wicked antagonist: "The Lord of Darkness . . . begins to work his evil alchemy. And the film . . . comes to seductive life." When the hero and heroine defeat the Lord of Darkness, Corliss claims, "their victory rings hollow," because while the evil lord was trying to lead the heroine astray, the film was "a bedtime story peopled with creatures of enticement and desire."

Another musical film featuring Curry's talents was 1988's *Pass the Ammo.* Though not a widely released film, it garnered good reviews, including that of Kael, who wanted to see more of Curry in it: "It's too bad that his role diminishes as *Pass the Ammo* gets underway." Curry portrayed a dishonest television preacher—as Kael reported, "his curly, dimply smile [is] so elfishly dirty that it's as if he were lighted by hellfire." But Curry has also had more serious, and less mischievous roles; he starred as the famous playwright in the British Broadcasting Corporation television biography of William Shakespeare, and provided the main voice for the animated children's film *Abel's Island.*

Selected discography

(With cast) *The Rocky Horror Picture Show* (includes "Sweet Transvestite" and "I Can Make You a Man"), Ode Records, 1975.
Read My Lips, A & M, 1978.
Fearless (including "I Do the Rock"), A & M, 1979.
Also recorded another album for A & M, c. 1981.
The Best of Tim Curry (compilation: on CD and cassette only)

Sources

New Yorker, April 4, 1988.
People, February 16, 1981; June 20, 1988.
Time, March 24, 1975; May 12, 1986.

—*Elizabeth Thomas*

Roger Daltrey

Singer

"The Who is the band that refused to die before it got old," stated Dave Marsh in *The Rolling Stone Illustrated History of Rock and Roll.* From their formation in the 1960s to their recent reunion tour, the Who have embodied some of the most basic elements of rock and roll—chaotic performances, destructive onstage behavior, and record-breaking noise levels—as well as taken music in new directions with trend-setting concept albums and rock operas. In a business where bands typically go through many personnel changes and rarely last for more than a few years, the Who are also remarkable for their stability and longevity. For more than twenty years, the group's lyrics have been effectively shouted out by vocalist Roger Daltrey.

Daltrey, bassist John Entwhistle, and guitarist Pete Townshend all grew up in the same neighborhood, a working-class section of London known as Shepherd's Bush. By the early 1960s, the three were playing together in a band called the Detours, which performed rhythm and blues and covers of early Beatles songs in local dance clubs. Late in 1963, the Detours hooked up with managers Pete Meaden and Helmut Gordon, who encouraged the band to cater to the British "mods"—young people dedicated to amphetamines, Vespa scooters, American rhythm and blues, and stylish clothing. Drummer Keith Moon joined the group, which had been renamed the High Numbers, and punched up their sound with his manic playing. They built up quite a following in the mods' favorite clubs, but their only recording, "I'm the Face," failed to sell.

Meaden and Gordon were soon replaced by Kit Lambert and Chris Stamp, two young filmmakers who discovered the band while looking for a movie subject. They were as much intrigued by the frantic crowds that came to hear the High Numbers as they were by the group's music. They carefully calculated ways in which the band could heighten its appeal, suggesting that they revert to a gimmicky name they had used in the past—the Who—and prodding them to make destruction a part of their act. Under their tutelage the Who began putting out "soul music pilled-up and riotous, played with none of the elegant perfection of the Rolling Stones, but with all the zealotry of garage-band amateurs," wrote Marsh. When Townshend began smashing his guitars onstage, and Moon kicked over his drum set, the mods loved it, and this type of flamboyance "saved the Who, who would never have gotten far trying to play R & B with the propriety of the Bluesbreakers or the Stones." They took volume to new levels (eventually being listed in the *Guinness Book of World Records* as the world's loudest band). Daltrey, who had "the mug, the posture, and the demeanor (permanently chipped shoulders) of a budding thug/aspiring John Dillinger,"

For the Record. . .

Full name Roger Harry Daltrey; born March 1, 1944, in London, England.

Founding member, with John Entwhistle, of rhythm and blues/ dance band the Detours, early 1960s; founding member of the Who (originally called the High Numbers) with Entwhistle, Keith Moon, and Pete Townshend, 1965—; solo artist, 1973—. Has also appeared in films, including *Tommy, McVicar, Lisztomania, Sextet,* and *The Legacy.*

Addresses: *Record company*—Atlantic Records, 75 Rockefeller Plaza, New York, NY 10019.

developed a commanding stage presence. He "twirled his mike like a lariat, marched in place, danced silly steps, stuttered, swaggered, screamed; he pounced on the crowd, half stand-up comic, half assailant."

The Who released their first single, "I Can't Explain," in 1965, but it didn't really take off until they appeared on the British music show "Ready Steady Go!" with their screaming mob of fans from the London clubs. From then on success was theirs. Yet, from the very first, the Who mocked their own popularity, with album titles such as *The Who Sell Out.* Despite their tongue-in-cheek attitude, they were real innovators. Their second album included a ten-minute mini-opera that eventually led to the first full-scale rock opera, 1969's *Tommy.* This story of a deaf, dumb, and blind pinball champion was considered pretentious by some, but was hailed as a masterpiece by many others, and it brought wealth, artistic respectability, and international fame to the Who. A second rock opera, *Quadrophenia,* explored the tortured inner lives of the mods the Who had once exploited to build their fame.

When *The Who by Numbers* was released in 1975, the group was as popular as ever, but its members, particularly Townshend, seemed to be undergoing an identity crisis. The most famous line from their first album had been "Hope I die before I get old," but they hadn't died, and they were uncertain as to what to do next. The group didn't record for three years while its members worked on individual projects. Daltrey had already released a solo album and appeared in the title role of the film version of *Tommy.* In 1975 he portrayed classical composer Franz Liszt in Ken Russell's *Lisztomania.* He later acted in *Sextet, The Legacy,* and *McVicar,* a film biography of train robber John McVicar. He also developed the script for *McVicar* from the robber's autobiography. His solo albums received mixed re-

views, with some critics commenting that Daltrey seemed to need Pete Townshend's lyrics to reach his peak.

The Who returned as a unit in 1978 with *Who Are You?,* but only a month after the long-awaited album was released, drummer Keith Moon was found dead in his apartment, overdosed on a drug which, ironically, had been prescribed to curb his alcoholism. The Who's future was thrown into doubt; but after much deliberation, Daltrey, Entwhistle, and Townshend decided to try to replace Moon and carry on. Kenny Jones of Small Faces was recruited, noted session man John "Rabbit" Bundrick joined the group on keyboards, and "finally, the Who came back onstage, with live shows that were more formal and less spontaneous but retained all of the old power and more of the enthusiasm than anyone had a right to expect," wrote Marsh. Unfortunately, the return of the Who was overshadowed by a tragedy that occurred when they played Cincinnati's Riverfront Coliseum: eleven concertgoers were crushed to death in a

> *Daltrey, who "had the mug, the posture, and the demeanor (permanently chipped shoulders) of a budding thug/aspiring John Dillinger," developed a commanding stage presence.*

rush for seats. The group put out four more albums, but announced their official breakup in 1983 after the release of *It's Hard.*

Although Who fans had hopes of a reunion tour in 1985, when the group agreed to perform at the Live-Aid benefit concert, it wasn't until 1989 that all the members agreed to participate. Daltrey, Townshend, and Entwhistle hit the road with fifteen musicians to back them up on "The Kids Are Alright 1989 Tour." "Extraordinary is the only word that comes to mind," *Boston Globe* reviewer Steve Morse wrote of the much-anticipated show. "The Who thoroughly aced their exam,. . .scoring in the upper 99th percentile on song selection, visuals, sound mix, performance, crowd rapport, and just about anything else you might want to judge a show by. . . .It was the best stadium show this writer has ever seen."

Selected discography

Albums with the Who

My Generation, Decca, 1966.
Happy Jack, Decca, 1967.
The Who Sell Out, Decca, 1968 (released in England as *A Quick One*).
Magic Bus—The Who on Tour, Decca, 1968.
Tommy, Decca, 1969.
Direct Hits, Track, 1969.
Live at Leeds, Decca, 1970.
Who's Next, Decca, 1971.
Meaty Beaty Big and Bouncy, Decca, 1971.
Quadrophenia, MCA, 1973.
Odds and Sods, MCA, 1974.
Portrait, Polydor, 1975.
The Who by Numbers, MCA, 1975.
Who Are You?, MCA, 1978.
The Kids Are Alright, MCA, 1979.
Quadrophenia (soundtrack), Polydor, 1979.
Face Dances, Polydor, 1981.
Hooligans, MCA, 1981.
Phases, Polydor, 1982.
It's Hard, Polydor, 1982.
Who's Last, Polydor, 1985.
Two's Missing, Polydor, 1987.

Solo albums

Daltrey, MCA, 1973.

Ride a Rock Horse, MCA, 1975.
One of the Boys, MCA, 1977.
McVicar (soundtrack), Polydor, 1980.
Best of Roger Daltrey, Polydor, 1981.
Best Bits, MCA, 1982.
Parting Should Be Painless, WEA, 1984.
Under a Raging Moon, Atlantic, 1985.
Can't Wait to See the Movie, Atlantic, 1987.

Sources

Books

Hardy, Phil, and Dave Laing, *Encyclopedia of Rock and Roll*, McDonald, 1987.
Jahn, Mike, *Rock: From Elvis Presley to Rock and Roll*, Rolling Stone Press, 1976.
Miller, Jim, editor, *Rolling Stone Illustrated History of Rock and Roll*, Rolling Stone Press, 1983.

Periodicals

Audio, February, 1986.
Boston Globe, July 13, 1989; July 15, 1989.
Boston Phoenix, July 21, 1989.
People, August 3, 1987.
Rolling Stone, February 28, 1985; August 27, 1987.

—Joan Goldsworthy

Terence Trent D'Arby

Singer

"At the very least," Mikal Gilmore wrote in *Rolling Stone*, "[Terence Trent] D'Arby is the hottest and smartest luminary that the trend-fixated British pop scene has witnessed all decade: a magnificent and rousing vocalist who can combine the sensual graininess of Sam Cooke and Otis Redding with the tonal dexterity of Marvin Gaye, Al Green and Smokey Robinson." And music writer Charles Shaar Murray, quoted in both *Rolling Stone* and *Village Voice*, observed that "D'Arby seems like something invented by three rock critics on the 'phone. Young black American, pretty. . . . Highly articulate, enormously well-read and gifted with an awesome knack for self-promotion. . . . Perfect."

Indeed, critics and reviewers have been almost unanimous in their praise of the American expatriate's vocal abilities. "There's only one hitch in all this," observed Gilmore. "D'Arby may possess a tremendous reserve of talent, ambition and good looks, but he also possesses a penchant for playing the role of an outspoken and unpredictable bad boy."

Even before the release of his debut album, *Introducing the Hardline According to Terence Trent D'Arby,* he announced "I can justifiably say that my first album will be one of the most brilliant debuts from any artist in the last 10 years," reported *People.* He later went even further, boasting "my album is better than *Sgt. Pepper['s Lonely Hearts Club Band],*" the Beatles' 1967 classic selected as the best album made between 1967 and 1987 by a panel of music critics and writers assembled by *Rolling Stone.*

The controversy D'Arby stirred wasn't limited to music, however. A star in Britain even before his album was released (thanks to a slick promotional drive by CBS Records), D'Arby told a British interviewer that in the United States "I obviously wouldn't say on nationwide TV that I thought America was racist, sexist, homophobic and violent if they asked me why I left. I would just say America wasn't a culture I felt comfortable in. But anybody with a brain would understand what I'm trying to say," *People* reported. And Daisann McLane's *Village Voice* profile of D'Arby quoted his philosophy of race in American music: "Prince introduced the theme of bisexuality because it makes [him] more palatable. Fathers don't feel threatened when they see posters of Prince on their [daughters'] bedroom walls.'"

Terence Trent D'Arby was born in Manhattan in 1962. His father, James Darby, had played guitar and been a fan of the early rock and roll until he received the calling and became a minister in the Pentecostal Church of Our Lord Jesus Christ. The family lived for a time in New Jersey and Chicago before settling in the comfortable

For the Record. . .

Surname originally Darby; born c. March 1962, in New York City; son of James Benjamin (a minister) and Frances (a teacher and counselor) Darby. *Education:* Attended the University of Central Florida, 1979-80.

Professional musician, 1981—; lead singer with musical group Touch, 1981-83. *Military service:* U.S. Army, 1980-83; served as a supply clerk with the Third Armored Division in West Germany.

Awards: Golden Gloves lightweight regional amateur boxing champion, c. 1979; nominated for British Grammy Award for newcomer of the year, 1987; nominated for Grammy Award for best new artist, 1988; named best new artist by British Phonographic Institute, 1988.

Addresses: *Home*—London, England. *Office*—CBS Records Group, 51 West 52nd Street, New York, NY 10019.

college town of DeLand, Florida, when D'Arby, then known as Terry Darby, was 11. In high school he wore glasses and was a member of the DeLand High School Modernaires singing group, and was a finalist in the Mr. DHS contest to find the most popular and talented boy in the school.

D'Arby also developed a love for boxing and won a Golden Gloves championship while in high school. He studied journalism at the University of Central Florida for a year and then, in 1980, joined the U.S. Army, where, recruiters promised, he could continue his education in boxing and at the same time receive star treatment in his unit.

What the recruiters didn't tell D'Arby was that he would have to undergo airborne training to become a paratrooper in order to be an Army boxer. When he decided he didn't want to box that badly, he was made a supply clerk and assigned to duty in Germany. D'Arby enjoyed the local nightlife and eventually joined a nine-man band, Touch, as its lead singer.

As the band became more successful, D'Arby's duties as a supply clerk became less and less appealing. Bored with Army life and hot on his newfound musical career, he went AWOL. "I was in hiding," he told McLean. "It was really romantic. Fugitive on the run. Serious rock and roll myth. Every gig I wondered, would they catch me? Would this be my last gig for years?"

After D'Arby signed a management contract with Klaus

Pieter Schleinitz, he turned himself in to Army authorities. It is not clear if he was court-martialed or not; Gilmore wrote: "According to the account D'Arby has given in previous interviews, the army court-martialed him with the aim of imprisoning him for up to five years, and only the clever and compassionate defense of a New York lawyer saved him." Others, including McLean, believe D'Arby was most likely given an "administrative reprimand."

D'Arby was discharged in April 1983. After a brief return to the United States to process out of the Army, he returned to Germany to rejoin Touch, but before long the band went their separate ways. "There was a lot of jealousy in the band," D'Arby told Gilmore. "I was the frontman, and to be honest, just wanted to be a star—I wanted a fast car and fast women. I just wanted to shake my butt onstage and get laid." Following the band's disintegration D'Arby moved to London, where he honed his singing skills and worked at becoming a star.

"I know that some people view me as a bit manufactured. But I can't be Whitney Houston: somebody who is polite and perfect and appeals to your mother and your grandfather."

When his first album was released in Britain, in mid-1987, it exploded to the top of the charts in a single week, prompting Simon Reynolds to comment in the British journal *New Statesman*, "D'Arby is one of those pop phenomena that seems vaguely *called for*, demanded into being by pop's climate of desire. In this case, a hankering for ye olde 'real soul' is married to the requisite '80s designer-socialist sense of image. D'Arby is another example of how soul—once a music of breakdown—has become a component of a *Cosmo*-style regimen of narcissism and self-actualisation. Soul as emotional work-out." "I know that some people view me as a bit manufactured," D'Arby told *Rolling Stone*. "But I can't be Whitney Houston: somebody who is polite and perfect and appeals to your mother and your grandfather."

Selected discography

Introducing the Hardline According to Terence Trent D'Arby
(includes "Wishing Well," "Sign Your Name," "As Yet Untitled,"
"If You Let Me Stay," "Dance Little Sister," "Let's Go Forward,"
and "If You All Get to Heaven"), CBS, 1987.
Neither Fish Nor Flesh, CBS, 1989.

Sources

Musician, June 1988.
New Statesman, August 21, 1987.
Newsweek, February 22, 1988.
People, November 16, 1987; May 9, 1988.
Rolling Stone, November 19, 1987; May 19, 1988; June 16, 1988.
Time, January 25, 1988.
Village Voice Rock & Roll Quarterly (supplement), April 5, 1988.

—*Michael L. LaBlanc*

Def Leppard

Rock band

Despite an average age of only eighteen, Def Leppard burst onto the heavy metal scene back in 1980 like a group of seasoned veterans. "This band frequently transcends the mundane through sheer musical energy and playing ability," wrote Jim Schwartz in *Guitar Player.* In a genre known for cliched riffs and monotonous beats, these heavy metalheads have created a sound of their own while becoming one of the top-selling groups in rock and roll.

All five original members, Joe Elliott, Pete Willis, Steve Clark, Rick Savage and Rick Allen, come from the steel-producing town of Sheffield, England. Before employment as a van driver, lead singer Elliott used to dream about forming a band in school, creating song lists, logos, and band names while others in his class were studying. "I figured out fairly early that I wasn't gonna be a brain surgeon or a nuclear physicist," he told *Rolling Stone,* "so I fantasized about rock and roll."

Guitarist Willis was studying engineering at college when he met fellow axeman Clark. Already playing with Savage on bass in the band Atomic Mass, Willis asked Clark to sit in and he soon joined the group. With the addition of Elliott and drummer Allen, they changed their name to Deaf Leppard and later dropped the *a.* In July of 1978 they made their debut at Westfield School in Sheffield earning a grand total of $12.00. With a twin guitar assault reminiscent of Wishbone Ash, they began gigging in bars with a repertoire that included 50% of their own originals. "We always thought our songs would be good enough to get us by," Allen told John Swenson in *Rolling Stone.*

Britain experienced a new wave of heavy metal as the '80s rolled in and Def Leppard was in a prime position to cash in. They recorded a privately-made EP, *Getcha Rocks Off,* which sold out its initial 24,000 copies. AC/DC manager Peter Mensch picked up the group and convinced Polygram to sign them to a deal. In 1980 the chartbreaking *On Through the Night* was released, climbing all the way to #51 in the US. "We actually wrote the first album nine months before ever playing a live concert," Willis told *Guitar Player.* "We wanted to do it right from the start and be polished." Songs like "Rock Brigade," "Hello America," "When the Walls Come Tumbling Down," "Overture," "Sorrow is a Woman," and "Wasted" were recorded in just eighteen days and made for a remarkably strong outing. "Displaying a wisdom beyond their years, Def Leppard take the timeworn basics of heavy metal, give them a punky Eighties overhaul and come up with, uh, heavy melody," stated David Fricke in *Rolling Stone. "On Through the Night* is awfully impressive for a band making its vinyl debut." The band then toured the UK opening for

For the Record...

Original band members included **Joe Elliott** (born August 1, 1959), vocals; **Steve Clark** (born April 23, 1960), guitar; **Pete Willis** (born February 16, 1960), guitar; **Rick Savage** (born December 2, 1960), bass; and **Rick Allen** (born November 1, 1963), drums. **Phil Collen** (born December 8, 1957), guitar, replaced Willis in 1982. All original members from Sheffield, England.

Willis and Savage formed Atomic Mass after completing schooling; Clark, Elliott and Allen joined, changed name to Def Leppard; released EP in 1979; signed with Polygram and released debut in 1980.

Addresses: 80 Warwick Gardens, London, W14 8PR, England.

Sammy Haggar and AC/DC before coming Stateside to warm up audiences for Ted Nugent.

Their follow-up LP, *High 'n' Dry,* was an even bigger seller breaking the Top 10. Their sound also expanded as "Bringin' on the Heartbreak" stretched the metal boundaries even further. In 1982 Willis was replaced by ex-Girl guitarist Phil Collen who told *Guitar World,* "We offer a lot more melody than most heavy rock bands, vocally as well as musically." Def Leppard was now a headline act after only two albums, and Collen's style differed enough from Willis's to create a unique combination with Clark.

They employed the services of ace producer Mutt Lange for 1983's *Pyromania,* another Top 10 LP which eventually sold over two million copies. The album also included three hit singles: "Photography"(#12), "Rock of Ages"(#16), and "Foolin' " (#28). By now the five members were being featured in teen magazines and ruling the MTV airwaves.

Tragedy struck the band on New Year's Eve 1984, when drummer Rick Allen severed his left arm in an auto accident. Refusing to accept the conventional wisdom that such an injury would certainly end his musical career, Allen determined to relearn to play with the aid of a special drum kit. In a show of loyalty, the band didn't replace Allen, deciding to remain on hiatus until he was able to return.

Lange was used again as producer on 1987's *Hysteria* LP and more hits followed. "Animal," "Women," "Hysteria," "Pour Some Sugar on Me," "Armageddon It," and "Rocket" each received substantial air-play. In 1988 Def Leppard issued a seventeen-cut video entitled *Historia* providing an excellent summary of their musical career. "With its intriguing perspective and loads of superb, hard-driving solos, *Historia* will hopefully inspire other bands to release similar projects," wrote Jas Obrecht in *Guitar Player.*

Selected discography

On Through the Night, Mercury, 1980.
High 'n' Dry, Mercury, 1981.
Pyromania, Mercury, 1983.
Hysteria, Mercury, 1987.

Sources

Books

The Rolling Stone Encyclopedia of Rock & Roll, edited by Jon Pareles and Patricia Romanowski, Rolling Stone Press/Summit, 1983.
The Harmony Illustrated Encyclopedia of Rock, Mike Clifford, consultant, Salamander, 1988.
Nite, Norm N., with Charles Crespo, *Rock On: The Illustrated Encyclopedia of Rock and Roll,* Volume 3, Harper, 1985.
Rock Movers & Shakers, edited by Barry Lazell with Dafydd Rees and Luke Crampton, Banson, 1989.

Periodicals

Guitar Player, March 1982; November 1988.
Guitar World, September 1983.
Rolling Stone, June 26, 1980; October 2, 1980.

—*Calen D. Stone*

Bo Diddley

Guitarist, singer, songwriter

Alongside Chuck Berry, Bo Diddley is recognized as one of the first and most influential rock guitarists. In a career that has spanned well over three decades, Diddley has remained true to his original style. As Jeff Hannusch wrote in *Guitar Player* in 1984, perhaps the greatest thing one can say about Diddley is that "he has never had to sound like anyone else but Bo Diddley." He was born Otha Ellas Bates in 1928 in Pike County, Mississippi. In 1934 his mother sent him to Chicago to live with her cousin, Gussie McDaniel. After the McDaniels adopted Otha, he dropped his first and last names and was known as Ellas McDaniel. However, he soon acquired his nickname and soon-to-be professional title, Bo Diddley, which *Guitars, From the Renaissance to Rock* refers to as a mischievous or bully boy. "That's how I got my name . . . from messin' 'round," stated Diddley in *Rock 100*.

Diddley studied violin under Professor O.W. Frederick for 12 years starting at age 7. He began teaching himself guitar in the early 1940s while attending Foster Vocational High School. At age 13 he was playing for change on Langley Avenue in Chicago with his friend Jerome Green. "I had a raggedy guitar, a washtub bass, a dude 'sanding' on a sheet of paper, and Jerome had maracas, shakin' 'em, and man . . . it was lovely," Diddley told *Guitar World*. Besides violin and guitar, Diddley was also a trombonist with the Baptist Congress Band. By the time he was 20, Diddley had formed The Langley Avenue Jive Cats, with legendary slide guitarist Earl Hooker, playing at the 708 Club in Chicago.

After graduating from Foster's, Diddley got married and began working odd jobs outside of music in construction and semi-pro boxing. He was laid off from the construction job for a spell and decided to take another shot at music. Diddley went out and bought an electric guitar for its volume potential in the rowdy clubs and then recorded a single on a disc cutter owned by one of his neighbors. Diddley pedaled the songs—"I'm a Man" backed with "Bo Diddley"—to various labels before arriving at the Chess brothers' (Leonard and Phil) label in Chicago, home label to blues stalwarts like Muddy Waters, Willie Dixon, Howlin' Wolf, and the chart-climbing Chuck Berry.

Chess saw a market for Diddley's sound but they insisted that he change the lyrics to "Bo Diddley," which were rather obscene, and rerecord it. Diddley agreed and signed a contract with Chess in 1955. The single was released on a subsidiary label, Checker, and skyrocketed all the way to number 2 on the national R & B charts but didn't even crack the pop charts. The album *Bo Diddley* was also released in 1955 and Diddley appeared on the Ed Sullivan television show

For the Record. . .

Legal name, Ellas McDaniel; born Otha Ellas Bates, December 30, 1928, in McComb (Pike County), Mississippi; son of Ethel Wilson; legally adopted by mother's cousin, Gussie McDaniel, 1934; married Ethel Mae Smith, 1946 (divorced); remarried; wife's name, Kay; children: (first marriage) two; (second marriage) two.

Formed Langley Avenue Jive Cats with Earl Hooker during early 1940s; did construction work and fought as a semi-professional boxer; signed to recording contract with Chess/Checker Records, 1955; owner and president of Bokay Productions (record distribution company); toured with the Clash, 1979, and Ron Wood, 1988; appeared in television commercial promoting athletic shoes, 1989—.

Awards: Member of Rock and Roll Hall of Fame; recieved *Guitar Player* magazine's Editors Award for Lifetime Achievement, 1990.

Addresses: *Home*—Hawthorne, Flordia. *Office*—c/o Otelsberg, 5530 Keokuk Ave., Woodland Hills, CA 92364.

before hooking up with Alan Freed's rock and roll package to tour the country.

The "Diddley beat" was a simple, yet extremely infectious, "shave and a haircut, two bits" (a.k.a. "hambone") pattern. *The Illustrated Encyclopedia of Rock* calls it an "idiosyncratic syncopated rhythm." Perhaps it was in Diddley's early influences (his mother was Cajun), this hypnotic guitar sound with little or no chord progressions being propelled by Jerome Green's pounding congas, maracas and bass. Diddley's lyrics were equally strange and laced with his odd sense of humor, "a view of all life . . . particularly sex, as a profound cosmic joke, played out at the expense of everyone, but particularly the solemn and pompous," wrote Dave Marsh in the *Rolling Stone Record Guide*. On stage, Diddley was backed by his equally bizarre stepsister, the Duchess, and her counterparts, Cookie and Sleepy King. "[Diddley's] Bo-dacious caricatures are pure diddley daydreams out of a dada Disneyland," reported *Rock 100*.

As appealing as the sound was, Diddley did little to vary from it and it took another four years for him to break Billboard's Hot 100 with "Crackin' Up" in 1959. That same year, "Say Man" made the Top 20 pop charts but Diddley has never had another single make it past number 50 since. "I had this idea that everybody would like everything I recorded, which was totally

wrong, and I had to learn that," he told Howard Mandel in *Guitar World*. During the ensuing lull in his career, Diddley was rediscovered by foreign rock and blues groups that comprised the British Invasion: the Rolling Stones, the Animals, and the Yardbirds. Their cover versions of Diddley tunes brought him somewhat back into the limelight. He continued to release a batch of albums during the sixties and seventies with jacket covers that portrayed him as everything from a gun-slinger to a black gladiator in Ben Hur garb.

As corny as his album covers and outlandish clothes may have seemed, when Diddley plugged in his axe, guitarists took note. His wild collection of instruments, custom-built for him alone by the Gretsch company, were years ahead of their time with their oblong, triangle, and star shapes sometimes covered in carpet or fur. They were as much a part of the show as the man himself. "Bo Diddley used the guitar as a part of a flashy strutting performance of flamboyance and obvious sexual suggestion," as stated in *Guitars, From the Renaissance to Rock*. Diddley tunes to an open D (D,A,D,F#,A,D),

> *As corny as his album covers and outlandish clothes may have seemed, when Diddley plugged in his axe, guitarists took note.*

which accounts for part of his signature sound, but his use of tremolo, volume, pick-scraping, and various electronics are what make him one of the true innovators of rock guitar. "Bo Diddley on acid . . . I always just wanted to be wilder than Bo Diddley—which hasn't happened yet, and probably is impossible," said Fabulous Thunderbirds guitarist Jimmie Vaughan in *Guitar Player*.

Living Blues quotes Diddley as having called his former boss and label head, Leonard Chess, a "thief." Writer Pete Golkin explained: "When Diddley, who during a difficult period years later sold the rights to his hit songs of the '50s, complains about not receiving money owed him, it is done with a certain air of confusion about the times in which he and other artists quickly rose to stardom." Having experienced the financial plight that so many musicians have fallen into, Diddley decided to take career matters into his own hands and can now be found distributing his records on his own through Bokay Productions. "I've really been ripped off so much in the past, I don't trust any of them anymore . . . I just got tired of beating my head against the wall. I don't know what these companies are looking for, but I'll tell you one thing: I'm going to sound like Bo Diddley until the day I die," he told *Guitar Player*.

Although his last charted single was "Ooh Baby" in 1967 (which only reached number 88), Diddley remains active by playing one-nighters with pickup bands and touring with his daughter's band, Offspring. In 1979, English punk rockers, the Clash, paid tribute to Diddley by having him open a series of shows for them and he toured with Rolling Stones guitarist Ron Wood on a double bill called The Gunslinger's Tour in 1988. "That term—rock and roll—has been misused," Diddley said in *Guitar World*. "A guy in the audience the other night, he kept buggin' me: 'Play some rock and roll!' But I looked at him, pulled him off to the side, and said 'Can I explain something' to you?' I had to school him. Because I was playin' the only thing I knew how, *my* type of rock and roll—which is where it came from, because I was the beginning."

Selected discography

Single releases

Single releases on Checker between 1955 and 1962 include "Bo Diddley"/"I'm a Man—Spell It M-A-N," "Who Do You Love?," "Say Man," "Mona," "Road Runner," "Hey Bo Diddley," "Crackin' Up," and "You Can't Judge a Book By the Cover."

LPs

Bo Diddley, Checker, 1955, reissued, Chess, 1987.
Have Guitar, Will Travel, Checker, c. 1960.
Bo Diddley Is a Gunslinger, Checker, c. 1960, reissued, 1989.
In the Spotlight, Checker, 1964, reissued, 1987.
Two Great Guitars, Checker, 1964.
Super Blues Band, Checker, 1968.
Black Gladiator, Checker, 1971.
The London Bo Diddley Sessions, Checker, 1973, reissued, 1989.
Got Another Bag of Tricks, Chess, 1973.
Another Dimension, Chess, 1975.
20th Anniversary, RCA, 1976.
I'm a Man, MF, 1977.

Sources

Books

Christgau, Robert, *Christgau's Record Guide,* Ticknor & Fields, 1981.
Dalton, David, and Lenny Kaye, *Rock 100,* Grosset & Dunlap, 1977.
Evans, Mary Anne, and Tom Evans, *Guitars, From the Rennaissance to Rock,* Facts on File, 1977.
Harris, Sheldon, *Blues Who's Who,* Da Capo, 1979.
Kozinn, Allan, Pete Welding, Dan Forte, and Gene Santoro, *The Guitar: The History, the Music, the Players,* Quill, 1984.
Logan, Nick, and Bob Wolffinden, *The Illustrated Encyclopedia of Rock,* Harmony, 1977.
The Rolling Stone Record Guide, edited by Dave Marsh with John Swenson, Random House/Rolling Stone Press, 1979.

Periodicals

Guitar Player, June 1984; July 1986.
Guitar World, July 1984.
Living Blues, September-October 1989.

—*Calen D. Stone*

The Doobie Brothers

Pop/rock group

The Doobie Brothers epitomized mainstream rock and roll throughout the 1970s with a string of platinum albums and top ten hits. Personnel and stylistic changes notwithstanding—and both were substantial—the Doobies packed concert halls worldwide for more than a decade. Today their work is a staple of the "classic rock" format radio stations, and members of the original group are playing live together again. Reflecting on the resurgent popularity of the California-based hard rock band, *Rolling Stone* contributor Jeffrey Ressner concludes: "While the group has gone through numerous evolutionary changes over the past two decades, it refuses to become extinct."

Like so many other rock bands, the Doobie Brothers formed in California around a nucleus of semi-seasoned professional performers. The original three members, Tom Johnston, John Hartman, and Dave Shogren, called themselves Pud and began jamming for a tough audience of Hell's Angels bikers in 1969. The trio became a foursome with the addition of Patrick Simmons, who was primarily a folk musician and rhythm guitarist.

Unlikely though the association of Simmons and Johnston seemed, it provided the group with an interesting mix for songwriting and instrumentation. The 1971 addition of Tiran Porter provided three-part vocal harmony that became one trademark of the band.

The name Doobie Brothers was derived from the slang term for a marijuana cigarette—a favorite indulgence of the group. The early Doobies were a hard-living lot who played the road houses that were frequented by motorcycle gangs and other California toughs. In 1971 the group signed with Warner Bros. records and released their first album, *The Doobie Brothers*. It did not sell well, and the band members found themselves back at their old California gigs. Johnston was undaunted, however. As *Rolling Stone* correspondent Timothy White puts it, he "rolled up his sleeves and resolved to create some salable music for his band."

The result was *Toulouse Street,* a 1972 album that had platinum sales and two top ten singles, "Listen to the Music" and "Jesus Is Just Alright."

White writes: "The Doobies had a formidable sound, Simmons' deft country-blues picking meshing with Johnston's penchant for thick chord riffing with an R&B bent. Underscored by drummer Hartman and bassist Shogren was a powerful rock-pop sound that was buoyant but blistering, mighty and yet melodic." A 1973 album, *The Captain and Me,* quickly went platinum and placed two singles, "China Grove" and "Long Train Runnin'," in the top ten. The Doobies further enhanced their popularity by touring incessantly, making as many as two hundred personal appearances in a year.

The Doobies' fourth album, *What Were Once Vices Are Now Habits,* demonstrated that the band did not wish to produce solely pop material. After a slow start the record went platinum on the strength of the bluesy single "Black Water," the first Doobie Brothers song to reach number one. Years of touring and drug use began to take a toll on the group, however, and the membership roster began to change frequently. Chief among the departures was that of founder Johnston, who suffered bleeding ulcers in 1975. Johnston was replaced by a former member of Steely Dan, Michael McDonald, who quietly steered the Doobie Brothers in a new direction.

Most of the Doobie Brothers hits after 1975 feature vocal performances by McDonald. His influence also transformed the Doobies' sound from rock to jazz, with keyboards challenging the guitars as lead instrument. McDonald wrote several hits for the Doobies, including "Takin' It to the Streets," "What a Fool Believes," "Minute by Minute," and "I Keep Forgetting." The Doobie Brothers entered the 1980s on a strong footing, even though Simmons was the only original member still associated with the group.

By 1982 solo contracts were beckoning McDonald and Simmons, so the Doobie Brothers disbanded after a "farewell tour." Simmons told *Rolling Stone* that he expected the band to be quickly forgotten and was therefore surprised when a number of early Doobies hits became staples of AOR radio. "My perception was that the public forgets fast, and the music business is fickle," Simmons said, "[But] apparently, a few of our songs have been considered timeless." In 1987 some members of the original band, including Simmons, Johnston, Tiran Porter, and Michael Hossack, gave a benefit concert that resulted in a clamor for reunification. Johnston reorganized the Doobie Brothers, signed a contract with Capitol, and the band released another album, *Cycles,* in 1989.

Critics quickly noted that the tunes on *Cycles* bear a great resemblance to the earliest Doobie Brothers work. Johnston admits that he wanted to appeal to the tried-and-true Doobies fans that had supported the band all along. "Over the years," he told *Rolling Stone,* "I've found it's best to stick with what you know and what you can do best rather than trying to modernize it to the point where you're not yourself anymore. . . . We wanted to be recognizable." A Doobie Brothers tour in 1989 played to sold out stadiums in America, Japan, Australia, New Zealand, and Europe. Johnston credited "classic rock radio" with the renewed interest in his group. "Classic radio is responsible for keeping people who were famous back then in the public eye," he said. "People who maybe want to come back now."

Selected discography

The Doobie Brothers, Warner Bros., 1971.
Toulouse Street, Warner Bros., 1972.
The Captain and Me, Warner Bros., 1973.
What Were Once Vices Are Now Habits, Warner Bros., 1974.
Stampede, Warner Bros., 1975.
Takin' It to the Streets, Warner Bros., 1976.
Best of the Doobies, Warner Bros., 1976.
Livin' on the Fault Line, Warner Bros., 1977.
Minute by Minute, Warner Bros., 1978.
One Step Closer, Warner Bros., 1980.
Best of the Doobies, Volume 2, Warner Bros., 1981.
Cycles, Capitol, 1989.

—*Anne Janette Johnson*

Bob Dylan

Singer, songwriter, guitarist

In the early 1960s Bob Dylan was heralded as the spokesman for his generation, writing and singing folk songs that were as deep and moving as those of any artist since his idol, Woody Guthrie. At the 1965 Newport Folk Festival Dylan shocked his following by going electric and venturing into rock and roll. He proved to be equally superior in that field also and by 1968 he was trying his hand at folk-rock, creating an impact that touched even the Beatles and the Rolling Stones. As the 1980s came around Dylan was undergoing a spiritual rebirth and his writing reflected a religious conviction that was truly heartfelt. Throughout a career that has seen the better part of three decades, Dylan has been pop music's master poet and an ever-changing performer.

Born Robert Zimmerman in Duluth, Minnesota, Dylan was raised in the northern mining town of Hibbing from the age of six. His earliest musical influences, Hank Williams, Muddy Waters, Jimmy Reed, Howlin' Wolf and John Lee Hooker, were brought to him via the airwaves of a Shreveport, Louisiana, radio station. He played in a variety of bands during high school, including the Golden Chords, before enrolling at the University of Minnesota in 1959. It was at college that he changed his name to Dylan (probably after the poet Dylan Thomas) and began creating his own mythological background, which made him out to be everything from an Indian to a hobo to Bobby Vee! After hearing the Kingston Trio and Odetta he began to explore folk music, learning older tunes and sitting in at local coffeehouses around campus.

Just one year into college, Dylan dropped out after hearing Woody Guthrie and hitchhiked to New York to meet the legendary singer who was in an East Coast hospital suffering from Huntington's disease. "Guthrie was my last idol," Dylan said in *Rock 100*. "My future idols will be myself." Obviously in little need of self-confidence, by April 1961 he was gigging at Gerde's Folk City in New York's Greenwich Village. With the folk scene booming, Columbia executive and talent scout John Hammond had just signed Pete Seeger; Dylan followed soon after.

His debut LP, *Bob Dylan,* was released in March 1962. Recorded for a mere $402, the album featured acoustic reinterpretations of old folk songs, but also included two Dylan originals, "Song for Woody" and "Talking New York." Within a year his second LP, *The Freewheelin' Bob Dylan*—containing self-penned compositions only—was released. Protest tunes like "A Hard Rain's a-Gonna Fall," "Masters of War," and "Don't Think Twice, It's Alright" were making listeners more conscious and aware; both politically and personally. The trio of Peter, Paul & Mary recorded a version of "Blowin' in the Wind" from the LP that helped put the spotlight on Dylan. In July of that year at the Newport Folk Festival he was crowned leader of the folk movement with Joan Baez as the reigning queen. The new voice of youth, "Dylan's albums were listened to as if they were seismic readings from an impending apocalypse," reported *Rock 100.*

The Times They Are a-Changin', with its title track and "The Lonesome Death of Hattie Carroll," broke in the new year of 1964. Imitators of his guitar/harmonica rig and odd singing (talking?) voice were sprouting up everywhere. "It's phrasing," Dylan told *Rolling Stone,* "I think I've phrased everything in a way that it's never been phrased before." In addition to his unique voice, lyrics, and meter, Dylan's physical image was just as intriguing with his wild conk of hair, stovepipe legs, and facial scowl. As much as the public and critics adored him, they also were frustrated as attempts to gain insight were met with toying word games and sometimes downright humiliation. Dylan began to question his role as guru on his fourth LP, *Another Side of Bob Dylan,* moving away from political themes and towards personal love songs. "My Back Pages" and "It Ain't Me Babe" signalled that a different Dylan had now arrived.

Bringing It All Back Home (1965) was a half-acoustic, half-electric outing that featured Dylan classics "Subterranean Homesick Blues," "Maggie's Farm," "Mr. Tambourine Man," and "It's Alright Ma (I'm Only Bleeding)." Dylan's first step into rock was also his first million-seller. Even so, his die-hard fans were not prepared for Dylan's performance at the 1965 Newport Folk Festival, when he appeared onstage backed by the electric Paul Butterfield Blues Band. Cries of "sellout" and "gone commercial" filled the air as he was booed off the stage only to return for a final acoustic number, "It's All Over Now, Baby Blue." Anyone who doubted his commitment only needed to check out the next LP, *Highway 61 Revisited,* which was able to leap off the turntable courtesy of Michael Bloomfield's stinging guitar lines. The album featured the songs "Desolation Row," "Just Like Tom Thumb's Blues," "Queen Jane Approximately," and perhaps Dylan's most popular tune yet, "Like a Rolling Stone" (which went all the way to number 2).

His masterpiece, *Blond on Blonde* (1966), is considered by some to be the finest rock album in history. A double LP recorded with Nashville session men, it is filled with an amazing display of Dylan's songwriting abilities: "Sad Eyed Lady of the Lowlands," "Absolutely Sweet Marie," "Rainy Day Women No. 12 & 35," "Memphis Blues Again," "I Want You," and others that firmly established Dylan as the most prolific stylist of all time. Just when it seemed he was in full force, Dylan was seriously injured in a motorcycle accident on July 29, 1966. He would spend the next year and a half recuperating from a broken neck in upstate New York. He recorded tracks with his backup group, the Band, but they would not be released until 1975 as *The Basement Tapes* (an LP that was bootlegged endlessly during the nine-year delay).

After flirting with death, Dylan's comeback album, *John Wesley Harding,* relied more on religious themes and a mellower country flavor. "All Along the Watchtower" became a hit shortly after for Jimi Hendrix while the entire mood of *JWH* sent an influential wave out that touched other artists of the time. Dylan carried the country style even further on *Nashville Skyline,* recording a duet with Johnny Cash, and the easy-going "Lay Lady Lay." His next release, however, was a commercial and critical disappointment. *Self-Portrait* was a double album consisting mainly of non-originals that seemed to be almost intentionally bad. *New Morning,* also from 1970, did not fare much better; Dylan's talent seemed to have peaked.

In 1973 Dylan's Columbia contract expired and he

signed with Asylum just after releasing his soundtrack to the movie *Pat Garrett and Billy the Kid,* which included one of his biggest hits, "Knockin' on Heaven's Door." (Dylan also played the part of Alias in the film. Actor Sam Shepard told *Rolling Stone* that Dylan "knows how to play a part. He and Billy Graham are the two greatest actors in the world.") As if in retaliation for his leaving, Columbia released *Dylan,* a collection of studio outtakes and cover tunes that accomplished little more than embarrassing Dylan. His two Asylum LPs, *Planet Waves* and *Before the Flood,* were both recorded with the Band; the first being a studio album and the second featuring live recordings of the ensuing tour in early 1974.

In 1975 Dylan re-signed with Columbia and recorded one of his best records yet, *Blood on the Tracks,* which seemed to harken back to his earlier style. "Tangled up in Blue," "Idiot Wind," "Shelter From the Storm," "Meet Me in the Morning," and "Buckets of Rain" amongst others had critics gushing with joy over yet another Dylan comeback. He then hit the road with a musically varied ensemble called the Rolling Thunder

---

In the early 1960s Bob Dylan was heralded as the spokesman for his generation, writing and singing folk songs that were as deep and moving as those of any artist since his idol, Woody Guthrie.

Revue: Mick Ronson, Joan Baez, T-Bone Burnett, Roger McGuinn, Ramblin' Jack Elliott, and David Mansfield, all blasting off on Dylan classics and material from his newest LP, *Desire.* That album topped both the British and U.S. charts riding a crest of popularity created by "Hurricane," Dylan's thumping plea for the release of the imprisoned boxer Ruben "Hurricane" Carter. In 1976 the live *Hard Rain* captured the revue on vinyl. Two years later he would release another fine studio effort, *Street Legal,* featuring "Where Are You Tonight," "Baby Stop Crying," and "Changing of the Guards."

Dylan's next phase can be summed up in three albums, *Slow Train Coming, Saved,* and *Shot of Love,* and one word: Christianity. In 1979 he became "born-again," as writers coined it, studying the Bible at the Vineyard Christian Fellowship school in California. Although raised a Jew, Dylan took his new-found belief to the point of righteousness. "Dylan hadn't simply found Jesus but seemed to imply that he had His home phone number as well," wrote Kurt Loder in his *Rolling Stone* review of *Slow Train Coming.* The LP revolved around Dylan's beliefs, but it also rocked with the aid of Dire Straits guitarist Mark Knopfler. Critics and the public were split over the newest Dylan. Jann Wenner explained his view of this period in *Rolling Stone:* "Dylan created so many images and expectations that he narrowed his room for maneuverability and finally became unsure of his own instincts."

A rejuvinated Dylan appeared in 1983 on *Infidels,* produced by Knopfler with ex-Rolling Stone Mick Taylor on guitar. Dylan had joined an ultra-Orthodox Jewish sect, Lubavitcher Hasidim, and the songs reflected the move (although more subtly than during his Christian phase). In the mid-1980s Dylan continued to record and toured with Tom Petty and the Heartbreakers and the Grateful Dead as his backup bands. In 1988 he appeared as one of the Traveling Wilburys alongside Jeff Lynne, Tom Petty, George Harrison, and the late Roy Orbison. More changes can probably be expected from this master of the unexpected; Dylan has stayed on top by keeping ahead of the pack, knowing where his audience wants to be next, and then delivering.

Compositions

Composer of numerous songs, including "All Along the Watchtower," "All I Really Want to Do," "Blowin' in the Wind," "Chimes of Freedom," "Desolation Row," "Don't Think Twice, It's All Right," "Highway 61 Revisited," "I Shall Be Released," "If Not for You," "It Ain't Me, Babe," "Just Like a Woman," "Knockin' on Heaven's Door," "Lay, Lady, Lay," "Like a Rolling Stone," "The Mighty Quinn," "Mr. Tambourine Man," "My Back Pages," "Positively 4th Street," "Rainy Day Women No. 12 & 35," "Subterranean Homesick Blues," "Tangled Up in Blue," "The Times They Are a-Changin'," "When I Paint My Masterpiece," "When the Ship Comes In," "With God on Our Side," and "You Ain't Goin' Nowhere."

Selected discography

All titles on Columbia, unless noted

Bob Dylan, 1962.
The Freewheelin' Bob Dylan, 1963.
The Times They Are a-Changin', 1964.
Another Side of Bob Dylan, 1964.
Bringing It All Back Home, 1965.
Highway 61 Revisited, 1965.

Blonde on Blonde, 1966.
Bob Dylan's Greatest Hits, 1967.
John Wesley Harding, 1968.
Nashville Skyline, 1969.
Self-Portrait, 1970.
New Morning, 1970.
Bob Dylan's Greatest Hits, Vol. 2, 1971.
Dylan, 1973.
Pat Garrett and Billy the Kid, 1973.
Planet Waves, Asylum, 1974.
Before the Flood, Asylum, 1974.
The Basement Tapes, 1975.
Blood on the Tracks, 1975.
Desire, 1976.
Hard Rain, 1976.
Street Legal, 1978.
Bob Dylan at Budokan, 1979.
Slow Train Coming, 1979.
Saved, 1980.
Shot of Love, 1981.
Infidels, 1983.
Real Live, 1984.
Empire Burlesque, 1985.
Knocked Out Loaded, 1986.
(With Tom Petty, George Harrison, Jeff Lynne and Roy Orbison)
   The Traveling Wilburys, Volume One, Warner Bros., 1988.
Down in the Groove, 1988.
Dylan and the Dead, 1989.
Oh, Mercy, 1990.

(Dylan has also appeared on numerous albums by other artists; for a more complete listing check Bob Spitz's *Dylan, A Biography,* McGraw-Hill, 1989.)

Sources

Books

Christgau, Robert, *Christgau's Record Guide,* Ticknor & Fields, 1981.
Dalton, David, and Lenny Kaye, *Rock 100,* Grosset & Dunlap, 1977.
Dylan, Bob, *Tarantula,* Macmillan, 1970.
Bob Dylan: The Illustrated Record, Harmony, 1978.
The Illustrated Encyclopedia of Rock, compiled by Nick Logan and Bob Woffinden, Harmony, 1977.
The Rolling Stone Illustrated History of Rock and Roll, edited by Jim Miller, Random House/Rolling Stone Press, 1976.
The Rolling Stone Record Guide, edited by Dave Marsh with John Swenson, Random House/Rolling Stone Press, 1979.
Shepard, Sam, *Rolling Thunder Logbook,* Viking Press, 1977.
Spitz, Bob, *Dylan, A Biography,* McGraw, 1989.
What's That Sound?, edited by Ben Fong-Torres, Anchor, 1976.

Periodicals

Detroit News, July 9, 1989.
Musician, September, 1986.
Oakland Press, July 2, 1989.
Rolling Stone, March 11, 1976; September 21, 1978; November 16, 1978; July 12, 1979; September 20, 1979; September 18, 1980; June 21, 1984; Summer 1986; College Papers, Number 3.

—Calen D. Stone

The Eagles

Rock group

Time magazine introduced the Eagles to readers in 1975 as having been "conceived in the teaching of Carlos Castaneda and his ephemeral medicine man, Don Juan." As individuals they, like Don Juan, wandered (in and out of different groups including Linda Ronstadt's back-up band) until they found what guitarist Glenn Frey called their "power spot" as the Eagles. Singer-composer Jackson Browne brought the group (then made up of Frey, Bernie Leadon, Don Henley, and Randy Meisner) to the attention of impresario David Geffen, who advanced them $100,000 and sent them to Colorado to put together an act. A month later, they were signed to the newly created Asylum Records, and by the end of the decade they had become one of the top groups of the 1970s.

Combining their unique flavor of hard-rocking music with solid production, the Eagles' 1972 self-titled debut album quickly became a bestseller, staying on the charts the last seven months of the year. Browne, another Asylum artist, aided them in one of their first hits, co-authoring "Take It Easy" with Frey. The album

also included successful singles "Witchy Woman" and "Peaceful, Easy Feeling." Repaying Geffen's advance with proceeds from their first three hit singles, the group went rapidly on to record another best-selling release in 1973. *Desperado,* considered by critics to be something of a conceptual album, cast the rock-and-rollers as Old West outlaws in songs such as "Outlaw Man" and the title track. Both songs, assessed *Time,* were "linked by loneliness, excess and self-destruction." Don Henley, the group's drummer, admitted, "the whole cowboy-outlaw rocker myth was a bit bogus. I don't think we really believed it; we were just trying to make an analogy.... We were living outside the laws of normality, we were out here in L.A., things were kind of Western, and we just decided to write something about it to try to justify it to ourselves."

On the Border (1974) continued in the successful trend already begun, yielding the group's first smash single, "Best of My Love." Social commentary had begun seeping into the group's work, with the title track a thinly-disguised piece about the troubles President Richard Nixon had gotten himself into, although, assessed Henley, "we weren't old enough or mature enough to make any sense out of it then." The group was maturing rapidly, however, forced to deal with internal tensions that resulted first in creative tension, later to self-destruction. Nonetheless, by the end of the year the Eagles' three albums had been certified gold and they were on the professional rise.

The group's following two albums, *One of These Nights* and *Hotel California,* were their most successful, with hits including not only the title tracks but also "Lyin' Eyes" (which won them their first Grammy in the category of best pop vocal performance by a duo or group), "Take It to the Limit," "New Kid in Town," and "Life in the Fast Lane." "Hotel California," commonly thought to epitomize and denounce the decadence of Southern California lifestyles (of which the Eagles themselves were said to partake), became an especially popular song for the group and featured the distinctive guitar work of Joe Walsh, who replaced Leadon in the group. Henley was later to report, however, that the song was meant "in a much broader sense than a commentary about California. I was looking at American culture, and when I called that one song 'Hotel California,' I was simply using California as a microcosm for the rest of America and for the self-indulgence of our entire culture." The song garnered a Grammy in 1977 for record of the year; the same year Randy Meisner departed, his place filled by former

> *"The [Eagles'] whole cowboy-outlaw rocker myth was a bit bogus. I don't think we really believed it; we were just trying to make an analogy."*
> —Don Henley

Poco bass guitarist Tim Schmit. The group, busy in the recording studio and reluctant to endorse award shows, did not attend the Grammys. Said Frey, "I have reasonable doubt about how accurately any kind of contest or award show can portray the year in music." Nevertheless, the group was genuinely delighted by news of the award.

Over two years and $800,000 went into the group's long-awaited sixth album. *The Long Run,* a curious departure from the group's earlier work, had already reached double-platinum status (for sales of over two million copies) when it was shipped to stores. Hailed by *Rolling Stone* as promising "to be the Eagles' weirdest" record, the album included the slow ballad "I Can't Tell You Why" and such unusual titles as "Teenage Jail," "The Disco Strangler," and the college fraternity favorite "The Greeks Don't Want No Freaks." The tone of the album was described by Henley as "tongue-in-cheek cynical. Most of the humor is so dry nobody will think it's funny." One single, "Heartache Tonight," won a 1979

Grammy for best rock vocal performance by a duo or group.

The Eagles' final group effort came in the form of a double-live set that included a major hit with "Seven Bridges Road" by Steve Young, and afterward, several of the members went on to lucrative solo careers. Of their success and time together, Henley told *Rolling Stone*, "I don't think we had any delusions that we were creating history or changing culture or anything. . . . We just wanted to do the work and be good at it and be respected by our fellow songwriters."

Selected discography

The Eagles, Asylum, 1972.
Desperado, Asylum, 1973.
On the Border, Asylum, 1974.
One of These Nights, Asylum, 1975.
Hotel California, Asylum, 1976.
The Long Run, Asylum, 1979.
Eagles Live, Asylum, 1980.

Sources

Books

Nite, Norm N., and Ralph M. Newman, *Rock On: The Illustrated Encyclopedia of Rock 'N' Roll,* Volume II, Crowell, 1978.
Stambler, Irwin, *Encylopedia of Pop, Rock, and Soul,* St. Martin's, 1974.

Periodicals

Rolling Stone, April 6, 1978; July 26, 1979; November 5-December 10, 1987.
Time, August 18, 1975.

—Meg Mac Donald

Lester Flatt

Singer, guitarist

Singer-guitarist Lester Flatt is widely considered one of the founding fathers of bluegrass music. As a member of the legendary Flatt and Scruggs and the Foggy Mountain Boys, Flatt did more to popularize bluegrass than almost any other musician; his group transformed the genre from a regional to a national favorite and assured it audiences for generations to come. At a time when country music in general struggled to compete with rock and roll, the Foggy Mountain Boys won fame with a strictly traditional sound, unhampered by drums, synthesizers, or electronic enhancements. This is not to suggest, however, that the Flatt and Scruggs sound lacked innovation. It actually helped create the distinction between *country* on one hand and *bluegrass* on the other.

One of nine children of a poor sharecropper, Lester Raymond Flatt was born in rural Overton County, Tennessee, in 1914. "Like all farm children in those difficult times," writes Neil V. Rosenberg in *Stars of Country Music,* "Lester grew up knowing about hard work, for everyone in the family pitched in to do the chores." In what little free time the Flatt family found, the members would gather for songfests; both of Lester's parents played banjo in the old clawhammer, or "frailing," style, and his father also played the fiddle. Lester gravitated to the guitar and began picking before he turned ten. He learned to sing in local church choirs and perfected his techniques by comparing them with songs he heard on the radio.

In 1931, at the age of seventeen, Flatt went to work in the textile mills. He felt lucky to have work during the Depression, and he stayed with mill work full-time throughout the decade. Music was a sideline, but one that he was devoted to; he and his wife liked to imitate their favorite duo, Charlie and Bill Monroe. By 1939 Flatt was playing radio gigs in Roanoke, Virginia, as a member of the Harmonizers. Then he met Clyde Moody, a former member of Bill Monroe's band, and they formed the Happy-Go-Lucky Boys, a regional favorite.

Flatt was highly honored when he was invited to become a member of Charlie Monroe's Kentucky Pardners in 1943. The Monroe brothers had split, each forming his own band, and Flatt moved into Charlie's act as a tenor and mandolin player (the role Bill Monroe had previously taken). The following year Flatt quit the music business, but only briefly. He was given an offer too good to refuse: the chance to perform with Bill Monroe and the Blue Grass Boys. Bill Monroe had become a regular on the Grand Ole Opry—the pinnacle of success for a country band—and Flatt eagerly accepted the offer to sing lead and play guitar with the group. He soon made friends with another newcomer to the act, banjo player Earl Scruggs.

Work with the Blue Grass Boys was very challenging for Flatt in particular. As Rosenberg explains, the tempo Monroe set in much of his music was daunting, and Flatt had to improvise to keep up. "Monroe was playing much of his music so fast that Lester had trouble keeping time on the guitar," writes Rosenberg. "He solved this problem by catching up at the ends of phrases with a guitar run which, in its fullest form in the key of G, slid from F-sharp to G on the sixth string, then from A to B on the fifth string, from D to E on the fourth and ended in a ringing open G note on the third string. Often only the end of the run was audible. This was a common phrase in country guitar playing long before Lester used it, but because he used it so frequently and effectively it became associated with him, and eventually with bluegrass music, as 'the Lester Flatt G run.'"

In addition to playing, Flatt was called upon to sing lead in many songs. He also became the master of ceremonies for the Blue Grass Boys, adopting an easy, friendly style onstage. Life with the Blue Grass Boys was never boring, to say the least—Monroe was an exacting artist and the pace of touring and radio work was exhausting. By 1948 both Flatt and Scruggs had decided to quit, even though their presence in the band had propelled it to new levels of popularity. Against Monroe's objections, they both resigned within two weeks of one another. They were not idle long. Only one month later they began to meet informally, just to play, and they

decided to take some local radio work. They signed with Mercury Records and made their first recordings in the summer of 1948.

Flatt and Scruggs and the Foggy Mountain Boys originally included fiddler Jim Shumate, bassist Cedric Rainwater, and tenor Mac Wiseman, all of whom had worked with Monroe. Wiseman soon left and was replaced by Curly Seckler. Thus from their earliest days the Foggy Mountain Boys drew on Monroe's influence, especially in terms of tempo and choice of material. The group differed from Monroe's, however, in two major respects: Scruggs's banjo virtuosity elevated that instrument to prominence for the first time, and Flatt's vocals lacked the piercing quality of Monroe's high tenor. Together, Flatt and Scruggs and the Foggy Mountain Boys became one of the hottest acts in the South. *Country Music U.S.A.* author Bill C. Malone calls the band's early work "the most exciting in the history of bluegrass music."

Touring and recording relentlessly, Flatt and Scruggs began to win a widespread popularity that had eluded

---

Lester Flatt did more to popularize bluegrass than almost any other musician.

Bill Monroe. This success was sealed in 1953 when the pair signed a lucrative contract for a daily morning show on WSM, the home of the Grand Ole Opry. The show was sponsored by the Martha White Flour Mills, and Flatt and Scruggs opened each segment with a ditty about their sponsor. Incredibly, the "Martha White Theme Song" has become one of the most famous pieces in the Flatt and Scruggs repertoire; some bluegrass radio shows open with it to this day. When Flatt and Scruggs were invited to join the Grand Ole Opry in 1955, they continued their relationship with Martha White Flour, and gratitude for the association was expressed by sponsor and performers alike.

Flatt and Scruggs and the Foggy Mountain Boys entered the 1960s as the most popular bluegrass band in America. Few bluegrass groups have ever enjoyed a genuine hit on the Billboard charts; Flatt and Scruggs had several, including "The Ballad of Jed Clampett," a theme they wrote for "The Beverly Hillbillies" television show. "The Ballad of Jed Clampett" made both the pop and country charts, staying at number one on the latter for several weeks. Flatt and Scruggs were also among the first country performers to appear at folk festivals, including the inaugural Newport Folk Festival in 1959. In the mid-1960s they gave a sold-out concert at New York's prestigious Carnegie Hall.

Friction developed between Flatt and Scruggs as the 1960s advanced. Scruggs wanted to take the group in new directions, but Flatt preferred the traditional sound. They disbanded the Foggy Mountain Boys in 1969, and Flatt formed his own band, Lester Flatt and the Nashville Grass. This group was a favorite of bluegrass purists, many of whom supported Flatt's decision to steer clear of rock influences. Flatt played with the Nashville Grass for ten years until a chronic heart condition hospitalized him. He died May 11, 1979, at the age of sixty-four. Just before his death, Flatt was reconciled with his longtime partner after a decade of estrangement. *Rolling Stone* contributor Chet Flippo notes in a eulogy that Lester Flatt, in his tireless way, "spread bluegrass far and wide." His music, Flippo concludes, was "unlike anything urban audiences had heard before."

Selected discography

With Earl Scruggs and the Foggy Mountain Boys

Country Music, Mercury, 1958.
Flatt & Scruggs with the Foggy Mountain Boys, Harmony, 1960.
Songs of the Carters, Columbia, 1961.
Songs of Our Land, Columbia, 1962.
Hard Travelin', Columbia, 1963.
Flatt & Scruggs at Carnegie Hall, Columbia, 1963.
Flatt & Scruggs at Vanderbilt University, Columbia, 1964.
The Original Sound of Flatt & Scruggs, Mercury, 1964.
Flatt & Scruggs with the Foggy Mountain Boys, Mercury, 1964.
The Golden Era of Flatt & Scruggs, Rounder.
Foggy Mountain Breakdown, Hilltop.
Flatt & Scruggs' Greatest Hits, Columbia, 1966.
Lester Flatt and Earl Scruggs, Columbia.
20 All-Time Great Recordings of Flatt & Scruggs, Columbia.
The World of Flatt & Scruggs, Columbia.
Foggy Mountain Chimes, Harmony.
Sacred Songs/Great Original Recordings, Harmony.
Bonnie and Clyde, Columbia.
Wabash Cannonball, Harmony.

The Mercury Sessions: Volume 1, 1948-1950, Volume 2, 1950, Rounder, 1985.
You Can Feel It in Your Soul, County, 1988.

With the Nashville Grass

Lester Raymond Flatt, Flying Fish, 1975.
The Best of Lester Flatt, RCA.
Flatt on Victor, RCA.
Kentucky Ridgerunner, RCA.
Country Boy, RCA.
Before You Go, RCA.
Flatt Out, Columbia.

Other

Lester Flatt Live with Bill Monroe, RCA.
(With Mac Wiseman) *On the Southbound*, RCA.
(With Wiseman) *Lester 'n' Mac*, RCA.
(With Wiseman) *Over the Hills to the Poorhouse*, RCA.

Sources

Books

Malone, Bill C., *Country Music U.S.A.*, revised edition, University of Texas Press, 1985.
Malone, Bill C. and Judith McCulloh, *Stars of Country Music*, University of Illinois Press, 1975.
Sandberg, Larry and Dick Weissman, *The Folk Music Sourcebook*, Knopf, 1976.
Shestack, Melvin, *The Country Music Encyclopedia*, Crowell, 1974.
Stambler, Irwin and Grelun Landon, *The Encyclopedia of Folk, Country, and Western Music*, St. Martin's, 1969.

Periodicals

Bluegrass Unlimited, January, 1968, February, 1968, January, 1971, November, 1971.
Esquire, October, 1959.
New York Times, July 19, 1959.
New York Times Magazine, June 13, 1970.
Rolling Stone, July 12, 1979.

—Anne Janette Johnson

Tennessee Ernie Ford

Singer

Several generations of fans have thrilled to the rich baritone-bass of Tennessee Ernie Ford, one of the first stars to have "crossover" hits in country and pop music. Ford's soothing voice and affable ways assured him constant employment on radio and television from the late 1930s until the 1970s, and his albums of religious music continue to sell well to this day. As Melvin Shestack puts it in *The Country Music Encyclopedia,* Ford is "a Good Old Boy with no rural edges left. . . . His rich voice and ability to put over songs (even some clinkers) has afforded him countless acres to cultivate solid gold peas."

Ernest Jennings Ford was born February 13, 1919, in the town of Bristol on the Tennessee-Virginia border. His father was a postal worker who liked to play the fiddle, and many of the Ford family members sang in the local church choir. Ford has said that his family's favorite song was "The Old Rugged Cross," a number he has recorded several times. As a youngster he loved to sing, appearing in high-school plays and taking part in the glee club. He also enjoyed listening to country music on the radio, and he made himself such a fixture at the Bristol radio station that after graduation he was offered a job. While attending Virginia Intermount College to study voice, he worked as an announcer for ten dollars a week. In the fall of 1939 he enrolled at the Cincinnati Conservatory of Music, but he returned to radio work before the school year ended.

Between 1939 and 1941 Ford served as a disc jockey and announcer on stations in Atlanta, Georgia, and Knoxville, Tennessee. He enlisted in the Air Corps soon after the Japanese bombing of Pearl Harbor, becoming a bombardier on heavy aircraft. Promoted to the rank of lieutenant, he was stationed in California as a flight instructor for most of the war, and in 1942 he married Betty J. Heminger. After the war, Ford decided to stay in California. He returned to radio work in a succession of stations in San Bernardino, Pasadena, and El Monte.

The postwar years saw California emerge as a strong market for country-and-western music, and Ford was able to capitalize on that demand. He became friends with Cliffie Stone, whose well-known variety shows "Dinner Bell Roundup" and "Hometown Jamboree" were havens for country talent. By 1948 Ford was a regular soloist on Stone's shows, and Stone helped him to land a recording contract with Capitol Records. The following year Ford had his first charted country hits, "Mule Train" and "Smokey Mountain Boogie." In 1950 Ford and Kay Starr recorded a duet, "I'll Never Be Free," that climbed both the country and pop charts. Thereafter the avuncular Ford's talents were in great demand. As television found its way into American homes, his popularity soared.

Ford had one last daily television show from 1962 until 1965 on ABC. After that, he confined himself to recording and touring, with an occasional television special and numerous appearances on others' shows. Early in his career Ford had discovered an enthusiastic audience for religious music, and as he aged he recorded more and more traditional Christian hymns. It is these works that have maintained his strong following, one that is independent of the vicissitudes of the pop and country markets. Ford's rich bass is particularly well suited to hymn singing, and his renditions of "Old Rugged Cross," "Rock of Ages," and "Faith of Our Fathers," among others, are classics. In 1963 he became one of the first religious performers to earn a platinum record, for the album *Hymns.*

> Ford is "a good Old Boy with no rural edges left. His rich voice has afforded him countless acres to cultivate solid gold peas."

Ford's modern recording work is almost exclusively hymns. He still does personal appearances in Nashville and elsewhere—he was one of the first country performers to tour the Soviet Union—but he now lives in semi-retirement on his ranch in northern California. *Coronet* magazine contributor Richard G. Hubler notes that Ford broke new ground as an entertainer when he brought "a satiric sophistication to hill-country wit; his offhand comments are those of a new type of minstrel-philosopher." *World-Telegram and Sun* reporter Harriet Van Horne has called Ford "an original—in thought, word, and deed," whose talent is "the kind . . . you can't weigh in gold."

Ford's biggest hit came early in 1956. He released "Sixteen Tons," a pessimistic pro-labor song about coal mining, just before Christmas, 1955. "Sixteen Tons" had originally been recorded by its author, Merle Travis, in 1947, but Ford added a soft-rock arrangement that gave the populist tune a snappy beat. In nine weeks "Sixteen Tons" had sold two million copies; it topped the charts throughout the spring months. Ford had his own daytime television show at the time, but the success of the single led to a prime-time variety show on NBC. Enigmatically entitled "The Ford Show," Ford's program was sponsored by the automobile manufacturer of the same name. After a rocky start it quickly gained popularity, running for six years. A *New York Times* critic has said of the show: "[Ford's] personable drawl, ingratiating smile, and unhurried manner provided a jovial and restful pleasant half-hour." Ford himself decided to cancel the show in 1961 when he retired briefly to be with his family.

Selected discography

Spirituals, Capitol, 1958.
Nearer the Cross, Capitol, 1958.
Gather 'Round, Capitol, 1959.
Sixteen Tons, Capitol, 1960.
Sing a Hymn, Capitol, 1960.
Civil War Songs of the North, Capitol, 1961.
Civil War Songs of the South, Capitol, 1961.
Hymns at Home, Capitol, 1961.
I Love to Tell the Story, Capitol, 1962.
Favorite Hymns, Capitol, 1962.

Sing a Hymn with Me, Capitol, 1962.
Sing a Spiritual with Me, Capitol, 1962.
This Lusty Land, Capitol, 1963.
Hymns, Capitol, 1963.
Tennessee Ernie Ford, Capitol, 1963.
We Gather Together, Capitol, 1963.
Long, Long Ago, Capitol, 1963.
Great Gospel Songs, Capitol, 1964.
Tennessee Ernie Ford's Country Hits, Capitol, 1964.
World's Best Loved Hymns, Capitol, 1965.
Favorite Hymns, Ranwood, 1987.

Other recordings

Christmas Special, Capitol.
Amazing Grace, Pickwick.
Jesus Loves Me, Pickwick.
Make a Joyful Noise, Capitol.
The Need for Prayer, Pickwick.
Rock of Ages, Pickwick.
America the Beautiful, Capitol.
Faith of Our Fathers, Capitol.
For the 83rd Time, Capitol.
Tennessee Ernie Ford Sings His Great Love, Capitol.
25th Anniversary, Capitol.
The Story of Christmas, Capitol.
The Star Carol, Capitol.
The Very Best of Tennessee Ernie Ford, Capitol.

(With Glen Campbell) *Ernie Sings and Glen Picks,* Capitol.
Precious Memories, Capitol.
He Touched Me, Capitol.
Tennessee Ernie Ford Sings 22 Favorite Hymns, Ranwood.
Swing Wide Your Golden Gate, Word.
Tell Me the Old Story, Word.
There's a Song in My Heart, Word.

Sources

Books

The Illustrated Encyclopedia of Country Music, Harmony, 1977.
Malone, Bill C., *Country Music U.S.A.,* revised edition, University of Texas Press, 1985.
Shestack, Melvin, *The Country Music Encyclopedia,* Crowell, 1974.
Stambler, Irwin and Grelun Landon, *The Encyclopedia of Folk, Country, and Western Music,* St. Martin's, 1969.

Periodicals

Coronet, August, 1956.
New York Times, October 6, 1956.
Saturday Evening Post, September 28, 1957.
World-Telegram and Sun, September 27, 1957.

—Anne Janette Johnson

Samantha Fox

Singer

B ritish pop singer Samantha Fox always dreamed of being a singer. She told *Teen* magazine, "I was one of those kids, singing into a hairbrush in front of my mirror, with a blowdryer for a wind machine." Years later, without the aid of hairbrush and blowdryer, she has raised eyebrows and pulses with her first three major-label recordings: *Touch Me* (1986), *Samantha Fox* (1987), and *I Wanna Have Some Fun* (1988). Appearing on the jacket covers posed in sexy outfits and singing behind danceable, synthesized disco tracks, Fox has become a popular success. Her first album went gold, its single "Touch Me (I Want Your Body)" selling more than four million copies around the world. Her second album yielded the top-ten hit "Naughty Girls" while her third album produced the number one "I Wanna Have Some Fun." But amid all her commercial popularity, revealing outfits, and come-hither looks, Fox has failed to impress the critics, who remain staunchly united in their disapproval.

Fox was first exposed to the public as a "Page Three Girl" for England's most popular tabloid, the *Sun.* In 1983, at the age of sixteen, she joined a bevy of beauties who would greet Britons every morning on the third page with a warm smile and a bare chest. Fox explained to *Creem*'s Iman Lababedi that "the Page Three Girl is the working class girl next door with a nice smile and a nice pair of boobs." Paul Mathur, in the English publication *Melody Maker,* was more descriptive in his interpretation of the affair: "She ripped off her cozzie, unleashed her double-D's and became just like your average girl next door. . . ." In the process, Fox became the *Sun*'s most popular pinup and unleashed a career earning four thousand dollars for each personal appearance. She also became popular enough to take part in celebrity/rock charities. Along with fellow Page Three Girls she helped raise one hundred thousand dollars under the title Bare-Aid to assist African Relief activist Bob Geldof's efforts.

In 1986, however, Fox decided to pursue her ambition of becoming a singer. But popular success is often not a barometer of critical approval, and Fox's debut album, *Touch Me,* did little to dispel this notion. "The only thing to note about this record is that in 'Suzie Don't Leave Me with Your Boyfriend,' it contains a title about as lyrically graceful as a Czechoslovakian telephone book," Mathur scoffed. With lyrics such as "I was beggin' for you to treat my body like you wanted to/ ooh, ooh," *People*'s Ralph Novak claimed that "all anybody could tell is that she sounds better than Howard Cosell."

Fox's follow-up album continued in the same musical vein and brought the same critical derision. Colin Irwin of *Melody Maker* called *Samantha Fox* "a small step for

For the Record. . .

Born in 1966, in England; daughter of Pat Fox (a music manager and former construction worker).

Modeled under contract to *Sun*, 1983-87; Pop singer, 1986—.

Addresses: *Record company*—c/o Jive/RCA, 1348 Lexington Ave., New York, N.Y. 10128.

man, a huge step for lip gloss." Attempting to upgrade her material with a song titled "If Music Be the Food of Love" (from Shakespeare's *Twelfth Night*) and a cover of the Rolling Stones' "(I Can't Get No) Satisfaction," Fox still failed to convince the critics. Novak stated that her version of the Stones' classic "shows an ability to make a sow's ear out of a silk purse," while Alanna Nash, writing for *Stereo Review,* labeled Fox "really less a singer than a sex fantasy." The fantasy was maintained on her next album, *I Wanna Have Some Fun.* With such titles as "Your House or My House," "Next to Me," and "Hot for You," Fox continued to explore the topics of love and lust. In reviewing this release, Nash described it as "airhead pop" and confessed a desire to simply "get back to an analysis of those jacket pictures."

Fox's concert appearances have done little to change the prevailing critical perception. A reviewer for *Variety,* in a play on one of her hit song's lyrics, stated that "naughty girls may need love, but in the video age they apparently don't need much talent if they happen to be beautiful," adding that Fox "was neither naughty nor terribly lovable during an amateurish hourlong set."

Fox, however, is undaunted by such criticisms. Quoted in the *Detroit Free Press,* she maintained, "I'm not U2. . . .I don't want to be taken seriously." While the battle between popular adoration and critical disdain wages on, perhaps the final word comes from Lababedi: "If the American teenage male can't get it up over Ms. Fox, there's something drastically wrong with the American teenage male. It's as simple as that."

Selected discography

Touch Me, Jive/RCA, 1986.
Samantha Fox, Jive/RCA, 1987.
I Wanna Have Some Fun, Jive/RCA, 1989.

Sources

Creem, May 1987.
Detroit Free Press, August 11, 1989.
Melody Maker, June 21, 1986; July 19, 1986; July 18, 1987.
People, November 3, 1986; January 12, 1987; October 19, 1987; December 19, 1988.
Stereo Review, February 1988.
Teen, June 1989.
Variety, June 7, 1989.

—*Rob Nagel*

Peter Frampton

Singer, songwriter, guitarist

For Peter Frampton, fame came swiftly and unexpectedly in 1976 with the release of a live album that succeeded in doing what his studio recordings could not: deliver the zeal of an immensely talented musician. The media, rushing to explain the phenomenon, and his advisers, rushing to make a buck, had much to do with Frampton's eventual downfall and his later insistence on governing his reemerging career. Said Frampton in a *Rolling Stone* interview: "I started out as a musician, and I ended up as a cartoon." Unlike many performers who never had the chance, Frampton learned from his mistakes, and acted on that knowledge.

Born April 22, 1950, in Beckenham, Kent, England, Peter Frampton made his musical debut, guitar in hand, at the age of 8 at a Boy Scout variety show. The audience responded so well he could not help but do an encore. By 16 he was playing with the English pop group The Herd, meeting now with the approval of adoring tennyboppers. "It was great and it was terrible all in the same time," Frampton said in a 1986 interview with *Rolling Stone*. "It was incredibly exciting to be screamed at, but on the other hand, it wears thin very quickly, and the music was being forgotten." Concerned about that, and about mismanagement of the band, Frampton left in 1969 to form Humble Pie. After several moderately successful studio albums, and despite the band's popularity, Frampton again severed ties. This time, while he was convinced the group would be big, the style of music—leaning toward a louder, harder sound—did not suit him.

As a session musician, Frampton worked with George Harrison on *All Things Must Pass*. His association with Ringo Starr, Klaus Voorman, and Billy Preston would provide him with a backup group in 1972 when he recorded his first solo album, *Winds of Change*. What followed was four years of concentrated touring in the United States, opening for such bands as ZZ Top, the J. Geils Band, and Humble Pie. His stage performance had a magical quality to it, but his albums sold poorly. Finally, in March of 1976, he released the live album *Frampton Comes Alive* and went on a vacation before a one-nighter in Detroit. That one-nighter became two when the first sold out in an hour, then three when the second sold out in half an hour, until Frampton had a five-night engagement awaiting him in the Motor City.

No longer an opening act, Frampton spent the summer of 1976 playing for audiences as large as 100,000; being joined on stage by well-known musicians like Stephen Stills and Carlos Santana. *Billboard* named him Artist of the Year, as did the readers of *Rolling*

For the Record. . .

Full name, Peter Kenneth Frampton; born April 22, 1950, in Beckenham, Kent, England; son of Owen (a cabinet-maker and head of a high school art department) and Peggy Frampton; married Mary Lovett, August 24, 1972 (marriage ended); married Barbara Gold, 1983; children (*second marriage*) Jade.

Singer songwriter, guitarist. Member of rock band the Herd, 1966-69; member of rock band Humble Pie, 1969-71; solo artist, 1972—. Appeared in motion picture *Sgt. Pepper's Lonely Hearts Club Band* in the role of Billy Shears, 1978.

Awards: Named *Billboard* magazine's artist of the year, 1976.

Addresses: *Office*—c/o Hit & Run Music Ltd., 81-83 Walton St., London SW3 2HR England.

had had his doubts from the beginning, consoling himself with the knowledge that Paul McCartney would be in the picture. In the end, though, Billy Preston played that part. "I'd transgressed the un-written law," Frampton said later. "I'd messed with the Beatles, something I swore I would never do. I'm sure a lot of people thought I was selling out." Just before the film was released, Frampton was involved in a serious car accident that left him with multiple fractures and lacerations.

Knowing that his next album needed to be stronger than the last did nothing to help him make it. *Where I Should Be* produced only one single, "I Can't Stand It No More." By 1979, instead of playing multiple nights at Madison Square Garden, he played only one. His next album, *The Art of Control* was put together with the help of songwriter Mark Goldenberg. "There was nothing I could do at that point," Frampton commented in his 1988 *Rolling Stone* interview, "to make it any better. And that was the time I realized that it was time to . . .

> *"I started out as a musician, and I ended up as a cartoon."*
> —Peter Frampton

---

completely start all over again." A few months after the release of *The Art of Control* in 1982, his record company dropped him.

Putting his life back together was a personal struggle for Frampton. He loathed the thought that people still confused him with the cartoon character, the caricature he felt that his manager and the media had created. In 1983, he began the transformation with his marriage to Barbara Gold. Their daughter, Jade, was born a year later. According to *Rolling Stone,* these events were crucial to Frampton: "It was additional proof that not all his hopes for a good life resided with his music. . . . He grabbed at any evidence that suggested he was still what he always most wanted to be, a songwriter and a guitar player who was respected by his peers."

In 1984, guitarist Steve Morse asked Frampton to help write a song for Morse's upcoming album. Encouraged to begin practicing again, Frampton amassed enough new material of his own by the end of the year to make

Stone. Said Frampton of this success: "At times I felt I was being thrown into the deep end, but I work very well in that situation . . . I never said no to anything. I told everything to everybody. I gave everything away, and when you give it all away, you have nothing left."

Throughout the rest of 1976, *Frampton Comes Alive* continued to top the charts, remaining at number one for seventeen weeks and ultimately selling over 15 million copies. Driven by his manager, he played as many as seven nights a week, boosting his fatigue with cocaine and liquor. At the end of the summer—again, at his manager's insistence—he reluctantly began recording another album. *I'm In You* did not hold up to the success of the live album. Fans knew it. Critics knew it. Frampton knew it. The following summer, though, he toured again at the same frantic pace, relying on much of the material from the previous summer's album for his stage show. According to *Rolling Stone,* Frampton finally reached the point of quitting. He was talked out of it. "The consensus of opinion was that if I pulled out, it wouldn't look good," he said. "What that really meant was that a lot of revenue wouldn't be coming in. . . . No one really thought about my health, except that I was starting to consider the fact that here I am alone in a room with a bottle of Remy Martin drinking myself to sleep."

After the *I'm in You* tour, work began with the Bee Gees on the movie *Sgt. Pepper's Lonely Hearts Club Band.* The film, a poorly received fantasy, featured 29 Beatle songs and spawned an accompanying album. Frampton

an album. Under new management, he recorded and released *Premonition* in early 1986 and struggled to "come alive" once again. "I think at some point I might have said it must be great to be as big as Elvis, but that wasn't a realistic dream. . . . My success is enjoying what I do, and if I can maintain that enjoyment, that is more success than however many albums I sell. The other kind of big success . . . that just isn't in my dreams."

Selected discography

With the Herd

Lookin' Through You, Fontana, 1968.

With Humble Pie

As Safe as Yesterday Is, Immediate, 1969.
Town and Country, Immediate, 1969.
Humble Pie, A&M, 1970.
Rock On, A&M, 1971.
Rockin' at the Fillmore, A&M, 1971.

Solo LPs

Winds of Change, A&M, 1972.
Frampton's Camel, A&M, 1973.

Somethin's Happening, A&M, 1974.
Frampton, A&M, 1975.
Frampton Comes Alive, A&M, 1976.
I'm in You, A&M, 1977.
Where I Should Be, A&M, 1979.
Breaking All the Rules, A&M, 1981.
The Art of Control, A&M, 1982.
Premonition, Atlantic, 1986.

Other

Sgt. Pepper's Lonely Hearts Club Band, 1978.

Sources

Books

Anderson, Christopher P., *The Book of People,* Putnam, 1981.
Nite, Norm N., and Ralph M. Newman, *Rock On: The Illustrated Encyclopedia of Rock 'N' Roll,* Volume II: *The Modern Years: 1964-Present,* Crowell, 1978.
Stambler, Irwin, *Encyclopedia of Pop, Rock, and Soul,* St. Martin's, 1974.

Periodicals

Newsweek, April 19, 1976.
New York Times, October 3, 1976.
Rolling Stone, July 26, 1979; July 3, 1986.

—Meg Mac Donald

Glenn Frey

Singer, songwriter, guitarist

The breakup of the Eagles resulted in most of the band members going solo. Only two, though—drummer Don Henley and guitarist Glenn Frey—were to find success quickly. Frey was the first to strike out on his own, soaring comfortably into an admirable new career unhindered by "the poisoned delights and sundown despair of the California dream" associated with the Eagles.

Frey's first solo album, *No Fun Aloud,* is characterized as having a "casually polished, r&b-tinged surface" that "barely conceals a prodigiously talented singer/ songwriter." Reviewers indicate much of the album is fun, like the rousing "Partytown" (complete with backup vocals from such revelers as controversial tennis star John McEnroe) and the "bullish" remake of "I've Been Born Again." The upbeat, unpretentious air is rounded out with the inclusion of sweet melodies and gentle lyrics in pieces like the Spanish-sounding "She Can't Let Go" and "The One You Love." Longtime friend and fellow Detroiter Bob Seger collaborated with Frey on "That Girl," a "weeper . . . in which Frey's understated vocal is dramatically colored by David Wolinski's distant organ trill and a string arrangement that sounds like a spring rain." While *Rolling Stone* suggests the album might have "benefited from more rhythmic punch," the reviewer thought it nonetheless will do nicely "if you're drinking a beer right now."

Despite an agressive and successful foray into the solo scene, Frey was to receive harsher critiques down the line. His third album, *Soul Searchin',* is a case in point. While the package looks good and the songs sound good to the casual listener, according to *People* reviewer David Hiltbrand, they were still "little gems that possess not a whit of warmth or sincerity." Comparing Frey to former Eagle Don Henley, Hiltbrand goes so far as to suggest Frey's work "doesn't have the intelligence and feeling that mark Henley's records." On *Soul Searchin'* in particular, he asserts, Frey's shifting vocals seem to underscore what otherwise appears to be sincerity. His talents do carry him through on such slick pieces as "True Love" with its "meaty organ licks and smoky horns," the Springsteenish "Working Man," and "70's bubblegum-soul"-sounding "Let's Pretend We're Still in Love," but they still seem, to Hiltbrand, contrived, the album title a farce. If Frey were to embark on a "soul search," Hiltbrand claims, "you can rest assured he'll be back empty-handed and in time for lunch."

For Frey, just being in the business after so many years is a good sign. He feels he is part of a group of musicians "none of whom thought we would be doing it this long." Part of their strength and continuing popu-

For the Record. . .

S urname pronounced "Fry"; born November 6, 1948, in Detroit, Mich.

Singer, songwriter, and guitarist; performed as member of backup bands for Bo Diddley and Linda Ronstadt; member of group Longbranch Penny Whistle; founding member of the Eagles, 1971-81; solo artist, 1981—. Also actor and commercial spokesperson.

Awards: Co-recipient (with other members of the Eagles) of Grammy Awards for best pop vocal performance by a group, 1975, for "Lyin' Eyes"; for record of the year, 1977, for *Hotel California;* for best arrangement for voices, 1977, for "New Kid In Town"; and for best rock vocal performance by a group, 1979, for "Heartache Tonight."

Addresses: *Office*—c/o Triad Artists Inc., 10100 Santa Monica Blvd., 16th Floor, Los Angeles, CA 90067.

music and his career. "I'm realistic enough about my own solo career so that I don't anticipate having the sort of success I achieved with the Eagles." The late 1980s also saw Frey branch out into acting, appearing in a dramatic role on NBC-TVs "Miami Vice" that was favorably reviewed by critics, and in television commercials promoting a national chain of health and fitness gyms.

Selected discography

Solo LPs

No Fun Aloud, Asylum, 1982.
Allnighter, MCA, 1984.
Soul Searchin', MCA, 1988.

Sources

High Fidelity, September 1982.
New York Times, September 14, 1988.
People, October 10, 1988.
Rolling Stone, August 5, 1982.

—*Meg Mac Donald*

larity, he asserts, comes from the fact that many fans from the early days are still with him, still wanting to rock and roll. They continue to share a similar outlook on life and "want people from their generation to speak for them." So Frey maintains a good attitude about his

James Galway

Flutist

Irish flutist James Galway is a superb interpreter of the classical flute repertoire and a consummate entertainer. His silky tone and masterful technique, charismatic personality, and varied programs appeal to audiences of all ages and musical tastes.

Galway was born on Carnalea Street in a working-class neighborhood of Belfast, Northern Ireland. His father, James, was a shipyard riveter, and his mother Ethel worked as a winder in a spinning mill in West Belfast. The Galways were a musical family: Galway's father played the flute and accordion in local bands and his mother taught herself to play piano. Jimmy's first instruments were a harmonica, an old violin, and a penny whistle, but it wasn't until he picked up a flute at about age nine that he seriously began to practice. He took informal lessons from his father and paternal grandfather and learned to read music from the leader of a local flute band. When he was ten years old he entered three solo competitions in the Irish Flute Championships and won them all.

While a student at the Mountcollyer Secondary Modern School, Galway came to the attention of Douglas and Muriel Dawn, who set him on the path to a musical career. A flutist with the BBC Northern Ireland Symphony Orchestra, Muriel gave Galway lessons in the rudiments of flute playing. Douglas found him a job as an apprentice piano tuner, arranged for him to perform with the Belfast orchestras, and was instrumental in the Belfast Education Committee's awarding the young flutist with a scholarship to study at the Royal College of Music in London. For three years Galway studied with renowned flutist John Francis before transferring to the Guildhall School of Music to study under Geoffrey Gilbert, whom Galway cites as one of the most important technical influences in his life. In the early 1960s Galway attended the Conservatoire National Superieur de Musique in Paris, where he studied with Gaston Crunelle, who also taught Jean-Pierre Rampal. Galway never completed a degree, however, because he failed to attend classes peripheral to his interests.

Upon his return to London, Galway played flute and piccolo in several orchestras: Sadler's Wells Opera Orchestra, the Royal Opera House Orchestra, the BBC Symphony Orchestra, and the London Symphony Orchestra (LSO). In the late 1960s, while on a tour of the United States with the LSO, Galway met and took some lessons with the celebrated French flutist Marcel Moyse, who was then living in Vermont. His lessons with Moyse inspired Galway to strive for greater artistry—particularly a greater variety of tone colors—in his playing.

For the Record. . .

Born December 8, 1939, in Belfast, Northern Ireland; son of James (a shipyard riveter) and Ethel Stewart (a textile mill worker; maiden name, Clarke) Galway; first wife's name, Claire; married second wife, Anna Christine Renggli, 1972; children: (first marriage) Patrick; (second marriage) Charlotte and Jennifer (twins). *Education:* Attended Royal College of Music; studied under Geoffrey Gilbert at Guildhall School of Music; studied under Gaston Crunelle at Conservatoire National Superieur de Musique (Paris).

Worked as an apprentice piano tuner; played with the Wind Band of the Royal Shakespeare Theatre at Stratford-upon-Avon; played flute and piccolo in Sadler's Wells Opera Orchestra, 1961-66, and the Royal Opera House Orchestra, 1965; played piccolo in the BBC Symphony Orchestra; principal flutist with the London Symphony Orchestra, 1966-67; with Royal Philharmonic Orchestra, 1967-69; principal solo flute with Berlin Philharmonic Orchestra, 1969-75; soloist, 1976—; has appeared as a guest performer on numerous recordings and television programs; teacher of music, 1976-77, and 1989—.

Awards: Order of the British Empire, 1977; received Grand Prix du Disque for his recording of Mozart concertos; presented record of the year awards from both *Billboard* and *Cashbox* magazines.

Addresses: *Manager and publicist*—ICM Artists, 40 West 57th Street, New York, NY 10019.

Since then Galway has become one of the most popular soloists on the international music scene. He tours widely to enthusiastic crowds that include flute students, flutists, and amateurs of classical and popular music alike. Galway programs concerts with particular audiences in mind and performs on any one of nineteen handmade gold flutes, which have become his trademark, and a penny whistle. Not hesitant to talk to audiences or appear in the media, Galway's lilting brogue, twinkling eyes, and quick wit are known to many who have seen him on "Live From Lincoln Centre," "Sesame Street," talk shows, or credit card commercials.

Galway's lengthy discography includes most of the masterpieces of the flute repertoire as well as forays into country, folk, jazz, and modern popular music. His more than 30 RCA Victor recordings are best-sellers—he has one platinum and several gold albums to his credit—and his hit records with John

> *Galway's lengthy discography includes most of the masterpieces of the flute repertoire as well as forays into country, folk, jazz, and modern popular music.*

Denver, Cleo Laine, and Henry Mancini have made him one of the most successful crossover artists of our time.

Ever attentive to the quality of his recorded works, Galway has refused to release albums that did not entirely satisfy him. His recording of the Mozart concertos, which won the Grand Prix du Disque, attests to his concern for quality. Although critics sometimes decry Galway's recording of popular tunes, Galway cites a famous precedent. "My own model is [violinist] Jascha Heifetz," he told Bob Porter in the *Dallas Times Herald.* "He recorded everything from Bach to 'Ave Maria.' He was the biggest influence on what I have done with my life."

Since the flute repertoire is limited, Galway has transcribed pieces originally composed for other instruments, such as Vivaldi's *The Four Seasons* and com-

Galway left the LSO to join the Royal Philharmonic Orchestra, and in 1969 he became principal flutist of the Berlin Philharmonic Orchestra under the world renowned conductor Herbert von Karajan. As Galway had for a long time been unsatisfied with orchestral performing, and even working with such a celebrated orchestra and conductor did not fulfill his need to express himself more fully, he began to accept extra-orchestral engagements. Michael Emmerson, a talent scout who has since become involved in managing RCA Red Label records, spotted Galway and offered to manage his solo career. In the summer of 1975, with Emmerson's encouragement, Galway struck out on his own. In his first year as a solo performer, Galway taught flute for a semester at the Eastman School of Music in Rochester, New York, toured widely, and made four records. By the end of that year it was obvious to everyone that Galway had found his niche.

missioned new pieces by composers Joaquin Rodrigo and John Corigliano, among others.

The lifestyle of a celebrity on tour takes its toll. Galway had become known as a serious carouser, and after he underwent a crisis of conscience in 1987, he adopted a stricter lifestyle, checking into a health farm to lose weight. He also returned to a more regular practice regimen and decided to cut short his fledgling conducting career as too time-consuming. In 1989—after a twelve-year hiatus—he resumed teaching. He teaches in his home in Lucerne, Switzerland, and conducts masters classes in the cities where he performs. Galway is also co-authoring a book on flute performance and technique with Australian flutist and writer Andrew Richardson. What advice does Galway give his students? "Practice all the time, just non-stop practice, and listen to other people in the same business; establish where you're at, where you're going and what you're going to do about it," he told Patricia Harty of *Irish America Magazine*.

Writings

James Galway: An Autobiography, enlarged edition, Chivers, 1980.
Flute, London, 1982.

Selected discography

Released by RCA on Victor Red Seal

"Annie's Song" and Other Favorites.
Bach Trio Sonatas.
Clair de Lune—The Music of Debussy.
The Classical James Galway.
Corigliano: *Pied Piper Fantasy.*
French Flute Concertos by Ibert, Chaminade, Poulenc, Faure, Charles Dutoit.
James Galway and the Chieftans in Ireland.
James Galway: Greatest Hits.
James Galway Plays Bach Flute Concertos—Concerto in A Minor, Concerto in E Minor, Suite No. 2 in B Minor.

James Galway Plays Mozart Concerto in C for Flute and Harp, Concerto in G.
James Galway Plays Schubert.
James Galway's Christmas Carol.
(With various artists) *James Galway's "Music in Time."*
Italian Serenade Works for Flute and Guitar.
The Magic Flute of James Galway.
Man with the Golden Flute.
Mozart: *Concerto No. 1 in G, Concerto No. 2 in D, Andante in C.*
Mozart: *The Two Flute Concertos.*
The Pachelbel Canon and Others.
(With Cleo Laine) *Sometimes When We Touch.*
Sonatas for Flute and Piano.
"Song of the Seashore" and Other Melodies of Japan.
Telemann: *Flute Concertos, Suite in A Minor, Concerto in G, Concerto in C.*
Vivaldi: *The Four Seasons.*

Sources

Books

Galway, James, *Autobiography*, enlarged edition, Chivers, 1980.

Periodicals

Baltimore Sun, March 18, 1987.
Bloomington Herald-Telephone, March 6, 1987.
Boston Herald, July 3, 1987.
Chicago Sun Times, April 23, 1989.
Dallas Times Herald, July 8, 1988.
Detroit Free Press, March 27, 1987.
Flute Talk, April 1989.
Gannett Westchester Newspapers, July 17, 1988.
Irish America Magazine, September 1986.
Music Magazine, February/March 1989.
New York Times, July 16, 1988.
Ovation, June 1987.
Portland Press Herald, March 15, 1987.
Raleigh News and Observer, April 2, 1989.

—Jeanne M. Lesinski

Roland Gift

Singer, songwriter

Roland Gift, lead singer of the Fine Young Cannibals, one of the most popular new groups of the late 1980s, has been compared by critics to such great vocalists as Sam Cooke, Al Green, Otis Redding, Nat King Cole, and even Frank Sinatra. "Gift draws portraits of heartache and longing," explained John Leland in *Vogue,* "as he slides from falsetto to a deep mournful moan." Reviewer Nicholas Jennings concurred in *Maclean's,* declaring that "the highlight of the Cannibals' sound. . .[is] Gift's plaintive voice." Also serving as the band's lyricist, Gift has contributed in large measure to the success of the Cannibals' first two albums, *Fine Young Cannibals* and *The Raw and the Cooked.*

Born in Birmingham, England, to a white mother and a black father, Gift grew up in the English seaside town of Hull. According to Marlaine Glicksman in *Film Comment,* Gift found the fishing port dull and "backward." He told her, "When I was really little, all I ever wanted was to be a cosmopolitan person." Perhaps accordingly, Gift's youthful ambition was to be an actor, and he constantly performed in school and community plays. He was also attracted to music, however, and recalled for Glicksman that "mostly the singers I used to listen to were soul singers—American black soul singers. When I see somebody has created something, it really excites me, I feel I can go out and do anything." Gift found Otis Redding particularly inspiring, but as he grew older, he became interested in the punk scene, admiring groups such as the Clash. At the age of sixteen he dyed his hair and gave up acting to join a punk band.

Gift's career as a musician before joining the Fine Young Cannibals included stints with the Akrylyx and the Bones; it was while with the former group that he opened for the popular ska group English Beat, whose members Andy Cox and David Steele would later seek him out as a vocalist for the Cannibals. For Akrylyx Gift played the saxophone, but he confided to Steve Dougherty of *People* that he was "so bad that people asked me to sing." According to Rob Tannenbaum of *Rolling Stone,* "at the end of the Akrylyx's set, Gift would sing a song." But Gift admitted to Tannenbaum: "It was just. . .awful, just shouting." Despite his punk influences, Gift still prefers the soul sound of the 1960s, before "guitars got really heavy and dominant, and singing went out the window," as he put it to Tannenbaum.

By 1983, the English Beat had broken up. Cox and Steele wanted to form a new group, but recognized that they needed a lead singer, preferably one with attractive looks as well as a good voice. According to Tannenbaum, the pair listened to over four hundred demo tapes in the course of their search. Once, they thought they had found the perfect candidate, but he

For the Record. . .

Born c. 1962 in Birmingham, England. Played with bands including the Akrylyx and the Bones until c. 1984; member of the Fine Young Cannibals, c. 1984—. Appeared in films, including *Tin Men, Sammy and Rosie Get Laid,* and *Scandal.*

Addresses: *Manager*—AGM Management, 1312 N. LaBrea Ave., Hollywood, CA 90028.

turned out to be "fifty-five, bald, and fat," in Tannenbaum's words. Finally, Cox and Steele remembered a band that had often opened for their concerts, and in particular remembered the saxophone player.

When Gift joined Cox and Steele, they chose their band's name from a 1960 film that none of them had ever seen, *All the Fine Young Cannibals.* They released their first album in 1985, entitled *Fine Young Cannibals.* Gift and the other Cannibals scored a dance hit in England with the album's "Johnny Come Home," and what Glicksman heralded as "a revved-up rendition of Elvis Presley's 'Suspicious Minds'" also did well in the band's homeland. *Fine Young Cannibals* brought its authors' musical talents to the attention of filmmakers, too. Jonathan Demme recruited the Cannibals to do a remake of the Buzzcocks' "Ever Fallen in Love," which Jimmy Guterman in a *Rolling Stone* review labeled an "instant classic," for use in his *Something Wild.* Director Barry Levinson was so impressed with the band and Gift's singing that he not only asked them to record songs for the film *Tin Men,* but included in it footage of the Cannibals portraying a 1960s group. Later, the cuts from *Tin Men* and "Ever Fallen in Love" helped make up Gift and the Cannibals' second release, *The Raw and the Cooked.* This album, whose unusual name comes from a book of the same title by Claude Levi-Strauss, also spawned the band's first number one single— "She Drives Me Crazy." "Good Thing," from *Tin Men,* was a follow-up hit.

Though Gift turned away from acting in his adolescence, he has since had an opportunity to express himself through the medium of his first career choice. Not only has his work with the Fine Young Cannibals become tied to the screen, but he has had respectable acting roles in motion pictures. After seeing Gift per-

form with the Cannibals on a British television music show, director Stephen Frears cast him as Danny in the 1987 cult film *Sammy and Rosie Get Laid.* Film offers began to pour in after that, and he won a major part in the British film *Scandal.* But Gift is picky about the roles he accepts: as Tannenbaum put it, "he's seen musicians destroy credibility in two fields with one bad part." Gift also finds there are not many non-stereotypical parts for black actors. "Obviously I don't like the stereotyping," he complained to Tannenbaum. He commented to Glicksman: "People. . .expect me to be black, to do the black thing. [It's] racist, really, expecting someone to behave a certain way. . . .I think it shouldn't be an issue, and I'd like it not to be an issue. I am black, but don't forget I'm half white." Gift plans to do further film work, plus take part in a Hull production of William Shakespeare's *Romeo and Juliet.*

Gift is also working on the Fine Young Cannibals' third album. Whether he concerns himself with music or acting, Gift summed up his attitude for Glickman: "I love performing because it's something that you never need to stop doing. You're always learning. If you're a craftsman and you can create, then it's always going to be different and always changing. It's more than wanting to be famous. It's more than wanting to be a star. It's about wanting to be involved in some kind of creation. That's what it's about."

Selected discography

Albums with the Fine Young Cannibals

Fine Young Cannibals (includes "Johnny Come Home" and "Suspicious Minds"), I.R.S., 1985.
The Raw and the Cooked (includes "She Drives Me Crazy," "Good Thing," "Ever Fallen in Love," "Tell Me What," and "As Hard As It Is"), I.R.S., 1989.

Sources

Film Comment, March/April, 1989.
Maclean's, March 6, 1989.
People, May 1, 1989.
Rolling Stone, March 9, 1989, April 20, 1989.
Vogue, April, 1989.

—Elizabeth Thomas

Boris Grebenshikov

Singer, songwriter, guitarist

It's a warm, muggy night in Moscow, and a hundred or so people are milling around the courtyard of one of the city's generic apartment complexes, which seems almost tenement-like by U.S. standards. Over to one side is a cluster, in the middle of which, smoking a cigarette and leaning against a brick wall, is Soviet rock star Boris Grebenshikov. It's 1987, and the lean, handsome singer-songwriter, who hails from Leningrad, is in the middle of one of the things he does best—talking to reporters. "I'm the darling of *glastnost*," he's declared, and there's no question that he's positioned himself well to reap the benefits of Mikhail Gorbachev's new policies of openness, tolerance, and reform. Though not the first Soviet rocker to reach the West, he was the first to land a big-time record contract; in June 1989, Columbia Records—the label of Bruce Springsteen, Bob Dylan, and George Michael—released Grebenshikov's *Radio Silence* album and put him on tour to spread the word about his distinctive but unquestionably Western-influenced music.

The album and tour were the result of a long and careful process of bringing Grebenshikov to U.S. audiences. The plan began in 1987, about the same time U.S. pop superstar Billy Joel journeyed to the Soviet Union to perform six concerts; Belka International, Inc., a company that puts together joint Soviet-American ventures—including the Space Bridge project—decided to bring Grebenshikov to the West to meet with American and British musicians and with U.S. record companies. Great interest was expressed, with ex-Police member and political activist Sting among the most vocal. The company's principals—Kenny Schaffer and Marina Albee—figured that of all the Soviet rock acts, Grebenshikov would be their best bet.

"[The interest] is definitely there for Boris," Albee told the *Detroit Free Press*. "There really aren't any other Russian bands now who have the right sound and can go to the U.S." Dave Snow of Opal Records, which has released albums by Soviet artists like Zvuki Mu and Djivan Gasparyan, agreed. "Its something with a Russian name that was really Westernized and made for Western tastes," he told the *Free Press*. Indeed, Grebenshikov's greatest advantage over his countrymen has more to do with marketing than music. He speaks crystal clear English—he started learning, at his parents' insistence, when he was eight years old—understanding the nuances and subtleties of the language. It makes him highly quotable and he speaks with an egoistic confidence and assurance reminiscent of the early days of Elton John or Boy George.

Rock and roll wasn't an early career goal for Grebenshikov. Little is known about his childhood, though his parents' ability to pay for English lessons indicates that the family was better off than many in Russia. And because he understood English, Grebenshikov was a step ahead in understanding the power of this new and, at that time, illegal art form. Rock and roll became a sensation on the Soviet black market, where albums and tapes were exchanged for outlandish prices. Tastes were largely behind the times—they've only caught up during the past three years—and Grebenshikov and his friends were drawn more towards the melodic British rock of the Beatles than to the grittier sounds coming from America. "Our music isn't as rhythmic," Grebenshikov, who formed his first band when he was 15, told the *Detroit Free Press*. "Russian songs are written in minor chord structures, with a lot of feeling and depth. It's not designed to be as instantly catchy as what you hear [in America]."

Rock certainly served to heal Grebenshikov's frustrations as he went on to study and earn a degree in applied mathematics at the University of Leningrad. At the time he appeared to be a proper Soviet citizen, even a member of Komsomol, the Communist Youth League. But underneath he was a rocker at a time when it was outlawed and illegal. Though he told the *Washington Post* that "nobody treated it seriously from the authority side . . . the state just ignored it completely," that changed in the mid-1970s, when the government discovered that Western rock was embracing politics, sex, and the drug culture.

Grebenshikov formed Aquarium in 1972, but he also had a day job as a mathematician and sociologist at the university. "When I graduated from school, I had to go somewhere, and it could be either the Army, which I didn't want to go into, or some kind of university. And so I spent six very nice years doing rock 'n' roll and all the antisocial things that I could possibly dream of, and getting by. It was the time of least resistance. That's how I became a mathematician."

Aquarium's activities, however, gave him more notoriety. It wasn't long before the group became the underground favorite in the Soviet Union, and as its leader, Grebenshikov became a cultural folk hero. The walls leading up the eight-story climb to the three-bedroom apartment he and his family—longtime companion Irina and his three children—share with two other families are lined with graffiti. "Boris is God." "Long live Boris." "Boris, I love you—I can't live without you." It's no wonder that his influence is often compared to that of Bob Dylan and Bruce Springsteen in the United States.

Because rock and roll was underground in the U.S.S.R. until recently, there are no record sales figures to track Grebenshikov's popularity. It's estimated that millions of homemade Aquarium tapes have passed hands since 1972. When Melodiya, the state-run record label, finally released an Aquarium album in 1987, it sold 3.5

> *Though not the first Soviet rocker to reach the West, Grebenshikov was the first to land a big-time record contract.*

million copies. Two more releases have experienced similar success. Grebenshikov, however, doesn't enjoy royalties relative to his status; he told the *Chicago Tribune* that he receives about 4,000 rubles for every million albums sold, about 300 times less than the average U.S. recording contract.

But money was the least of his worries in the early days of Aquarium. In 1972, Grebenshikov was kicked out of Komsomol because of his rock and roll activities. In 1980, after playing a rock festival in the Soviet republic of Georgia, he lost his job at the university. Aquarium—and other Soviet bands—maintained, playing clandestine concerts and often dodging the arm of Soviet law. "If you're playing for free, you could spend the night in jail he told the *Chicago Tribune*. "But if you were caught with some money in your hands, well, I've heard of some people who spent several years in jail."

In 1985 Mikhail Gorbachev came to power in the Soviet Union, bringing with him reform. Soviet society opened, slowly and with no small amount of suspicion on the part of its citizenry—particularly oppressed artists. "There was no trust," Grebenshikov told the *Washington Post*. "He was just another name, and we had three or four of them right before. It was 'When will he die?'" Gorbachev proved to be good for Soviet rock and roll, however. The once-underground performers were "recognized" by state agencies governing recording and performing. And plain old business sense allowed rock to become part of the culture. "We've learned there's a lot of money to be made from these bands," Melodiya executive Victor Solomatzin told the *Detroit Free Press*. "The young people are the ones who buy records, and this is the music they want."

So the ultra-popular Grebenshikov, who had already received exposure in *People* and *Rolling Stone* magazines, was positioned perfectly to benefit from the new openness. He came to America in December 1987, and was introduced to Western superstars, including Lou Reed, David Bowie, Frank Zappa, and even boxer Mike Tyson. Bowie took him out nightclubbing, but Grebenshikov told *Newsday* he found it "boring. I don't like to shout over the din of any club. When I talk with people, I talk with them. When I sit back and listen to music, I sit back and listen to music. I don't feel the need to do these things simultaneously."

Working with Eurythmics member and producer Dave Stewart, *Radio Silence*—which also features guest appearances from Stewart's partner Annie Lennox and Pretenders leader Chrissie Hynde—was recorded throughout 1988 and early 1989 at several Western studios. What many critics found refreshing was a switch from the blatantly sexual orientation of most Western hitmakers. "Russian culture doesn't relate to sex at all," Grebenshikov told the *Washington Post*. "No one can conceive of a song with sexual overtones like in black music and rock 'n' roll, which are based on sex. I can't imagine a Russian rock 'n' roll song being based on sex. We just don't have the language for it, and I don't think we need to because Russians are something different and that's what makes it a thing apart. Russian writers would rather tackle philosophical or political subjects." For Grebenshikov, one of those future topics might be how a Soviet man of the people copes with Western life. He now doesn't leave home without his American Express Card, and he has a bank account, which is a true rarity in the Soviet Union. Such luxuries can't help but put a dent in his street credibility.

Still, that's something he saw coming in 1987, when his drive to the West began. *Radio Silence* hasn't exactly made him a superstar on these shores, which he said was enough of a humbling experience to keep his head below the clouds for the time being. "I'm doing my thing and letting God provide," he told the *Los Angeles Times*. "I'm not looking to leave Russia. It's my home. I don't want to live anywhere else. I'm not after the money. I'm looking for spiritual gratification."

Selected discography

Red Wave (one of four acts featured on album), Gold Castle Records, 1986.
Radio Silence, Columbia, 1989.

With group, Aquarium, featured on numerous underground and black market recordings in the Soviet Union during 1970s and 1980s and on three sanctioned albums released by Melodiya, the Soviet state-run record company, during the late 1980s.

Sources

Associated Press, August 19, 1987.
Boston Globe, August 7, 1989.
Chicago Tribune, June 3, 1989.
Chicago Tribune Sunday Magazine, February 19, 1989.
Detroit Free Press, June 11, 1989.
Los Angeles Times, August 19, 1989.
Newsday, April 17, 1989; August 6, 1989.
New York, March 20, 1989.
New York Times, April 17, 1989.
People, April 6, 1989.
United Press International, July 28, 1989.
Washington Post, July 16, 1989; August 3, 1989.

—*Gary Graff*

Nanci Griffith

Singer, songwriter, guitarist

In *Sing Out!,* singer/songwriter Tom Russell related that he first encountered Nanci Griffith at a folk festival in 1976. One evening around a campfire, with people spread out on a grassy hill into the darkness, guitars and wine being passed around, a gruff voice yelled from the darkness, "Let *her* play one." From the edge of the campfire light came a waif-like young girl. She began to play and sing in a voice Russell said possessed "a wild, fragile beauty." When she finished and the echo of the applause drifted away, the voice spoke again: "That was Nanci Griffith. She writes songs."

In the contemporary music world, where the drum machine is the musical backbone, dancing is the answer to social problems, and lyrics speak only of vacuous, pubescent angst, Nanci Griffith stands at the edge of light. At a time when popular music is, as *Detroit News* music critic Susan Whitall observed, "bankrupt of inspiration," Griffith offers songs of love, stories of broken dreams, observations of people living lives that are neither heroic nor pathetic. "The people residing within the lines of her songs," *Connoisseur* reviewer Jared Lawrence Burden stated plainly, "are the salt of the American earth." According to Stephen Holden of the *New York Times,* Griffith "sings lyrics redolent of the American landscape."

Southern literature and folk music inform Griffith's vision of this landscape. Born in Austin, Texas, in 1954, she grew up reading various writers and listening to jazz, folk, and country. But more than others, the fiction of Eudora Welty, the voice of folk singer Carolyn Hester, and the songs of country singer Loretta Lynn imbued her with a passion for struggling human relationships, dreams, and a sense of place; with, in the opinion of Peter Nelson of *Rolling Stone,* a "forthrightness and clarity of heart"; and with, as Griffith explained to Holden, a desire to tell "incredibly vivid stories that hit their subjects right on the nail's head."

The combination of these influences has given rise to a unique Griffith style, which she terms "folkbilly," and which the *New York Times* defined as a "songwriting style steeped in the rich mixture of Southern literary tradition, folk music, and country." But Griffith is not just a songwriter, "she writes songs," and her songs are stories. Russell explained the difference: "Nanci's musical roots are based in folk music, but her writing style always carried evidence of a prose writer's skills. She has a poet's eye and a novelist's sense of time and place." Griffith told James Ring Adams of the *Wall Street Journal* that the venerable Nashville songwriter Harlan Howard, with whom she studies, said to her: "You're a writer. You're a writer first. You just happen to be a writer who can sing."

As a result, Griffith's lyrics and themes are reportorial

For the Record...

Born 1954 in Austin, Texas; daughter of Griff (a printer and publisher) and Ruelene (in real estate) Griffith. *Education:* Education major at University of Texas at Austin.

Began playing bars in Austin, Texas, at age 14; taught kindergarten and first grade in Austin school system briefly during mid-1970s; first recorded for small Texas-based label, B.F. Deal, 1977; recording artist, 1978—; began musical collaboration with band Blue Moon Orchestra on third album, *Once in a Very Blue Moon,* 1985.

Addresses: *Residence*—Nashville. *Management*—Vector Management, P.O. Box 128037, Nashville, TN 37212. *Record company*—MCA Records, Inc., 70 Universal City Plaza, Universal City, CA 91608.

and realistic. *Stereo Review's* Alanna Nash pointed out how Griffith crafts songs "with a more conversational feel, focusing more on character development than outside events." Burden offered a panorama of the focus in her songs: "There is a black middle-class woman living in Houston, caught at a moment of pride and wonder about her marriage. There is a couple arguing at the airport about their lost love. In one of her strongest and best-known songs, 'Love at the Five and Dime,' two lovers' romance is rekindled by memories of the days when they were courting." The aim of these songs is not self-aggrandizement. In the best literary tradition, Griffith gives a voice to the inarticulate, the uninspired, the unheard. She told Paul Mather of *Melody Maker,* "I want to celebrate the South again. . . . There's a dignity and beauty there that's not often pointed out."

Her celebration of life is not confined only to songs. When Griffith is not on the road, she writes stories and novels. So far she has completed one manuscript, *Two of a Kind Heart,* spanning three generations of a Texas family, and is working on a second, *Love Wore a Halo Before the War.* There is no division between the focus of Griffith's songs and her prose. Often she turns a story into a song. "Love at the Five and Dime" was originally a short story while "Love Wore a Halo (Back Before the War)," which appears on *Little Love Affairs,* is drawn from the corresponding novel.

In concert, Griffith combines both mediums. She tells stories both through and between her songs. "Her stories," Mather said, "are sometimes ordinary, sometimes magical, invariably enchanting." He went on to add that "despite the often upbeat seduction, the last-

ing memory is of a beautiful sadness." A reviewer for *Variety* was left with the impression of "an unusual talent, a winsome, almost strangely pure-voiced singer whose style and sound bear little taint of commercialization or contrivance, marked instead by a quirky, honest individuality and soulfulness that connect in gentle, often bewitching ways."

Some critics, however, do indeed consider Griffith's individuality to be contrived. According to Nash, there are some who deem her material "overly sentimental and precious, as affected as the white cotton anklets she wears with the old-fashioned dresses she makes from prints bought on sale from Woolworth's." Griffith's devoted following, on the contrary, feels she is more affective than affected. Mather explained: "Nanci Griffith gives us dreams . . . that affect because of, rather than despite, their traditionalism. There's no urge here to reinvent, to introduce a new pop vocabulary, simply a pure joy in her own ability to make music that touches all those places that make you sigh and stuff." In the end, perhaps all that matters is Griffith's ability to step

> *Griffith offers songs of love, stories of broken dreams, observations of people living lives that are neither heroic or pathetic.*

into the light and touch her audience. Burden observed: "As she talks, the young men in the audience are wishing that Nanci Griffith were their girlfriend, the older men are wishing she were their daughter, and the women are wishing that they, too, could play guitar and sing."

Selected discography

There's a Light Beyond These Woods, Philo/Rounder, 1978.
Poet in My Window, Philo/Rounder, 1982.
Once in a Very Blue Moon, Philo/Rounder, 1985.
Last of the True Believers, Philo/Rounder, 1986.
Lone Star State of Mind, MCA, 1987.
Little Love Affairs, MCA, 1988.
One Fair Summer Evening, MCA, 1988.
Storms, MCA, 1989.

Sources

Connoisseur, February 1989.

Detroit News, November 12, 1989.

High Fidelity, June 1988.

Melody Maker, March 19, 1988; April 23, 1988; April 30, 1988.

New York Times, February 10, 1988; April 3, 1988; September 17, 1989.

People, March 7, 1987; March 7, 1988; September 11, 1989.

Rolling Stone, May 7, 1987; March 24, 1988.

Sing Out!, Fall 1986.

Stereo Review, May 1988; June 1988; March 1989.

Time, July 25, 1988.

Variety, March 23, 1988.

Wall Street Journal, April 14, 1987.

—Rob Nagel

Vince Guaraldi

Pianist, composer, arranger

Vince Guaraldi is perhaps best known for writing and playing the jazz-oriented scores that accompany the "Charlie Brown" television specials. He defined for an entire generation, and subsequent generations, the sound and feel that accompanies the *Peanuts* gang. It is his composition, "Linus and Lucy," that breaks the entire group into spontaneous dance. And it is his composition, "Christmas Time Is Here," that follows Charlie Brown on his lonesome and burdensome quest for the perfect Christmas tree. But these works alone do not define Guaraldi. During his short life he had other achievements. Bob Doerschuk, profiling Guaraldi in *Keyboard,* offered this wide-ranging definition: "Throughout his career, Vince was an explorer, peering down unfamiliar paths in search of new changes, new rhythms, yet never forgetting his own voice, which spoke best in the language of melodic simplicity."

Vincent Anthony Guaraldi was born in San Francisco on July 17, 1928, into a musical family. His uncles, Muzzy Marcellino (a television music director) and Joe Marcellino (a violinist and bandleader), piqued his early interest in music, and by the age of seven he began piano lessons with his mother, continuing to play throughout his high school years. After graduation and a tour in Korea, Guaraldi apprenticed at the San Francisco *Daily News*. While working there in 1949, he suffered an accident in which he almost lost a finger, an occurrence that proved to be a pivotal point in Guaraldi's life. Doerschuk noted that "it was this incident, along with his family's encouragement and his own desire to develop his talent, that committed him to the music world full-time."

Later that year Guaraldi began classes at the San Francisco Conservatory of Music and played his first professional outing. During the next decade, Guaraldi performed, toured, and recorded with various groups and soloists, including vibraphonist Cal Tjader, trombonist Bill Harris and bassist Chubby Jackson, Woody Herman and his Thundering Herd, and Howard Rumsey's Lighthouse All Stars. In addition, he also formed his own trio (piano, guitar, and drums) and recorded his first album, *Vince Guaraldi Trio,* for Fantasy Records in 1956.

Guaraldi's musical style at that time was extremely energetic, influenced by boogie woogie and bebop. But late in the 1950s he came upon bossa nova, a musical hybrid of Brazilian samba and cool jazz with subdued, subtle harmonies and light syncopation. "It was during a trip to New York with Tjader that Vince had his first exposure to Latin American music, a style that was to have a profound effect on his own playing," Doerschuk reported. "Years before most American musicians were even aware of bossa nova, Guaraldi was looking for ways to blend the piano into the hypnotic rhythms and soft textures that music required."

Interest in this style of music and in the bossa nova-like soundtrack to the 1959 French/Brazilian film *Black Orphans,* which updated the legend of Orpheus and Eurydice against the carnival of Rio de Janeiro, led Guaraldi to record *Jazz Impressions of "Black Orpheus"* in 1962. This album gave Guaraldi national exposure and earned him commercial success. Ironically, what garnered attention was not the single from that album, "Samba de Orpheus," but the B-side, "Cast Your Fate to the Wind." Included as filler because the album was originally too short, "Cast Your Fate to the Wind" caught on after a California disc jockey played it repeatedly, and it was awarded the Grammy Award for Best Original Jazz Composition for 1962. "With its unpretentious, almost stark framework, catchy theme, and tastefully restrained performance, the disc established Guaraldi's sound in the ears of many young record buyers who had only been exposed to rock," Doerschuk noted. "Cast Your Fate to the Wind" was one of the first jazz records to enter into the national Top 40 list. It also spawned further exposure through the film "Anatomy of a Hit," produced by noted jazz critic

Full name, Vincent Anthony Guaraldi; born July 17, 1928, in San Francisco, Calif.; son of Carmella Marcellino Guaraldi; died February 6, 1976, in Menlo Park, Calif. *Education:* San Francisco Conservatory of Music.

Pianist, composer, arranger. Performed and recorded with vibraphonist Cal Tjader, 1950-52; played in sextet led by trombonist Bill Harris and bassist Chubby Jackson, 1953-56; toured with Woody Herman and his Thundering Herd, 1956-57, and 1959; again played with Cal Tjader, 1957-59; played with Howard Rumsey's Lighthouse All Stars, 1959; played with his own trio, also worked as a composer, arranger, and performer (piano) for television shows and motion pictures, 1960-76.

Awards: Grammy Award for Best Original Jazz Composition for "Cast Your Fate to the Wind," 1962; nominated for an Academy Award for Best Music Scoring for the film "A Boy Named Charlie Brown."

Ralph Gleason for public television in 1963, which profiled Guaraldi and analyzed his hit.

Because of the increased acclaim this record brought, Guaraldi felt compelled to explore new settings for his music. When he was approached by the California Episcopal Archdiocese to produce a celebration of the Holy Eucharist with music in the jazz medium, Guaraldi responded. On May 25, 1965, the Guaraldi *Mass* was celebrated, and recorded, at Grace Cathedral in San Francisco. A two hundred-voice choir performed Gregorian-like chants while Guaraldi and his trio accompanied with jazzy improvisations. Despite a few detractors who felt it inappropriate, the *Mass* received wide coverage and acclaim from such sources as *Time* magazine and Bishop James A. Pike, head of the diocese of California.

A new setting for Guaraldi's music also came through his soundtracks for the *Peanuts* television specials and film. Ralph Gleason introduced Guaraldi to *Peanuts* producer Lee Mendelson, who had wanted a jazz track to accompany the cartoons, differentiating them from others done previously. Their collaboration spanned sixteen half-hour shows and one movie, "A Boy Named Charlie Brown," for which Guaraldi was nominated for an Academy Award for best music scoring of a feature film in 1970. In 1981, Mendelson told Doerschuk, "I think Vince's music was one of the contributions that made the Charlie Brown shows successful. . . . Vince gave it a sound, an individuality, that no other cartoon

had ever had. I'd say that over the last fifteen years we've received as much mail asking about the music as we have about anything else in the shows."

Despite the success of the series, Guaraldi failed to produce another hit record. He returned to playing in clubs and bars around San Francisco where he continued to expand his vision, playing with verve and intensity. Shirley Lewis Harris saw Guaraldi perform in 1971 and reported in *Billboard* that he "is still playing the same kind of jazz he did years ago, but with more guts than ever. This man can turn a piano into the closest thing to a human being just by putting his hands on the keys. He makes the piano laugh, cry, sigh, be coy or intellectual."

Guaraldi played his last gig at Butterfield's Bar in Menlo Park, California, on February 6, 1976, when he suffered a fatal heart attack between sets. Although it came as a shock to his fans and relations, the situation under which he passed away seemed ironically appropriate. His mother, Carmella Guaraldi, explained to Doerschuk: "When it happened down at Butterfield's, when the end finally came, he went the way he would have wanted to go, with the piano." Philip Elwood, in an obituary notice for *Rolling Stone*, defined Guaraldi's achievements: "Deep down, Guaraldi was a jazzman. He was never comfortable if the artistic milieu was restrictive or his colleagues weren't putting out. He was an experimenter, an improvisor, a creator. What more can we ask of an artist?"

Selected discography

Vince Guaraldi Trio, Fantasy, 1956.
Jazz Impressions of "Black Orpheus," Fantasy, 1962.
Vince Guaraldi, Bola Sete, & Friends, Fantasy, 1963.
Latin Side, Fantasy, 1965.
Vince Guaraldi at the Grace Cathedral, Fantasy, 1965.
A Charlie Brown Christmas, Fantasy, 1965.
At El Matador, Fantasy, 1967.
Oh, Good Grief, Warner, 1968.
A Boy Named Charlie Brown, Fantasy, 1969.
Greatest Hits, Fantasy, 1980.

Sources

Billboard, August 21, 1971.
down beat, February 25, 1965; April 8, 1976.
Keyboard, July, 1981.
Music Journal, November, 1966.
Rolling Stone, March 25, 1976.

—*Rob Nagel*

Lynn Harrell

Cellist

Lynn Harrell is one of the leading cellists of his generation and is especially popular in the United States and Great Britain. He is known for his broad and big-toned performance style and technical mastery, as well as his geniality and delight in music making.

Although Harrell was born into a musical family—his father was Mack Harrell, a baritone with the Metropolitan Opera, and his mother, Marjorie Fulton, was a violinist—his parents did not pressure any of their three children to play musical instruments. Harrell began to play the piano at age eight and—not liking it—much later decided to play the cello after he saw one at an informal chamber music concert at his home. Since the boy chose the cello because he was big for his age and it was the biggest instrument he knew, Harrell often quips that he might have become a bassist if he had known of the instrument's existence.

The Harrell family moved from New York City to Dallas when Mack Harrell accepted a position as artist-in-residence at Southern Methodist University. Lynn excelled at the cello at a price. "When I stopped playing sports in school," he recalled to John Farrell of *USC Magazine,* "baseball, basketball and football, when I decided I wanted to practice the cello instead, I gave up popularity, friends. I was suddenly a leper. No one was the same to me. And that was very, very hurtful. Very lonely." When four years later his father died of cancer, the young cellist found consolation in his music, pouring all his feelings into the cello in what he calls a "very complicated emotional relationship." His cello again received his sorrow when Harrell's mother was killed in an automobile accident in 1963.

Harrell studied cello with Lev Aranson in Dallas, Leonard Rose at the Juilliard School in New York, and Orlando Cole at the Curtis Institute in Philadelphia. In 1961 he made his Carnegie Hall debut with the New York Philharmonic Orchestra. Harrell also attended master classes with two of the most renowned cellists in the world: Gregor Piatigorsky in Dallas (1962) and Pablo Casals in Malboro, Vermont (1963). At age eighteen Harrell was a finalist in the Tchaikovsky Competition in Moscow and beame the youngest member of the Cleveland Orchestra under the world famous conductor George Szell. Three years after joining the orchestra, Harrell was promoted to first chair. Harrell recalls those years as a sort of apprenticeship. "But it was like having a class on music in the best sense," he told Gordon Emerson of the *New Haven Register.* "That's when I really got a working knowledge of how to put a piece together for a performance and it's been very valuable."

In 1971 Harrell struck out on his own, but it was only following a joint recital in 1972 with James Levine—

For the Record. . .

Full name, Lynn Morris Harrell; born January 30, 1944, in New York City; son of Mack (a baritone with the Metropolitan Opera) and Marjorie (a violinist; maiden name, Fulton) Harrell; married Linda Blanford (a journalist), September 7, 1976; children: Eben and Katherine (twins). *Education:* Studied cello at the Juilliard School of Music and at the Curtis Institute of Music.

Made debut with the New York Philharmonic Orchestra, 1961; first cello with the Cleveland Orchestra, 1963-71; made recital debut at Tully Hall, New York City, 1971; taught at the University of Cincinnati College-Conservatory of Music, 1971-76; taught at the Juilliard School of Music, New York City, 1977; featured soloist with numerous major symphony orchestras in the United States and Europe; became first holder of the Piatigorsky Chair of Cello at the University of Southern California (USC), 1987; appointed to the International Chair of Cello Studies at the Royal Academy of London, 1988.

Awards: Co-recipient (with Murray Perahia) of the first Avery Fisher Prize, 1975; Grammy Awards (with Itzhak Perlman and Vladimir Ashkenazy) for best chamber music performance, 1981, for Tchaikovsky's *Piano Trio in A Minor,* and (with Perlman and Ashkenazy) 1987, for *Beethoven: The Complete Piano Trios.*

Addresses: *Office*—c/o Columbia Artists Management, 165 West 57th Street, New York, NY 10019. *Publicist*—Herbert H. Breslin, Inc., 119 West 57th Street, New York, NY 10019.

Touring is lonely and fatiguing, and after the number of his performances peaked at 130 in a single year, Harrell decided to limit them to about 100 to allow for more family time. When Harrell was playing concerts in London with Ashkenazy, he met his future wife—Linda Blandford—an English journalist who came to interview the duo. They were married in 1976 and have twins, Katharine and Eben, with whom they live in Beverly Hills.

Harrell takes teaching seriously. His first teaching appointment was with the Cincinnati College Conservatory of Music before he began his solo career. Since then he has taught at the Juilliard School, was appointed to the International Chair of Cello Studies at the Royal Academy of London, and in 1987 became the first holder of the prestigious Piatigorsky Chair of Cello at the University of Southern California in Los Angeles (USC). "As I have been given, so it has always seemed to me, I was obliged to give to others," he wrote

> *Since he chose the cello because he was big for his age, and it was the biggest instrument he knew, Harrell often quips that he might have become a bassist if he had known of the instrument's existence.*

whom he had met when Levine was an intern with the Cleveland Orchestra—that his career was launched. Since then he has performed with many of the world's greatest orchestras and soloists. He owns a 1720 Montagnana cello and a 1673 Stradivarius cello, fine instruments by world renowned makers. He is equally comfortable performing in solo recitals, chamber music concerts, and solo appearances with the orchestra. He has made a number of televised appearances: "PBS Gala of the Stars," "Live from Lincoln Center," and the "Metropolitan Opera Gala," among others.

Harrell's discography includes more than two dozen albums on a number of labels, including RCA, EMI/Angel, Deutsche Gramophone, and CBS. In 1981 he and violinist Itzhak Perlman and pianist Vladimir Ashkenazy were awarded a Grammy for their recording of the Tchaikovsky *Trio in A Minor,* op. 50. In 1986 Harrell signed an exclusive contract with London/Decca to record works by Tchaikovsky, Brahms, Bach, and others.

in the *Instrumentalist.* "I have always felt that I owed others a huge musical debt and that I was to pay it through the next generation." Harrell rarely gives private lessons, preferring instead the master-class format. He finds that teaching enriches and inspires his own playing.

Between performing, recording, and teaching, Harrell maintains a hectic schedule. He has conducting ambitions, and he may also write a book and make a videotape on cello technique. But in putting his goals in perspective, he emphasizes non-musical activities as well. "My goals," Harrell told Farrell, "are just to get the music right, to get it better. But in the last five years or so, I've also become much more concerned with my quality of life. When I come to the end of my career, I want to feel I've had a good and satisfying life. I want to feel content with what I've done, not sorry for missing out on the pleasure that one can derive from living life to the fullest. For me much of that has to do with making music. But it's more than music too. It's family and students and friends. I want to live a life that's very rich and full and happy to the end."

Selected discography

C.P.E. Bach: *Cello Concerto in A Major;* Couperin: *Pieces en Concert,* Angel/EMI.

J.C. Bach, Mozart, Stamitz, Wanhal: *Oboe Quartets,* Angel/EMI.

J.S. Bach: *Six Suites for Solo Cello,* London/Decca.

J.S. Bach: *Sonatas for Viola da Gamba and Harpsichord,* London/Decca.

Beethoven: *Sonatas for Cello and Piano* (with James Levine), RCA.

Beethoven: *Sonatas for Cello and Piano* (with Vladimir Ashkenazy), London/Decca.

Beethoven: *Trio No. 7 in B Flat* "Archduke," Angel/EMI.

Beethoven: *Piano Trios,* Angel/EMI.

Beethoven: *Serenade,* Op. 8; Dohnany: *Serenade,* Op. 10, CBS.

Boccherini: *Quintet for Strings in E Major,* Vanguard.

Brahms: *Sonatas for Cello and Piano, No. 1 in E minor,* Op. 38, *No. 2 in F Major,* Op. 99, London/Decca.

Brahms: *Double Concerto for Violin and Cello,* CBS.

Dvorak: *Concerto in B Minor,* Op. 104; Bruch: *Kol Nidrei,* Op. 47, London/Decca.

Dvorak: *Concerto in B Minor,* Op. 104, RCA.

Elgar: *Concerto,* Op. 85; Tchaikovsky: *Rococo Variations,* Op. 33; *Pezzo Capriccioso,* London/Decca.

Haydn: *Cello Concertos, No. 1 in C Major, No. 2 in D Major,* Angel/EMI.

Herbert: *Cello Concertos,* London/Decca.

Lalo: *Concerto in D Minor;* Saint-Saens: *Concerto No. 2 in D Minor,* Op. 119; Faure: *Elegie,* Op. 24, London/Decca.

Mozart: *Piano Quartet in G Minor,* K. 478, RCA.

Prokofiev: *Sonata in G Major,* Op. 119; Debussy: *Sonata;* Webern: *Drei Kleine Stucke,* Op. 11, RCA.

Rachmaninoff: *Sonata for Cello and Piano,* Op. 19; *Vocalise,* Op. 34, No. 14, London/Decca.

Schoenberg: *Pierrot Lunaire,* Op. 21, CBS.

Schubert: *Arpeggione Sonata,* D. 821; Mendelssohn: *Sonata in D Major,* Op. 58, RCA.

Schubert: *Quintet for Strings in C Major,* DG.

Schumann: *Concerto in A Minor,* Op. 129; Saint-Saens: *Concerto No. 1 in A Minor,* Op. 33, London/Decca.

Schostakovich: *Concerto No. 1,* Op. 107; Bloch: *Schelomo,* London/Decca.

Strauss: *Don Quixote,* Op. 35, London/Decca.

Tchaikovsky: *Piano Trio in A Minor,* Op. 50, Angel/EMI.

Villa-Lobos: *Bachianas Brasileiras No. 5 For Soprano and Cellos,* London/Decca.

Vivaldi: *Concerto in G Major,* P. 120, *Concerto in G minor,* P. 369.

Sources

Instrumentalist, April 1988.
Keynote, May 1988.
Los Angeles Daily News, July 17, 1988.
New Haven Register, October 4, 1987.
Ovation, March 1986.
Raleigh News and Observer, January 15, 1988.
USC Magazine, January 1988.

—Jeanne M. Lesinski

George D. Hay

Country music promoter

George Hay never sang a single song or plucked a single tune, but he exerted an immense influence on the development of country music as an entertainment form. Hay was the founder of the "Grand Ole Opry," the informal showcase of country and western talent that has become the industry's signature program. Listeners across America were introduced to country music by way of powerful WSM Radio in Nashville; the show survives to this day on its parent station and in syndication. Hay, who called himself the "Solemn Ol' Judge," saw radio as an important medium for the popularization of rural music. Although his Opry became increasingly glamorous and professional over the years, it has never lost the intimate "barn dance" quality he sought to preserve.

George Dewey Hay was born in Attica, Indiana, in 1895. In his early twenties he moved south to Memphis, Tennessee, where he gained a job as a reporter for the Memphis *Commercial Appeal.* When the newspaper branched out into commercial radio, Hay switched formats, serving as an editor and an announcer. By 1924 he was being heard over the air on WLS in Chicago, a station that reached listeners throughout the South and Midwest. WLS hired Hay to serve as master of ceremonies for a show of hillbilly music modeled on the old-fashioned barn dances so popular in all of America's rural regions. Hay had been strongly influenced by hoedowns he had attended in the Ozark Mountains and elsewhere, and he strove to re-create that exciting, informal atmosphere in the studio.

The "WLS Barn Dance," soon renamed the "National Barn Dance," was an immediate success, and Hay found himself named top radio announcer of 1924 in a *Radio Digest* poll. In *Country Music U.S.A.,* Bill C. Malone notes that Hay, "calling himself the 'Solemn Ol' Judge,' and blowing blasts from a steamboat whistle,. . .helped to give the new *Barn Dance* show an authentic, homey atmosphere." The "National Barn Dance" featured stringbands, fiddlers, square-dance callers, other country performers, as well as more mainstream crooners and balladeers. It too enjoyed a long run on WLS and later WGN in Chicago, finally going off the air in 1968.

Late in 1925, Hay moved to WSM, a new station in Nashville, Tennessee. Although WSM had only a seventy-five-mile range, Hay found the offer attractive because he was named director of the station. His employers, National Life and Accident Insurance Company, had rather high-brow aspirations, but Hay asserted himself and found air time for another barn dance show. The original "WSM Barn Dance" had its debut November 28, 1925, with Hay as master of ceremonies, and a fiddler, eighty-year-old Uncle

For the Record. . .

Full name George Dewey Hay; born November 9, 1895, in Attica, Ind.; died May 9, 1968, in Virginia Beach, Va.; children: Margaret, Cornelia.

News reporter for the Memphis *Commercial Appeal,* Memphis, Tenn., c. 1920; radio announcer on WMC, Memphis, 1923-24. Announcer and master of ceremonies on the "National Barn Dance," WLS Radio, Chicago, Ill., 1924-25. Founder, announcer, and master of ceremonies on the "Grand Ole Opry" (originally titled "The WSM Barn Dance"), WSM Radio, Nashville, Tenn., 1925-56.

Awards: Named top announcer in the United States by *Radio Digest,* 1924; elected to the Country Music Hall of Fame, 1966.

Jimmy Thompson, as the sole performer. Within weeks the station was deluged with local bands who wanted air time; Hay obliged them, sometimes giving them down-home names such as the Possum Hunters, the Clod Hoppers, and the Fruit Jar Drinkers.

Much of WSM's programming came from an NBC affiliate in New York City. Therefore Hay found his show following a long stretch of classical music and grand opera. One night Hay opened his barn dance by announcing: "Folks, you've been up in the clouds with grand opera; now get down to earth with us in a. . .shindig of Grand Ole Opry!" The name stuck, and by 1926 the barn dance was formally known as the Grand Ole Opry.

Soon the Opry was expanded to three hours in length. Performers were paid very little for appearances, but the honor of a Grand Ole Opry gig could lead to invitations for tours and bigger public performances. Hay never found himself at a loss for talent. In 1932 WSM expanded to 50,000 watts, bringing the station a listening area that included all of the eastern United States, the Midwest, and parts of Canada. The Grand Ole Opry's influence grew accordingly, and many of its stars went on to national fame. Such artists as Roy Acuff, Eddy Arnold, Ernest Tubb, Uncle Dave Macon, Minnie Pearl, and Bill Monroe found their careers boost-

ed by regular Opry appearances, and by the 1950s a stint on the Opry was an absolute prerequisite to fame in the country format.

Malone writes: "In the years that followed, Hay introduced the show each Saturday night with his steamboat whistle and his warm command, 'Let her go, boys'. . .But the mood of spontaneous simplicity could not last, because the barn dances had demonstrated that country music could sell. Judge Hay lived long enough to see his 'down-to-earth' show become a national institution and the longest-lasting program on American radio. The popularity of the *Grand Ole Opry* and other barn dance shows presaged country music's coming commercial success—and its incorporation into the American popular culture mainstream."

Hay retired from the Grand Ole Opry in 1956 and spent the rest of his life living quietly with his daughter in Virginia. In 1966 he returned to Nashville one last time for his induction into the Country Music Hall of Fame. His death at home on May 9, 1968, was first announced on WSM, in honor of his pioneering work there. The Grand Ole Opry now originates from its own theatre at Opryland Park in Nashville. It is still heard over the air on Saturday nights and still follows the format Hay initiated—each artist plays for fifteen or twenty minutes in front of a live audience, in an atmosphere both intimate and informal. The long tenure of the Grand Ole Opry—sixty years and counting—would no doubt please the Solemn Ol' Judge.

Sources

Books

Malone, Bill C., *Country Music U.S.A.,* revised edition, University of Texas Press, 1985.

McDaniel, William R., and Harold Seligman, *Grand Ole Opry,* Greenburg, 1952.

Stambler, Irwin, and Grelun Landon, *The Encyclopedia of Folk, Country, and Western Music,* St. Martin's, 1969.

Periodicals

New York Times, May 10, 1968.

—*Anne Janette Johnson*

Michael Hedges

Singer, songwriter, guitarist

"**M**ichael Hedges is one of the most brilliant singer-songwriters I have ever encountered," declared David Crosby, of Byrds and Crosby, Stills, Nash, and Young fame, in the *Windham Hill Records Catalog and Occasional.* "I haven't been this excited about an up-and-coming talent since Joni Mitchell and Jackson Browne. He is also probably the reigning king of the acoustic guitar." In a profile of Hedges for *Frets,* Mark Hanson and Phil Hood further defined his impact and standing: "A powerful rhythmic player, with the touch and sensitivity of a classical guitarist, Hedges is causing a major rethinking of the solo steel-string guitar's capabilities. . . .The fact that his first three albums were recorded 'live' is a testament to his considerable talents as a composer and an innovator in guitar technique."

Born on New Year's Eve, 1953, in Enid, Oklahoma, Hedges began his musical studies very early in life, playing piano at four years old. His influences, however, were far from the traditional classic orientation. As Hedges told Jonathan Rowe of the *Christian Science Monitor,* "I'm the guy who grew up in the Midwest, and all I knew was pop music." Inspired by popular music figures such as the Beatles and Ian Anderson of the rock group Jethro Tull, Hedges followed the piano with studies on the flute, guitar, cello, and clarinet. Musical education in a more formal setting came at Phillips University in Oklahoma, where he studied flute and composition; during summers at the National Music Camp in Interlochen, Michigan; and later at the Peabody Institute in Baltimore, where Hedges initially began studying classical guitar and electronic music. But his interest in steel-string guitar (he played it in bars at night while studying at the conservatory during the day) prevented him from devoting sufficient time to the classical guitar. Hedges subsequently switched majors, earning his degree in composition. He then traveled to California, where he studied at Stanford's Center for Computer Research and Musical Acoustics.

Leading a double life again—studying during the day and performing in bars and cafes at night—led to his discovery and eventual signing by Windham Hill founder and guitarist William Ackerman. On the videocassette *Windham Hill in Concert,* Ackerman explained that while seeing Hedges perform at the Varsity Theater in Palo Alto, "Michael did to me what he does to everyone, just sort of tore my head off watching the guitar being reinvented."

Hedges's first album on the Windham Hill label, *Breakfast in the Field* (1981), brought immediate praise from fellow guitarists. *Guitar Player* contributor Dan Forte quoted guitar great Larry Coryell: "I heard Michael Hedges's record, and I fell down. Couldn't believe it." What Coryell and others were astonished by was Hedges's playing technique. As Forte described it: "Michael employs full-chord hammer-ons and pull-offs (sometimes using both hands), artificial harmonics, two-hand tapping techniques, and utterly unorthodox tunings." The resulting sound was both percussive and lyric. Other guitarists, most notably jazz guitarist Stanley Jordan and rock guitarist Eddie Van Halen, use this technique of tapping the neck of the guitar with both hands, but not to the same compositional end as Hedges. Whereas others might employ the hammer-on technique on one string at a time, producing a straight melody line, Hedges will hammer-on two or three strings, giving a more chordal effect. Kevin Lynch, writing for *down beat,* defined the difference: "His harmonic sense is more vertical than linear. Hedges considers each string for its sonic possibilities, to be isolated and juxtaposed as an electronic composer might. That means re-tuning strings, introducing new musical relationships." Hedges explained his approach to Hanson and Hood: "I try to add one note that is a little more colorful. That's kind of my crusade, I guess. I just want to hear new voicings."

Aerial Boundaries (1984), Hedges's follow-up album,

For the Record. . .

Born December 31, 1953, in Enid, Oklahoma; son of Thayne and Ruth Hedges; married, wife's name Mindy Rosenfeld Hedges. *Education:* attended Phillips University, the National Music Camp at Interlochen, Michigan, and the Stanford University Center for Computer Research and Musical Acoustics; earned degree in composition, Peabody Institute.

As a member of the Windham Hill fraternity, has appeared in concert as a solo act and with other members, such as Liz Story, Will Ackerman, and Montreux. Has toured on a shared billing with Leo Kottke and opened for Suzanne Vega.

Awards: Grammy Award nomination for *Aerial Boundaries* (1984), for best engineered recording—non-classical.

Addresses: *Record Company*— Windham Hill Records, P.O. Box 9388, Stanford, CA 94305.

Other projects by Hedges include the original musical score for the popular television special "Santabear's First Christmas" and the solo composition "Because It's There" for the sound track of a Japanese production on the life of explorer and mountain climber Naomi Uemura. Employing his classical training, Hedges transcribed, arranged, and performed J. S. Bach's "Prelude to Cello Suite #1 in G Major" on harp guitar (a rare, hybrid instrument with six guitar strings on a bottom neck and five bass strings on a top) for inclusion on the Windham Hill artists' compilation *A Winter's Solstice II.* And on David Crosby's 1989 release, *Oh Yes I Can,* Hedges arranged and played guitar on one cut, and played guitar and provided background vocals on another.

Even though Hedges's vocal outings have garnered mixed reviews, his guitar technique, compositional abilities, and concert performances continue to impress and amaze. A concert reviewer for *Variety* admitted that "Hedges's acoustic instrumentals are taking modality into ranges that, when successful, represent abstract

introduced not only new techniques and voicings but an entire package that Forte labeled "a landmark acoustic guitar effort." According to Rowe, the ethereal title cut "has become a Hedges standard, like Bob Dylan's 'Blowin' in the Wind.' Snippets appear as filler on National Public Radio's 'All Things Considered,' and on TV ads." One track from the album that has attracted considerable attention is "Spare Change." Originally recorded with pianist Liz Story and bassist Michael Manring for *An Evening with Windham Hill Live,* Hedges this time constructed the entire piece note by note using tape techniques. Michael Tucker, of *Jazz Journal International,* called the piece "an uncommonly moving experience" with its "processed, eerie rifts and tempo changes."

Hedges was unable to maintain such commercial and critical success with his third album and vocal debut, *Watching My Life Go By* (1985), which also featured him on flute, synthesizer, and acoustic and electric basses. Even with the aid of acclaimed jazz vocalist Bobby McFerrin, who gave Hedges vocal lessons and provided his trademark chants on one track, the album was not received well. While one reviewer for *Variety* called Hedges's lyrics "flaccid," others, such as Rowe, saw positive signs: "His singing does not equal his guitar work, especially when he's in his jazzy Joni Mitchell mode," but "what he lacks in vocal ability, he makes up in sheer sincerity and conviction." And on his live release, *Live on the Double Planet* (1987), Rowe believed Hedges captured "his urgency much better than the earlier release."

> *"I heard Michael Hedges's record, and I fell down. Couldn't believe it."*
> *—Larry Coryell*

impressionism in the aural realm." And Lynch, upon seeing Hedges perform, defined the duality that has marked Hedges's life since his academic years: "Inside him a rock and roller wrestled with a conservatory-trained musician—and out came strong, innovative music."

Selected discography

Breakfast in the Field, Windham Hill, 1981.
Aerial Boundaries, Windham Hill, 1984.
Watching My Life Go By, Open Air, 1985.
Santabear's First Christmas, Windham Hill, 1986.
Live on the Double Planet, Windham Hill, 1987.

Also provided compositions and performances for the following Windham Hill releases: "Spare Change" (accompanied by Liz Story and Michael Manring) for *An Evening with Windham Hill Live,* 1983; "Because It's There," "Aurora/Nevermore" (introduction by Philip Aaberg), and "Requiem for a Mountain Climber" (by Philip Aaberg, with Michael Hedges and William Ackerman) for *The Shape of the Land,* 1986; "Prelude to Cello Suite #1 in G

Major" (by J. S. Bach, arranged by Michael Hedges) for *A Winter's Solstice II,* 1988.

Sources

Periodicals

Christian Science Monitor, September 22, 1987.
down beat, November 1985.
Frets, November 1986.
Guitar Player, February 1985.
Jazz Journal International, October 1986.
Variety, February 17, 1988.
Windham Hill Records Catalog and Occasional, summer 1989.

Videocassettes

Windham Hill in Concert, production of Windham Hill Productions, Inc. and Laserdisc Corporation, 1986.

—Rob Nagel

Don Henley

Singer, songwriter, drummer

After the dissolution of the Eagles in 1981, Don Henley emerged as a strong soloist playing the part of both "romantic raconteur" and "commentator with a conscience." While the initial draw to rock and roll might have been excitement and money, for Henley it became something more important: a vehicle for change. Even during his years with the Eagles, Henley felt it was important to produce work that was more than entertainment. That commitment became even stronger after the group broke up. "Keeping in mind that a good love song never hurts on an album," Henley told *Rolling Stone,* "I try to get as much information as I can gracefully get into a song without making it a pedantic treatise."

Born July 22, 1947, in Linden, Texas, Henley was an only child, son of an elementary school teacher and an "auto-parts salesman-farmer." He grew up listening to country music and later spent six years playing in a band that had formed during high school. He also played in Linda Ronstadt's backup band, out of which, according to some sources, the Eagles arose. College-educated with a love for good literature and a penchant for finding just the right word in lyrics, Henley explained the logical influence of country music on the otherwise rocking Eagles this way: "I was in a big Emerson and Thoreau frenzy [after college], living that Sixties idyllic flower-child kind of life from a rural perspective . . . rediscovering that whole American agrarian myth." California in 1970 still had the flavor of the West about it and was accepting of long-haired musicians who liked rock and roll. "It seemed the logical place to go," Henley said, and the Eagles did, launching a successful career studded with seven award-winning albums.

Henley's first solo album, *I Can't Stand Still,* features a curious combination of political and personal themes that was to continue on subsequent albums. Side one handles the latter, with love songs expressing something quite different from the "see ya later" mentality the title track suggests. Henley explores loneliness and longing, his treatment of male-female relationships more sensitively handled than was often the case with the Eagles. Asked about the anti-woman charge brought against the group in earlier years, Henley told *Rolling Stone,* "Um, Glenn [Frey]'s attitude toward women was a little different than mine sometimes. I'll just let it go there." Side two of the LP includes one of the album's toughest tracks, "Johnny Can't Read," an intentional shot at the dilemma of illiteracy. Other issues confronted are the nuclear threat, in "Them and Us," and what *Rolling Stone* reviewer John Milward termed "the exploitative nature of TV news" in "Dirty Laundry." Unfortunately, Milward suggests Henley preaches too much, and has a credibility problem in being a comfortably living artist contemplating the problems of the common man. According to Milward, "Henley's social concerns don't bleed half as much as his personal ones."

Building the Perfect Beast, released in 1985, fared better in the eyes of critics and record buyers. As with his first album, *Beast* was a collaborative effort, but Henley's voice and direction are unmistakable as he crosses the boundary between rockers with shrill, biting lyrics (as in the title track) and soft, bittersweet ballads (as in "Sunset Grill" and "The Boys of Summer") with ease. It was "The Boys of Summer," described as "a romantic song full of nostalgia and vitriol," that garnered him a Grammy, not to mention almost continual airplay.

But, as usual, the general public may not have understood Henley's intentions any better on *Beast* than they had years before on *Hotel California.* Nostalgia was part of it, but there was more. "We raised all that hell in the Sixties, and then what did we come up with in the Seventies?" Henley commented to *Rolling Stone.* "Nixon and Reagan . . . I don't think we changed a damn thing, frankly. That's what the last verse of "The Boys of Summer" was about . . . we thought we could change things by protesting and making firebombs and growing our hair long and wearing funny clothes. But . . . after all our marching and shouting and screaming didn't work, we withdrew and became yuppies.

Four-and-a-half years passed before the release of Henley's third album. "I've got to learn how to do this faster," he told *Rolling Stone,* "but I don't know if I can.

Songs have to arise from life." On The End of the Innocence, they do. Again, much of the album has a tough, rocking sound, with some songs bordering on the savage—"manicured savagery" according to *Time*—but savagery nonetheless. Henley delivers harsh criticism about social and political issues in "Little Tin God," "If Dirt Were Dollars," and "New York Minute." Yet even as he kicks and snarls his way through pieces like "I Will Not Go Quietly," the album has an atmosphere of sanity and not the "jaded swagger that often got the Eagles branded as a slick bunch of SoCal libertines." Not all of the album roars, of course. "The Heart of the Matter" is considered an especially sensitive classic-sounding song, and the title track, a remarkably evocative, wistful "love" song with an excruciating undertone of disenchantment, longing, and loss—of innocence, of youth, of faith in country and family.

The combination of personal and political themes rises out of Henley's belief that the two are permanently intertwined. "I think that how we relate to each other as men and women, or as *people* has something to do with the way things are going in general." He feels that where there is disillusionment, distrust, and suspicion in and about the "system," so too will it exist in personal relationships. Sensitive to the world around him, Henley continues to draw on experience and emotions to express himself, though the process is not always an easy one. "You have to dredge up all kinds of feelings and emotions and wear them right on the surface of your skin," he says, "and I don't like to do that sometimes."

When asked to comment on the overall effectiveness of rock music as a vehicle for change, Henley seems pessimistic. "I wish I could say it has changed things, but I'm afraid it's been used largely as an escape. And when it comes to political issues, most rock & roll artists are living in the Dark Ages . . . they practically deny the existence of, and do not participate in, our democratic system." Despite the lack of progress made on issues of concern to him, like the homeless and jobless, Henley maintains a certain hopefulness. "I *do* have hope. I mean, inside every cynic there's an idealist trying to get out. At least in my case there is." And, in this case, the idealist is not keeping his ideals to himself.

Selected discography

Solo LPs

I Can't Stand Still, Asylum, 1982.
Building the Perfect Beast, Geffen, 1985.
The End of the Innocence, Geffen, 1989.

Sources

New York Times, July 5, 1989; July 9, 1989.

Rolling Stone, October 14, 1982; December 19, 1985; November 5-December 10, 1987; July 13, 1989.

Time, July 31, 1989.

—*Meg Mac Donald*

Bruce Hornsby

Singer, songwriter, pianist

Success long eluded rock performer Bruce Hornsby. While many in the recording industry considered his work promising, he was rejected by all the major labels. "I was going nowhere fast," he told Dennis Hunt of the *Los Angeles Times*. "I was writing these formula pop songs. It wasn't what wanted to do." In 1985 Hornsby decided to follow his instincts. He and his brother, John, began writing music that blended jazz, country-folk, and New Age. The result, an album titled *The Way It Is,* earned Hornsby and his four-man band, the Range, a Grammy Award.

A native of Williamsburg, Virginia, Hornsby grew up wanting to be a professional basketball player. While in high school he learned to play piano. He later studied at the University of Miami School of Music, where he learned classical and jazz piano. After receiving his degree, Hornsby returned to Virginia and formed a rock cover band that played in bars and clubs throughout the South. In 1980 he moved to Los Angeles, where he worked as a staff composer for 20th Century Fox.

During this time he recorded and distributed demo tapes. Some of the biggest names in the music industry took notice, and several record companies expressed interest. But Hornsby received no contract offers, so he enlisted in Sheena Easton's road band for two years. In 1985 Hornsby recorded another demo. This time, he ignored the advice given him by industry insiders; he was tired of trying to write what other people thought was commercial. The tape consisted of four songs written by Hornsby and his brother, and it featured Hornsby, alone, singing and playing acoustic piano, bass, drums, and accordion. There was no electronic music. "I just wanted a tape to sound exactly like I heard the music in my head and not have to compromise with anybody about any of it," he explained to Pam Lambert of the Wall Street Journal. The tape led to a contract with RCA.

The debut album of Bruce Hornsby and the Range, *The Way It Is,* went platinum. Its title track, a song about racial prejudice, topped the Billboard chart. Another single, "Mandolin Rain," reached the top ten. Hornsby produced six of the album's songs, three others were produced by Huey Lewis, an early champion of Hornsby's work. The album's style, which Lambert described as "jazz-tinged folk-rock," and socially conscious material struck a chord with audiences and critics. Huey Lewis has called Hornsby's music "rural Southern highbrow." A *People* reviewer wrote: "With their small-town settings and common heroes, Hornsby's are the sort of heartland tunes that just might knock a chip in the Springsteen-Mellencamp monopoly." At the 1987 Grammy Awards Hornsby and his group were named best new artist.

A second album, *Scenes from the Southside,* has also sold millions. Hornsby's music has been influenced by jazz pianist Keith Jarrett and country singer George Jones; his lyrics are drawn from current events and social trends. Mostly, his work reflects his southern roots. "I guess this sounds pompous, but we want to create our own sort of microcosm of a place, "he told *Rolling Stone.* "Kind of like Faulkner, I guess, had a county where all his things were set. If there's anything special about what we're doing, that's what it is."

Selected discography

The Way It Is, RCA, 1986.
Scenes from the Southside, RCA, 1988.

Sources

Christian Science Monitor, February 23, 1987.
Detroit Free Press, March 31, 1987.
Los Angeles Times, June 21, 1987.
Minneapolis Star and Tribune, March 13, 1987.
New York Times, September 19, 1988.
People, October 13, 1986; November 17, 1986.
Rolling Stone, February 12, 1987.
Stereo Review, December 1986.
Wall Street Journal, February 19, 1987.

—*Denise Wiloch*

Billy Idol

Singer, songwriter

A product of the late '70s British punk movement, Billy Idol has become one of the most popular and successful vocalists in contemporary rock. His group, Generation X, was extremely popular in the UK while his subsequent solo career has developed a worldwide following. Along with his guitarist, Steve Stevens, he has been creating hard-driving albums, electrifying live shows, and unique videos.

Idol was born William Broad in Stanmore, England, and spent four years with his family in Long Island, New York, before returning to his homeland. At the age of ten his grandfather bought him a guitar at London's Woolworth store and he soon began learning chords from an instruction book. As a teenager he listened to American artists like Iggy and the Stooges, Lou Reed, the New York Dolls, and the Doors. Soon he was writing his own tunes in a similar vein. After dropping out of college Idol began hanging out at Malcolm McClaren's Sex clothes shop on King's Road (a popular hangout for local punkers who were known as the Bromley Contingent: Siouxsie and the Banshees, the Clash, and the Sex Pistols amongst others).

Idol put an ad in *Melody Maker* stating simply "I want to form a group." Bassist Tony James answered it and in August of 1976 they formed Chelsea with vocalist Gene October. The group only lasted two months, however, but Idol and James started another band, Generation X, the following year. In August 1977 they released their self-titled debut LP of which Dave Marsh wrote in *The Rolling Stone Record Guide,* "Billy Idol was a bit too slick to be effective."

Even though they never were big in the States, Generation X became extremely popular in England. They recorded seven hit singles including "Ready Steady Go," "Your Generation" (in answer to the Who's "My Generation") and "Wild Youth" while becoming the first punk band to appear on the British Top of the Pops television show. Even then Idol could see that the punk attitude would soon burn itself out. He told Paul Gambaccini in *Rolling Stone,* "We have to open ourselves up as human beings. We can't just yell out our frustrations. . . What we left out was how we feel about things, rather than how we think about things. That's what we're trying to do now; put more soul, more emotion, into our music."

Because of management hassles, Idol would not be able to fulfill his plan with Generation X as the band eventually folded after their third LP. In March of 1981 he moved to Greenwich Village, New York. "I came looking for new people to play with," he said in *Rolling Stone*. "I'd been hanging out in London for ages; it was a closed scene." He released a mini LP, *Don't Stop,* and the cut "Dancing with Myself" was soon heard in the city's nightclubs while the LP stayed on the charts for fifty weeks. He ran into Steve Stevens on and off for about nine months when the guitarist finally left his group, Fine Malibus, and the two began writing tunes together.

In May of 1982 *Billy Idol* was released and, on the strength of "Hot in the City" (#23), "White Wedding" (#36), and "Come On, Come On," stayed on the charts for over a year and a half. They toured the country with Phil Feit on bass and Steve Missal on drums before bringing in a new rhythm section for Idol's second LP, *Rebel Yell*. The album made the Top 10 as keyboardist Judy Dozier, bassist Steve Webster, and drummer Tommy Price provided support on three more hits: "Rebel Yell," "Eyes without a Face" (#4) and "Flesh for Fantasy" (#29). Idol's Presley-like sneer and gut-wrenching vocals were a perfect match for Steven's uniquely fresh guitar playing. With an arsenal of equipment he's able to create sounds rather than licks, as on the title track with its machine-gun spitting notes. Also acting as Idol's musical director, Stevens told *Guitar World*, "He's such a rock and roll fan, if he brings me something with three chords it's got so much *spirit* that it makes it really exciting to work with him." The two cowrote eight of *Rebel Yell*'s tunes.

It would be three more years for the next LP from Idol, *Whiplash Smile*. The single, "To Be a Lover" received heavy airplay on both MTV and FM radio and topped out at #6 on the charts. They embarked on a massive arena tour which featured a spread eagle female backdrop with the drum kit as the center of attention. The group now consisted of Susie Davis on keyboards and

Kenny Aaronson on bass as well as Price continuing as drummer. Despite a reputation for being rude, nasty, and stuck-up, Idol is perhaps just putting on a front. "I don't want to mess with Billy's image," Aaronson told *Guitar Player*, "but he is easily the nicest 'star' I've ever worked with."

In 1987 Chrysalis issued a greatest hits package, *Vital Idol*, that produced two more hits for the singer: "Mony Mony" (which made it all the way to #1 in the US) and "Sweet 16" (#17 in the UK).

Selected discography

Solo LPs

Don't Stop (mini LP), Chrysalis.
Billy Idol, Chrysalis, 1982.
Rebel Yell, Chrysalis, 1983.
Whiplash Smile, Chrysalis, 1986.
Vital Idol, Chrysalis, 1987.

With Generation X

Generation X, Chrysalis, 1977.
Valley of the Dolls, Chrysalis, 1979.
Kiss Me Deadly, Chrysalis, 1981.

Sources

Books

Christgau, Robert, *Christgau's Record Guide*, Ticknor & Fields, 1981.
Nite, Norm N., with Charles Crespo, *Rock On, The Illustrated Encyclopedia of Rock & Roll*, Volume 3, Harper, 1985.
The Harmony Illustrated Encyclopedia of Rock, Mike Clifford, consultant, Salamander, 1988.
Rock Movers & Shakers, edited by Barry Lazell with Dafydd Rees and Luke Crampton, Banson, 1989.
The Rolling Stone Illustrated History of Rock & Roll, edited by Jim Miller, Random House/Rolling Stone Press, 1976.
The Rolling Stone Record Guide, edited by Dave Marsh with John Swenson, Random House/Rolling Stone Press, 1979.

Periodicals

Guitar Player, November 1984; May 1986.
Guitar World, May 1986; July 1987.
Rolling Stone, July 13, 1978; March 29, 1984; January 31, 1985.

—*Calen D. Stone*

Indigo Girls

Folk/pop duo

The Indigo Girls are "ideal duet partners," announced Jerry Guterman in *Rolling Stone*. "Their voices soar and swoop as one. . .and when they sing. . .they radiate a sense of shared purpose." The duo, made up of Amy Ray and Emily Saliers, have enjoyed tremendous success with the release of their first album on a major label, *Indigo Girls*. "Closer to Fine," an upbeat single from the disc, has proved especially popular, and its accompanying video has seen much airplay on video stations such as MTV and VH-1. Despite the darker tones of many of the album's other numbers—tones which led a *People* reviewer to call listening to *Indigo Girls* "in one sitting a rather grim experience"—Ray and Saliers have received much critical acclaim for their 1989 effort.

Both women sing, compose, and play acoustic guitar, and both started practicing their arts as youngsters. Saliers, who spent her earlier years in New Haven, Connecticut, before her family relocated to the Atlanta suburb of Decatur, Georgia, began composing songs when she was nine. She confessed to a *People* reporter, however, that her lyrics "made no sense." Ray performed at parties given by relatives in her youth, and her grandmother tried unsuccessfully to gain her an audition for the country music variety show "Hee Haw." The future partners met during grade school in Decatur but had little to do with each other. "We had this unspoken competition because we both played the guitar," Saliers explained in *People*.

When the two young women reached high school, however, they began performing as a team. Calling themselves simply Saliers and Ray, they played in an Atlanta bar on amateur nights. Their repertoire at this point predominantly consisted of folk standards, but they would occasionally slip in their own compositions. Eventually, when they both found themselves attending Atlanta's Emory University—Ray studying religion and Saliers English—they decided to change their moniker. "I found [indigo] in the dictionary," Ray told *People*. "It's a deep blue, a root—real earthy."

As the women prepared to graduate from Emory, Ray was totally committed to a musical career, but Saliers wavered. Moira McCormick reported in *Rolling Stone* that Ray handed her partner "an ultimatum, and Saliers chose the group." As the latter told McCormick, "from then on, we were making career decisions." Saliers further explained that Ray then felt that "we needed to play rock & roll clubs instead of folk clubs," because the Indigo Girls were being stereotyped as pop-folk artists. Despite their good intentions, however, the perception persisted. A *Stereo Review* critic included in his assessment of *Indigo Girls* the compliment, "This is red-blooded folk music with no holds barred."

Wanting their music to remain completely independent of others' control, the Indigo Girls began recording on their own Indigo label. They cut "Crazy Game," a single, in 1985; an extended-play record in 1986; and an album entitled *Strange Fire* in 1987. This strategy "was working," Ray claimed to McCormick. "We were making a living. But we had so much to do, we were just falling apart." So the duo signed a contract with Epic Records in 1988, but only after the company had reassured them on the issue of artistic control. In the meantime, the Indigo Girls had acquired successful musicians among their growing number of fans, including the groups R.E.M. and Hothouse Flowers, both of which contributed their talents to the duo's first Epic album. *Indigo Girls* was helped in its accomplishment of selling over five hundred thousand copies by the fact that its artists served as the opening act for several R.E.M. concerts.

With the Indigo Girls' popularity established, Epic planned to reissue their extended-play effort and to release an altered version of *Strange Fire*. As for new material, according to McCormick, Saliers answers critics' charges of over-seriousness thus: "It's possible

For the Record. . .

Group originally formed as Saliers and Ray, 1980; name changed to the Indigo Girls, c. 1983; recording artists, 1985—. Members are **Amy Ray**, born c. 1964, daughter of a radiologist and a homemaker; and **Emily Saliers**, born c. 1963, daughter of a theology professor and a librarian. *Education:* Both Ray and Saliers graduated from Emory University.

Addresses: *Record Company*—Epic Records, 51 West 52nd Street, New York, NY 10019.

that in the future we'll write more songs with comic relief. But we've just been writing what we felt."

Selected discography

Albums

Strange Fire, Indigo, 1987.
Indigo Girls (includes "Closer to Fine," "Secure Yourself," "Kid Fears," "Prince of Darkness," and "Blood and Fire"), Epic, 1989.

Also released single, "Crazy Game," on Indigo, 1985, and an extended-play record on Indigo, 1986.

Sources

Periodicals

People, March 27, 1989; July 24, 1989.
Rolling Stone, May 4, 1989; September 21, 1989.
Stereo Review, July 1989.

—*Elizabeth Thomas*

Freddie Jackson

Singer, songwriter

Since 1985 singer Freddie Jackson has recorded a string of pop hits, his romantic ballads especially capturing the hearts of female listeners. His debut album, *Rock Me Tonight,* was the number-one soul album for sixteen straight weeks, and his second LP, *Just Like the First Time,* also went platinum. *Rolling Stone* record critic Rob Hoerburger described Jackson as the "perfected . . . vocal persona of the smooth-sailing love man eager to please and be pleased." In his article for *Rolling Stone* on the new male soul singers, Vince Aletti similarly observed that like fellow love balladeer Luther Vandross, Jackson taps the "pure pop romanticism that's at the heart of contemporary soul." But where Vandross distinguishes his love songs with his vocal virtuosity, "Jackson is more the pillow-talking love man," wrote Aletti, trading "showoffy moves" for "hushed intimacy" and "trust-in-me sincerity." *New York Times* writer Peter Watrous agreed: "Mr. Jackson . . . is one of black pop's most elegant performers, a singer who can turn a heartbreak ballad into a world view."

The third of five children, growing up poor in New York's Harlem, Jackson got his musical start as a gospel singer at Mt. Nebo Baptist Church. A child soloist, the singer sometimes moved the congregation to tears—learning early how to captivate an audience. Later discovered by singer Melba Moore while performing in a New York nightclub, Jackson toured with her as a back-up vocalist in the mid-1980s, his cameo solos sparking the interest of industry heavyweights and audiences alike. As a solo artist, Jackson has enjoyed consistent success with best-selling recordings and sold-out concerts (often showcasing the work of rising young songwriters), his polished presentation and pure tones appealing to both blacks and whites.

Aletti views Freddie Jackson's mainstream success as a continuation of the 1980s phenomenon of black "crossover" artists. Led by Michael Jackson and Prince with their megahits *Thriller* and *Purple Rain,* Freddie Jackson joins the ranks of pop stars Lionel Richie and Whitney Houston, enjoying the fame and fortune that mainstream popularity brings. Detecting a renewed appreciation in eighties listeners for "the richness of soul vocal styling"—a "nostalgia for stylized, well-crafted vocals in a modern, unironic, often lushly emotional mood"—Aletti holds this "neoclassicism" responsible for the ease with which Freddie Jackson, and other black vocalists like him, have climbed both soul and pop charts. While the singer acknowledged some difficulties in "crossing over" in his interview with Watrous (black radio, for instance, has pressured him for more ethnocentric music), Freddie Jackson explained: "My music is for people who like to hold hands in con-

For the Record. . .

Born c. 1958; raised in New York, N.Y.

Child Soloist at Mt. Nebo Baptist Church in Harlem; later sang at White Rock Baptist Church in Harlem; worked as a word processor; nightclub performer in New York; back-up vocalist and cameo soloist touring with singer Melba Moore, c. 1984; performed and recorded with Los Angeles funk group Mystic Merlin prior to launching solo career; solo recording artist and concert performer, 1985—; concert appearances include Radio City Music Hall, Madison Square Garden and Broadway's Lunt-Fontanne Theater; composer of songs with Paul Laurence; appeared in motion picture *King of New York*.

Awards: American Black Gold Award for outstanding male artist, 1986.

Addresses: *Home*—New York, N.Y.; and Poconos Mountains, Pa.

Record Company—Capitol Records, 1750 N. Vine St., Los Angeles, Calif., 90028.

cert. . . . It's intimate. With all the racial tension going on today, all the hate, my songs, which are about love, make more sense than ever."

Selected discography

Solo LPs

Rock Me Tonight, Capitol, 1985.
Just Like the First Time, Capitol 1987.
Don't Let Love Slip Away, Capitol, 1988.

Sources

Ebony, November, 1988, February, 1989.
Jet, November 4, 1985.
New York Times, September 6, 1989.
People, September 5, 1988, June 26, 1989.
Rolling Stone, March 12, 1987, October 6, 1988.
Variety, May 13, 1987.

—*Nancy Pear*

Janet Jackson

Singer

Janet Jackson stepped out from the shadow of her famous musical brothers, including superstar Michael Jackson, with the release of her 1986 album, *Control*. Though she had recorded two albums previously, and acted in several television series, she was primarily regarded as Michael's baby sister until her two hits, "What Have You Done for Me Lately" and "Nasty," began vanishing from record stores, propelling *Control* to the top of *Billboard*'s album charts. Proving that she was no fluke, Jackson handily followed her 1986 success with the critically acclaimed 1989 album *Rhythm Nation 1814,* which featured the popular "Miss You Much."

Born in the mid-1960s in Gary, Indiana, Janet was the last of Joseph and Katherine Jackson's nine children. By the time she was four, five of her brothers had risen to nationwide fame as the Jackson Five; eventually this fame led to the family's move to a suburb of Los Angeles, California. According to Aldore Collier in *Ebony,* Janet's childhood desire to become "a horse-racing jockey" was quickly pushed to the side after her father heard her voice on tape. But singing was not the first avenue that brought her to the attention of audiences. When Janet was nine, a television appearance on one of her brothers' variety specials led to producer Norman Lear's recruiting her for his situation comedy, "Good Times." On the show she played Penny, an abused child adopted by one of the regular characters. Later Janet portrayed Charlene, the girlfriend of Willis on "Diff'rent Strokes." And in her late teens, she joined the cast of the syndicated television series "Fame." As Collier phrased it, Janet grew up "before the television-viewing public, almost like a slowly blooming rose."

Meanwhile, Janet Jackson also released two albums. But they were both, in the words of *People* reporter Suzanne Stevens, "coolly received. . .co-produced by the Jackson family machine and aimed at the bubble gum set." Jackson made the first break from her wholesome, teen-idol image in 1984, however, when she surprised her family by eloping with James DeBarge. A member of another family singing group, DeBarge had been a friend of Janet since she was ten years old. Nevertheless, the marriage ended in less than a year. Speculations as to the cause of the breakup included Jackson's youth, but she told Collier: "That had nothing to do with it." Stevens claimed that "after eight months of hounding," John McClain, an executive at A&M Records, "persuaded [Janet] to annul the pact" for fear the marriage would hurt her career. Jackson blamed the heavy demands of both her and her spouse's work. She confided to Collier: "It was really hard and it just couldn't go on that way. You have to really have that free time together."

For the Record. . .

Born c. 1966, in Gary, Ind.; daughter of Joseph (a music manager and former crane operator) and Katherine (Corse) Jackson (a homemaker and sales clerk); married James DeBarge, September 1984, (annulled, 1985).

Actress in television programs, including "Good Times," "Diff'rent Strokes," and "Fame," beginning c. 1975; recording artist and concert performer since adolescence.

Awards: Two platinum albums.

Addresses: *Home*—4641 Hayvenhurst Ave., Encino, Calif. 91436. *Record company*—A&M Records, 1416 N. La Brea, Los Angeles, Calif. 90028.

"close relationship with her mother" as a benefit of this living arrangement, despite Katherine Jackson's misgivings about her daughter's sexier image. One of *Control*'s songs in particular, "Funny How Time Flies" provoked Mrs. Jackson to remark: "I don't like that moaning at the end. I don't like it when my baby does that," according to Collier.

Though it is difficult to measure up to an album as successful as *Control*, Jackson appears to have done so with her fourth effort, *Rhythm Nation 1814.* In addition to selling well, *Rhythm Nation* was given an excellent rating by critic Vince Aletti of *Rolling Stone.* The disc is a concept album that takes on the issues of illiteracy, prejudice, homelessness, and other social problems interspersed with dance tunes; Jackson's music and themes on *Rhythm Nation* have evoked comparisons with Sly and the Family Stone and the late Marvin Gaye. Aletti praised the record's "simplicity and directness" and concluded that "nothing sounds slight, and everything clicks."

Shortly after she left DeBarge, Jackson began work on *Control.* According to Stevens, the new image that permeates the album and the accompanying videos was a lot of work: "McClain put Janet on a diet, sent her to voice and dance coaches for three months and shipped her to Minneapolis to record under the tutelage of [singer/songwriter] Prince proteges Jimmy Jam and Terry Lewis." The result, however, was worth it. In addition to quickly selling a million copies, *Control* was labeled "a better album than Diana Ross has made in five years" by *Rolling Stone* reviewer Rob Hoerburger. Though *People* reviewer Ralph Novak complained of what he perceived as the album's over-instrumentation, he did comment that Jackson "can sing with such sweet clarity that it's a puzzle why anyone would insist on burying her." He also concluded that she was "clearly making a strident declaration of independence" with *Control.*

That "declaration," however, did not prevent Jackson from moving back to the family home after her marriage ended. She told Collier that she enjoys early morning conversations with her brother Michael, and shares his enthusiasm for exotic pets. Collier also cited Janet's

Selected discography

Solo LPs

Control (includes "Control," "Nasty," "What Have You Done for Me Lately," "Let's Wait a While," and "Funny How Time Flies"), A&M, 1986.
Rhythm Nation 1814 (includes "Miss You Much," "Livin' in a World," and "Someday Is Tonight"), A&M, 1989.

Also released *Dream Street* and *Janet Jackson.*

Sources

Ebony, September 1986.
Newsweek, July 21, 1986.
People, March 24, 1986; July 7, 1986.
Rolling Stone, April 24, 1986; October 19, 1989.

—*Elizabeth Thomas*

Joan Jett

Singer, songwriter, guitarist

Many people in the rock establishment felt that Joan Jett's musical career was finished after the Runaways, the group in which she got her start, disbanded when Jett was just nineteen years old. But the raucous young singer/guitarist proved her critics wrong by launching a solo career and developing into "one of rock's most contemporary women—both serious and trashy, tough and tender," in the words of *Rolling Stone* contributor Rob Tannenbaum, who adds, "In this decade, Chrissie Hynde, Joan Armatrading, and Annie Lennox are the only other women who have confronted rock stereotypes as successfully and interestingly as Joan has."

Jett's family moved from the East Coast to Southern California when she was fourteen, and that same year, she was given her first guitar as a Christmas gift. She loved the British glamour rockers T. Rex, Slade, Sweet, and Gary Glitter, but her most important inspiration was Suzi Quatro, whose tough-girl stance she sought to imitate. She got her chance to act out her fantasies at the age of fifteen, when she met producer-manager Kim Fowley. He had come up with the idea for the Runaways after meeting Kari Krome, a thirteen-year-old lyrist with a repertoire of songs about sex. Krome asked Jett, an acquaintance of hers, to join the group Fowley was forming. Sandy West, Lita Ford, Cherie Currie and Jackie Fox were soon recruited through newspaper advertisments, and Fowley won them a contract with Mercury.

"They were presented as five hot, tough high-school-age girls out for sex and fun (a fairly novel idea in pre-punk days)," according to the *Rolling Stone Encyclopedia of Rock and Roll*. In May 1976, their debut album, entitled simply *The Runaways,* was released. Their lack of musical experience was painfully evident on the album, however. With their amateurish playing, "the stigma of Fowley-as-Svengali, and a blantantly sexual presentation—lead singer Cherie Currie wore lingerie onstage—they often seemed more like tease objects than real musicians." Conflicts within the band caused Currie and Fox to quit in mid-1977, and Jett, who already wrote most of the group's material, took over Currie's role as lead singer. The Runaways became immensely popular in Japan, where three of their records went gold, but they continued to be largely ignored in their own country, where they were dismissed as "jailbait rockers." Some of the only favorable notices they ever received in the United States came after they served as the opening act for the Ramones' 1978 tour. The Runaways played their last gig in San Francisco, on New Year's Eve, 1978. After that, Jett, who felt that they were turning too much in the direction of heavy metal, quit the group, which collapsed shortly thereafter.

For the Record...

Born September 22, 1960, in Philadelphia, Pa.

Singer, guitarist, and songwriter; founding member of the Runaways, 1975-78; solo artist, 1980—. Actress in film *Light of Day*, 1987.

Addresses: c/o Epic Records, 51 W. 52nd St., New York, NY.

In the spring of 1979, Jett went to England to try to establish a solo career, but with little result. She cut three songs with former Sex Pistols Paul Cook and Steve Jones, but the songs were released only in Holland. Returning to Los Angeles, she produced an album for a punk group known as the Germs, then played the lead in the film *We're All Crazy Now*, which was loosely based on the Runaways. Although the film was never released, it proved to be very important to Jett's career, for while working on it, she met record producer Kenny Laguna and producer-writer Ritchie Cordell. Laguna had worked with a variety of groups, from the Archies to the Steve Gibbons Band; Cordell was a bubblegum legend who had co-written the Shondells' "I Think We're Alone Now" and "Mony Mony." The two men offered to help Jett with her career, but their plans were delayed when she was diagnosed as having a heart-valve infection and pneumonia, which kept her hospitalized for six weeks.

By 1980, Jett had recovered and began putting together her solo album, with Laguna and Cordell producing. The completed product, entitled *Joan Jett,* featured the songs she'd cut earlier with Paul Cook and Steve Jones, as well as new material. Released exclusively in Europe, it was enthusiastically praised by U.S. reviewers, but in spite of all the good press, it was rejected by every American record company. Laguna finally retitled the album *Bad Reputation* and brought it out independently in January 1981, but it didn't sell. Undaunted, Jett assembled a new band, the Blackhearts, and recorded an album that rocked even harder than her first. *Joan Jett and the Blackheart* shot up the charts, thanks to the popularity of the single "I Love Rock 'n' Roll," a remake of an old Arrows tune that became a number-one hit. Another single, "Crimson and Clover," also reached the top ten, and Jett's version of "Little Drummer Boy," included on pre-Christmas editions, further boosted the album's popularity. Later albums such as *Glorious Results of a Misspent Youth* solidified Jett's position as the queen of good-natured, hard-driving rock.

Reviewing one of Jett's more recent offerings, *Up Your Alley,* Rob Tannenbaum commented in *Rolling Stone:* "Though coarse stomps like 'Bad Reputation' and 'Cherry Bomb' have established Joan Jett as an eternal teen rebel who loves rock and roll for its simple beat and insolent stance, she has grown into a multidimensional songwriter....Maybe if Jett didn't look and act like a cover girl for *Outlaw Biker,* tough-talking tracks like 'Little Liar' and 'Back It Up' would be recognized for their underlying strength and dignity and Jett would get more recognition for her reliability."

In 1987, Jett appeared with Michael J. Fox in Paul Schrader's film *Light of Day.* In it, she plays Patti Rasnick, the daughter of a working-class Cleveland family, who breaks free of her oppressively moralistic upbringing by becoming the leader of the Barbusters, a rowdy band that plays in rundown taverns. The film received mixed notices, but most reviewers concurred that Jett was the best thing in it. "Jett provides the movie's fire," asserted David Ansen in *Newsweek.* "She doesn't have a professional actor's technical finesse. But she has something more important: a riveting tough-girl charisma and blunt emotional honesty....she connects with the audience in a primal way." Richard Corliss of *Time* magazine also noted Jett's powerful performance. "Try watching someone else when she's on screen," he challenged. "It can't be done."

Selected discography

LPs

Joan Jett, Blackheart, 1980, rereleased as *Bad Reputation,* Epic, 1981.
Joan Jett and the Blackhearts, Epic, 1981.
Album, Epic, 1983.
Glorious Results of a Misspent Youth, Epic, 1984.
Good Music, Epic, 1986.
Up Your Alley, Epic, 1988.

LPs; with the Runaways

The Runaways, Mercury, 1976.
Queens of Noise, Mercury, 1977.
Waitin' for the Night, Mercury, 1979.
And Now the Runaways!, Mercury, 1979 (released in the United States as *Little Lost Girls,* Rhino, 1981).
Best of the Runaways, Mercury, 1982.

Sources

Books

Laing, Dave, and Phil Hardy, *Encyclopedia of Rock,* McDonald, 1987.
Miller, Jim, editor, *Rolling Stone Encyclopedia of Rock and Roll,* Rolling Stone Press, 1983.

Periodicals

Ms., July 1985.
Newsweek, February 9, 1987.
New York, March 2, 1987.
People, December 1, 1986.
Rolling Stone, August 11, 1988.
Time, February 9, 1987.

—Joan Goldsworthy

Elton
John

Singer, songwriter, pianist

Elton John emerged in the 1970s as a hugely successful pop performer, the kind of star who often flies high but fades fast. John, however, has been able to maintain his career for nearly twenty years, largely because his music "has become the repository of a million escapist dreams," to quote *Time* correspondent David DeVoss. Once a flamboyant feather-clad rocker with several hundred pairs of gimmick glasses, John has entered midlife as a more sober but no less artistic performer who still generates hit records and sellout concert crowds. He is one of the rare pop singers who is able to reach mainstream audiences while still earning the respect of rock critics; this is because John's original compositions exhibit piano virtuosity and an easy familiarity with rockabilly, gospel, blues, and both soft and classical rock. DeVoss calls John an entertainer of "astonishing versatility" whose "appeal knows no demographic limits." DeVoss also finds John "the symbol of the often battered, never completely shattered juvenile faith that no one is too short, too fat, too awkward or parentally despised to be transformed into someone who is not only famous and rich, but—infinitely more important—loved by the multitudes." The critic concludes that the central appeal of John's music is its "sweet, pensively expressed sense of sadness over human connections missed or lost."

Elton John was born Reginald Kenneth Dwight on March 25, 1947, in Pinner, Middlesex, England. He recalls his childhood as cheerless; he was overweight, unpopular, and plagued at home by a repressive father who wanted him to be a banker. Young Reg Dwight had one solace—a love for music. He learned to play the piano at the age of four and earned a fellowship to the Royal Academy of Music at eleven. Predictably, his father banned pop and rock recordings from the home, but his mother smuggled them in anyway. "I couldn't believe how great they were," John told *Circus* magazine. "From then on rock 'n' roll took over. I used to play Jerry Lee Lewis and Little Richard on the piano and just thump them out." At seventeen John dropped out of school to become a professional musician. He played piano for several bands in the London area, the most notable of which was Bluesology, the group that backed singer John Baldry. It was during this time that Reginald Dwight became Elton John by combining the two first names of performers he admired—Baldry and saxophonist Elton Dean. "Changing the name helped me a lot," John told *Circus*. "I'm still the same person as Reg Dwight, but Elton John gave me a feeling of confidence."

"Nobody expected Reg to become anything big," Baldry told *Time*. "He was a shy person, almost introverted onstage." Bespectacled and obese, John had few illusions about his potential as well. Still, in 1967, he answered a trade paper ad for songwriters and com-

For the Record. . .

Full name, Elton Hercules John; name originally Reginald Kenneth Dwight; born March 25, 1947, in Pinner, Middlesex, England; son of Stanley (a Royal Air Force squadron leader) and Sheila Eileen Dwight; married Renate Blavel, February 14, 1984 (divorced, 1988). *Education:* Attended Royal Academy of Music, 1959-64.

Member of group Bluesology, 1965-66; began writing songs with lyricist Bernie Taupin, 1967; solo performer, 1967—; recording artist, 1969—; concert performer, 1970—. Appeared in film "Tommy," 1975; subject of television documentary, "Say Goodbye, Norma Jean," 1974.

Awards: Named to *Playboy* Jazz and Pop Hall of Fame, 1975; winner (with Dionne Warwick, Gladys Knight, and Stevie Wonder; under name Dionne & Friends) of Grammy Award for best pop performance by a duo or group with a vocal, 1986, for "That's What Friends Are For."

Addresses: *Office*—c/o John Reid Enterprises, 51 Holland St., 2nd Floor, London W8 7JB, England.

to epitomize the "me generation" that replaced flower children in the so-called youth market. His excesses were legion—fleets of luxury cars, diamond-studded glasses, shopping sprees on several continents, lavish homes in London and Los Angeles, brief love affairs with men and women. His antics may have amused some, but his music appealed to nearly all, just as Bender predicted. From 1973 until 1977 he dominated the pop charts with a string of hits most notable for their variety—and for the fact that few people could sing John's songs the way he could. His work included old-style rockers like "Crocodile Rock," and "Saturday Night's Alright for Fightin'," and "The Bitch Is Back," fantasy outings like "Rocket Man," and "Bennie and the Jets," message music such as the gospel "Border Song" and the whistful "Goodbye Yellow Brick Road," and love ballads like "Your Song" and "Tiny Dancer." The John-Taupin partnership was responsible for more than a dozen gold records before it dissolved in 1977. John set a punishing pace for himself in the early

> *Once a flamboyant feather-clad rocker with several hundred pairs of gimmick glasses, Elton John has entered midlife as a more sober but no less artistic performer.*

posers and received a call from a record company executive. The executive had matched John's melodies with lyrics by an equally unknown writer, Bernie Taupin. John and Taupin were not offered a contract, but they went into partnership anyway. Eventually they were hired by Dick James, a music publisher who helped the Beatles early in their career. For some months John and Taupin labored unsuccessfully to churn out commercial jingles and songs for Englebert Humperdinck and Lulu. They tired of this quickly and, in 1969, they began to produce their own songs—with John doing vocals and piano—in a London basement. Their first album, *Empty Sky,* was a modest success in England, and their second, *Elton John,* crossed the ocean and caught on in the American market. The catalyst in John's success was ultimately the singer himself. Having finally shed his excess weight, he also lost his reluctance to give live performances. His 1970 American debut at the Troubador Club in Los Angeles found him clad in outrageous clothing and clowning joyously onstage—in effect making up for the dull childhood he had endured. Quickly he was hailed as the harbinger of a new era in rock—a performer whose "high-talented, low-keyed protest-free approach to life and sound [would] appeal equally to the flower child in the young and the gardener of verses in the old," to quote *Time* contributor William Bender.

Indeed, as the 1970s progressed, Elton John seemed

1970s—he toured America ten times between 1970 and 1976—and finally the toll began to tell. In 1978 he announced his retirement, claiming "there was no burning spark left."

If John's retirement decision was short-lived (he returned to concert touring in 1979), some fundamental changes in his lifestyle were not. The 1980s have seen a less flamboyant Elton John, one who has eschewed the glittering costumes and onstage acrobatics. His best known 1980s hits, with the exception of the defiant "I'm Still Standing," reflect a greater interest in the blues and ballad forms and a more mellow vocal sound. According to Jim Gladstone in the *Philadelphia Inquirer,* however, John's live performing talents "remain in bloom after 20 years." In *People* magazine, John suggested that diversity is the key to a long career in entertainment. He said: "I can see myself singing at 50 and 60 and hope I will always have something to contribute."

Selected discography

Empty Sky, MCA, 1969.
Elton John, MCA, 1970.
Tumbleweed Connection, Uni, 1970.
17-11-70, MCA, 1971.
Friends, Paramount, 1971.
Madman Across the Water, MCA, 1971.
Honky Chateau, MCA, 1972.
Don't Shoot Me, I'm Only the Piano Player, MCA, 1973.
Goodbye Yellow Brick Road, MCA, 1973.
Caribou, MCA, 1974.
Captain Fantastic and the Brown Dirt Cowboy, MCA, 1974.
Greatest Hits, MCA, 1974.
Rock of the Westies, MCA, 1975.
Here and There, MCA, 1976.
Blue Moves, MCA, 1976.
Greatest Hits 2, MCA, 1977.
Single Man, MCA, 1978.
Victim of Love, MCA, 1979.
Live Collection, Pickwick, 1979.
21 at 33, MCS, 1980.
The Fox, Geffen, 1981.
Jump Up!, Geffen, 1982.
Too Low for Zero, Geffen, 1983.
Breaking Hearts, Geffen, 1984.
Your Songs, MCA, 1986.
Live in Australia with the Melbourne Symphony Orchestra, MCA, 1987.
Leather Jackets, Geffen, 1987.
Greatest Hits 3, Geffen, 1987.
Ice on Fire, Geffen, 1988.
Reg Strikes Back, MCA, 1988.
Sleeping with the Past, MCA, 1989.

Sources

Books

Simon, George T., The Best of the Music Makers, Doubleday, 1979.

Periodicals

Circus, December, 1970.
Look, July 27, 1971.
New York Times, May 12, 1974.
People, August 26, 1974; January 16, 1978.
Philadelphia Inquirer, October 5, 1988.
Rolling Stone, November 21, 1974.
Time, December 14, 1970; July 7, 1975.

—Anne Janette Johnson

Janis Joplin

Singer, songwriter

Janis Joplin, one of the most influential women singers of the late 1960s, first came to the attention of rock fans as the vocalist for the San Francisco, California-based band, Big Brother and the Holding Company. Compared to music greats like blues artist Bessie Smith and soul singer Aretha Franklin, most critics agree that she was the main reason for the group's success with songs like "Piece of My Heart" and "Summertime." Renowned for her performance at the 1967 Monterey Pop Festival, and later for her solo appearance at the Woodstock festival in 1969, Joplin nevertheless failed to achieve a chart-topping single until her rendition of country composer Kris Kristofferson's "Me and Bobby McGee" was released posthumously in 1971.

Joplin was born January 19, 1943, in Port Arthur, Texas. Though her family was middle-class, as a teenager she showed signs of the unconventional woman she would become. She was something of a loner, and, unlike her siblings and neighborhood peers, she listened to folk and blues music. Joplin's favorite artists included Odetta, Leadbelly, and Bessie Smith, and she was greatly influenced by them in her own vocal style. By the time she was seventeen, she had decided to become a singer, and she left home.

At first Joplin found work in country and western clubs in Houston and other Texas cities. Gradually she formed the goal of saving enough money from her gigs for bus fare to California, and after a few years she accomplished this and arrived on the Pacific coast. Joplin enrolled in several different colleges while singing folk songs for little money, but her attempts at continuing her education never lasted long. She also tried living in various communes, and eventually settled in San Francisco for a few years.

Ironically, a disheartened Joplin went back to Texas in early 1966, right before a friend of hers, Chet Helms, became manager of a new rock group called Big Brother and the Holding Company. The band needed a female vocalist, and Helms thought of Joplin. He contacted her and convinced her to return to San Francisco. Though Joplin had not had much previous experience singing rock music, the combination of her gravelly, bluesy voice with Big Brother's hard rock sound was a success. The group quickly became popular in the San Francisco area, and by the time the Monterey International Pop Festival took place in 1967 in Monterey, California, Big Brother and the Holding Company were a featured attraction. Joplin's performances at this festival and at Woodstock in 1969 are considered by many specialists in the music of the late 1960s to have been classic moments in the history of rock. As Geoffrey Stokes reported in his portion of the book *Rock of Ages:*

Born January 19, 1943, in Port Arthur, Tex.; died October 3, 1970, in Hollywood, Calif.; father was a canning factory worker, and mother was a registrar at a business college. *Education:* Attended various colleges for short periods during the 1960s.

Sang in various small clubs in Texas and California, c. 1960-66; vocalist for Big Brother and the Holding Company, 1966-68, 1970; solo recording artist and concert performer, 1968-70.

Awards: One gold album with Big Brother and the Holding Company for *Cheap Thrills;* two gold albums as a solo artist for *I Got Dem Ol' Kozmic Blues Again Mama* and *Pearl.*

Addresses: *Record company*—Columbia/CBS Records, 51 W. 52nd St., New York, N.Y. 10019.

The Rolling Stone History of Rock and Roll, at Monterey, "Janis Joplin walked away with an afternoon blues show."

Big Brother's triumph at Monterey gained them a recording contract with Mainstream, a small label, with whom they released their debut album, *Big Brother and the Holding Company.* Also, Joplin and the rest of the band were in demand on a national scale; they toured many areas of the United States and Canada, including New York City. Increasingly, Joplin was the member of Big Brother who was singled out for critical acclaim; for instance, a *Village Voice* reviewer lauded one of her concert performances thus: "She sure projects. . . .She jumps and runs and pounces, vibrating the audience with solid sound. The range of her earthy dynamic voice seems almost without limits." With critiques like that, it is not surprising that Joplin left Big Brother to go solo in 1968, soon after the group recorded their second album, *Cheap Thrills,* for Columbia.

The first group of musicians Joplin recruited to back up her solo career was dubbed the Kozmic Blues Band; with them she released her first album on Columbia, *I Got Dem Ol' Kozmic Blues Again Mama.* Though it contained no overwhelmingly successful single, *Kozmic Blues* went gold, and Joplin's popularity as a concert performer continued. After a brief reappearance with

Big Brother and the Holding Company in early 1970, she formed yet another back up group, the Full-Tilt Boogie Band. They played on Joplin's last album, 1970's *Pearl* (the nickname the singer's closest friends called her). Besides her acclaimed version of Kristofferson's "Me and Bobby McGee," *Pearl* included cuts like "Get It While You Can"—which she considered one of her theme songs, "Cry Baby," and the humorous "Mercedes Benz," a song she composed herself.

But before *Pearl* could be released, what Stokes called "a drug she'd had an on-and-off affair with for most of her performing life" brought about Joplin's death. On October 4, 1970, the singer's body was found in the Landmark Motor Hotel in Hollywood, California. Joplin had died the day before from an overdose of heroin. She was cremated and her ashes were scattered off the California coast.

Selected discography

LPs

(With Big Brother and the Holding Company) *Big Brother and the Holding Company* (includes "Women Is Losers" and "Down on Me"), Mainstream, 1967.
(With Big Brother and the Holding Company) *Cheap Thrills* (includes "Piece of My Heart," "Ball and Chain," "Turtle Blues," and "Summertime"), Columbia, 1968.
I Got Dem Ol' Kozmic Blues Again Mama, Columbia, 1969.
Pearl (includes "Me and Bobby McGee," "Get It While You Can," "Cry Baby," and "Mercedes Benz"), Columbia, 1971.

Sources

Books

Dalton, David, *Piece of My Heart: The Life, Times, and Legend of Janis Joplin,* St. Martin's, 1986.
Friedman, Myra, *Buried Alive: The Biography of Janis Joplin,* Morrow, 1973.
Ward, Ed, Geoffrey Stokes, and Ken Tucker, *Rock of Ages: The Rolling Stone History of Rock and Roll,* Summit Books, 1986.

Periodicals

Texas Monthly, March 1988.

—Elizabeth Thomas

Mark Knopfler

Singer, songwriter, guitarist

At a time when much of rock and roll lacks the stamp of individuality, Mark Knopfler, producer, lead guitarist, singer, and songwriter long associated with the group Dire Straits, has crafted a guitar-based rock sound that reflects his respect for rock's roots while still displaying his own originality and inventiveness. No one disputes that the success of Knopfler and Dire Straits comes from his highly defined musical aesthetic. Yet it is important to emphasize that although Dire Straits has gone through a number of personnel changes since its founding in 1977—only Knopfler and bassist John Illsley remain from the original four—Knopfler has always viewed the group as a rock and roll band and not a superstar vehicle. For him, playing rock music is a way of life, a total commitment.

Knopfler and Dire Straits have consistently received high praise from the usually cynical rock press—with only a few dissenters. Their debut album, *Dire Straits,* was released in 1978 at the height of New Wave popularity. "It's almost as if they were aware that their forte has nothing to do with what's currently happening in the industry, but couldn't care less," wrote Ken Tucker in *Rolling Stone. Stereo Review* announced, "they're so good, it's scary," and later added, "The first Dire Straits disc was, frankly, almost too good to be true: a complete fully rounded stylistic statement from a young band that sounded as if it had been woodshedding for years. *down beat* agreed, calling Knopfler "the most distinctive guitar voice to come along since Jimi Hendrix." Gene Lyons, writing in *Newsweek,* judged Knopfler to be "perhaps the most influential guitar stylist since Chuck Berry."

Mark Knopfler was born in Glasgow, Scotland, on August 12, 1949, the son of an English mother and a Hungarian Jewish father, whose Communist sympathies forced him to flee his native land. His father was an architect and his mother a schoolteacher, but Knopfler grew up poor in a family that could not afford a car or television. The Knopflers relocated in Newcastle, England, when Mark was nine and, as a child, he took music lessons—piano and violin—from his father. "I would just play by ear, and as soon as it got difficult, I was in trouble," Knopfler told *Rolling Stone.* Like so many innovative rock musicians, Knopfler does not read music. "I go by my ears. I can't relate music to those dots. I heard my uncle Kingsley play boogie-woogie when was about eight years old. That was one of the most beautiful things I had ever heard. Those three chords, the logic of it. So I just used to slam out boogie-woogie on the piano, drive everybody nuts."

Knopfler left home at 17 to attend journalism school and then worked for two years as a cub reporter with the *Yorkshire Evening Post* and even reviewed local bands.

Born August 12, 1949, in Glasgow, Scotland; son of an architect and a teacher; married second wife, Lourdes Salamone. *Education:* Attended journalism school; degree in English literature from University of Leeds, 1973.

Reporter and rock music critic for *Yorkshire Evening Post,* 1968-70; lecturer at Loughton College, 1973-77; while attending school and teaching, performed in clubs in London, England, with various bands, including Brewer's Droop and Cafe Racers; founder, 1977, member of group Dire Straits, 1977—.

Awards: Grammy Award, with Dire Straits, for best performance by a group, and two MTV Video Music awards, with Dire Straits, for best group video and best video of the year, all 1986, all for "Money for Nothing."

Addresses: *Residence*—London, England; and New York, N.Y. *Office*—c/o Warner Bros. Records Inc., 3300 Warner Blvd., Burbank, CA 91505.

"I liked the music but hated the writing—I wasn't cut out to be a rock-and-roll critic," he told Ken Tucker of the Knight-Ridder News Service, quoted in the *Springfield News-Sun.* The last story he wrote was Jimi Hendrix's obituary. "I was stunned. I don't recall what I wrote. I said some stuff, left the paper and got drunk." The newspaper experience gave Knopfler a perspective that has served him well, especially in writing socially powerful lyrics. "You learn the way society works, the way business works. You come across life and death," he said in *People.*

Knopfler returned to school and earned a degree in English from the University of Leeds in 1973. "The day I finished university, I went to London and joined a band-and promptly ended up completely destitute, divorced [from his first wife] and selling guitars to stay alive." He joined Brewer's Droop, an "obscene" R&B Cajun outfit. "After that, I just starved to death, basically. It got pretty tough until I got hold of this teaching job that saved my life," he recounted for *Rolling Stone.* The job was at Loughton College and Knopfler taught English and guitar privately. "I was pretty good at it but felt uncomfortable acting as the sort of role model a teacher is supposed to be. After all, what I liked best was playing in bars with my friends," he said to Tucker. At that time he was with the group Cafe Racers, who played in neighborhood pubs around Loughton College.

In 1977 Knopfler decided to become a full-time musi-

cian. He settled in London and shared an apartment with his younger brother, David, and John Illsley. With Knopfler on lead guitar, David on rhythm, Illsley on bass, and session drummer Pick Withers, Dire Straits—the band's name came from its members' economic predicament—was born. They invested $180 earned from pub engagements and cut a five-track demo tape that was sent to most major American record companies with no success. The fortunes of Dire Straits changed, however, when BBC disc jockey Charlie Gillett played "Sultans of Swing," a Knopfler song about jazz musicians who play for love and not money, on his "Honky Tonkin" show. Public response was immediate and enthusiastic.

By Christmas 1977, Dire Straits had a record contract with Warner Bros., which soon translated into a Top Ten hit and a platinum LP. Success for Knopfler came at 28, old for the rock world but not for Knopfler, considering the tendency of rock musicians to self-destruct if fame comes too young and too easy. "We'd probably be dead by now, or definitely on the casualty list. We couldn't have handled it," he told Kurt Loder in *Rolling Stone.* One casualty of Dire Straits' sudden success was David Knopfler. The younger Knopfler left the band to pursue a solo career after Dire Straits' second album was recorded. The unhappy breakup was obviously painful and difficult for Mark Knopfler to discuss. "One of the problems was having this huge, great specter of a big brother writin' tunes and tellin' everybody what to do with them. It's probably much better that I should leave him to grow up in his own way. I certainly wouldn't want to tell him how to do that," Knopfler explained to *Rolling Stone* in 1983. "I'm not sure how much he would be prepared to go through all the things that I was. . . . Dave was never into guitar as much as I was. Dave plays only keyboards now." Dire Straits has gone through a number of personnel changes (drummer Pick Withers, the other original member, left the band in 1982), reflecting, in part, Knopfler's demanding standards.

But to conclude that Knopfler is insensitive to the desires of other musicians is unfair. Part of Dire Straits' lore is how guitarist Jack Sonni came to join the band. Sonni, who worked at Rudy's Music Stop, a guitar store on 48th Street in Manhattan, first saw Dire Straits when the group played the Bottom Line club in 1979. Sonni became a friend of the Knopfler brothers when they started visiting Rudy's regularly, even being invited to visit them in England. Then in December 1984 Mark Knopfler approached Sonni about joining the band on its world tour, replacing Hal Lindes, who had been fired. The transition from working in a guitar store to playing in a world-class rock and roll band is, on one level, incomprehensible, and on another, typical of the confidence Knopfler has in himself to back up his musical risks and personnel decisions. "It's nice to play Father Christmas," *Musician* reported Knopfler telling his manager. "I said to [Sonni], 'Just one condition. Whatever I do, man, try your damnedest not to let it affect our friendship.'" Sonni and Dire Straits gelled. "He was *born* to it. Born to boogie, born to rock; pick your cliche, they all fit Sonni," said Knopfler.

In 1985 rock's social consciousness—personified by Bob Geldof's Live Aid, Willie Nelson's Farm Aid, the Lionel Richie-Michael Jackson anthem, "We Are the World," for USA for Africa, and Bruce Springsteen's gritty working-class persona—captured international attention, propelling the phenomenon of rock and roll beyond its immediate audience and into the daily lives of millions worldwide. But 1985 was also the year that Dire Straits received the kind of attention in the United States that it had garnered in the rest of the world since its founding in 1977. Dire Straits' fifth studio album, *Brothers in Arms,* earned Knopfler and the band eight Grammy nominations, the most for any single individual or group, winning for best rock performance by a group for the song "Money for Nothing" and for best engi-

---

For Knopfler, playing rock music is a way of life, a total commitment.

---

neered album. Knopfler also made the cover of *Rolling Stone* and *Musician.*

Knopfler's musical activities have not been limited to Dire Straits. He is in great demand as a session guitarist—he has played on Van Morrison's *Beautiful Vision,* Steely Dan's *Gaucho,* and Bryan Ferry's *Boys and Girls,* to name a few—and covets the opportunity to play with rock icons like Bob Dylan and Phil Everly. Dire Straits played the Knopfler composition "Private Dancer" on Tina Turner's comeback album, with Jeff Beck filling in for the guitar solo for the absent Knopfler. As a record producer for other artists, Knopfler brought his talent to Dylan's *Infidels* and Aztec Camera's *Knife.* He also wrote the scores for the movies *Cal, Local Hero,* and *Comfort and Joy,* which testifies to his musical versatility.

Knopfler is married to Lourdes Salamone, the daughter of a Hilton Hotels executive. They divide their life between two residences, in New York's Greenwich Village and London's West End. On the future of Dire Straits, Knopfler told Tucker he has no definite plans: "I don't know what Dire Straits will do after this. Who knows? We might come back a year from now with a choir and a couple of trombone players, but it'll still be Dire Straits." Whatever the future, Knopfler already has envisioned his last days: "I think it's England. I'd like to die with my boots on. I don't see myself dying in some place where they play dominoes. It'll probably be in a little club. I'll be playing guitar, an old walking stick hung up over me amp."

Selected discography

With group Dire Straits; released by Warner Bros.

Dire Straits (includes "Sultans of Swing," "Down to the Waterline," "In the Gallery," "Water of Love," "Setting Me Up," "Six Blade Knife," "Southbound Again," and "Wild West End"), 1978.

Communique (includes "Communique," "Once Upon a Time in the West," "News," "Where Do You Think You're Going?," "Lady Writer," "Angel of Mercy," and "Portobello Belle"), 1979.

Making Movies (includes "Tunnel of Love," "Romeo and Juliet," "Hand in Hand," "Les Boys," "Skateaway," "Expresso Love," and "Solid Rock"), 1980.

Love Over Gold (includes "Love Over Gold," "Telegraph Road," "Private Investigations," "Industrial Disease," and "It Never Rains"), 1982.

Twisting by the Pool (includes "Twisting by the Pool," "Badges," "Posters," "Stickers," "T-Shirts," "Two Young Lovers," and "If I Had You"), 1983.

Alchemy (live album; includes "Once Upon a Time in the West," "Romeo and Juliet," "Expresso Love," "Private Investigations," "Sultans of Swing," "Going Home," "Two Young Lovers," "Solid Rock," "Tunnel of Love," and "Telegraph Road"), 1984.

Brothers in Arms (includes "Brothers in Arms," "The Man's Too Strong," "Money for Nothing," "So Far Away," "One World," "Your Latest Trick," "Ride Across the River," "Walk of Life," and "Why Worry?"), 1985.

With others

Slow Train Coming (with Bob Dylan), Columbia, 1979.
Solo In Soho (with Phil Lynott), Warner Bros., 1980.
Gaucho (with Steely Dan), MCA, 1980.
Beautiful Vision (with Van Morrison), Mercury, 1982.
Infidels (with Dylan; also producer), Columbia, 1983.
Boys and Girls (with Bryan Ferry), Warner Bros., 1985.
Missing . . . Presumed Having a Good Time (with the Notting Hillbillies), Warner Bros., 1990.

Composer of song "Private Dancer," recorded by Tina Turner; producer of album *Knife,* recorded by Aztec Camera.

Also composer and performer of soundtrack for British television documentary, "In Private and Public: The Prince and Princess of Wales," 1986.

Motion picture soundtracks

Local Hero, 1983.
Music from the Film "Cal," Mercury, 1984.
Comfort and Joy, Phonogram, 1985.

Sources

Dayton Daily News, February 26, 1986.
Detroit Free Press, September 8, 1986.
down beat, June 1983; July 1984.
Guitar Player, December 1982; June 1984; September 1984.
High Fidelity, December 1982; January 1984.
Musician, September 1985.
Newsweek, November 4, 1985.

New York Times, November 14, 1980; November 13, 1983; August 24, 1984; August 26, 1984; March 3, 1985; September 4, 1985.
People, November 22, 1982; February 25, 1985; September 2, 1985; September 30, 1985; September 22, 1986.
Playboy, July 1985.
Rolling Stone, January 25, 1979; February 5, 1981; January 20, 1983; May 26, 1983; May 24, 1984; March 14, 1985; November 21, 1985.
Saturday Review, October 1985.
Springfield News-Sun (Springfield, Ohio), February 24, 1986.
Stereo Review, May 1979; August 1979; February 1981; February 1983; September 1983; August 1984; September 1985; November 1985.

—*Jon Saari*

Gordon Lightfoot

Singer, songwriter, guitarist

An eloquent composer, Gordon Lightfoot pens contemporary ballads that could easily be the envy of historic bards entrusted to record the world around them in all its beauty, harshness, and poignancy. Said Jack Batten, in the Toronto *Globe and Mail,* Lightfoot fills the role of "journalist, poet, historian, humorist, short-story teller, and folksy recollector of bygone days." From love songs to depictions of Canadian history and wilderness, Lightfoot's songs, many of which became virtual overnight standards ("If You Could Read My Mind," "Sundown," "Carefree Highway"), touch the listener on more levels and in more ways than most musicians could ever dream of.

Born in Orillia, Ontario, on November 17, 1938, Lightfoot displayed vocal ability early on, noticed by his mother, who encouraged him to sing before women's clubs and at Kiwanis festivals. Later he studied classical piano, performed in plays, operettas, and barbershop quartets, played drums and sang in a dance band, and, finally, taught himself the basics of folk guitar. At Westlake College in Los Angeles he studied orchestration, earning his living doing vocal arrangements, demo records, and commercial jingles. In 1960 his attention was captured by the growing folk movement. Encouraged by Canadian friend Ian Tyson (of Ian and Sylvia), Lightfoot pursued the guitar seriously. He wound up performing in coffee houses in eastern Canada, where his distinctive voice and compositions were first noticed by the public.

A number of Lightfoot's original works were covered throughout the 1960s by folk and country musicians including Peter, Paul and Mary, Judy Collins, and Johnny Cash, and he garnered a series of hit singles himself: "Remember Me," "I'm Not Saying," and "Black Day in July." Before success, though, he worked on a number of musical assignments including a stint on the Canadian television show "Country Hoedown." Of his experience he said in *Canadian Composer,* "I'm not particularly proud . . . but it sure taught me a lot of things. I don't envy the kids who make it overnight. . . . There's no security in this business, but experience and training sure helps."

Lightfoot had written some seventy-five songs, most of which "didn't really mean anything," before he heard wordsmith Bob Dylan for the first time and had his viewpoint about composing changed dramatically. His work became more personal, reflecting his own identity. When he made his New York City debut in 1965, the *New York Times* praised his "rich, warm voice" and "dexterous guitar technique." Continued reporter Robert Shelton, "With a little more attention to stage personality, he should become quite popular."

The following year, United Artists released Lightfoot's

Full name, Gordon Meredith Lightfoot; born November 17, 1938, in Orillia, Ont., Canada; son of Gordon Meredith and Jessie Vick (Trill) Lightfoot; divorced; children: Fred, Ingrid. *Education*—Attended Westlake College of Music, 1958.

Began performing while a child; did vocal arrangements, demonstration records, and commercial jingles in Los Angeles while studying orchestration at Westlake College, 1958; singer, songwriter, guitarist, 1959—; began performing in coffee houses in eastern Canada; debuted in New York City, 1965; signed first recording contract, 1966.

Awards: Winner of Canadian Juno Awards for top folk singer, 1965, 1966, 1968, 1969, 1973, 1974, 1975, 1976, and 1977, for top male vocalist, 1967, 1970, 1971, 1972, and 1974, and for composer of the year, 1972 and 1976; recipient of awards from ASCAP for songwriting, 1971, 1974, 1976, and 1977; decorated Order of Canada, 1970; "Sundown" named pop record of the year, 1974, by Music Operators of America; recipient of Vanier Award by Canadian Jaycees, 1977; named Canadian male recording artist of the decade (1970s), 1980; named to Juno Hall of Fame, 1986.

Addresses: *Office*—c/o 1365 Yonge St., # 207, Toronto, Ont. M4T 2P7 Canada.

---

which Lightfoot sings of the fate of the ship and crew of an ore carrier sunk on Lake Superior in 1975, appeared on his 1976 release, *Summertime Dream.*

Despite having written over four hundred songs—a number of which received regular airplay—and having a number of best-selling albums and several Grammy Award nominations, Lightfoot did not score another Top 40 hit. In 1987, after a three-year hiatus from the recording industry, he returned with *East of Midnight,* the slickly produced pop ballad "Anything For Love," and a new stage show featuring more folk music. Contemplating retiring, Lightfoot told *Maclean's,* "When your albums aren't selling, it's not practical for a man to spend his life chained to a desk and to a recording studio. You have to grow up and realize that there is a new generation of recording artists out there." New artists can, however, cause problems.

In April of 1987, Lightfoot filed a lawsuit against Michael Masser, alleging that Masser's song "The Greatest Love of All" (recorded by Whitney Houston) stole twen-

> *Lightfoot has been honored as Canada's top folksinger often, receiving the prestigious Juno Award sixteen times.*

ty-four bars from Lightfoot's 1969 hit "If You Could Read My Mind." According to *Maclean's,* Lightfoot commented, "It really rubbed me the wrong way. I don't want the present-day generation to think that I stole my song from him." Unlikely, though Lightfoot himself has always remained cautious and questioning about the industry. Said Toronto promoter Bernie Fiedler, "I don't think Gordon realizes that he has a tremendous talent. When intelligentsia of the music business courted him, he felt threatened. He's a cautious man who won't take chances."

Lightfoot has been honored as Canada's top folksinger often, receiving the prestigious Juno Award sixteen times before being inducted into the country's Hall of Fame. "Gordie is completely original," said singer-songwriter Murray McLauchlan. "He can spin a great yarn—in the gothic sense—and write bittersweet ballads that are very poignant." Despite having traveled all across North America, Britain, Australia, and other places, Lightfoot remains an essentially private man granting few interviews and disliking having his

---

first album, *Lightfoot,* and he was named Canada's top folksinger. In 1967 he moved into the position of top male vocalist, and in 1970 he was awarded Canada's Medal of Service, celebrating his positive general contribution to the good of Canada. After four more respectably selling albums, Lightfoot signed with Warner to record a number of albums on their Reprise label, including *If You Could Read My Mind* (originally released as *Sit Down Young Stranger,* which featured both title tracks as well as the melodic "Approaching Lavender"), *Old Dan's Records,* and *Endless Wire.* Several collections of Lightfoot's songs, including music and lyrics, were published by Warner Bros. Publications.

By 1976 Lightfoot had earned eight gold albums and one platinum album—for *Sundown,* the title track of which brought him considerable popularity in the United States. The album sold over 1,500,000 copies during its first year of release (1974), replacing *If You Could Read My Mind* as a favorite of fans and critics and eventually holding a place on both the rock and country music charts. One of his best-known songs, the haunting ballad "The Wreck of the Edmund Fitzgerald," in

picture taken. His troubadour image is enhanced by his reedy voice and his timeless, thought-provoking lyrics of life and love and sorrow. What Milton Okun observed in his book *Something to Sing About* remains true: "He seems to offer the sort of restrained self-composure so often seen in highly talented performers. He has no need to shout, because he feels he has something of musical and poetic validity to say." And Gordon Lightfoot has said it well.

Selected discography

Lightfoot, United Artists, 1966.
Way I Feel, United Artists, 1967.
Did She Mention My Name, United Artists, 1968.
Back Here On Earth, United Artists, 1969.
Early Lightfoot, United Artists, 1969.
Sunday Concert, United Artists, 1969.
If You Could Read My Mind (originally released as *Sit Down Young Stranger*), Reprise, 1970.
Summerside of Life, Reprise, 1971.
Don Quixote, Reprise, 1972.
Old Dan's Records, Reprise, 1972.
Sundown, Reprise, 1974.
Cold on Shoulder, Reprise, 1975.
Gord's Gold, Reprise, 1975.
Early Morning Rain, Sunset, 1976.
Summertime Dream, Reprise, 1976.
Endless Wire, Warner Bros., 1978.
Dream Street Rose, Warner Bros., 1980.
Salute, Warner Bros., 1983.
East of Midnight, Warner Bros., 1986.
Gord's Gold, Volume II, Warner Bros., 1989.

Sources

Books

Anderson, Christopher P., *The Book of People,* Putnam, 1981.
Nite, Norm N., *Rock On,* Volume 2, Harper, 1978.
Okun, Milton, *Something to Sing About,* Macmillan, 1968.
Stambler, Irwin, *Encyclopedia of Pop, Rock and Soul,* St. Martin's, 1974.

Periodicals

Maclean's, March 16, 1987.
Globe and Mail (Toronto), May 4, 1970.
Village Voice, February 14, 1974.
Washington Post, December 27, 1974.

Other

Liner notes from album *Gord's Gold,* Reprise, 1975.

—Meg Mac Donald

Kenny Loggins

Singer, songwriter

Kenny Loggins has made a name for himself in several areas of the music industry: first as a songwriter, then as a partner to Jim Messina in the duo Loggins and Messina, and finally as a solo artist. His first involvement with music was in a parochial school in Alhambra, California, where he learned to play the guitar. He joined a folk group while in college, but by the late 1960s he had gravitated to rock.

Loggins spent time in two groups, Gator Creek and Second Helping, which were under contract to Mercury and Viva records, respectively, but neither gained much notice. In 1969, Loggins left Viva to work for one hundred dollars a week as a songwriter for ABC Wingate, the publishing division of ABC records. Some of his most notable work there was recorded by the Nitty Gritty Dirt Band. Their album *Uncle Charlie and His Dog Teddy* contained four of Loggins's songs, including the very popular "House at Pooh Corner."

In 1971, Loggins was offered an artist's contract with Columbia Records, and Jim Messina was chosen to be his producer. Messina had formerly played bass for Buffalo Springfield and lead guitar for Poco, but had grown tired of touring and planned to concentrate his energies on studio work and production. To produce Loggins's solo album, Messina recruited ex-Sunshine Company rhythm players Larry Sims and Merel Bregante, keyboardist Mike Ornartian, and hornmen Al Garth and Jon Clark.

During the recording sessions, Messina realized that Loggins's musical style and his own were very complementary, and he ended up playing on the record as well as producing it. The completed album, *Kenny Loggins with Jim Messina Sittin' In,* climbed the charts slowly but steadily. Thanks to "Vahevala," an FM hit with a Caribbean feel, and "Danny's Song," which became popular after Anne Murray covered it, *Sittin In'* eventually went gold.

Encouraged by their popularity, Loggins and Messina began touring with all the members of their studio band except Ornartian. "The Kenny Loggins Band with Jim Messina," as they were billed, was received so enthusiastically by audiences that they soon cut another album, entitled *Loggins and Messina.* One of its country-rock songs, "Your Mama Don't Dance," became a major hit, and the album quickly went gold. Loggins and Messina cut five more albums during the 1970s and, although some music critics felt that they lacked the intensity of the first two albums, nearly all sold over a million copies. The exception was *So Fine,* which featured reworkings of classic songs of the 1950s. Fans didn't appreciate the departure from good-time country-rock, and the duo returned to their usual sound on their 1976 offering, *Native Sons.* In November 1976, Loggins and Messina announced that they would no longer be performing together. Despite the success of their partnership, they had maintained separate contracts and had never expected to make so many albums together.

Jim Messina returned almost exclusively to production work, and Loggins finally became the solo performer he'd set out to be earlier in the decade. His first solo album, *Celebrate Me Home,* was an extension of the country-tinged pop-rock sound of Loggins and Messina. Its follow-up, *Nightwatch,* was a platinum seller, as was 1979's *Keep the Fire.* Despite becoming an album-oriented rock superstar in his own right, Loggins has continued to write for other performers. In recent years he has also devoted considerable time to writing songs for movie sound tracks, including "Footloose," from the film of the same title, "I'm Alright," from *Caddyshack,* "Danger Zone," from *Top Gun,* and "Meet Me Half Way," from *Over the Top.*

Selected discography

LPs with Jim Messina; all for Columbia

Kenny Loggins with Jim Messina Sittin' In, 1972.
Loggins and Messina, 1972.
Full Sail, 1973.
On Stage, 1974.
Mother Lode, 1975.
So Fine, 1975.
Native Sons, 1976.
Best of Friends, 1977.
Finale, 1977.

Solo LPs; all for Columbia

Celebrate Me Home, 1977.
Nightwatch, 1978.
Keep the Fire, 1979.
Alive, 1980.
High Adventure, 1982.
Vox Humana, 1985.
Back to Avalon, 1988.

Sources

Books

Hardy, Phil, and Dave Laing, *Encyclopedia of Rock and Roll,* McDonald, 1987.
Jahn, Mike, *Rock: From Elvis Presley to Rock and Roll,* Rolling Stone Press, 1976.
Nite, Norm N., *Rock On: The Illustrated Encyclopedia of Rock n' Roll,* Crowell, 1978.

Periodicals

People, September 26, 1988.
Stereo Review, November 1988.

—Joan Goldsworthy

Bob Marley

Singer, songwriter, guitarist

In his brief life, Bob Marley rose from poverty and obscurity to international stardom, becoming the first Third World artist to be acclaimed to that degree. It was largely through him that the world became familiar with reggae music and Rastafarianism, the religion embraced by much of Jamaica's black underclass. According to *New York Times Magazine* contributor Jon Bradshaw, Marley became an influential political force in his native country by articulating "the plight of the Jamaican ghettos—urging change and preaching revolution should change not come." Because "exact and obvious" analogies to the situation in Jamaica were applicable in so many parts of the world, Marley eventually became a heroic figure to poor and oppressed people everywhere.

Robert Nesta Marley was born to Cedella Malcolm Marley when she was barely nineteen years old. The child was the result of her clandestine affair with the local overseer of crown lands in the rural parish where she lived. Captain Marley, a white man more than twice Cedella's age, married the girl to make the birth legitimate, but he left the countryside the day after his impromptu wedding in order to accept a post in the city of Kingston and had almost no contact with his wife and son for several years. As the infant grew, he became the pet of his grandfather's large clan. He was known as a serious child and had a reputation for clairvoyance.

When Bob was about five years old, Cedella received a letter from her estranged husband asking that his son be sent to Kingston in order to attend school. Bob's mother reluctantly agreed and put her young son on the bus to Jamaica's largest city. Captain Marley met the child, but, for reasons unknown, he took him to the home of an elderly, invalid woman and abandoned him there. Bob was left to fend almost entirely for himself in Kingston's ghettos, which are generally considered some of the world's worst. Months passed before Cedella Marley was able to track down her child and bring him back to his country home. Before long, however, mother and child had returned to Kingston, where Cedella believed she had a greater chance of improving her lot. With them were Bob's closest friend, Bunny Livingston, and Bunny's father Thaddeus.

Jamaican society held few opportunities for blacks. Bob and Bunny grew up in an environment where violent crime was glorified by many young people as one of the few ways of getting ahead. Music was seen as another means of escape. Like most of their contemporaries, the two boys dreamed of becoming recording stars and spent their days coming up with songs and practicing them to the accompaniment of makeshift guitars they fashioned from bamboo, sardine cans, and electrical wire. By 1963, Marley's dream had come

For the Record. . .

Full name, Robert Nesta Marley; born February 6, 1945, in Nine Miles, Saint Ann, Jamaica; died of cancer May 11, 1981, in Miami, Fla., buried in Nine Miles, Saint Ann, Jamaica; son of Norval Sinclair Marley (a British army captain) and Cedella Marley Booker (formerly a shopkeeper, now a singer; maiden name Malcolm); married Alpharita Constantia Anderson (a singer), on February 10, 1966; children: David, Cedella, Stephen, and Stephanie; he also had seven other legally recognized children with seven different women: daughters Karen and Makeda Jahnesta, and sons Rowan, Robbie, Kimani, Julian, and Damian. *Religion:* Rastafarian.

Worked as a welder, Kingston, Jamaica, briefly in 1961; lab assistant at Du Pont, forklift driver in a warehouse, and assembly-line worker at Chrysler, all in Delaware, 1966; owner of a record store, Wailin' Soul, Kingston, Jamaica, 1966; formed Tuff Gong recording label, 1970; recording artist, 1962-81; founding member, with Peter Tosh and Bunny Livingston, of musical group the Wailers (originally known as the Teenagers, then as the Wailing Rudeboys, then the Wailing Wailers), early 1960s.

Awards: Special citation on behalf of Third World nations from United Nations, 1979; Jamaica's Order of Merit, 1981.

---

true—he'd released his first single, "Judge Not." Soon he and Bunny had teamed with another singer, Peter Tosh, to form a group known as the Wailers. Through talent shows, gigs at small clubs, and recordings, the Wailers became one of the most popular groups in Jamaica.

Their early success was based on popular dance hits in the "ska" music style, but as time passed, they added social commentary to their lyrics, and were instrumental in transforming the light, quick ska beat into the slower, bass-heavy reggae sound. The three men also came under the influence of Rastafarianism. This complex set of mystical beliefs holds that Emperor Haile Selassie I of Ethiopia (whose given name was Ras Tafari) is the living God who will lead blacks out of oppression and into an African homeland. It was once considered the religion of outcasts and lunatics in Jamaica, but in the 1960s it came to represent an alternative to violence for many ghetto dwellers. Rastafarianism lent dignity to their suffering and offered them the hope of eventual relief. Rejecting the standards of the white world that led many blacks to straighten their hair, Rastas let theirs mat up into long, ropy "dreadlocks." They follow strict dietary rules: abhor

alcohol and drugs, but revere "ganja" (marijuana) as a holy herb that brings enlightenment to users. The Wailers soothed ghetto tensions with lyrical messages of peace, love, and racial reconciliation but, at the same time, they warned the ruling class of "imminent dread judgement on the downpressors."

For all their acclaim in Jamaica, the Wailers saw few profits from their early recording careers, as unscrupulous producers repeatedly cheated them out of royalties and even the rights to their own songs. In the early 1970s, Marley sought an alliance with Chris Blackwell, a wealthy white Jamaican whose record company, Island, was the label of many major rock stars. At the time, reggae was still considered unsophisticated slum music that could never be appreciated by non-Jamaican audiences. Blackwell had a deep interest in the music, however, and because he felt that the Wailers were the one group who could popularize reggae internationally, he offered them a contract and marketed their first Island album, *Catch a Fire,* just as he would any rock band. Tours of Britain and the United States helped the Wailers' sound to catch on, but perhaps the most important catalyst to their popularity at this time was Eric Clapton's cover of Marley's composition, "I Shot the Sheriff," from the Wailers' 1973 album *Burnin'.* Clapton's version became a worldwide hit and led many of his fans to discover the Wailers' music.

As their popularity increased, the original Wailers drew closer to a parting of the ways. Bunny Livingston (who had taken the name Bunny Wailer) disliked leaving Jamaica for extended tours, and Peter Tosh resented Chris Blackwell's efforts to make Bob the focus of the group. Each launched solo careers in 1975, while Marley released *Natty Dread,* hailed by *Rolling Stone* reviewer Stephen Davis as "the culmination of Marley's political art to this point." The reviewer continued: "With every album he's been rocking a little harder and reaching further out to produce the stunning effect of a successful spell. *Natty Dread* deals with rebellion and personal liberation. . . .The artist lays his soul so bare that the careful listener is satiated and exhausted in the end." *Rastaman Vibration* was released the following year to even more enthusiastic reviews. It was full of acid commentary on the worsening political situation in Jamaica, including a denouncement of the CIA's alleged involvement in island politics that brought Marley under surveillance by that and other U.S. intelligence organizations. His prominence in Jamaica reached messianic proportions, causing one *Time* reporter to exclaim, "He rivals the government as a political force."

Although Marley regarded all politicians with skepticism, considering them to be part of what Rastafarians call "Babylon," or the corrupt Western world, he was known to favor Michael Manley of the People's National Party over Edward Seaga of the right-wing Jamaican Labour Party for the post of Prime Minister of Jamaica. When Manley asked Bob Marley to give a "Smile Jamaica" concert to reduce tensions between the warring gangs associated with the two parties, the singer readily agreed. On December 3, 1976, shortly before the concert was to take place, seven gunmen, suspected to be henchmen of the Jamaican Labour Party, stormed Marley's home. Marley, his wife Rita, and their manager Don Taylor were all injured in the ensuing gunfire. Despite the assassination attempt, the concert went on as scheduled. An audience of 80,000 people was electrified when Marley, bandaged and unable to strum his guitar, climbed to the stage to begin a blistering ninety-minute set. "At the close of his performance, Bob began a ritualistic dance, acting out aspects of the ambush that had almost taken his life," reported Timothy White in *Catch a Fire: The Life of Bob Marley.* "The last thing [the audience] saw before the reigning King of Reggae disappeared back into the hills was the

> *In his brief life, Bob Marley rose from poverty and obscurity to international stardom, becoming the first Third World artist to be acclaimed to that degree.*

image of the man mimicking the two-pistoled fast draw of a frontier gunslinger, his locks thrown back in triumphant laughter."

Immediately after the "Smile Jamaica" concert, Marley left the country in self-imposed exile. After a period of recuperation, he toured the United States, Europe, and Africa. Reviewing his 1977 release, *Exodus,* Ray Coleman wrote in *Melody Maker:* "This is a mesmerizing album. . . .more accessible, melodically richer, delivered with more directness than ever. . . .After an attempt on his life, Marley has a right to celebrate his existence, and that's how the album sounds: a celebration." But *Village Voice* reviewer Roger Trilling found that *Exodus* was "underscored by deep personal melancholy, a musical echo of the rootless wanderings that followed [Marley's] self-exile from Jamaica."

In 1978, Marley injured his foot during an informal soccer game. The painful wound was slow to heal and finally forced the singer to seek medical help. Doctors informed him that he had an early form of cancer and

advised amputation of his damaged toe. He refused, because such treatment was not in keeping with Rasta beliefs. Despite worsening health, Marley continued to perform until September 1980 when he collapsed while jogging in New York's Central Park during the U.S. leg of a world tour. Doctors determined that tumors were spreading throughout his lungs and brain. He underwent radiation therapy and a controversial holistic treatment in the Bavarian Alps, but to no avail. After his death on May 11, 1981, he was given a state funeral in Jamaica, which was attended by more than 100,000 people. Prime minister Edward Seaga remembered Marley as "a native son. . .a beloved and departed friend." "He was a man with deep religious and political sentiments who rose from destitution to become one of the most influential music figures in the last twenty years," eulogized White in *Rolling Stone.* He was "an inspiration for black freedom fighters the world over. . . .When his death was announced, the degree of devastation felt beyond our borders was incalculable."

Selected discography

LPs

Soul Rebel, Trojan, 1971.
Catch a Fire, Island, 1973.
Burnin', Island, 1973.
African Herbsman, Trojan, 1973.
Best of Bob Marley and the Wailers, Studio One, 1974.
Natty Dread, Island, 1974.
Rasta Revolution, Trojan, 1974.
Live! Bob Marley and the Wailers, Island, 1975.
Rastaman Vibration, Island, 1976.
Birth of a Legend, Calla, 1976.
Reflection, Fontana, 1977.
Exodus, Island, 1977.
Kaya, Island, 1978.
Babylon by Bus, Island, 1978.
In the Beginning, Psycho, 1979.
Survival, Island, 1979.
Bob Marley and the Wailers, Hammer, 1979.
Uprising, Island, 1980.
Crying for Freedom, Time-Wind, 1981.
Chances Are, Cotillion, 1981.
Soul Revolution, Part II, Pressure Disc, 1981.
Marley, Phoenix, 1982.
Jamaican Storm, Accord, 1982.
Bob Marley Interviews. . ., Tuff Gong, 1982.
Confrontation, Island, 1983.
Legend, Island, 1986.
Bob Marley, Urban-Tek, 1989.

Sources

Books

Davis, Stephen, *Bob Marley,* Doubleday, 1985.

Davis, Stephen, *Reggae Bloodlines: In Search of the Music and Culture of Jamaica,* Anchor Press, 1979.

Goldman, Vivian, *Bob Marley: Soul Rebel—Natural Mystic,* St. Martin's, 1981.

White, Timothy, *Catch a Fire: The Life of Bob Marley,* Holt, 1983.

Whitney, Malika Lee, *Bob Marley, Reggae King of the World,* Dutton, 1984.

Periodicals

Black Stars, July 1979.

Crawdaddy, July 1976; August 1977; May 1978.

Creem, August 1976.

down beat, September 9, 1976; September 8, 1977.

Encore, January 1980.

Essence, January 1976.

First World, Number 2, 1979.

Gig, June-July 1978.

Interview, August 1978.

Melody Maker, May 1, 1976; May 14, 1977; November 18, 1978; September 29, 1979.

Mother Jones, July 1985; December 1986.

New York Times Magazine, August 14, 1977.

People, April 26, 1976.

Playboy, January 1981.

Rolling Stone, April 24, 1975; June 1, 1978; June 15, 1978; December 28, 1978; January 11, 1979; March 18, 1982; May 27, 1982; June 4, 1987.

Sepia, March 1979.

Stereo Review, July 1975; September 1977; February 1982.

Time, March 22, 1976; December 20, 1976.

Village Voice, June 27, 1977; April 17, 1978; November 5, 1979.

Obituaries

Jet, May 28, 1981.

Maclean's, December 28, 1981.

Newsweek, May 25, 1981.

New York Times, May 12, 1981; May 21, 1981.

Rolling Stone, May 28, 1981; June 25, 1981.

Time, May 25, 1981.

Variety, May 20, 1981.

—Joan Goldsworthy

Ziggy Marley

Singer, songwriter, guitarist

Ziggy Marley has barely entered his twenties, but he has already been praised as one of the most important figures in reggae music today, as well as potentially one of the biggest international stars of the 1990s. His musical precociousness is hardly surprising, as he is the son of two of Jamaica's leading musicians, Bob and Rita Marley. That background does present certain problems, however—such as creating his own identity and enduring continual comparisons to his father.

It was Bob Marley who familiarized the world with reggae music and the Rastafarian faith; his early death was deeply mourned by the many people from all races and religions who regarded him as a prophet. His death plunged the Jamaican music scene into a malaise that persists today. Ziggy was only twelve when his father died, but even then the resemblance between the two was uncanny. Gregory Stephens observed in *Whole Earth Review* that "Ziggy is like a reflection of his father Bob, a young echo. As time goes on it is almost scary how this reflection seems to grow more and more like the original, in spirit if not always in style." And since the younger Marley has continued with the musical career on which his father launched him at the age of ten, he is now "the one who many people hope will be reggae music's redeemer," according to *Rolling Stone* contributor Anthony DeCurtis.

"Ziggy has in fact been groomed for the role of Bob Marley's successor from an early age," stated Stephens. "As Marley's eldest son, he was widely seen as heir to the heritage, and he was given moorings for the journey by a mixture of strict but worldly Rastas and Jesuits." This privileged upbringing, which included occasional world travel and onstage appearances with the Wailers, was in sharp contrast to Bob Marley's youth. He grew up fending for himself in Kingston's ghettoes and earned a reputation as "Tuff Gong" the street fighter long before he was known as a singer. By the time his children were born, however, he was Jamaica's favorite musician. He had the means to protect his family and was eager to do so. Yet even Ziggy, the so-called "Crown Prince of Reggae," could not completely escape Jamaica's pervasive violence: in 1975 both his parents were wounded by gunshots in a politically related attack, and in later years he would see several of his father's associates slain under similar circumstances.

Bob Marley's desire to shield his children from the seamier side of the music industry led him to ban them from the recording studio when they were very young. Yet as early as 1975 he had written something with them in mind: "Children Playing in the Streets," a melodic protest song detailing the desperate conditions under which most of Jamaica's children live. In 1979, aware of the cancer that would soon take his life, he personally brought Ziggy into the studio to record the song, perhaps as a way of handing down his musical legacy. Backing vocals were provided by Sharon Marley (Rita's oldest daughter, whom Bob had adopted) and two of the couple's other children, Cedella and Stephen. All proceeds from the sale of the single were donated to the United Nations Children's Fund.

For several years the family quartet, known as the Melody Makers, performed mainly on special occasions, such as Bob Marley's state funeral in 1981. Ziggy had begun to write original material for the group, however. From the start, his lyrics reflected his unusual upbringing and serious outlook. Stephens declared, "The images that have come out of this man-child's imagination remind me of the paintings done by the children of Guatemala and El Salvador. They are all images of a world at war." In 1985 the Melody Makers released their first album, *Play the Game Right,* followed in 1986 by *Hey World!* Neither was particularly successful; in spite of the social consciousness and political commentary evident in Ziggy Marley's lyrics, the Melody Makers' young voices led many in the music industry to dismiss them as just another "kiddie group." Jordan Harris, formerly an executive with A & M Records, attributes the lackluster sales of *Play the Game Right* and *Hey World!* to poor handling by record company EMI America. He recalled in *Rolling Stone* that he was terribly disappointed when A & M lost the bid for the Melody Makers' contract to EMI: "What bothered me most is not that I wasn't able to sign the band then. . .but that the people that signed them I don't think understood what they had. I think they thought they were signing Musical Youth or some lightweight pop-type thing."

Rita Marley was of a similar mind. Besides failing to provide adequate promotion for the Melody Makers, EMI was pushing Ziggy to leave his brothers and sisters behind for a solo career. Ziggy emphatically rejected this idea. He told DeCurtis: "Blood t'icker than water. . . .I am not a youth who is on any trip to become a big star. You come to know how important family is around you. I've been with my family singing from 1979 until this day, and now you walk up to me and say I must leave them alone and come to myself? What purpose would that serve? Me wouldn't feel good about that, and then the music wouldn't feel good about that either." Accordingly, Rita took her children to Virgin Records, which was committed to keeping the Melody Makers intact. Jordan Harris, who had since moved from A & M to Virgin, was elated. He expressed the utmost confidence in the Melody Makers' future: "I really think *this* sound and *this* music could be the music of the Nineties. Three years, five years from now, Ziggy Marley could be one of the most important musicians in the world."

Alex Sadkin was scheduled to produce the Melody Makers' first album for Virgin, but he was killed in an automobile accident near Kingston before the project got underway. Production was turned over to Tina Weymouth and Chris Frantz, the husband-and-wife team from the group Talking Heads. They were familiar with Sadkin's approach, as he had worked on the Talking Heads' *Speaking in Tongues* album, and they had worked with reggae artists before on their Tom Tom Club recordings. Under their direction, much of the recording for the Melody Makers' third album, *Conscious Party,* was done in New York. Deeply religious and heavily influenced by daily Bible readings, Ziggy shocked many New Yorkers at casual jam sessions with his impromptu lyrics warning against drinking and premarital sex. When finished, *Conscious Party* was an example of cultural cross-fertilization. It included some of Jamaica's most distinguished reggae artists as well as guest contributions from Keith Richards, Jerry Harrison of the Talking Heads, the Ethiopian band Dalbol, and the cast of the Broadway musical *Sarafina!*

Weymouth and Frantz strove to augment rather than to change the Melody Makers' sound, delivering what *Rolling Stone's* David Wild called perhaps "the best-sounding reggae album you'll ever hear—both pleasantly high-tech and appropriately rootsy." *Audio* reviewer Michael Terson also praised the producers for creating an "ingenious" sound that "delivers strength on the reggae backbeat and on the rock downbeat," but noted that they "wisely stayed pretty much out of the way of Ziggy, his siblings, and the band. . . .In the end, it all comes down to Ziggy Marley. Here, his charisma blooms. He sounds eerily like Father Bob, but Ziggy's songs are so strong that they blunt any sound-alike criticism. . . .Marley is about to become a huge international star. He's got it all, and so does *Conscious*

Party." Wild also emphasized that *Conscious Party* represented a personal triumph for the young songwriter: "There's one hell of a shadow hanging over Ziggy Marley, and it is testament to the beauty and strength of *Conscious Party* that instead of being an object of morbid fascination the album is one of the brightest, most life-affirming records in recent history."

The enthusiastic critical reception of *Conscious Party* marked a turning point for Ziggy Marley, when he began to be accepted on his own terms. Pondering the musician's future in *Whole Earth Review*, Stephens noted that, thus far, Marley's lyrics have consisted mainly of "strident calls to action and 'bald slogans.' They are catchy, but limited by the abstracted idealism of a youth who has an unusually broad, but also somewhat insular, view of the world. It will be interesting to hear what Ziggy comes up with when he comes home from the battlefield to write about love and other shades

---

Ziggy Marley has barely entered his twenties, but he has already been praised as one of the most important figures in reggae music today, as well as potentially one of the biggest international stars of the 1990s.

---

of gray." He concluded that Marley was bound to become even more popular, stating: "Anyone who can't see the economic as well as artistic potential of. . .Ziggy Marley hasn't yet understood the Messianic fervor that runs among Third World peoples, especially in Jamaica. Jamaican music has been able to infect nerve centers around the world—particularly New York and London—spreading a less severe case of Messianic expectations among American Dream refugees and entertainment consumers. So there is a potentially immense audience for a young, sexy, fashionable, implicitly spiritual Third World superstar."

Marley is also a key figure in a fierce struggle currently taking place in Jamaica's musical world. Since Bob Marley's death, traditional reggae, with its weighty sociopolitical and religious messages, has been largely supplanted by a bawdy, rap-related music known as "Dance Hall." Traditionalists hope that Ziggy Marley can attract Jamaica's youth to the spiritual values of

Rastafarianism, much as his father did in the 1970s. Jimmy Guterman remarked in *Rolling Stone* that "as children of the late Bob Marley, David 'Ziggy' Marley and the Melody Makers practically carry the mantle of reggae themselves." That is a responsibility which they are well qualified to handle, however, as the writer asserts in his review of their latest release, *One Bright Day:* "This is a formidable band even if you toss aside ideas about tradition. Ziggy sounds as much like his father as Julian Lennon sounds like John, but Ziggy has found a way to use that as a springboard: He accepts the familiarity and tries to add something new. At his best, Ziggy displays a voice that is his alone." Asked by DeCurtis if he found the endless comparisons to his father to be an oppressive burden, Marley replied stoically, "I am myself. . .and I have been myself every time. I never try to run from the truth. . . .Me and my father have something in common which you can't hide and you can't run from, you know?"

Selected discography

Singles

"Children Playing in the Streets," Tuff Gong, 1979.
"Sugar Pie," Tuff Gong, 1980.
"Trodding," Tuff Gong, 1980.
"What a Plot" (two-song EP), Shanachie, 1983.

LPs

Play the Game Right, EMI America, 1985.
Hey World!, EMI America, 1986.
Conscious Party, Virgin, 1988.
The Best of Ziggy Marley and the Melody Makers, EMI America, 1988.
One Bright Day, Virgin, 1989.

Sources

Books

White, Timothy, *Catch a Fire: The Life of Bob Marley,* Holt, 1983.

Periodicals

Audio, August 1988.
down beat, August 1989.
Maclean's, October 27, 1986.
New Statesman and Society, July 28, 1989.
Newsweek, May 30, 1988.
People, March 28, 1988.
Rolling Stone, March 24, 1988; May 7, 1988; September 7, 1989.
Whole Earth Review, summer 1988.

—*Joan Goldsworthy*

Richard Marx

Singer, songwriter, guitarist

Richard Marx, once hailed as "rock's newest *wunder*kid" by Steve Dougherty of *People,* worked for years singing backup and writing songs for stars like Lionel Richie and Kenny Rogers before landing a solo recording contract in 1986. His first album, aptly titled *Richard Marx,* spawned four hit singles and earned him a Grammy nomination. Marx's good looks have brought him what Dougherty labeled "a herd of young female fans," but he has also been praised as a "serious, articulate musician" by Ann Elliot in *Mademoiselle* and a "great singer" by reviewer J. D. Considine in *Rolling Stone.*

Marx was born in Chicago to parents who both earned their livelihoods in the commercial jingle business—his father composed and his mother sang. As a small child he often accompanied them to the studio where they worked. Marx told reporter Steve Hochman in *Rolling Stone:* "I loved to be in a recording studio. Any excuse to hang out. Get coffee for people, sharpen pencils, anything. And so when I got to sing, it was even cooler." And sing he did; when he was about five Marx began singing commercials for products including peanut butter and candy bars.

His interest in music continued during his adolescence. As Marx recalled for Hochman: "Some of my friends used to watch Beatles or Elvis movies for the plot and I watched them for the music. When those songs came on, I would be up and I would fake the guitar and I would *be* Elvis, you know? None of my friends got off on it like I did." At about the same time, the youngster began writing his own songs—"about girls [who] wouldn't go out with me in high school," Marx confided to Dougherty.

By the time he was eighteen Marx's songwriting talents had improved to the point where he got a response when he sent a demo tape through an odd series of acquaintances to pop star Lionel Richie. "A friend of mine [who] was going to school in Atlanta, [Georgia], was roommates with a guy who grew up with a guy who was then working for the Commodores," a group Richie was then a member of, Marx explained to Hochman. Richie encouraged Marx to move to Los Angeles, California, to enter the music business.

He followed Richie's advice. In Los Angeles, Marx sang backup on some of Richie's hits, including "All Night Long" and "Running With the Night." He also wrote "What About Me" for country star Kenny Rogers, and composed music for the group Chicago. When Marx was nineteen, he was recruited to write a song for the film *Staying Alive.* While doing this, he met the film's female lead, actress and dancer Cynthia Rhodes. Though she at first rejected his romantic overtures because he was seven years her junior, they eventually married.

Meanwhile, Marx's quest to become a solo artist was initially frustrating. Primarily involved in a more mellow, ballad-oriented sound for his backup work with other artists, in his free time he wrote rock songs. And Marx had the discouraging experience of having a friend who was a music producer tell him: "'You're never going to get a record. You're not an artist,'" Marx admitted to Dougherty. Despite this judgment, and the fact that he "was turned down by every record company at least three times," as he put it to Dougherty, the young singer-songwriter kept trying. Finally, in 1986, Marx was signed by Manhattan Records after an audition with the president of the company.

Richard Marx, the resulting album, was a rapid success. The hit singles from it include "Don't Mean Nothing," "Should Have Known Better," and "Endless Summer Nights." Though it took Marx until 1989 to release his second effort, *Repeat Offender,* his music continues to be extremely popular. Though *Rolling Stone* critic Considine labeled *Offender* "disappointing," he conceded that "the songs go down as easily as chocolate milk." Perhaps more important, however, is the fact that Marx's second album has already scored two chart hits—the energetic "Satisfied" and the ballad "Right Here Waiting." The young artist is philosophical, though, about his status as a pop star. Marx told Dougherty: "It could be the next single or 20 singles from now, but eventually I'm going to put out a song that is going to stall and go double plywood. But I won't freak out, because I can always work as a producer."

Selected discography

Richard Marx (includes "Don't Mean Nothing," "Should Have Known Better," and "Endless Summer Nights"), Manhattan, 1987.
Repeat Offender (includes "Satisfied" and "Right Here Waiting"), EMI, 1989.

Sources

Mademoiselle, June 1989.
People, March 7, 1988.
Rolling Stone, September 24, 1987; June 29, 1989.

—Elizabeth Thomas

Bobby McFerrin

Singer

In Germany they call him *Stimmwunder* (wonder voice); in America Bobby McFerrin is considered the most innovative jazz vocalist to emerge in twenty years. Singing solo and a cappella, he uses his four-octave voice to "play" a variety of instruments—such as the guitar, the trumpet, and the drums. "I like to think of my voice as being my body," he told Micheal Bourne in *down beat.* "That's my equipment." A triple Grammy winner, McFerrin recently topped the popular-music charts with his single "Don't Worry, Be Happy."

The son of opera singers (his father was the first black man to perform regularly with the Metropolitan Opera), McFerrin was born in New York City. In 1958 his family moved to Los Angeles. McFerrin attended Sacramento State University and Cerritos College, but dropped out to play piano for the Ice Follies. Over the next few years, he played keyboard with lounge acts and for dance troupes. In 1977 McFerrin decided, suddenly, to become a singer. "I was in a quiet moment when a simple thought just came into my head: 'Why don't you sing?' It was as simple as that, but it must have had some force behind it because I acted on it immediately," he explained to Bourne. He sang with various bands and was eventually discovered by singer Jon Hendricks. While on tour with Hendricks, McFerrin was again discovered—this time by comedian Bill Cosby.

Through Cosby, McFerrin was booked in Las Vegas and at the Playboy Jazz Festival in Los Angeles. He later performed at New York's Kool Jazz Festival and began touring or recording with such jazz greats as George Benson and Herbie Hancock. In 1982 he released his first album, *Bobby McFerrin.* His fans were disappointed: "He sang with some of his vocal pyrotechnics fully alight," *Horizon*'s Leslie Gourse wrote, "but he had loud electronic instrumental accompaniment that essentially was pop." McFerrin learned from his mistake; his next effort, *The Voice,* was widely praised. Recorded live during a solo concert tour of Germany, the album is all a cappella and displays the singer's virtuosity. "McFerrin coaxes up a daffy assortment of vocal effects and characterizations on *The Voice,*" Francis Davis noted in *Rolling Stone.* "His circular breathing technique enables him to sing while inhaling and exhaling, thus allowing him to be his own background choir on 'Blackbird' and 'T. J.' He slaps himself into a percussive frenzy on 'I Feel Good' and creates the sound of static between frequencies on 'I'm My Own Walkman.'"

McFerrin's later works have also been well received. Of *Spontaneous Inventions* Susan Katz of *Newsweek* wrote: "[It] shows off his ability to Ping-Pong between sweet falsetto melody and what sounds like a walking-bass accompaniment. . . .McFerrin delivers a cappella improvisations on everything from Bach to 'The Beverly Hillbillies' theme song." Similarly, his more recent album, *Simple Pleasures,* contains versions of old pop and rock tunes, such as "Good Lovin'," "Suzie Q," and "Sunshine of Your Love." *Interview's* Glenn O'Brien found that "the way he does these near chestnuts makes them new and restores the power that made them parts of your memory banks in the first place." So far, the album has sold over one million copies, and one of its tracks, "Don't Worry, Be Happy," has become a hit single.

McFerrin has received three Grammy Awards, two for his work on "Another Night in Tunisia," recorded by Manhattan Transfer. His third, as Best Male Jazz Vocalist, was for "'Round Midnight," the title song of the 1986 movie. McFerrin has also recorded the theme for "The Cosby Show" and the sound track for "Just So," an animated series of specials that aired on cable television. He has appeared on "The Tonight Show" and "Sesame Street," and he provides the vocals for Levi's commercials. McFerrin tours extensively as well. During his concerts, he often improvises his material. Spontaneity is an important part of McFerrin's music: "I like being an improviser, expecting the unexpected," he told Bourne. "Even when something is rehearsed, I want it to be spontaneous."

Selected discography

Bobby McFerrin, Elektra Musician, 1982.
The Voice, Elektra Musician, 1984.
Spontaneous Inventions, Blue Note, 1986.
Simple Pleasures, EMI Manhattan Records, 1988.

Sources

Periodicals

Christian Science Monitor, April 17, 1987.
down beat, May 1985.
Horizon, July/August 1987.
Interview, August 1988.
Newsweek, October 6, 1986.
New York Times, November 20, 1987.
People, September 21, 1987.
Rolling Stone, March 28, 1985.
Time, October 17, 1988.

—Denise Wiloch

Bill Medley

Singer, songwriter

Bill Medley first rose to stardom during the 1960s as one-half of the Righteous Brothers—the duo that became the epitome of the phrase "blue-eyed soul." With partner Bobby Hatfield, he was responsible for hits like "You've Lost That Lovin' Feelin'" and "Soul and Inspiration." When Medley broke up with Hatfield in 1968, however, his career languished despite boosts from occasional Righteous Brothers reunions. But in 1987 he scored a huge success with singer Jennifer Warnes in their duet from the film *Dirty Dancing*—"The Time of My Life."

Born William Thomas Medley on September 19, 1940, in Santa Ana, California, he displayed an interest in music early in his life. Despite the fact that every attempt by his parents to get him to play an instrument—saxophone, trumpet, and piano—ended with Medley's protests after a few lessons, he was active in his church choir as a young boy. His devotion to this mode of musical expression lasted until his last few years of high school, when he began to listen to rock and roll. In his senior year, Medley formed a band with some of his classmates; they played at school dances and small clubs.

Medley was still playing those small clubs in Southern California when he made the acquaintance of Bobby Hatfield in 1962. The two men quickly became friends and decided to team up in their musical efforts. Despite their white middle-class backgrounds, they called themselves the Righteous Brothers and chose the genres of rhythm and blues and soul to express their talents. They signed with the small company Moonglow Records, and their debut album, *The Righteous Brothers,* was released in 1963. Medley and Hatfield soon attracted a following, predominantly among black music fans, but enjoyed only moderate success with wider audiences. They did, however, score a small hit with the single "Little Latin Lupe Lu."

The Righteous Brothers' careers received a huge boost when they became involved with record producer extraordinaire Phil Spector. Spector recruited Medley and Hatfield for his own recording label, Philles, and in 1965 the duo released its biggest smash, "You've Lost That Lovin' Feelin'." Geoffrey Stokes described the classic recording thus in the book *Rock of Ages: The Rolling Stone History of Rock and Roll*: "Medley's baritone—warm, sexy, almost relaxed—sang the opening verse; Hatfield's tenor—brassy, strangled, passionate—entered on the chorus. Its highly charged emotionalism seemed to prod Medley into passion of his own. Behind their inflamed call and response, the strings soared and dipped. . . . After the crescendo, the silence, broken only by single notes sustained on a lone base, was as sudden as a plunge off . . . a cliff. But this wasn't the end, merely a gathering of strength so the whole process could be repeated—on, if possible, a level of even greater intensity. Whenever 'Lovin' Feelin' ' came on the radio," Stokes concluded, "it reduced, for its three-minute span, the Supremes to little girls, the Beatles to fey pretenders." Needless to say, "Lovin' Feelin' " rose to the top of the charts.

Medley and Hatfield had other successful singles on the Philles label, including "Unchained Melody," "Ebb Tide," and "Just Once in My Life," but like many other Spector protegees, they felt a lack of artistic control over their work. By 1966 the Righteous Brothers had left Philles for Verve Records, and they scored a hit the same year with the mournful love ballad "Soul and Inspiration."

But a short two years later, Medley disbanded the duo, feeling that it was restricting both his creativity and Hatfield's. Medley went on in pursuit of a solo career, and Hatfield—obviously of a different opinion—retained the "Righteous Brothers" name and recruited a new partner. Neither fared well in comparison with their previous status as a team, but Medley put out several albums on the MGM label, such as *Someone Is Standing Outside* and *Nobody Knows* before moving to A & M Records in 1971. He also proved a popular attraction on the nightclub circuit.

In 1974, however, Medley reunited with Hatfield; they made their second debut on national television on "The Sonny and Cher Show." Though brief, the partnership lasted long enough to give them another top ten hit, "Rock and Roll Heaven." Later reunion appearances in the 1980s produced no hits but attracted attention due

to the nostalgia for 1960s music that swept the United States.

But Medley finally experienced a great popular achievement without Hatfield in 1987. Ironically, however, it came through another duet performance. With pop and country artist Jennifer Warnes, he recorded "Time of My Life" on the RCA label. The theme from the motion picture *Dirty Dancing*, the song was helped by the film's huge box office sales and rose to number one on the *Billboard* chart. A critical success as well, "Time of My Life" garnered Medley and Warnes a Grammy Award for Best Pop Performance by a Duo or Group With Vocal. Medley also went on tour with many of the other artists featured on the *Dirty Dancing* soundtrack album, and his newfound celebrity has sparked further interests in Righteous Brothers concert appearances.

Selected discography

Singles with Hatfield, except as noted

"Little Latin Lupe Lu," Moonglow, 1963.
"You've Lost That Lovin' Feelin'," Philles, 1965.
"Unchained Melody," Philles, 1965.
"Ebb Tide," Philles, 1965.
"Just Once in My Life," Philles, 1965.
"Soul and Inspiration," Verve, 1966.
"Rock and Roll Heaven," Haven, 1974.
(With Jennifer Warnes) "The Time of My Life," RCA, 1987.

LPs with Hatfield

Righteous Brothers, Moonglow, 1963.
Some Blue-Eyed Soul, Moonglow, 1965.
You've Lost That Lovin' Feelin', Philles, 1965.
Just Once in My Life, Philles, 1965.
Back to Back, Philles, 1965.
Soul and Inspiration, Verve, 1966.
Go Ahead and Cry, Verve, 1966.
Sayin' Somethin', Verve, 1967.
Greatest Hits, Verve, 1967.
Greatest Hits Volume 2, Verve, 1967.
Souled Out, Verve, 1967.
Standards, Verve, 1967.
One for the Road, Verve, 1968.
Give It to the People, Haven, 1974.
Sons of Mrs. Righteous, Haven, 1975.

Solo LPs

100% Bill Medley, MGM, 1968.
Soft and Soulful, MGM, 1969.
Gone, MGM, 1970.
Someone Is Standing Outside, MGM, 1970.
Nobody Knows, MGM, 1970.

A Song for You, A & M, 1972.
Wings, A & M, c. 1972.
Smile, A & M, 1973.
Sweet Thunder, Liberty, 1980.
The Best of Bill Medley, MCA, 1989.

—*Elizabeth Thomas*

Wes Montgomery

Guitarist

"Listening to [Wes Montgomery's] solos is like teetering at the edge of a brink," composer-conductor Gunther Schuller asserted, as quoted by *Jazz & Pop* critic Will Smith. "His playing at its peak becomes unbearably exciting, to the point where one feels unable to muster sufficient physical endurance to outlast it." Legendary guitarist Joe Pass simply says this about Montgomery's place in musical history: "To me, there have been only three real innovators on the guitar—Wes Montgomery, Charlie Christian, and Django Reinhardt," as cited in James Sallis's *The Guitar Players*. This high praise is a testament to the ability of a man of contradictions: Montgomery was a musician who never learned to read music, and he enjoyed commercial success rarely afforded to jazz musicians during the 1960s, while suffering critical—and personal—disapproval.

Born John Leslie Montgomery on March 6, 1923, in Indianapolis, Indiana, Montgomery showed no early musical aptitude or desire. At the age of nineteen, shortly after he was married, Montgomery heard a recording of "Solo Flight" by the Benny Goodman Orchestra with Charlie Christian on guitar. The impression was such that Montgomery immediately purchased an electric guitar, an amplifier, and as many Christian recordings as he could find, listening carefully to the guitar solos and learning to play them note for note. Montgomery's neighbors complained about the noise, however, so he abandoned the guitar pick in favor of plucking the strings with his thumb. He found the resulting sound mellow and pleasing. Later, while experimenting with different styles and approaches, he discovered the technique that would become his signature. Gary Giddins, in *Riding on a Blue Note,* explains: "Almost as an extension of that dulcet, singing tone, he began to work in octaves—voicing the melody line in two registers."

Within a year, Montgomery played in local clubs, imitating Christian solos. Exposed to other musicians and musical ideas, he developed his own concepts, and in 1948 was asked to join Lionel Hampton's big band. As a sideman, Montgomery toured and recorded with this group until 1950 when, having missed his wife and children, he returned home to work as a welder for a radio parts manufacturer. However, as Rich Kienzle pointed out in *Great Guitarists,* "His desire to play music. . .was strong. His shift was from 7 A.M. to 3 P.M.; he'd rest for a while, then play at the Turf Bar from 9 P.M. to 2 A.M., moving to a second gig at another club, the Missile Room, from 2:30 A.M. to 5 A.M." Montgomery continued this pace for six years, joining the group Mastersounds, composed of his brothers Monk (on bass) and Buddy (on piano and vibraphone), in 1957. A few recordings were made by the group on the West

Coast, but they failed to attract much attention, and Montgomery returned home to play in clubs.

In 1959, Montgomery received his big break. While performing at the Missile Room, he impressed saxophonist Cannonball Adderley, who subsequently contacted Orrin Keepnews of Riverside Records. Montgomery was immediately signed and traveled to New York to record his first album, *The Wes Montgomery Trio*. "From the beginning of his belated 'discovery,' the critical reception ranged from euphoria to hyperbole," Giddins explained. "No one had ever heard a guitar sound like Wes Montgomery's." This critical euphoria reached a fevered pitch with the release of Montgomery's follow-up album, *The Incredible Jazz Guitar of Wes Montgomery* (1960). It was not just the sound that Montgomery produced, but, as Sallis says, "the *intensity* of his music one responded to, the power and personality of it. When Wes hit a string you felt it, and it wasn't just a note, a C sharp or a B flat, it was part of a story he was telling you." This recording won Montgomery the *down beat* critics' New Star Award for 1960, and he topped the guitar category in both *down beat* readers' and critics' polls in 1961 and 1962.

For the next couple of years, Montgomery performed and toured with various groups, including his brothers, John Coltrane, Wynton Kelly's trio, and his own trio. Kienzle remarked that "by this time Wes had gained the eminence due him in the jazz world, producing a steady, high-quality level of music regardless of the context. His flow of ideas, soulful articulation, and effortless technique confronted other influences."

But in 1964, Riverside Records went bankrupt (following the death of president Bill Grauer), and Montgomery signed with Verve Records, headed by Creed Taylor. This move precipitated Montgomery's fall from grace with the jazz world and concurrent rise in the popular music world. Giddins explains: "Creed Taylor realized something about Montgomery's talent: it was octave technique and lyric sound, not his audaciously legato eighth-note improvisations with their dramatic architectural designs, that appealed to middle-of-the-road ears. So he set Montgomery on a course of decreasing improvisation and increasingly busy overdubbed arrangements, while the octaves, once used so judiciously, became the focus of his new 'style.'" Montgomery's 1965 release, *Goin' Out of My Head*, was a huge popular success, went gold, and earned him a Grammy award as the best instrumental jazz performance of the year.

Commercial success continued to escalate with subsequent albums on the Verve label, and in 1967, after having moved with Taylor to A&M Records, Montgomery recorded *A Day in the Life*. The title track not only became a popular hit, but the album became the best-selling jazz album of 1967 and one of the best-selling jazz albums of all time.

Remaking pop hits with a jazz feel increased his audience, but decreased his acclaim in jazz circles. Adrian Ingram, in an article for *Jazz Journal International*, noted that "hard core jazz fans began to desert him, complaining bitterly of over-orchestrated arrangements, sub-standard material (pop tunes) and constricted solo space." Sallis offered an explanation for his decline: "He was a victim of his own popularity, or of the trivialization of his talent, depending on how you perceive it, and as a result that talent went largely unheard for the last years of his life."

Montgomery was aware of the growing dissatisfaction in the jazz community with his supposed commercialization, and he tried to make a distinction between his earlier work and his more popular work. "There is a jazz concept to what I'm doing, but I'm playing popular music and it should be regarded as such," Montgomery said, as quoted by Giddins. His approach to music had always been one of feeling rather than one of technique. His inability to read music led to his development of a fine ear; he heard music rather than saw it on a page. And this was most important in his relation with his audience. "Wes believed that the music should be communicated, that the audience was part of the band, and the *feeling* of the music was more important to him than playing every note correctly," Jimmy Stewart wrote in *Guitar Player*. Regardless of the style of, or the audience for, the music, Montgomery played with feeling and conviction. Of *Road Song,* his last recording for A&M before his death, *down beat*'s Pete Welding said, "He couldn't play uninterestingly if he wanted to. Time and time again throughout this collection his supple sense of rhythm, his choice and placement of notes, his touch and tone raise what might have been in lesser hands merely mundane to the plane of something special, distinctive, masterful."

Even with his quoted defense of playing popular music, Montgomery, as Ingram noted, "began to feel trapped by both the music business in general and non-jazz audiences who would tolerate only note perfect renditions of the most popular tunes from his Verve albums."

"Wes Montgomery believed that the music should be communicated . . . the feeling of the music was more important to him than playing every note correctly."

Montgomery longed to return to the playing of his earlier style. This was no more evident than when he performed live. A month before Montgomery's death, Giddins saw him perform and described what he heard: "Surrounded by four rhythm players, his regular group, he immediately shot off a single chorus of 'Goin',' and followed it with the most fiery, exquisite set of guitar music I've ever heard. . . .Clearly, he had compromised only on disc and would eventually be recorded more seriously." Unfortunately, this did not occur. At the peak of his career, Montgomery suffered a fatal heart attack in his hometown on June 15, 1968.

"While Montgomery's place in jazz history was earned through his early recordings—his jazz recordings— his talent was encompassing enough to enable him to take on the requirements of 'commercial' music and execute it with utter elan, unerring taste, musicianship, and true distinction," Welding wrote. In a review for *down beat* of a posthumous release, Don DeMicheal

offered this statement on Montgomery's lasting ability: "Montgomery could do no wrong when his muse was hot upon him, and it often led him to try and accomplish things that few others could even conceive." But it is perhaps this quote from Ingram that succinctly defines the achievements and losses of Montgomery: "Even when he was immersed in blatantly commercial surroundings, Montgomery never lost his ability to create sophisticated, tasteful jazz. He could turn tap water into vintage wine, though it is sad he was forced to do so, so often."

Selected discography

Finger Pickin', Pacific Jazz, 1957.
Montgomeryland, Pacific Jazz, 1958-59.
The Montgomery Trio, Riverside, 1959.
The Incredible Jazz Guitar of Wes Montgomery, Riverside, 1960.
Movin' Along, Riverside, 1960.
So Much Guitar!, Riverside, 1961.
Full House, Riverside, 1962.
Fusion, Riverside, 1963.
Boss Guitar, Riverside, 1963.
Movin' Wes, Verve, 1964.
Bumpin', Verve, 1964.
Goin' Out of My Head, Verve, 1965.
Smokin' at the Half Note, Verve, 1965.
Tequila, Verve, 1966.
California Dreaming, Verve, 1966.
A Day in the Life, A&M, 1967.
Down Here on the Ground, A&M, 1967.
Road Song, A&M, 1968.
Willow, Weep for Me, Verve, 1969.

Sources

Books

Britt, Stan, *The Jazz Guitarists,* Blandford Press, 1984.
Giddins, Gary, *Riding on a Blue Note,* Oxford University Press, 1981.
Kienzle, Rich, *Great Guitarists,* Facts on File, 1985.
Sallis, James, *The Guitar Players,* Morrow, 1982.

Periodicals

down beat, January 9, 1969; March 6, 1969.
Guitar Player, April, 1977.
Jazz, November, 1966.
Jazz & Pop, August, 1968.
Jazz Journal International, July, 1986.

—Rob Nagel

Jim Morrison

Singer, songwriter

Hard rock, mysticism, lyrical poetry and theatrics merged in the music of Jim Morrison and the band he fronted, the Doors. During the group's existence in the late 1960s, critics were sharply divided in their opinions of its worth. Some dismissed Morrison as a mediocre, self-indulgent vocalist who sold out to the demands of the pop music market as soon as his group became popular. Others praised him as both a powerful singer and poet and believed that the Doors' unique sound represented a brilliant fusion of jazz, rock, blues, and pop sounds. Today the Doors' music remains popular—and influential, and it seems obvious that much of the controversy surrounding the band arose from the contradictions inherent in Morrison himself. As Toby Goldstein wrote in *Feature,* his life "was filled with the events of which legends are made. No mere rock singer, he was both godlike and pompous, sensual and piggish, never existing on a middle ground."

Morrison was born into a family with a long history of career militarists. His mother stood passively by while his stern, authoritarian father ordered the children about. After leaving his family, Morrison would claim that both his parents were dead. In 1964 he headed for the West Coast to study film at UCLA. Once there, he felt a great sense of release which he later described as "the feeling of a bowstring being pulled back for 22 years and suddenly being let go." Besides his film studies, he delved into poetry and philosophy, particularly the work of Friedrich Nietzsche and William Blake. Classmates recall Morrison as a brilliant student, but before long he drifted away from school and into the Venice Beach culture, where he dropped acid freely and worked on his poetry. One night on the beach he met Ray Manzarek, a classically-trained musician Morrison already knew from his art classes at UCLA. He mentioned to Manzarek, a pianist in a local blues band, that he had written some songs, which Manzarek asked to hear. "When he sang those first lines—'Let's swim to the moon/ Let's climb through the tide/ Penetrate the evening/ That the city sleeps to hide'—I said, 'That's it,'" Manzarek recalled. "I'd never heard lyrics like that to a rock song before. . . .We decided to get a group together and make a million dollars." Manzarek enlisted a jazz drummer, John Densmore, and ex-jugband guitarist Robbie Krieger to complete the group. The Doors' name came from the title of Aldous Huxley's study of mescaline, *The Doors of Perception,* and from a William Blake quote, "There are things that are known and unknown; in between are doors."

The newly-formed group practiced for five months before debuting at a Sunset Strip club called the London Fog, where each member made five dollars on weeknights and ten dollars on the weekends. Their strange new sound was too much for the club's owner,

Full name, James Douglas Morrison; born December 8, 1943, in Melbourne, Fla.; died July 3, 1971, in Paris, France; son of George Stephen (rear admiral in the U.S. Navy) and Clara Clarke Morrison; married Pamela (died 1974). *Education:* Attended St. Petersburg Junior College, 1961-62; attended Florida State University, 1962-63; attended University of California at Los Angeles, 1964-65.

Vocalist, songwriter, poet, and filmmaker. Founding member (with Ray Manzarek, John Densmore, and Robbie Krieger) of the Doors, 1965-71. Author of poetry books, including *The Lords and the New Creatures,* Simon & Schuster, 1970; *The Bank of America of Louisiana,* Zeppelin, 1975; *Wilderness: The Writings of Jim Morrison,* Villard Books, 1988; and of film scripts, including "Feast of Friends," 1969, and "Highway," 1970.

marized Morrison's message: "To become more real, to become a better person, cut your ties to your establishment past, swim in your emotions, suffer symbolic death and rebirth—rebirth as a new man, psychologically cleansed." *Strange Days,* also released in 1967, "was one of the first concept albums. . .and certainly the most subtle," noted Michael Cuscuna in *down beat.* Amid the minor-key songs of loneliness and alienation was a raucous sexual shout, "Love Me Two Times," a song which "breaks the solemnity of the album, and points out a Doors anomaly," wrote Terry Rompers in *Trouser Press.* "Only they could play pure pop and still make a deep poetic statement on one side of an LP without skipping a beat or losing their commitment to either genre."

At the height of their popularity, the Doors played to hysterical audiences in every major rock palace in the United States. Morrison believed that these shows were more than mere opportunities to promote his hit songs. To him they were electronic musical rituals, designed to reveal his innermost fantasies and to whip the audience

> "No mere rock singer, [Jim] Morrison was both godlike and pompous, sensual and piggish, never existing on a middle ground."

into a purifying frenzy. His skintight leather clothes and the predominance of reptiles in his lyrics led to his being known as the "Lizard King," and in "Not to Touch the Earth," he proclaimed, "I am the Lizard King. . . . I can do anything." Morrison's original fans, however, felt that he had done little of note since breaking out of the underground. By the time the Doors' third album, *Waiting for the Sun,* was released in 1969, the national mood of liberation and psychic exploration that had contributed to the Doors' popularity began to crumble. Many began to see Morrison's emotional angst as somewhat absurd and overblown.

The singer's excesses were all too real, however. He was drinking heavily, and was arrested several times for disorderly conduct. When he realized that numerous policemen had been sent to cover a Doors concert in New Haven, Connecticut, Morrison began baiting them from the stage. He was arrested on charges of obscenity, but was later acquitted. The group was banned from auditoriums in Phoenix and Long Island after Morrison allegedly incited his audience to riot. "I

who let them go after four months. The Doors were on the verge of disbanding before they found their next gig, at the Whisky A-Go-Go. There they began to build a following. As they added more original songs to their repertoire, Morrison developed into a sensually powerful, extroverted stage performer. His intensity is revealed by musician Jack Ttana's description of a slow night at the Whisky, when he and Morrison's wife Pamela were the only people in the audience. Ttana recalled, "He's into 'When the Music's Over,' and he comes to the part where he freaks out and throws the mike stand on the ground—and he really did it. Even more than that. And they went offstage and Pam said, 'Why'd you do all that?' And Jim said, 'You never know when you're giving your last performance.'" On another night at the Whisky, Morrison went into an Oedipal improvisation during the song "The End," shrieking, "Father, I want to kill you. . . . Mother, I want to [piercing screams]." This was too much for the Whisky's owner, who promptly fired the group. Jac Holzman of Elektra records had been in the audience that evening, however, and he offered the Doors a lucrative recording contract with his company.

The Doors, released in 1967, rapidly sold over one million copies, and skyrocketed the band to fame. This album, with its hit single "Light My Fire," contained all the elements of the classic Doors sound: Morrison's rich imagery and preoccupation with sex and death, Manzarek's classical/rock keyboards, Krieger's versatile guitar work, and Densmore's energetic, jazz-influenced percussion. A *Disk Review* writer called it "hard rock with slippery, psychedelic overtones" and sum-

always try to get them to stand up," he explained later, "to feel free to move around anywhere they want to. It's not to precipitate a chaos situation. . . . How can you stand the anchorage of a chair and be bombarded with all this intense rhythm and not want to express it physically in movement? I like people to be free." Law enforcement officials took a dim view of Morrison's sentiments, however. He was arrested again in March 1969 after a concert in Miami where he was said to have committed "lewd and lascivious acts" onstage. After a two-month trial, he was convicted of drunkenness and exposure. That incident exacted a heavy toll from the band. Court costs were immense, numerous concert dates were cancelled, and the Doors, creatively drained, nearly disbanded.

Instead, they went back into the studio to record three more gold albums by 1971. Most music critics reacted favorably to these efforts, particularly *L.A. Woman,* which Lester Bangs called in *Rolling Stone* "the supreme statement from an uneven, occasionally brilliant band" and R. Meltzer considered the group's "greatest album." But Morrison, disillusioned with life as a rock star, left the United States for an indefinite stay in Europe. After traveling through Spain, Morocco and Corsica, he settled in Paris, where he began to write poetry and screenplays once again. He died suddenly and mysteriously on July 3, 1971, at the age of twenty-seven. Official reports stated that he had suffered a heart attack while bathing, but because his body was seen by no one but his wife, a legend has arisen that Morrison is not really dead and will someday return. His tomb is in the Poets' Corner of the Pere Lachaise cemetery in Paris, near the graves of Balzac, Moliere, and Oscar Wilde. "The significance of the Doors should not be underestimated," stated Lester Bangs. "Jim Morrison was one of the fathers of contemporary rock."

Selected discography

The Doors, Elektra, 1967.
Strange Days, Elecktra, 1967.
Waiting for the Sun, Elektra, 1968.

The Soft Parade, Elektra, 1969.
Morrison Hotel, Elektra, 1970.
Absolutely Live, Elektra, 1970.
The Doors—13, Elektra, 1970.
L.A. Woman, Elektra, 1971.
Weird Scenes Inside the Gold Mine, Elektra, 1972.
American Prayer, Elektra, 1978.

Sources

Books

Dalton, David and Lenny Kaye, *Rock 100,* Grosset & Dunlap, 1977.
Hardy, Phil and Dave Laing, *Encyclopedia of Rock,* McDonald, 1987.
Hopkins, Henry and David Sugarman, *No One Here Gets Out Alive,* Warner Books, 1980.
Jahn, Mike, *Rock: From Elvis Presley to the Rolling Stones,* Quadrangle, 1973.
Miller, Jim, editor, *The Rolling Stone Illustrated History of Rock,* Rolling Stone Press, 1976.
Williams, Paul, *Outlaw Blues,* Dutton, 1969.

Periodicals

Crawdaddy, January, 1989.
down beat, May 28, 1970.
Feature, February 1979.
Jazz & Pop, October 1969; October 1970.
Melody Maker, August 3, 1968; October 10, 1971; March 11, 1972; October 20, 1973.
Rolling Stone, October 26, 1968; July 12, 1969; August 23, 1969; April 30, 1970; October 1, 1970; January 7, 1971; May 27, 1971; January 25, 1979; October 6, 1988.
Stereo Review, April 1979.
Trouser Press, April 1979; September-October, 1980.
Village Voice, January 8, 1979.

—Joan Goldsworthy

Van Morrison

The release of Van Morrison's album *Astral Weeks* in 1969 firmly established his reputation as a uniquely gifted musician. The album has been widely praised for its music, an upbeat synthesis of jazz and rock; its romantic lyrics; and most of all for Morrison's singing, which reveals him to be "part Celtic bard, part soul singer, and part ecstatically scatting mystical visionary," according to Mike Jahn in *Rock: From Elvis Presley to Rock and Roll*. Through twenty years of experiments and stylistic phases, Morrison has retained the respect of music critics. He "remains a singer who can be compared to no performer in the history of rock and roll, a singer who cannot be pinned down, dismissed, nor fitted into anyone's expectations," wrote Greil Marcus in the *Rolling Stone Illustrated History of Rock and Roll*.

Morrison was immersed in music from his earliest childhood. His father was an avid collector of classic jazz and blues records, and his mother was a jazz singer. Morrison learned to play harmonica, guitar, and saxophone when he was quite young, and by the time he reached his teens, he was playing professionally with various jazz, blues, and rock bands around his hometown of Belfast, Northern Ireland. He even spent some time in a country and western group known as Deanie Sands and the Javelins. At fifteen, he left school to tour Europe as the saxophonist with the Monarchs, a Belfast rhythm and blues band. After the tour, Morrison remained in Germany where a director had cast him as a sax player in a movie, but the project fell through long before completion. Morrison returned to Belfast, where he opened a rhythm and blues club in the Maritime Hotel. He and some friends served as the house band, Them.

Them's intense sound quickly made them a local sensation. In 1964 they recorded two singles; one, a cover of Joe Williams's "Baby Please Don't Go," garnered a great deal of British airplay and eventually made the British top ten. Them moved to London to work with record producer Bert Berns. One of the songs Morrison wrote for the band, "Here Comes the Night," went to the number-two slot on the British record charts and broke into the U.S. top thirty. Recording with sessionmen like Jimmy Page, Them made a few more minor hits, including "Mystic Eyes" and Morrison's "Gloria," before embarking on a tour of the United States. The tour was only moderately successful, however. Morrison returned to England disgruntled by the inner workings of the music industry. He soon stopped performing altogether and returned to Belfast.

Bert Berns had moved to New York and formed Bang Records while Them toured. Upon hearing about Morrison's disillusionment, he sent the singer a plane ticket and an invitation to come to New York and record some singles for Bang. Morrison accepted the producer's offer and flew to New York in 1967. One of the singles recorded at this time, "Brown Eyed Girl," became a top-ten hit in the United States that summer. Morrison was touring when he discovered that Berns had capitalized on the success of "Brown Eyed Girl" by releasing the other singles and demos that had been cut for Bang as an album, *Blowin' Your Mind.* Although the singer was infuriated by the move, *Blowing' Your Mind* was one of "the most exciting records of the time," according to Greil Marcus, and it is still considered a classic. Berns died suddenly in December 1967, leaving Van Morrison more wary of the music business than ever and in professional limbo. Despite the popularity of "Brown Eyed Girl," his popularity vanished. Unfocused and unsure of what direction to take, he toured the East Coast briefly, playing small clubs. Then, "brooding and drinking hard, Morrison moved to Boston, where, in an incomprehensible Belfast accent, he pestered late-night DJs for John Lee Hooker sides," reported Marcus. "Once he was booed off the stage when a group that would later make up part of the J. Geils Band called him out of the audience to front their version of 'Gloria.' 'Don't you know who this man is?' Peter Wolf shouted at the hissing crowd. 'This man *wrote the song!'* But they didn't know."

Morrison appeared completely burnt out when he returned to Belfast several months later, but his hometown seemed to revitalize him. He wrote a set of introspective songs about childhood, initiation, death, and sex. Meanwhile, Warner Brothers had picked up his contract, and in 1968 he went into the studio with master jazz drummer Connie Kay of the Modern Jazz Quartet, bassist Richard Davis, and other top musicians to record the music he'd written in Belfast. In two days he cut one of the least classifiable and most enduring albums in rock, *Astral Weeks.* It is "a strange, disturbing, exalting album," according to Marcus, "for which there was little precedent in rock and roll history when it was re-leased. . . . Tempered by jazz restraint . . . and three levels of string arrangements, the disc moved with a rock beat and a rock feel. It was as serious an album as could be imagined, but it soared like an old Drifters 45. With *Astral Weeks,* Morrison opened the way to a new career, and established himself as a performer who deserved to be ranked with the creators of the very best rock and roll music."

Many people rank *Astral Weeks* among the top five or ten greatest rock albums of all time and as Morrison's best. Dave Laing and Phil Hardy wrote in their *Encyclopedia of Rock:* "It remains unique amongst his work: fresh, subtle and infinitely delicate. The lyrics are stream-of-consciousness romanticism, magically evoking a wealth of moods, feelings, locations, all superbly enhanced by the music. Tumbling and swelling gently, guitar, flute, sax, drums, and flowing acoustic bass create a finely textured backdrop for Morrison's vocals, which in turn make brilliant use of scat and repetition." Besides winning unreserved critical praise, *Astral Weeks* sold fairly well. The followup, *Moondance,* was even

> *Many people rank* Astral Weeks *among the top five or ten greatest rock albums of all time and as Van Morrison's best.*

more popular. It combined the light, jazzy style of *Astral Weeks* with the emotional vigor of Them's rhythm and blues.

In the early 1970s, Morrison married Janet Planet and moved to Marin County, California, where she had grown up. His music mellowed, reflecting his domestic contentment. The hard edge of his lyrics gave way to a romantic celebration of marital bliss, but Morrison's creativity remained intact. The influences of country music as well as blues, soul, and jazz surfaced on albums such as *Tupelo Honey* and *St. Dominic's Preview.* On his 1973 tour of Europe and North America, he was accompanied by his Caledonia Soul Orchestra, an eleven-piece group that included a string quartet. Things changed dramatically late in 1973. Morrison's marriage crumbled, and he disbanded the Caledonia Soul Orchestra to return to Belfast for the first time since 1966. After recording *Veedon Fleece,* a return to the profound ambiguities of *Astral Weeks,* he dropped out of the music scene and led a secluded life for four years.

His comeback album, 1977's *A Period of Transition*, featured short jazz and rhythm and blues tunes. It was considered disappointing by some reviewers but his next album, *Wavelength,* was solidly acclaimed. In it, Morrison expressed a new serenity, reflecting his embrace of born-again Christianity. The lyrics in "Common One," "Into the Music," "Beautiful Vision," and "Inarticulate Speech of the Heart" were filled with spiritual longing. Mark Peel related in *Stereo Review* that after this "string of brilliant, synthesizer-based albums, . . . Morrison returned to laid-back, acoustic soul-mantras and Celtic mysticism of albums like the mid-Seventies 'Veedon Fleece' on 1985's 'A Sense of Wonder.' " In 1988, Morrison collaborated with the Chieftains for another highly praised album, *Irish Heartbeat.* "It would be hard to imagine a more natural merger of pop and folk than this collaboration between Van Morrison and Ireland's preeminent old-wave traditional band, the Chieftains," wrote a *Rolling Stone* reviewer. "Yet even those expectations don't prepare one for the splendor and intense beauty of *Irish Heartbeat,* a collection of ballads that finds both acts at the top of their form."

Van Morrison's concert career has been marked by temperamental performances and chronic stage fright. At a 1979 show in New York's Palladium, he stormed offstage in the middle of a set and refused to return. Mike Jahn characterized him in *Rock: From Elvis Presley to Rock and Roll* as "a painfully introverted figure who rarely gives interviews and is at a loss to explain his own lyrics. In the studio, he can sing like a soul man getting the spirit; onstage, he tends to baffle and alienate audiences by rushing through songs and remaining noncommunicative betweeen them." But Laing points out that "at his best, Morrison is a compelling performer. Nervous, intense, he stands motionless midstage, eyes closed, while his voice seems first to take him over, then enraptures the entire theatre. Above everything, Van Morrison is a great singer. He can take a few phrases and repeat them over and over, weaving his voice around the music, gradually working his way deeper into the listener's consciousness. . . . His music is truly spellbinding."

Selected discography

Singles; with Them

"Gloria," Parrot, 1965.
"Here Comes the Night," Parrot, 1965.
"Mystic Eyes," Parrot, 1965.

Singles; for Warner Brothers, except as noted

"Brown Eyed Girl," Bang, 1967.
"Come Running," 1970.
"Domino," 1970.
"Blue Money," 1971.
"Call Me Up in Dreamland," 1971.
"Wild Night," 1971.
"Tupelo Honey," 1972.
"Jackie Wilson Said," 1972.
"Redwood Tree," 1972.
"Moon Dance," 1977.
"Wavelength," 1978.

LPs; with Them

Them (released in England as *Angry Young Men*), Parrot, 1965.
Them Again, Parrot, 1966.
Them Featuring Van Morrison, 1972.

Solo LPs; for Warner Brothers, except as noted

Blowin' Your Mind, Bang, 1967.
The Best of Van Morrison, Bang, 1967.
Astral Weeks, 1969.
Moondance, 1970.
His Band and the Street Choir, 1970.
Tupelo Honey, 1971.
Saint Dominic's Preview, 1972.
Hard Nose the Highway, 1973.
It's Too Late to Stop Now, 1974.
T.B. Sheets, Bang, 1974.
Veedon Fleece, 1974.
A Period of Transition, 1977.
Wavelength, 1978.
Into the Music, 1979.
Common One, 1980.
Beautiful Vision, 1982.
Inarticulate Speech of the Heart, 1983.
Live at the Grand Opera House, Belfast, Polygram, 1984.
A Sense of Wonder, Polygram, 1985.
No Guru, No Method, No Teacher, Polygram, 1986.
Poetic Champions Compose, Polygram, 1987.
Live for Ireland, Polygram, 1988.
Irish Heartbeat, Polygram, 1988.
Avalon Sunset, Polygram, 1989.

Sources

Books

Hardy, Phil, and Dave Laing, *Encyclopedia of Rock,* McDonald, 1987.
Jahn, Mike, *Rock: From Elvis Presley to the Rolling Stones,* Quadrangle, 1973.

Miller, Jim, ed., *The Rolling Stone Illustrated History of Rock and Roll,* Rolling Stone Press, 1976.

Periodicals

Boston Globe, July 20, 1989.
Rolling Stone, August 27, 1987; December 3, 1987; August 11, 1988.
Stereo Review, November 1986.

—*Joan Goldsworthy*

New Kids on the Block

Pop group

The 1989 pop music charts were absolutely dominated by a young group from Boston, Massachusetts, the New Kids on the Block. The New Kids—who are reported to be earning in excess of a million and a half dollars *per week*—topped the 1989 *Billboard* list for sales of both albums and singles and became the first group since 1984 to have two songs in the top ten simultaneously. Teenage fans thrill to the New Kids' sound, a well-produced pastiche of funky, obliquely sexual street music, and young girls in particular adore the clean-looking, attractive singers. *Rolling Stone* reporter Dave Wild summed up the New Kids' appeal in a *Baltimore Sun* profile, calling the group "the center of teen culture. If you're 12, they're godheads. Their faces are on the Mount Rushmore of Cuteness."

Most critics dismiss the New Kids on the Block as a "weenie band" with little genuine talent and even less originality. *Baltimore Sun* critic J. D. Considine, for one, finds the New Kids' work "more a marketing ploy than a musical statement, professionally sung but essentially silly." The group's army of female fans respectfully

disagree with this opinion, however. Considine quotes a letter he received after panning a New Kids album, written by two young ladies in Baltimore. "We feel that the New Kids are excellent singers and very talented performers (and so does the rest of America)," the letter stated. "Maybe they *are* gorgeous hunks, but we also love the street sound they produce in their music. We feel that the New Kids are trying to set a positive example to all teenagers."

The name notwithstanding, the New Kids on the Block are no strangers to the music industry. The group formed in 1985 under the management and leadership of Maurice Starr, a black musician who had engineered the success of another teenaged band, New Edition. According to Joe Logan in the *Philadelphia Inquirer,* Starr "decided that the world needed a squeaky-clean group to appeal to the millions of adolescents who live to buy records and to worship teen idols. But Starr decided that this wouldn't be just any group. It would be white, but it had to have funk. To draw from another era, this group had to be as hip as the Jackson Five but as down-home as the [Osmond Brothers]."

Starr held a city-wide talent search in Boston, auditioning numerous acts before stumbling across Donnie Wahlberg, a fifteen-year-old shoe salesman. "You could tell right away he was a genius," Starr said in the *Inquirer.* "I asked him if he could rap and he went on nonstop. He had a cool walk, a cool talk. It was beautiful." Wahlberg then introduced Starr to a few of his friends in his Dorchester neighborhood—Danny Wood and Jordan Knight. Knight brought in his older brother, Jon. The youngest member of the group, Joe McIntyre, was added to replace a singer whose parents didn't

want him to become involved in show business. Starr took this group—all teenagers at the time—and began rehearsing them relentlessly. He wrote the music, designed the dance steps, and negotiated the 1986 contract with Columbia Records.

Starr gave his young proteges a genuine baptism by fire. He signed them to live performances before black audiences—traditionally tough critics—and saw to it that they would appeal across racial lines. In fact, the New Kids were signed to Columbia's black music division, as were their predecessors George Michael and Michael Jackson. A debut album, *New Kids on the Block,* did not sell well, although the single "Be My Girl" was well-received. Undaunted, Starr and his group returned to the studio to cut *Hangin' Tough,* and they toured extensively, playing both small gigs and opening for teen star Tiffany. *Hangin' Tough* was released early in 1989, and Logan writes that when it hit, it "began to generate hysteria among teenagers. . . . When it happened, it happened fast and it happened big."

> *"We don't do drugs, we don't drink and we don't smoke. We do have water fights, but we don't tear up hotel rooms."*
> —New Kid Danny Wood

Within months, the New Kids had earned three number-one singles, "Please Don't Go Girl," "You've Got It (The Right Stuff)," and "I'll Be Loving You (Forever)." Two more songs, "Cover Girl" and "Didn't I (Blow Your Mind)" also eventually made the top ten. Concert venues in every major city sold out in record time, and extra money was generated by video sales, souvenirs, and a 900 line telephone number. Logan concludes that the New Kids, "with the help of astute management, have created a veritable money machine by combining their scrubbed good looks, acrobatic dance steps and soulful vocals with a wholesome anti-drug image. Already, they have earned untold millions as unrivaled superstars among the jump-rope set." Business analysts estimate that the New Kids on the Block will earn seventy-five million dollars in 1990.

Critics and fans agree on one proposition: the New Kids are positive role models who have somewhat singlehandedly made drinking and drug-taking seem out of vogue. All of the members are from working-class families (Wahlberg and McIntyre have eight siblings, the Knights have four, and Wood has five), they live with their parents, and they refuse any involvement with alcohol or drugs. Wood explained the image in the *Philadelphia Inquirer.* "I don't think we're clean-cut," he said. "I mean, we're clean, but we still have an edge. . . . That's the way we were before we got successful and that's how we are now. I'm not saying we're the cleanest group out there working, but we don't do drugs, we don't drink and we don't smoke. We do have water fights, but we don't tear up hotel rooms."

If history repeats itself, the future may not be too rosy for the New Kids on the Block. Traditionally, teen bands lose popularity almost as fast as they earn it. Wild told the *Baltimore Sun* that the New Kids' biggest threat is "time," adding: "It's very hard to be a teen idol—ask Bobby Sherman. Ask Shaun Cassidy." Perhaps realizing this, the New Kids are reported to be frugal with their earnings, investing rather than spending the largesse that has come their way. Speaking for his mates, Wood told the *Philadelphia Inquirer:* "I'm not a looking-to-the-future kind of guy. I just can't say what we'll be doing [in the future]. I don't know when the group will end. It is on

my mind that we might not have success forever, so I'm trying to learn to write music, producing and playing the keyboard. Hopefully, we can last."

Selected discography

New Kids on the Block, Columbia, 1986.
Hangin' Tough, Columbia, 1989.
Merry, Merry Christmas, Columbia, 1989.

Sources

Baltimore Sun, December 31, 1989.
Detroit Free Press, November 30, 1989.
Detroit News, November 30, 1989.
Philadelphia Inquirer, November 26, 1989; November 27, 1989.
Seventeen, September 1989.
Teen, January 1989; July 1989.

—*Anne Janette Johnson*

Sinead O'Connor

Singer, songwriter

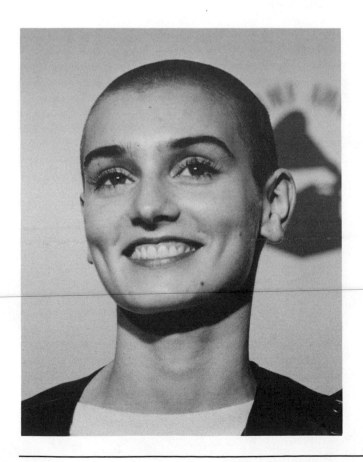

Sinead O'Connor's music is as distinctive and startling as her appearance. The debut album by this young Irishwoman, who offsets her feminine features with shapeless workclothes and a clean-shaven head, is a unique blend of pop, jazz, and Celtic sounds. Its title, *The Lion and the Cobra,* refers to a psalm about overcoming adversity—something with which O'Connor has a great deal of personal experience. After her parents separated when she was nine years old, O'Connor ran wild in the streets of Dublin. She was arrested several times for shoplifting and expelled from a series of Catholic schools before landing in reform school at the age of fourteen. "I have never—and I probably will never—experienced such panic and terror and agony over anything," she stated in *Rolling Stone.* In this "very Dickensian" place, troublemakers were punished by being forced to sleep on the floor of a hospice for the dying that was also housed in the building. "You're there in the pitch black," she recalled. "There were rats everywhere, and. . .old women moaning and vomiting," she recalled in *People.*

Ironically, O'Connor's first musical break came out of this nightmarish predicament. She had begun strumming a guitar and making up songs for emotional release; a teacher overheard and asked O'Connor to sing at her wedding. The bride's brother then asked her to cut a song with his band, In Tua Nua. O'Connor was released shortly thereafter and sent to a boarding school in Waterford, where she promptly landed in trouble again—this time for singing in pubs when she was still underage. She ran away to Dublin, where she joined a band and supported herself by busking, waitressing, and delivering telegrams in a French-maid costume.

Nigel Grainge heard O'Connor sing in 1985 and immediately asked the young performer-songwriter to come to London and record a demo tape for his company, Ensign Records. When he listened to the completed product, it was "shivers-down-the-spine-time," he told Janet Lambert in *Rolling Stone.* While waiting to begin work on her album, O'Connor met U2's guitarist, the Edge, and began working with him on the soundtrack for the 1986 film *The Captive.* Their collaboration led to her being tagged a "U2 protege," but in fact, O'Connor does not care for the group's music, which she finds "too bombastic." Simplicity, she insists, is her ideal.

When the time came to record her album in the fall of 1986, O'Connor found her plain style at odds with her producer's fondness for lush string arrangements behind lilting Celtic melodies. "I just wanted to keep it as simple as possible, with none of this mucking about with violins," explained O'Connor in *People.* Friction between artist and producer resulted in an album so

For the Record. . .

Given name pronounced Shin-ADE; born 1967 in Dublin, Ireland; daughter of a barrister and a dressmaker; one child, Jake, by John Reynolds.

Singer, songwriter. Sang on street corners and in a band in Dublin, Ireland, in the early 1980s; collaborated with the Edge on soundtrack for the 1986 film *The Captive;* recorded first album, 1987.

Addresses: c/o Chrysalis Records, 3300 Warner Blvd., Burbank, Calif., 91510.

terrible that Ensign scrapped it and let O'Connor return to the studio to produce herself. Critics had high praise for the finished product, immediately ranking O'Connor with two other boundary-stretching female vocalists, Laurie Anderson and Kate Bush. Within seconds, wrote Richard J. Grula in *Interview,* O'Connor's voice moves from "an ethereal whisper hanging over your shoulder" to "a torrid scream raging outside your window."

"[*The Lion and the Cobra*] covers an unusually wide range of ground," Lambert commented in *Rolling Stone.* "There's light, Pretenders-style pop on the first single, 'Mandinka,' syncopated dance funk on 'I Want Your (Hands on Me)' and symphonic strings on the six-and-a-half minute 'Tray.' O'Connor twists conventional song structure and stretches pop singing while maintaining her melodic sense: on 'Just Call Me Joe' her voice is a lullaby croon; on 'Never Get Old' it soars above the jazzy piano chords into ecstatic, wordless cries. There's a faint Irish aura throughout, whether in the spoken Gaelic that dramatically opens 'Never Get Old,' in the occasional snatches of folk airs or in the effective use of drone. But what really holds *Lion* together is the strong individuality of O'Connor's voice."

O'Connor, who delivered a child by her drummer, John Reynolds, shortly after completing her album, treats her accomplishments lightly. "I'm just a girl . . . I'm not different than anybody else," she insisted in *People.* "I don't ever want to get in the position where I think I'm something special just because I wrote a damn song." She maintains that her unusual hairstyle is a reflection of her love of simplicity, rather than a publicity stunt. "It makes me feel womanly because I feel natural," she explained. "It's just *there.* I don't wear makeup or jewelry except for a few rings. Inside, I don't feel simple, but I feel I look simple and I like that."

Selected discography

The Lion and the Cobra, Chrysalis, 1987.
(Contributor) *Stay Awake: Various Interpretations of Music from Vintage Disney films,* A & M, 1988.
I Do Not Want What I Haven't Got, Chrysalis, 1990.

Sources

High Fidelity, March 1988.
Interview, March 1988.
People, May 16, 1988.
Rolling Stone, April 21, 1988, January 26, 1989.
The Washingtonian, December 1988.

—*Joan Goldsworthy*

Ozzy Osbourne

Singer, songwriter

As the lead vocalist with Black Sabbath in the 1970s and throughout his solo career in the 1980s, Ozzy Osbourne has been one of the top performers in the rock and roll field known as heavy metal. With a reputation for bizarre acts and occult lyrics, he has both delighted fans and outraged critics.

Osbourne hails from Aston, a blue-collar section of Birmingham, England. He credits/blames his strange behavior to heredity, coming from a family in which lunacy was not uncommon. Osbourne has also attempted suicide on several occasions beginning as far back as age 14. After spending two months in Winson Green Prison for burglary he worked for a short period in a slaughterhouse.

In January of 1969 he formed Black Sabbath with guitarist Tommy Iommi, bassist Geezer Butler, and drummer Bill Ward. The group was originally called Polka Tulk and then Black Sabbath Earth before settling on Black Sabbath, the title of a Boris Karloff film. Although critics slammed the group, they became one of the first successful British bands patterned after the Led Zeppelin style of crunching guitars and thunderous beats. Others, including Uriah Heep and Mountain, soon followed and now, after twenty years, heavy metal is still one of the most popular styles in rock.

Osbourne sang vocals on seven Sabbath LPs as tunes like "Paranoid," and "War Pigs," and "Iron Man" soon became metal classics. Osborne claims to have been heavily into drugs, mainly LSD, during this period and his lyrics revolved around black magic and the mystical world. In *Rock 100* he stated, "We're all just simple, ordinary people who became . . . this." Osbourne left Black Sabbath on unfriendly terms in 1978 and was replaced by Dave Walker.

A few years later he signed a solo contract with Jet records and began assembling a new band to support him. The group, Blizzard of Oz, included Lee Kerslake on drums, Bob Daisley on bass (both later joined Uriah Heep) and a young guitarist named Randy Rhoads. Unfairly labeled as an Eddie Van Halen clone, Rhoads was a brilliant axeman in his own right. He proved to be innovative and imaginative in his use of the vibrato arm and fingerboard tapping and employed classical techniques as well.

Osbourne released his debut LP, *Blizzard of Oz,* in 1981 and enjoyed successful sales thanks in part to Rhoads's unique work on the tune "Crazy Train." At a Los Angeles meeting of Columbia record executives Osbourne pulled his now-famous stunt of biting the head off a dove. Delighted with the shocked reaction he had received, he tried it again a few months later at a Des Moines, Iowa, concert with a bat. It backfired, however, as the bat in turn bit Osbourne, who had to undergo a series of painful rabies shots.

Diary of a Madman (taken from the title of Aleister Crowley's autobiography and later used for Osbourne's own story) was also released in 1981 and the single "You Can't Kill Rock" received heavy FM airplay. Once again Rhoads's pyrotechnics were highlighted as "Flying High Again" sent future metalheads to their woodsheds trying to learn his guitar licks. Tragically, just twenty-five-years old, the promising guitarist's life ended on March 19, 1982 in Orlando, Florida, when the airplane he was in crashed into Osbourne's tour bus. "Randy was so unique that I don't think people will ever fully realize what a talent that guy was—not only in rock and roll, but in every other field," Osbourne told *Guitar Player*, ". . .he was the most dedicated musician I ever met in my life. He was a master of his art."

After the loss of Rhoads, Osbourne revamped his entire band by bringing in guitarist Brad Gillis (later of Night Ranger), bass player Rudi Sarzo, and Tommy Aldridge behind the drums. In 1982 the double-live LP *Speak of the Devil,* which included versions of older Black Sabbath material, was released. Gillis was replaced by yet another hot new guitarist, Jake E. Lee, for 1983's *Bark at the Moon,* which eventually reached the platinum status. The single "So Tired" was a Top 30 hit back in Osbourne's homeland of England. In May of 1983 the group was one of the many top live acts to play at California's US Festival.

Osbourne put aside his personal differences with former bandmates of Black Sabbath for a reunion gig at the July 1985 Live Aid concert in Philadelphia. Four years later Osbourne would donate a sizable chunk of the proceeds from another Philadelphia performance to AIDS research. Despite his obviously weird imagina-

tion, even Osbourne was shocked by its impact. "No one could have ever dreamed up a more insidious and evil disease," he said in the *Detroit Free Press.*

Meanwhile Osbourne was battling problems of his own. He entered both the Betty Ford Center and Hazelden Foundation in his continuing bouts with alcoholism. Although he was eventually cleared, Osbourne also faced charges after a California teen, John McCollum, took his own life after alledgedly listening to Osbourne's "Suicide Solution" from the *Blizzard* LP. He continued

> **At a Los Angeles meeting of Columbia record executives Osbourne pulled his now-famous stunt of biting the head off a dove.**

recording and in 1986 released the highly successful *Ultimate Sin* album. A single from the LP, "Shot in the Dark," went on to break the British Top 20. Osbourne paid homage to Rhoads in 1987 by issuing *Tribute,* containing previously unreleased tracks featuring the guitarist. Osbourne also discovered Zakk Wylde, his newest guitar sensation, who played on 1989's *No Rest For the Wicked* LP. Ozzy Osbourne remains one of the true madmen of heavy metal.

Writings

Author of an autobiography, *Diary of a Madman.*

Selected discography

With Black Sabbath

Black Sabbath, Warner Bros., 1970.
Paranoid, Warner Bros., 1970.
Master of Reality, Warner Bros., 1971.
Black Sabbath, Vol. 4, Warner Bros., 1972.
Sabbath, Bloody Sabbath, Warner Bros., 1973.
Sabotage, Warner Bros., 1975.
Technical Ecstasy, Warner Bros., 1976.

Solo LPs

Blizzard of Oz, CBS, 1981.
Diary of a Madman, CBS, 1981.
Speak of the Devil, CBS, 1982.
Bark at the Moon, CBS, 1983.

The Ultimate Sin, CBS, 1986.
Tribute, CBS, 1987.
No Rest for the Wicked, CBS, 1989.

Sources

Books

Christgau, Robert, *Christgau's Record Guide,* Ticknor & Fields, 1981.

Dalton, David, and Lenny Kay, *Rock 100,* Grosset & Dunlap, 1977.

Nite, Norm N., and Charles Crespo, *Rock On,* Volume 3, Harper, 1985.

The Harmony Illustrated Encyclopedia of Rock, Salamander, 1988.

The Illustrated Encyclopedia of Rock, compiled by Nick Logan and Bob Woffinden, Harmony, 1977.

Rock Movers and Shakers, edited by Barry Lazell with Dafydd Rees and Luke Crampton, Banson, 1989.

The Rolling Stone Encyclopedia of Rock and Roll, edited by Jon Pareles and Patricia Romanowski, Rolling Stone Press/Summit, 1983.

The Rolling Stone Record Guide, edited by Dave Marsh with John Swenson, Rolling Stone Press/Random House, 1979.

Periodicals

Detroit Free Press, May 1, 1989.
Guitar Player, November 1982; April 1983.
People, July 10, 1989.

—*Calen D. Stone*

K.T. Oslin

Country singer

Kay Toinette Oslin's sudden success as a vocalist marks a new trend in country music. Well into her forties—and just slightly overweight—Oslin hardly projects the image of beauty and submissiveness long associated with female country singers. Her songs too follow a different path: rather than "standing by her man," she extols the virtues of ogling young cuties and offers tributes to mature womanhood. Oslin labored in obscurity and poverty for more than twenty years, and was on the verge of quitting before her 1987 album, *80's Ladies,* went gold. Since then she has ridden the top of the country charts, both with her debut effort and with her follow-up album, *This Woman.*

"With K.T.'s years of struggle as their foundation," writes a *Ladies Home Journal* contributor, "both *80's Ladies* and *This Woman* give the perspective of a mature woman of experience." Oslin writes her own songs, drawing upon her life as she ages for themes. *Life* magazine correspondent Karen Emmons describes Oslin's work as "laments for girlhood, bleats of woe and wrenching love, but the voice and the point of view are distinctive and anything but forlorn. She may be a hurtin' woman, but she still knows how to have fun." Emmons adds that the number one song "80's Ladies," Oslin's first chart-topper, "[swept] a generation of former girls like a subliminal anthem." If there is anything subliminal in Oslin's songs, it is the suggestion that women can continue to have passion and promise as they enter middle age. Country music fans—both male and female—seem ready to embrace that idea.

Oslin was born in Crossit, Arkansas, to a working-class family. Her father died when she was five, and she was raised by her mother and grandmother, "two women who had to make their own way in life," to use her words. Oslin's mother had had show business ambitions, but she put them aside to work as a lab technician. Oslin was not so inclined. After studying drama at a small Texas college, she landed a job with the chorus of the *Hello, Dolly!* touring company. Eventually she found her way to New York City, where she earned chorus roles in such Broadway musicals as *West Side Story* and *Promises, Promises.* "New York spelled terror for me," Oslin told *People* magazine. "I'm from the suburbs. I'm from yards. My first apartment had five locks on the door and a bathtub in the kitchen."

Oslin soon found herself making television commercials, many of which pictured her as a happy housewife "babbling about my husband's hemorrhoids." Such work paid the bills—barely—but it did not satisfy Oslin's creative longings. Surprising even herself, she began to write country songs. She had never been a great fan of country music, she told *People,* but when she began to write, her pieces "were very definitely country. . . . They just came out that way." Oslin sold several songs to other recording artists before landing an Elektra contract in 1980. The single she released for Elektra, an early version of "Younger Men," failed to make the charts, so she lost her contract. At that point, Oslin told *People,* she was almost ready to give up. "I got real fat and I got real depressed," she said.

In a last-ditch effort to launch a career, Oslin borrowed $7000 from her aunt and mounted a showcase for Nashville's record executives. The 1986 production was well attended, but it failed to win her a contract. Desperate, she sent a copy of *80's Ladies* to RCA Records, and within months her first album was released. Nine years after writing her first song, Oslin found herself in the limelight at last. Her debut album climbed the country charts at a record-setting pace, she won the coveted Grammy Award for country vocal performance, and she was invited to tour with Alabama. She was forty-four at the time.

Oslin has no illusions about her success. "There are a million beautiful young women singers," she told *People.* "I am not one of them. Writing is the key to all of this success for me." Oslin's themes—once deemed too depressing by at least one Nashville executive—are indeed the strong point of her work. However, she possesses a strong, well-trained voice and a charming stage presence, both of which add to her performance. Her backup band, "Live Bait," consists of four handsome young men. Oslin tells audiences that her band members were chosen for their looks, because "I spend a lot of time on the bus, and I ain't gonna look at no ugly boys."

Oslin actually believes that her age has worked to her advantage in an industry where youth has traditionally been a prerequisite. "I let people know forty isn't the age to pack it in," she told the *Ladies Home Journal.* In *People* she expressed her gratitude and wonder another way. Now, when she performs, she said, "young 20-year-old boys come up to me and give me flowers. I'm talkin' real cuties." Asked if she regrets all the years she spent in obscurity, Kay Toinette Oslin responded, "I'd rather be starting now than ending now."

Selected discography

80's Ladies, RCA, 1987.
This Woman, RCA, 1989.

Sources

Ladies Home Journal, November 1988.
Life, October 1988.
People, June 6, 1988.

—*Anne Janette Johnson*

Donny Osmond

Singer

Donny Osmond has seen success in many guises during his career as a singer. Beginning as a member of the Osmonds with his older brothers in the mid-1960s, he branched out to become a solo teen idol during the 1970s. With his sister, Marie Osmond, he also hosted a television variety series for three years. After a long period of fading popularity due to what David Wild in *Rolling Stone* called his "squeaky-clean image," Osmond grabbed the spotlight again with his 1989 album, *Donny Osmond,* which has yielded two hit singles—"Soldier of Love" and "Sacred Emotion."

Born Donald Clark Osmond December 9, 1957, in Ogden, Utah, to Mormon parents, the singer's story really begins with his older brothers. Alan, Wayne, Merrill, and Jay Osmond had already garnered some measure of fame by the time Donny was ready to join their group. They had begun performing in church; as their reputation spread, the Osmonds sang at Mormon houses of worship throughout the western United States. Eventually they won a stint crooning at Disneyland, and appeared on Andy Williams's television variety show. Their specialty—for secular performances—was barbershop-style harmony, but a few years after Donny made the Osmonds a quintet, they won a contract with MGM Records and became pop-oriented.

With Donny as their lead singer, the Osmond Brothers scored their first big hit in 1971, the number-one single "One Bad Apple." During the same year, Donny launched his solo career with the top ten hit "Sweet and Innocent" and the even more successful "Go Away Little Girl," a remake of a song that had already been a hit twice—once for Steve Lawrence and once for the Happenings. For the remainder of the early 1970s Donny divided his musical efforts, continuing to record with his brothers, but also making several solo albums, including *To You With Love, Too Young,* and *Alone Together*. He scored chart hits with the singles "Puppy Love"—a remake of the old Paul Anka song, "Why," and "Too Young."

From 1974 to 1979, the most successful facet of Donny Osmond's career was that involving his sister, Marie. She had come to solo success in the country music genre with the 1973 smash "Paper Roses," and had a follow-up hit, "I'm Leaving It All Up to You," with Donny the next year. They made a total of five albums together; after the first two, however, they were signed by the American Broadcasting Corporation (ABC) to host a television variety show. Though the series proved popular enough to last three years—an impressive accomplishment during the late 1970s—Donny and the other Osmonds were having problems with their image. As Wild put it, they "were so unhip as to be anachronisms." Because of the Osmond family's commitment to the Church of Latter-day Saints (Mormons), Donny and his

and leather jacket, which led many critics to make comparisons with pop artist George Michael. Osmond denies Michael's influence.

All of Osmond's efforts have paid off, however, for his 1989 album *Donny Osmond* is a resounding success. The first single, "Soldier of Love," which Wild described as "an infectious . . . dance-rock number," reached the number two position on the charts. He scored a follow-

---

"The show was great—we had to stop it twice on opening night for standing ovations. Then the reviews came out. All they could talk about was my image."
—Donny Osmond

---

up hit with the love ballad "Sacred Emotion." Another cut from the album, "Secret Touch," was inspired by Osmond's courtship of his wife; he says that he had to date her in secret for three years because of the constant attention he received as a teen idol. Osmond is thrilled by the airplay that his 1989 hits have received. "This is the first time radio people are playing my record[s] because they *want* to," he commented to Wild. "Back in the Seventies, they played 'em because they had to."

siblings wished to put forth only wholesome entertainment, suitable for the entire family. This attitude was seen as old-fashioned and unrealistic by critics, and by much of the music audience. Donny (and the other singing Osmonds) always, however, managed to hold on to a small but devoted following for their records.

In 1980 the Osmond Brothers stopped recording for two years; when they came back together, Donny did not join them. Instead, he concentrated on the production aspect of the music industry, and one of his more noteworthy accomplishments in this area was directing a television special for pop and jazz artist Grover Washington, Jr. He also starred in a revival of the Broadway musical "Little Johnny Jones," but the problem of his wholesome reputation followed him to the stage. Osmond told Wild: "The show was great—we had to stop it twice on opening night for standing ovations. Then the reviews came out. All they could talk about was my image." The show was thus shortlived.

But according to Wild, the experience brought home to Osmond just how big an obstacle he had to overcome to regain success. Nevertheless, he remained determined, and fought hard for another chance at recording. He was almost chosen as the lead singer for a fledgling group called Air Play, and he made a cameo appearance in a video for fellow musician Jeff Beck. But Osmond credits rock star Peter Gabriel with helping him back to the charts. Not only did he allow Osmond to use his recording studio in Bath, England, but "he gave me credibility," Osmond admitted to Wild. Osmond also took on a new look in hopes of defeating his image problem, featuring a stubbly beard, jeans,

Selected discography

Solo LPs

The Donny Osmond Album, MGM, 1971.
To You With Love, MGM, 1971.
Portrait of Donny, MGM, 1972.
Too Young, MGM, 1972.
Alone Together, MGM, 1973.
Disco Train, Polygram, 1976.
Donald Clark Osmond, Polygram, 1977.
Donny Osmond (includes "Soldier of Love," "Sacred Emotion," and "Secret Touch"), Capitol, 1989.

LPs; with the Osmond Brothers

The Osmonds, MGM, 1971.
Homemade, MGM, 1971.
Phase III, MGM, 1972.
Crazy Horses, MGM, 1972.

The Plan, MGM, 1973.
Around the World Live in Concert, MGM, 1976.
Osmonds' Christmas Album, Polygram, 1976.
Brainstorm, Polygram, 1976.
Osmonds' Greatest Hits, Polygram, 1977.
Steppin' Out, Mercury, 1978.

LPs; with Marie Osmond

I'm Leaving It All Up to You, MGM, 1974.
Make the World Go Away, MGM, c. 1975.
New Season, Polygram, 1976.
Winning Combination, Polygram, 1978.
Goin' Coconuts, Polygram, 1978.

Sources

Books

Daly, Marsha, *Osmonds: A Family Biography,* St. Martin's, 1983.
Dunn, Paul H., *The Osmonds,* Avon, 1977.

Periodicals

Rolling Stone, August 10, 1989.

—Elizabeth Thomas

Mandy Patinkin

Singer; actor

Mandy Patinkin is "the greatest singer of theater music that we have," according to critic Daniel Okrent in *Esquire*. His first singing role on Broadway, that of Che Guevara in the popular musical "Evita," won him the coveted Antoinette Perry (Tony) Award. He has since increased his fame through performances in Stephen Sondheim's "Sunday in the Park with George," on soundtrack recordings of Sondheim's "Follies," and Rogers and Hammerstein's "South Pacific." His 1989 debut solo album of show tunes was not only acclaimed by reviewers, but turned in impressive sales figures as well. But singing is not Patinkin's sole talent. As Okrent revealed, he is a powerful screen and stage presence as well: "Watch Patinkin act, and it's too easy to forget how brilliantly he sings." His film roles have included such diverse parts as the earnest swashbuckler Inigo Montoya in *The Princess Bride* and a ruthless, McCarthy-era lawyer in *The House on Carroll Street*.

Patinkin was born Mandel Patinkin in Chicago, Illinois, during the early 1950s, to Jewish parents in the scrap metal business. He began singing at his synagogue when he was eight years old. As he told Cathleen McGuigan of *Newsweek,* there is still "a certain cry that I get like the cry a cantor makes." When Patinkin grew a little older, his mother encouraged him to participate in community theater. But when the young man decided to pursue a career in acting, his parents worried—they considered scrap metal a much more dependable source of income than dramatic talent. After a few years attending classes at the University of Kansas, Patinkin transferred to New York City's famed school, Juilliard.

When Patinkin auditioned for the 1979 play "Evita," he had not concentrated on singing for eight years. Nevertheless, he won the role and quickly became a renowned feature of the Broadway scene. But after he won the Tony Award he lost no time furthering his career as an actor in nonsinging parts. One of his first major film roles was that of Avigdor, the romantic lead in singer-actress Barbra Streisand's *Yentl*. John Stark quoted Streisand on the subject of Patinkin in *People* magazine: "He totally surprised me with his original approach. He was unpredictable, emotionally volatile and very gifted, and that was exciting for me as a director." Other films followed, including two based on E. L. Doctorow novels, *Ragtime* and *Daniel*. In the latter, Patinkin played a character based on Julius Rosenberg, an American communist accused of treason and executed. Sidney Lumet, who directed *Daniel,* told Nora Peck in *Cosmopolitan:* "Mandy is just a bolt of lightning. He's a giant actor, a blinding talent."

Patinkin has more or less divided his professional time between singing and acting. Another of his Broadway triumphs was the long-running "Sunday in the Park with

George," which a *People* critic hailed as "a show to see, savor, and see again." The same critic pronounced Patinkin's performance as Impressionist painter Georges Seurat, "perfect." Patinkin's talent is so wide-ranging that he even garners rave reviews as a Shakespearean actor; Jack Kroll critiquing him in a 1989 production of "A Winter's Tale" showered him with praise in *Newsweek:* "Mandy Patinkin gives one of those rare performances that's both truly American and deeply Shakespearean. [He] is really scary as the jealous Leontes." Echoing such sentiments in *New Republic,* reviewer Robert Brustein labeled Patinkin's appearance in the play "riveting."

But Patinkin's excellence in performance is purchased at a high price. He revealed to Stark that he is too much of a perfectionist for his own good. As Stark phrased it, Patinkin is "a standout worrier in a profession known for its neurotics. . . . He is quite capable of worrying himself sick, and his constant anxiety about his career and how to portray a given role correctly, has, on more than one occasion, driven employers, friends and Patinkin him-

self to distraction." Speaking of the first solo singing appearance he made at New York City's Public Theater to coincide with the release of his debut album *Mandy Patinkin,* he confided to Stark: "Two days before the concert I broke out in hives and welts. They were ready to medicate me." He also said, about any of his live performances, "if you're coming to see me, don't ever tell me. If I know someone is coming, be it a cabdriver, the doorman or a relative, I'll freak."

In the instance of the Public Theater concert, Patinkin's fears were totally unwarranted. Stark called it "two and a half hours of Broadway and Tin Pan Alley tunes delivered with an emotional wallop that could make even Liza Minnelli seem limp." As for Patinkin's 1989 album, it is a more permanent showcase for his voice, which has been variously described as "a fine, clean tenor" by McGuigan, and as simply "gorgeous" by Peck. Cuts like "Over the Rainbow" and "Soliloquy" from "Carousel" have been singled out for praise by both McGuigan and Okrent; other standout tunes include "No One Is Alone," from Sondheim's "Into the Woods," and "Once upon a Time." Okrent summed the singer thus: "He has impeccable phrasing, his diction [is] nearly supernatural, his shining tenor [is] an instrument of absolute purity."

Selected discography

LPs

Mandy Patinkin (includes "Over the Rainbow," "Soliloquy," "Into the Woods," "Once upon a Time," "Sonny Boy," "Puttin' on the Ritz," and "I'll Be Seeing You"), CBS Records, 1989.

Also featured on soundtrack albums of "South Pacific" and "Follies."

Sources

Cosmopolitan, January 1988.
Esquire, April 1989.
New Republic, May 8, 1989.
Newsweek, February 20, 1989; April 3, 1989.
People, February 17, 1986; May 8, 1989.

—*Elizabeth Thomas*

Minnie Pearl

Comedienne; singer

With her trademark straw hat dangling its price tag and her raucous "How-dee!" Minnie Pearl has established a forty-year reign as the queen of country comedy. The decidedly down-home Minnie is the alter ego of Sarah Colley Cannon, a refined and educated native of Centerville, Tennessee. Cannon began performing as Minnie Pearl in 1940 on the Grand Ole Opry, and some might argue that her face and voice are the most famous ever to emerge from that show. "Minnie Pearl seems indestructible," writes Leah Rozen in *People* magazine. "There may be newer and hipper characters, but for . . . years now the nation has settled back happily and laughed every time Minnie has barged onstage."

Sarah Ophelia Colley was born October 25, 1912, the youngest of five daughters. Her family was among the most well-to-do in tiny Centerville because her father owned the local lumber business. Reared in a home where education and refinement were paramount—a situation she finds ironic today, given the hayseed nature of her comic character—Colley was expected to do well in school and to attend college. At eighteen she entered Ward-Belmont College, an expensive finishing school in Nashville, where she majored in drama and dance. A flair for comedy had taken root by that time, quite against her will. "Even when I did serious parts I got laughs," she told *People*.

After graduation Colley returned to her hometown, where she taught dancing and drama for two years. Decorum demanded that she reach the age of twenty-one before she could travel on her own, and she spent the two years dreaming of a Broadway career. When she finally turned twenty-one she took employment with the Wayne P. Sewall Production Company, an Atlanta-based outfit that sent directors to small communities to stage plays and variety shows. Colley worked for the company for six years, from 1934 until 1940, and she travelled throughout the South into all the tiniest mountain villages. As she journeyed from place to place she picked up stories, songs, and impressions that she stored with no particular purpose in mind.

"I went on the road, and put on these amateur shows, and I met a lot of Minnie Pearls," she remembered in *Behind Closed Doors: Talking to the Legends of Country Music*. "I met a lot of country girls who didn't win the beauty contest, but wanted to be funny, and wanted to be loved and wanted to love people." Gradually, Sarah Ophelia Colley realized that she too was one of these women. She began doing small bits of comedy, adopting Minnie Pearl because it combined two popular Southern names. The final inspiration for Minnie Pearl came from a mother of sixteen who lived in a cabin on Brenlee Mountain in Alabama. "I came away from there

For the Record. . .

Full name Sarah Ophelia Colley Cannon; born October 25, 1912, in Centerville, Tenn.; daughter of Thomas K. (a lumber mill owner) and Fannie (Tate) Colley; married Henry Cannon (a pilot), 1947. *Education:* Graduate of Ward-Belmont College, Nashville, Tenn.

Travelling director and drama coach for Wayne P. Sewall Production Co., Atlanta, Ga., 1934-40; comic-singer on Grand Ole Opry and elsewhere, 1940—. Regular performer on "Hee Haw," 1969—, and "Nashville Now." Appeared on "Comic Relief" special to aid the homeless, Home Box Office, 1986.

Awards: Named Nashville's Woman of the Year, 1965; elected to Country Music Hall of Fame, 1975; recipient of the Courage Award from the American Cancer Society and the Pioneer Award from the Academy of Country Music, both 1987.

Addresses: Other— Halsey, 1111 Sixteenth Avenue South, Nashville, TN 37212.

Minnie Pearl was nominated to the Country Music Hall of Fame fourteen times before she was finally inducted in 1975. The long wait for the industry's highest honor was no doubt related to the fact that Minnie Pearl has done little real singing over the years; only once, in 1966, did she place a song, "The Answer to Giddyup Go," on the country charts. Her inclusion in the Country Music Hall of Fame—and a subsequent Pioneer Award from the Academy of Country Music—reflect the fact that Minnie Pearl's brand of hayseed comedy is an art form with a tradition as honorable as any musical one.

Having celebrated her fiftieth anniversary as Minnie Pearl in 1990, Sarah Ophelia Colley Cannon plans to keep performing, at least on the Opry. Describing her character, whom she views as an eccentric sister, Colley Cannon said: "Minnie Pearl is just as wild as a can of crab. She's nutty as a fruitcake. She doesn't care whether school keeps or not. She's great. I'm stupid, but she's great. And the reason she's great is because she doesn't try to be serious. She just worries about whether we're going to have the church social on Friday night or Saturday night or Sunday night. And about what she's going to wear, and if a feller is going to kiss her on the way home. Most of the time he doesn't. But she thinks next time he will."

imitating her," Colley said. "Not mocking her, but imitating her. That's when Minnie Pearl was actually born."

Colley was earning a sparse living from the Works Progress Administration in 1940 when she entertained a banker's convention as Minnie Pearl. One of the conventioneers paved her way to an audition at the Grand Ole Opry, and soon she was a regular. She would appear on the Opry at night and then travel all week with one of the touring units; often she was the only woman in the group. Her trademark price tag became a part of the act quite by chance, when she literally forgot to cut the tag off some plastic flowers she had added to her straw hat. The price—$1.98—has never changed.

Colley had been working as Minnie Pearl at a grueling pace for seven years when she met her husband, Henry Cannon. Cannon was a licensed pilot who owned a charter service, and after their marriage he flew his popular wife and her co-workers to their live concerts. Thus marriage hardly altered Minnie Pearl's busy schedule. Over the years, as she played bigger venues and moral standards changed, Minnie became slightly more racy and much rowdier. Her costume has not been altered, however, and many of her one-liners are resurrected from scripts that are decades old. "All those dumb jokes," she recalled in *People.* "They're all old. They're all dumb. The minute I look at a joke, it comes back to me."

Selected discography

Minnie Pearl, Everest.
Monologue, RCA.
How To Catch a Man, RCA.
Cousin Minnie, Starday.
(With Grandpa Jones) *Grand Ole Opry Stars,* RCA.
(Contributor) *Stars of the Grand Ole Opry,* RCA.

Sources

Books

The Illustrated Encyclopedia of Country Music, Harmony, 1977.
Nash, Alanna, *Behind Closed Doors: Talking with the Legends of Country Music,* Knopf, 1988.
Shestack, Melvin, *The Country Music Encyclopedia,* Crowell, 1974.
Stambler, Irwin and Grelun Landon, *The Encyclopedia of Folk, Country, and Western Music,* St. Martin's, 1969.

Periodicals

People, October 26, 1987.

—Anne Janette Johnson

Teddy Pendergrass

Singer

Teddy Pendergrass's fame and fortune were built on his provocative stage presence and the intimate rapport he established with his audiences. Female fans frequently swooned or tossed their undergarments onstage in response to his earthy baritone and forthright sexuality; one fan even went so far as to shoot another in a struggle for a scarf the singer had used to wipe his face. Pendergrass was at the height of his popularity when a car accident left him a quadriplegic—unable to feed or dress himself, let alone execute his charismatic stage moves. He could still sing, however, and within two years of the accident he had released his comeback album. His fans remained loyal, and many critics declared that Pendergrass's tragedy had brought new depth to his music.

Pendergrass began his career in 1968, not as a singer, but as the drummer for Harold Melvin and the Blue Notes. Within two years he had ascended to lead vocalist, and his personal sound came to define the group. In their *Encyclopedia of Rock,* Dave Hardy and Phil Laing described Pendergrass's singing on Blue Notes hits such as "The Love I Lost," "I Miss You," and "If You Don't Know Me by Now," as "tough, powerful . . . mixing the styles of gospel and blues shouters whose intense delivery blended bravado and impassioned pleading in equal measure." He combined an "earthy, sexual insistence on the more aggressively paced pieces with mellow, moodier vocal work on ballads, which he'd gradually infuse with wilder, improvised and often quite histrionic outbursts."

In 1977, Pendergrass left the Blue Notes to pursue a solo career. Women were even more enthusiastic about seeing him alone on stage than they had been about watching him front the Blue Notes. They flocked to special "For Women Only" midnight shows to hear Pendergrass sing "Close the Door," "Turn Off the Lights," and other hits. As a solo performer, Pendergrass expanded his range to attract new listeners: a *Stereo Review* writer noted that while he still "belted out his funky amorous entreaties with a raw virility that set many female libidos a-quiver," he had also learned to "set aside his club and loincloth to sing tenderly," thereby "reaching both those who like sweetness and those who prefer swagger." Nearly all his albums went platinum, and Pendergrass was acknowledged as the premier black sex symbol of the late 1970s.

Things changed dramatically on March 18, 1982. While Pendergrass was driving his Rolls-Royce through Philadelphia's Germantown section, the vehicle jumped the center median and crashed into a tree. Pendergrass told *Life:* "[After] the initial bang I opened my eyes, and I was still there. For a while I was conscious. I know I had broken my neck. It was obvious; I tried to make a move

From the outset, he was determined that his handicap would not stop his career. "I thrive on whatever kind of challenge I have to face" he told Charles L. Sanders in *Ebony*. "My philosophy has always been 'Bring me a brick wall, and if I can't jump over it I'll run right through it." After months of special therapy, including exercising with a heavy weight on his stomach in order to build up his weakened diaphragm, Pendergrass recorded *Love Language*. It became his sixth platinum album, affirming both his musical abilities and his fans' loyalty. Another milestone in the singer's recovery came at the 1985 Live Aid concert, when he made his first stage appearance since the accident, singing "Reach Out and Touch" with Ashford and Simpson. "I don't know how to fully describe those few moments onstage," he confessed in *People*. "Before I went on, I was scared,

and I couldn't." Pendergrass was correct in thinking that his neck was broken; his spinal cord was also crushed, and bone fragments had severed some vital nerves. Movement was limited to his head, shoulders, and biceps. When the full extent of the damage became apparent and doctors told him that his paralysis would probably be permanent, Pendergrass cried until his "eyes looked like golf balls," he told *Life*. He was further informed that injuries such as his usually affect the breathing muscles and, consequently, the ability to sing. Several days after the accident, Pendergrass cautiously tested his voice by singing along with a coffee commercial on television. "I could sing," he remembered, "and I knew that anything else I had to do, I could do."

Pendergrass's first task was to ride out the ugly rumors that surrounded his mishap. He had been driving on a suspended license, and stories quickly spread that he was drunk or drugged when it occurred. After investigating the incident, Philadelphia police announced that they found no evidence of substance abuse in connection with it, although they speculated that reckless driving and excessive speed were involved. Next, it was revealed that Pendergrass's passenger, Tenika Watson, who was not seriously injured in the crash, was a transsexual entertainer. The former John F. Watson admitted to some thirty-seven arrests for prostitution and related offenses over a ten-year period. This news was potentially very damaging to Pendergrass's image as the ultimate macho man, but his fans quickly accepted his statement that he had merely offered a ride to a casual acquaintance and had no knowledge of Watson's occupation or history.

Once released from the hospital, Pendergrass faced the difficult period of adjustment to his new limitations.

> *Pendergrass was at the height of his popularity when a car accident left him a quadriplegic.*

afraid of the unknown. Afterward I felt like I was larger than anybody there. It reaffirmed one very important fact to me, that it wasn't important that I shook my booty right or that I had legs that turned a certain way. What the audience most appreciated was what I was saying in the song."

"I ain't going to lie, this thing's a bitch," Pendergrass said of his paralysis. "You go through living hell, through all kinds of anxieties, and you suffer enormous apprehensions about everything. At first you don't know how people will accept you, and you don't want to be seen. You don't want to do anything. Given thoughts like that, you don't want to live. But . . . you have an option. You can give it up and call it quits, or you can go on. I've decided to go on."

Selected discography

Solo LPs

Life Is a Song Worth Singing, Philadelphia International, 1978.
Teddy, Philadelphia International, 1979.
T.P., Philadelphia International, 1980.
Live Coast to Coast, Philadelphia International, 1980.
It's Time for Teddy, Philadelphia International, 1981.
Teddy Pendergrass, Philadelphia International, 1982.
This One's For You, Philadelphia International, 1982.

Heaven Only Knows, Philadelphia International, 1983.
Greatest Hits, Philadephia International, 1984.
Love Language, Asylum, 1984.
Workin' It Back, Asylum, 1985.
Joy, Asylum, 1988.

Sources

Books

Hardy, Phil and Dave Laing, *Encyclopedia of Rock,* Macdonald, 1987.

Periodicals

Ebony, September 1984; February 1989.
Jct, December 18, 1980; April 5, 1982; April 19, 1982; May 17, 1982; May 31, 1982; July 6, 1987; July 20, 1987.
Life, June 1984.
People, January 13, 1986; June 27, 1988.
Stereo Review, December 1982; March 1984; June 1986.

—Joan Goldsworthy

Petra

Christian rock band

From the Greek word for "rock," Petra, one of the strongest voices in popular Christian music, takes its name and its purpose. The group is committed to delivering "quality, no compromise Christian music" that runs the gamut from hard rock to lyrical ballads and lush harmonies. Petra was founded by Bob Hartman in 1972 while he was attending the Christian Training Center in Fort Wayne, Indiana. With three other students, Hartman began playing around the Fort Wayne area, meeting opposition from many churches whose attitude toward rock music was decidedly negative. To many Christians the rock and roll sound was considered, very simply, evil. Petra disagreed. Said Paul Jackson, the group's business manager, "To say that rock and roll is evil is to give Satan credit for creating it. Satan created nothing. Satan robs and steals. We ask anyone to look at the fruit . . . these are young people whose lives have taken positive directions because of the minsitry of this band."

With the backing of their college the group managed to play some venues, and gradually, according to the

Petra press kit, they became "more aware of the potential of their music." Late in 1973 the band auditioned for Word Records and was accepted onto their newly formed contemporary label, Myrrh. Their subsequent recordings, a self-titled album released in 1974 followed by *Come and Join Us* in 1977, met with modest success, opening the door to a brand new market. Reported Michael Levans in the *Chicago Tribune,* "This wasn't the same old church hymn or gospel sing-along; this was music that carried the Christian message to a younger generation through the same crunching rock chords and hip phrasing that was being used by other bands in the early '70s." It wasn't until 1979 that, as the lead act on Star Song Records, Petra achieved a hit. "Why Should the Father Bother," from their *Washes Whiter Than* album, provided the band with the airplay needed to popularize them on a national level.

The following year drummer Louie Weaver joined the band, and in 1982 the group spent 300 days on the road promoting their *Never Say Die* album, which features Petra standards "The Coloring Song" and "For Annie," a gently rendered but pointed ballad about the tragedy of teen suicide. In 1983 the band did a marathon 240-day tour promoting *More Power To Ya* and *Not of This World,* both widely varied in their use of heavy metal sounds of pounding drums and sharp-edged vocals ("Second Wind" and "Judas Kiss") as well as melodic ballads with strong harmonies ("More Power To Ya," "Road to Zion," "Not of This World"). Remarkably, Petra's songwriters, including the band's own Hartman and lead singer Greg Volz, showed the keen ability to combine verbatim passages from Bible scriptures with the music most appealing to the young audiences the band sought to reach. With the release

of these albums, the group became an "'overnight success' after ten hard years of struggle."

While their next album would not be out until 1985, 1984 marked the first time Petra's work began to be recognized by the music industry. They received both a Grammy nomination (contemporary gospel group) and two nominations for the Dove Award from the Gospel Music Association. Many more would follow.

In 1985 Petra added John Lawry, a top Christian keyboardist formerly of the Joe English Band, and recorded *Beat The System,* a slick, fast-paced contemporary-sounding rock album that might easily do well on a secular radio station's playlist, given the chance. "It Is Finished," a driving, almost militant retelling of the Crucifixion of Christ, became one of the group's most popular live performance songs, with concertgoers joining in on the thundering chorus. "Hollow Eyes" effectively laments the situation of children starving in Nigeria; "Witch Hunt" attacks subgroups within the Christian faith who are off on "another Witch

> *"Petra remains the biggest name [in Christian music] with the least amount of Christian radio play."*
> —Evan James

Hunt looking for evil wherever [they] can find it; off on a tangent, hope the Lord won't mind it."

The band's next change in personnel resulted when Greg Volz made the decision to pursue a solo career. The slot was quickly filled by John Schlitt, a former member of the secular rock band Head East. According to *Performance,* after becoming a Christian, Schlitt had almost given up rock entirely until Bob Hartman contacted him. Wrote Jackson, "John Schlitt has brought a new dimension into the band. . . . There has in the past been a certain . . . well, mystique about Petra, not that that was deliberate; it just turned out that way. Now we are trying to make the band more accessible."

Making Petra more accessible has included the band's participation in school assemblies and speaking to youth groups. Their 1986 album, *Back to the Street,* reflects this slight change in direction—moving back from the slick, high-tech earlier efforts to a more straightforward rock and roll sound. All the same, the album is professional through and through, the music and lyrics just as creative, as precise and telling as in the past. *This Means War!,* released in 1987 and climbing immediately into the number one position on national Christian album sales charts, continued in what could be labeled a "back to basics rock and roll" direction. According to the Petra press kit, *This Means War!* outsold "the number two album by as wide a margin as three to one in some parts of the country and remained at the top spot on the charts throughout the end of 1987 and into 1988." The strength of the band's message and international appeal became apparent when, in 1988, the album was named Holland's contemporary Christian album of the year.

That year also marked the arrival of the band's new bass guitarist, Ronny Cates, a native of Shreveport, Louisiana. He joined in time to play on the *On Fire!* album, which has been called the "hardest rocking Petra album ever." Singles "First Love" and "Mine Field" filled the number one and three slots of *Musicline's* four airplay charts as the group prepared for an international tour that would take them across the United States, Australia, and Europe. Said Evan James, program director of a Cleveland radio station, "this recording captures a raw musical power that reaches all the way into the headbanger's realm—'All Fired Up,' 'Hits You Where You Live' . . . however, [it] does not totally abandon the Petra 'power pop' stronghold . . . 'First Love' and 'The Homeless Few' satisfy the need for softer cuts."

Despite their popularity and numerous honors and awards, opposition to the group continues. Petra's sound (but not content) is often faulted for being too secular. Said James, "Petra remains the biggest name with the least amount of Christian radio play." In response, the group's members simply rock on, emphasizing a ministry that reaches young people, delivering a message to them in a language they can understand. The message, according to Hartman, is twofold. First is the ministry. The second part is the music as the device to deliver the message in a direct, "hit-you-where-you-live" manner. "Being on fire for God is not some ethereal state of mind that we psych ourselves into," Hartman asserts, "Neither is it a one-time experience that we receive from God. It is a daily dying to self that begins in the inner man and works its way out into our lives. We become a 'defector' from our previous habits, our concept of Christian charity will be readjusted, . . . and we will truly be a light to a world that is 'dying to know He lives.'"

Selected discography

Petra, Myrrh, 1974.
Come and Join Us, Myrrh, 1977.
Washes Whiter Than, Star Song, 1979.
Never Say Die, Star Song, 1982.
More Power To Ya, Star Song, 1983.
Not of This World, Star Song, 1983.
Beat The System, Star Song, 1985.
Captured In Time and Space, Star Song, 1986.
Back To The Street, Star Song, 1986.
This Means War!, Star Song, 1987.
On Fire!, Star Song, 1988.

Sources

Chicago Tribune, May 25, 1989.
Contemporary Christian Music, November 1988.
GMN, August 1987.
Performance, 1987.
Petra Press Kit, Atkins-Muse and Associates, Inc.
The Tennessean, April 18, 1988.

—*Meg Mac Donald*

Harvey Phillips

Tuba player

Harvey Phillips is considered by many to be the best tubist in the world. His prodigious technical command of the tuba, musical sense, and rapport with the audience have made him in great demand as a performer. Through his efforts as a teacher, commissioner of new works, and popularizer of the tuba, he has been largely responsible for the present-day renaissance of interest in tuba performance and literature.

The youngest of ten children, Harvey was born on December 2, 1929, in Aurora, Missouri, to farmers Jesse and Lottie Phillips. The Phillips lost the family farm due to the Depression and became tenant farmers, finally settling near Marionsville, Missouri. Harvey began to study music in high school with retired circus bandleader Homer Lee, who introduced him to the sousaphone, the rap-around version of the tuba used in marching bands. "I had always wanted to play a brass instrument, but my folks couldn't afford to buy one." Phillips told the *News-Sun*. "So I fell in love with it. I thought it was the greatest thing that ever happened to me."

After graduating in 1947, Phillips got a summer job playing tuba with the King Brothers Circus. Nine weeks later he left to go to the University of Missouri, where he had a scholarship, but he was unhappy there and gladly joined the Ringling Brothers and Barnum & Baily Circus band when he received an offer from Merle Evans, the band's leader. Phillips stayed with Ringling Brothers until 1950.

His time with the circus proved to be very beneficial as he learned to play many kinds of music to accompany different acts and in his first year he visited every state in the Union. During his second visit to New York City, he met William Bell, then tubist with the New York Philharmonic Orchestra. Phillips later studied under Bell, and with his support attended the Juilliard School of Music, in New York, where he received a four-year scholarship.

Except for a two-year stint with the U.S. Army Field Band in Washington, D.C., Phillips remained in New York, attending classes at the Manhattan School of Music and performing with a variety of ensembles: the Sauter-Finegan Orchestra, the New York City Opera, the New York City Ballet, and the Goldman Band. Upon the request of Gunther Schuller, then president of the New England Conservatory in Boston, from 1967 to 1971 Phillips served as Schuller's vice-president for financial affairs. During his tenure there, he helped raise more than $6 million to rescue the conservatory from bankruptcy.

In 1971 Phillips joined the faculty of the Indiana University School of Music, in Bloomington, upon the retire-

For the Record. . .

Full name, Harvey Gene Phillips, Sr.; born December 2, 1929, in Aurora, Mo.; son of Jesse Emmett (a farmer) and Lottie Amber (Chapman) Phillips; married Carol Ann Dorvel, February 22, 1954; children: Jesse Emmett, Harvey Gene, Jr., Thomas Alexander. *Education:* Attended the University of Missouri, 1947-48, the Juilliard School of Music, 1950-54, and the Manhattan School of Music, 1956-58.

Played tuba with the King Brothers Circus, 1947; and with Ringling Brothers and Barnum & Baily Circus, 1948-50; member of U.S. Army Field Band, Washington, D.C., 1954-56; has performed with numerous musical ensembles, including New York City Opera, New York City Ballet, and the Goldman Band; served as vice-president for financial affairs for the New England Conservatory, Boston, Mass., 1967-71; Indiana University School of Music, professor of music, 1971-79, Distinguished Professor of Music, 1979—; co-founder of numerous musical ensembles, including Orchestra U.S.A. and New York Brass Quintet; founder of numerous musical festivals, including TUBA-CHRISTMAS and OCTUBAFEST; founder of Tubists Universal Brotherhood Association (TU-BA); founder and president of the Harvey Phillips Foundation.

Awards: Recipient of numerous awards, including American Music Conference Award and inclusion into the Circus Hall of Fame Band.

Addresses: *Home and office*—TUBARANCH, 4769 South Harrell Rd., Bloomington, IN 47401.

ment and recommendation of Bell, and by 1979 he was made a Distinguished Professor of Music, the highest professorial rank. Phillips has taught many master classes and clinics, been featured at dozens of national and international music conferences, and served on many committees and panels. He strives to instill pride, commitment, and professional ethics in all his students.

Phillips aspires to expand performance opportunities in every musical discipline, eradicate musical prejudice and misunderstanding, and broaden the base of audience support for the performing arts. To these ends Phillips organized the Tubists Universal Brotherhood Association (T.U.B.A.), which has a mailing list of 12,000, and other societies to promote brass instruments. He has co-founded such ensembles as Orchestra U.S.A., the New York Brass Quintet, the Matteson-Phillips Tubajazz Consort, and Twentieth Century Innovations, and has performed widely in the United States, Canada, Europe, Australia, and Japan.

To generate audience support, in 1973 Phillips originated the annual TUBA-CHRISTMAS, which later engendered OCTUBAFEST, TUBAEASTER, and SUMMERTUBAFEST, festivals held across the country to celebrate the tuba. TUBA-CHRISTMAS originated when Phillips wanted to honor his teacher, Bell, who was born on Christmas day. Phillips arranged for tuba players to come to the skating rink at Rockefeller Center to perform Christmas carols in what has now become a tradition. OCTUBAFEST, held annually at Phillips's TUBARANCH in Bloomington, attracts as many as 4,000 participants.

Invented in the early 1830s, the tuba was a relative newcomer to the orchestra. It was a vast improvement over its predecessors—the serpent and the ophicleide—and quickly assumed its role in the orchestra. It was not until 1954, however, when Ralph Vaughn Williams composed *Concerto for Bass Tuba and Orchestra* that the

> *Phillips has been directly responsible for the composition of more than 600 works for tuba. He has inspired, cajoled, and coerced works from many composers and has directly commissioned more than 100 others.*

tuba's solo capabilities were made known. Nevertheless, the solo repertoire increased little until Phillips decided to take matters into his own hands. Phillips has been directly responsible for the composition of more than 600 works for tuba. He has inspired, cajoled, and coerced works from many composers—including Vincent Persichetti, Morton Gould, Gunther Schuller, and Alec Wilder—and has directly commissioned more than 100 others. Sometimes payment has taken various forms, such as a case of gin, and when Phillips found himself deeply in debt from commissions and festivals, he set up the Harvey Phillips Foundation to support his musical activities.

Indefatigable in his efforts on behalf of the tuba and tubists, Phillips maintains a hectic schedule of performing, teaching, and consulting. Though he is satisfied that people are beginning to appreciate, play, and compose for the tuba with appropriate enthusiasm, he sees no reason to slow his pace.

Perhaps Gunther Schuller, a horn player and conductor of renown, who has throughout the years worked with Phillips on many projects, describes him best: "Harvey Phillips is not only a supreme artist on the tuba, but through his multiple activities as a teacher, clinician, commissioner of new works, and organizer of tuba and brass festivals, he has been an indefatigable 'philosopher of the tuba.' His efforts on behalf of other musicians never cease. More than anyone else he has tenaciously proselytized the notion that the tuba can, in the hands of fine musicians, communicate the entire gamut of musical emotions and expressions.

For his missionary zeal and his exemplary performance record, Mr. Phillips has won the respect of all his colleagues, as well as countless composers whose works he has premiered, championed and performed. Harvey Phillips, in short, is the major progenitor in his field, and already two generations of younger players are forever indebted to him."

Selected discography

Baker: *Sonatina;* Gould: *Suite* (New York Horn Trio), Golden Crest.
Benson: *Helix,* Golden Crest.
Downey: *Tabu,* Gasparo.
Persichetti: *Seranade No. 12 for Solo Tuba;* Wilder: *Sonata for Horn, Tuba, and Piano,* Golden Crest.
Ross: *Concerto* (Cornell University Wind Ensemble), Cornell University.
Vaughan Williams: *Concerto;* Schuller: *Capriccio* (New England Conservatory Symphony), GM.
Wilder: *Suite No. 2 for Horn, Tuba, and Piano;* Heiden: *Variations* (Valhalla Horn Choir), Golden Crest.

Sources

New York Times, December 16, 1985; July 22, 1986.
New Yorker, December 15, 1975.
News-Sun, March 8, 1987.

—*Jeanne M. Lesinski*

Bonnie Raitt

Singer, songwriter, guitarist

onnie Raitt first garnered acclaim and attention with her self-titled debut album in 1971. Performing in the rock-blues traditions, many felt she would meet with the same level of success that pop-country phenomenon Linda Ronstadt achieved during the 1970s. But despite Raitt's maintaining a faithful following of fans, she did not obtain truly widespread popularity until the release of her tenth album, *Nick of Time.* Both the title track and the single "Thing Called Love" scored hits for her.

Raitt was born on November 8, 1949, to musical parents. Her father, John Raitt, was a Broadway singing star famed for performing the male lead in "Carousel," and her mother, Marjorie, was a talented pianist. Raitt taught herself to play guitar when she was only nine years old; she confided to Kim Hubbard in *People* that her choice of instrument was influenced by her belief that "I'd never be as good on piano as my mother." As Raitt grew older, supported by her politically active, Quaker parents, she became interested in protest music. She played political songs in parks and "thought [folk and protest singer] Joan Baez was just about God," she told Hubbard.

Her interest in both politics and music continued when she matriculated at Radcliffe College. In addition to protesting the Vietnam War, Raitt studied African culture with the goal of becoming a social worker in Tanzania. But she also played in coffeehouses near Radcliffe, and became acquainted with many well-known blues artists, including Junior Wells. As Raitt said to Hubbard, she was "hangin' out with 70-year-old blues guys who drank at 10 in the morning. My parents were a little concerned."

Eventually Raitt's love for music proved stronger than her will to work in Africa, and she dropped out of Radcliffe without graduating. Not long afterwards, she signed with Warner Brothers Records. Her first album, *Bonnie Raitt,* was primarily composed of traditional blues standards, and was well received, bringing her favorable comparisons with early 1970s peers like Ronstadt and Maria Muldaur. Raitt followed with other successes, 1972's *Give It Up* and 1973's *Takin' My Time,* but afterwards, though she remained at least somewhat popular with folk and blues fans, she put out six albums that Hubbard avowed "left critics lukewarm." Even so, many of the negative reviews blamed Raitt's material and the records' production rather than the singer's talent. While complaining that on an entire side of her 1986 album *Nine Lives* "the mix is off," James Hunter in *Rolling Stone* praised the "powerfully lucid traces of [rhythm and blues] in her voice" and admitted that Raitt's singing "at its best . . . [blows] away both her influences and her competition." In the

For the Record. . .

Born November 8, 1949; daughter of John (a Broadway singer) and Marjorie Haydock (a pianist) Raitt. *Education:* Attended Radcliffe College.

Vocalist, guitarist; performed in small clubs beginning 1967, recording artist and concert performer, 1971—.

Awards: Four Grammys for Album of the Year, Best Pop Female Performance, Best Rock Female Performance, and Best Traditional Blues Recording (with John Lee Hooker), 1990, all for *Nick of Time.*

Addresses: 7323 Woodrow Wilson Drive, Los Angeles, Calif. 90046.

same vein, a *People* reviewer groused about *Nine Lives'* "numbing similarity of tempo across most of the LP's 10 tracks," while affirming that "Raitt is still a vibrant, aggressive singer."

Apparently the decline of Raitt's albums in critical favor coincided with struggle in her personal life. After devoting herself during the late 1970s to playing for causes such as the anti-nuclear movement, she found herself "depressed by how conservative [the United States] had become," according to Ron Givens in *Newsweek.* In addition, she ended a longtime love relationship, drank heavily, and put on weight. Raitt explained to Hubbard: "I wasn't kicking and screaming into dementia, but I did have a complete emotional, physical and spiritual breakdown."

But in 1987 Raitt agreed to work on a project with pop superstar Prince, one that included making a video. She was ashamed of her weight, and this inspired her to get her life into better order. "It's one thing to go onstage if you're a little chunky," Raitt told Hubbard, "it's another to make a video with a guy who's known for looking foxy. I decided to lose weight, which you can't do if you're drinking all the time." Though the project

with Prince was never completed, Raitt continued with her good intentions, joining Alcoholics Anonymous. "I still stay up and jam," she explained to Givens. "It's just that I can remember everything I did the next day and I don't have to feel sick."

Paralleling Raitt's personal achievements, her 1989 effort *Nick of Time* not only won back critical favor for her but brought her greater popularity than she had ever experienced before. When the word "comeback" came up, she quipped to Givens: "I never had a hit record, so how can I come back?" But now she has several, including the album's title track, a song about coping with the aging process. A *People* reviewer lauded the entire disc, saying that "throughout, the sound is intimate, clear, honest." Though thrilled with her newfound success, Raitt is more pleased with her potential for longevity. "I think my fans will follow me into our combined old age," she told Hubbard. "Real musicians and real fans stay together for a long, long time."

Selected discography

Bonnie Raitt, Warner Bros., 1971.
Give It Up, Warner Bros., 1972.
Takin' My Time, Warner Bros., 1973.
Street Lights, Warner Bros., 1974.
Home Plate, Warner Bros., 1975.
Sweet Forgiveness, Warner Bros., 1977.
The Glow, Warner Bros., 1979.
Green Light, Warner Bros., 1982.
Nine Lives (includes "No Way to Treat a Lady," "Freezin'," "Crime of Passion," and "Angel"), Warner Bros., 1986.
Nick of Time (includes "Thing Called Love" and "Nick of Time"), Capitol, 1989.

Sources

Newsweek, March 13, 1989.
People, September 22, 1986, April 4, 1989, April 24, 1989.
Rolling Stone, November 20, 1986, April 20, 1989.

—*Elizabeth Thomas*

Charlie Rich

Singer, songwriter, pianist

No singer's career illustrates the vicissitudes of country-music stardom better than that of Charlie Rich, the "Silver Fox." Rich achieved superstardom as a "crossover" artist in 1973 with two hit singles, "Behind Closed Doors" and "The Most Beautiful Girl," but for two decades before that he had struggled to find the right sound and style. The years since 1973 have been almost as daunting, because Rich, a blues and rock aficionado, has never been comfortable with the label "country star." All categories aside, Rich appeals to a broad audience with his soul-wrenching vocals. "I don't really like happy music," he told *Newsweek*. "I don't think it says anything."

Like many of his contemporaries in country music, Rich grew up in poverty on a cotton farm, miles from the glittering promise of Nashville. He was born and raised in Colt, Arkansas, population 312. Before he finished high school he was earning wages as a cotton picker for his father and other local farmers. Music was a sideline—one that was strictly monitored by his Baptist missionary parents. Rich was allowed to play the tenor saxophone in the high school band, but playing at dances and playing for money were forbidden.

Rich was a serious music student who developed a taste for jazz, especially the works of Stan Kenton and Oscar Peterson. For some time he attended the University of Arkansas, where, as a music major, he perfected his blues and jazz techniques on horn and piano. In 1952 he enlisted in the Air Force and was stationed in Enid, Oklahoma. There he joined a jazz group and began moonlighting in the local honky-tonks and clubs. During this period he met and married his wife, Margaret Ann, also a jazz buff and singer. Upon his discharge he returned to his father's cotton farm, but Margaret Ann had other ideas. She took a demo tape to the Sun Records studios, where producer Sam Phillips was working with the likes of Jerry Lee Lewis, Johnny Cash, Elvis Presley, and Roy Orbison. Phillips's associate Bill Justis listened to the tape and hired Rich as a session musician.

Justis and Phillips were candid with Rich: his sound was too jazzy and too elegant for success as a solo performer. He would have to loosen up and start composing and singing in the Jerry Lee Lewis vein. Rich obliged, even to the extent of writing a hit for Lewis, "I'll Make It All Up to You." Although Phillips predicted at one point that Rich's future in music looked as promising as Presley's, Rich had only one charted single on the Sun label, "Lonely Weekends." Rich wrote and sang the tune, which has since been recorded by a wide variety of country and rock artists. The singer told *Newsweek* that he had become quite disenchanted with Sun Records by the early 1960s. "Sam Phillips had

Born December 14, 1934, in Colt, Arkansas; son of a cotton farmer; married, wife's name Margaret Ann; three children. *Education:* Attended University of Arkansas, majored in music.

Professional singer-songwriter, piano and horn player, 1955—. Signed with Sun Records, ca. 1957, had first hit, "Lonely Weekends," 1959. Moved to RCA Records, 1963, Smash Records, 1965, and Epic Records, 1968. Had first number one country hit, "Behind Closed Doors," 1973. *Military service:* U.S. Air Force, 1952-55, stationed in Enid, Oklahoma.

Awards: Best male vocalist, song of the year, and album of the year from the Country Music Association, all 1973, all for *Behind Closed Doors.*

Addresses: *Home—* 8229 Rockcreek Parkway, Cordova, TN 38018.

gotten wealthy," he said, "and was more interested in Holiday Inn stock than the record business." Rich switched to Groove, a subsidiary of RCA, in 1963 and earned his second charted hit, "Big Boss Man."

The 1960s found Rich groping for a marketable style as he returned to the honky-tonk circuit. He had a brief period of success with Smash Records, where he recorded the rhythm-and-blues hit "Mohair Sam," but again subsequent albums failed to sell. In 1968 he signed with Epic Records and worked with up-and-coming producer Billy Sherrill.

Gradually Rich began to integrate his blues, rock, and country influences into a cohesive sound. Sherrill directed him more toward country music, feeling that country fans would respond to his mature years better than the youth-oriented rock audience. The 1972 *Best of Charlie Rich* and the 1973 *Behind Closed Doors* brought Rich the elusive stardom he had sought so long—and, ironically, *Behind Closed Doors* sold to pop fans as well as to the country market. Overnight the silver-haired Rich became a sought-after headliner, with million-selling singles such as "Behind Closed Doors" and "The Most Beautiful Girl."

Sherrill was right in one respect: country fans *are* more loyal than pop-rock fans. Rich has been the recipient of that loyalty for almost twenty years, remaining a favorite in Nashville despite his penchant for jazz and the blues. Drawing from eclectic sources as it does, Rich's work

has been dubbed "countrypolitan," and the singer has been likened to Frank Sinatra for his middle-of-the-road sexiness. *Country Music Encyclopedia* author Melvin Shestack quotes Peter Guralnik on the enduring appeal of the "Silver Fox": "The music that [Rich] does, his approach to the music, his ability to make each song a unique and personal vehicle for individual expression is something which in a way is lost to the star who is as much concerned with panoply as performance, who is forced by his image to be something he is not. . . . Charlie Rich is free to be whatever he likes. He feels none of the terrible restraints of stardom."

Selected discography

The Best of Charlie Rich, Epic, 1972.
Behind Closed Doors, Epic, 1973.
Collector's Series: Charlie Rich, RCA, 1985.
Greatest Hits/Best of Charlie Rich, Columbia, 1986.
American Originals, Columbia, 1989.
Best of Times, Epic.
The Early Years of Charlie Rich, Sun.
Entertainer of the Year, Pickwick.
Golden Treasures, Sun.
Lonely Weekends, Sun.
Memphis Sound, Sun.
She Loved Everyone But Me, RCA.
Silver Fox, Epic.
Charlie Rich Sings Hank Williams, Hi.
Songs for Beautiful Girls, Pickwick.
There Won't Be Anymore, RCA.
She Called Me Baby, RCA.
Time for Tears, Sun.
Tomorrow Night, RCA.
Very Special Love Songs, Epic.
Silver Linings, Epic.
The World of Charlie Rich, RCA.
Take Me, Epic.

Sources

Books

The Illustrated Encyclopedia of Country Music, Harmony, 1977.
Shestack, Melvin, *The Country Music Encyclopedia,* Crowell, 1974.

Periodicals

Newsweek, November 26, 1973.

—*Anne Janette Johnson*

Jimmie Rodgers

Singer, songwriter, guitarist

Jimmie Rodgers was the first country music singer who achieved national fame, international recognition, and superstar status. Today the laconic Rodgers is known as the "Father of Country Music," even though his career spanned a brief six years (but consisted of over one hundred recordings). Rodgers was a truly eclectic musician who was able to combine the popular tunes of urban dance clubs and Tin Pan Alley with rural instrumentation and vocals; he punctuated his best-known songs with an original "blue yodel" that has since been widely imitated in both country and bluegrass music. In the midst of the Great Depression, when 78 r.p.m. records cost a staggering seventy-five cents, each Rodgers release sold nearly a million copies. Unfortunately, Rodgers died of tuberculosis at the height of his fame, relinquishing his place on the stage to a host of imitators.

According to Chris Comber and Mike Paris in *Stars of Country Music,* Rodgers "popularized country music by taking it out of its rural environment and setting it firmly on the road to the multimillion-dollar industry it is today. He did this by fusing many of the accepted styles in popular music and mixing them with his own brand of genius." Rodgers could play guitar and banjo, he wrote some of his songs and adapted all the others to suit him, and he borrowed styles from such widely-scattered sources as blues, ballads, vaudeville entertainment, and Hawaiian numbers. Small though it is, the Rodgers repertory contains every sort of song associated with country music today, from lovelorn lament to railroad misadventure to good-natured travelling tunes.

Rodgers was more than a competent musician, however. He was an endearing entertainer whose easy stage presence was captured on his recordings. He created a believable—if not terribly admirable—stage persona that reached audiences in the Deep South and beyond. As Bill C. Malone puts it in *Country Music U.S.A.,* Rodgers "brought into clear focus the tradition of the rambling man which had been so attractive to country music's folk ancestors and which has ever since fascinated much of the country music audience. This ex-railroad man conveyed the impression that he had been everywhere and had experienced life to the fullest. His music suggested a similar openness of spirit, a willingness to experiment, and a receptivity to alternative styles." Comber and Paris offer a similar observation. Rodgers's informal approach, they write, "gave each listener something with which he could identify. Rodgers's sad songs were for those who were sad, his railroad songs were for the railroaders, his hobo songs were for the hoboes, his love songs with their tender lyrics were for lovers, and his bawdy songs were for those who could still enjoy themselves in times of adversity. Jimmie Rodgers was genuine. He had lived

Full name, James Charles Rodgers; born September 8, 1897, in Meridian, Miss.; died of tuberculosis May 26, 1933, in New York, N.Y.; son of Aaron W. (a railroad section foreman) and Eliza (Bozeman) Rodgers; married second wife, Carrie Williamson, April 7, 1920; children: (second marriage) Carrie Anita.

Left school in 1911 to work on the railroad; began as water boy for Mobile and Ohio line, became callboy and brakeman; retired due to ill health, 1924. Began professional music career, 1925, working as black-face singer-banjo player with travelling show; formed band the Jimmie Rodgers Entertainers, 1926, had radio debut on WWNC (Asheville, N.C.), 1926. Signed with Victor records, 1927, had first hit "Blue Yodel Number One (T is for Texas)," 1928.

dance band style introduced [Rodgers] to the melodies of popular music, many of which he later incorporated into his recordings, and allowed him to spend some time with his sister-in-law, who was a talented musician and composer."

By 1927 Rodgers had a modest musical career under way, with a short stint on an Asheville, North Carolina, radio station as the high point. That year an executive for Victor Records, Ralph Peer, announced that he would audition local talent at a portable studio in Bristol, Virginia. Rodgers was one of a number of entertainers who descended on Bristol, but at the last moment his backup band deserted him. Thus he appeared before Peer as a solo artist. Rodgers sang "The Soldier's Sweetheart" and "Sleep, Baby, Sleep" to his own guitar accompaniment, and Peer signed him to a contract. Rodgers's first record was released in October, 1927, and even though it presented nothing particularly original, it sold well. Within five weeks of the Bristol session,

all his lyrics: he had been sad, glad, gay, blue, broke, and in love. He had been a railroad man, and he had hoboed when he had to. Thus his recordings told of true-life experiences in a down-to-earth, unaffected way."

James Charles Rodgers was born in Meridian, Mississippi, on September 8, 1897. His mother died of tuberculosis when he was four, and he himself was a sickly child who often missed school. Because his father worked as a section foreman on the Mobile and Ohio railroad, Rodgers was passed from relative to relative in various small Mississippi towns. In 1911 he dropped out of school and went to work with his father on the railroad, beginning as a water boy. There, as he brought water to the black laborers, he began to pick up the music that was part of every railroader's day. On noon lunch breaks the black musicians taught him the rudiments of banjo and guitar, and he began to dream of a career as a performer.

Dogged by ill health, Rodgers worked on the railroads for more than fourteen years. He was primarily employed as a brakeman, and his work took him from the South to the Rocky Mountains. During one of his numerous periods of unemployment he tried to support his wife and daughter by singing in blackface in a minstrel show. He was diagnosed with tuberculosis in 1924 and almost died when a lung hemorrhaged. The illness— one of the most feared in those days—forced Rodgers to retire permanently from railroading. As an alternative he formed a dance band with his sister-in-law, Elsie McWilliams, and a violinist named Slim Rozell. Comber and Paris write: "This short-lived excursion into the

> *Jimmie Rodgers was the first country music singer who achieved national fame, international recognition, and superstar status. Today Rodgers is known as the "Father of Country Music."*

Rodgers travelled to New York City quite on his own initiative and pressured Peer to make more records. It was then that Rodgers recorded "T is for Texas," an original blue yodel that is better known as "Blue Yodel Number One."

Comber and Paris note that when "T is for Texas" was released early in 1928, it "caught on like wildfire." Rodgers's income leaped from nearly zero to more than $2000 per month in just six months, and he quite willingly began to cut a number of records. The blue yodels proved especially popular, leading some to call Rodgers "America's Blue Yodeler," but other tunes found wide audiences as well. In 1929 Rodgers appeared in a short film, *The Singing Brakeman*, that provided his other nickname. By that time he had called in his sister-in-law with her library of music, and he was recording as fast as his ill health would allow. Needless to say, Rodgers was in great demand as a live performer, but he was never able to maintain the rigorous pace that touring demanded. When he did appear live—

usually in the Deep South near his Texas home—he played for no more than twenty minutes. This acknowledged frailty only increased Rodgers's popularity, especially when he sang "T.B. Blues" and "Whippin' That Old T.B."

Rodgers found fantastic fame and prosperity even as the Great Depression descended. He indulged in every extravagance, delighting those in his audience who could barely afford to buy his records. Radio helped to propel his career, and a veritable army of aspiring country singers began to emulate their idol. Tragically, Rodgers's tuberculosis worsened every time he tried to exert himself, and by 1933 he was hospitalized with little expectation of survival. In April, 1933, he rallied just long enough to travel to New York for one last session. Between takes he rested on a cot, attended by a private nurse. Just as the session ended he suffered a serious hemorrhage and died in his room at the Taft Hotel. The whole nation mourned, and no less than four testimonial songs about him became best-sellers.

Malone writes: "In assessing Jimmie Rodgers' influence on American folk music and on a later generation of commercial performers, one can safely use the adjective 'phenomenal.' Indeed, one would be hard pressed to find a performer in the whole broad field of pop music—whether it be Al Jolson, Bing Crosby, or Frank Sinatra—who has exerted a more profound and recognizable influence on later generations of entertainers. No one as yet has made a full-scale attempt to determine how many of his songs have gone into popular or folk tradition, and there is no way to measure the number of people, amateur and professional, who have been inspired by him to take up the guitar or try their luck at singing. With the emergence of Jimmie Rodgers, country folk finally had one of their own to use as a model—a personification of the success that might be possible in the world of music, and the possessor of a magnetic style and personality that might be used to attain that success." Malone cites Rodgers for that distinctly country characteristic, an "effortless informality, marked by a very personal approach which insinuated its way into the hearts of listeners, making them feel that the song was meant just for them."

Jimmie Rodgers was the first inductee into the Country Music Hall of Fame when it opened in 1961. Many of his recordings are still available on the RCA label.

Selected discography

The Best of Jimmie Rodgers, MCA, 1988.
Best of the Legendary Jimmie Rodgers, RCA.
Country Music Hall of Fame, RCA.
Jimmie the Kid, RCA.
Jimmie Rodgers, RCA.
My Rough and Rowdy Ways, RCA.
My Time Ain't Long, Victor.
Never No Mo' Blues, RCA.
The Short but Brilliant Life of Jimmie Rodgers, RCA.
This Is Jimmie Rodgers, RCA.
Train Whistle Blues, RCA.

Sources

Malone, Bill C., Country Music U.S.A., revised edition, University of Texas Press, 1985.
Malone, Bill C. and Judith McCulloh, Stars of Country Music, University of Illinois Press, 1975.
Rodgers, Carrie, My Husband, Jimmie Rodgers, Ernest Tubb Publications, 1935.
Shelton, Robert and Burt Goldblatt, The Country Music Story: A Picture History of Country and Western Music, Bobbs-Merrill, 1966, reprinted, Arlington House, 1971.

—Anne Janette Johnson

The Rolling Stones

Rock group

Often billed as "the world's greatest rock and roll band," the Rolling Stones have earned the title; if not for their musical prowess, then certainly for their longevity. Formation of the group began back as early as 1949 when Keith Richard and Mick Jagger, both from Dartford, England, went to school together. It would take another eleven years, however, before their paths would cross again. To their amazement, they discovered that both of them had grown up listening to the same great American bluesmen and rockers like Chuck Berry and Bo Diddley. The two formed a friendship that was based around one common interest; music.

At the time, Jagger was attending London's School of Economics while Richard was struggling at Sidcup Art College. Soon they found out about a local musician named Alexis Korner who held blues jams at the Ealing Club. After Jagger began to sing for Korner's Blues Incorporated, he decided to join a group that Richard was putting together. Other members included Ian Stewart, Dick Taylor, Tony Chapman and a guitar player named Brian Jones.

Jones was quite different from the rest of the lads. Although only one year older than Jagger and Richard, he had already parented two illegitimate children by the time he was sixteen. And while Richard was more into the Berry school of rock guitar, Jones was pure blues and often refered to himself as Elmo Lewis (in reference to the slide guitarist, Elmore James).

Charlie Watts was already making a fair living drumming for a jazz combo when he was persuaded to replace Tony Chapman. The oldest member, a rocking bassist, Bill Wyman, hooked up immediately after to complete the rhythm section. With the shrewd talents of manager/publicist Andrew Loog Oldham, they began opening for Blues Inc. at London's Marquee Club in 1963, billed as "Brian Jones and Mick Jagger and The Rollin' Stones" (after a Muddy Waters tune). Dick Taylor was no longer in the band at this time.

With hair longer than any other group and an attitude that made the Beatles look like choir boys, the Stones took full advantage of their image as "the group parents love to hate." "That old idea of not letting white children listen to black music is *true*," Jagger told Jonathan Cott, "cause if you want white children to remain what they are, they mustn't." Their negative public image was constantly fueled by Oldham, who also decided that Stewart's neanderthal presence did not fit in with the rest of the band and so delegated him to the background, never seen but often heard.

Oldham quickly secured the Stones a contract with Decca Records and in June of 1963 they released their first single, a cover of Chuck Berry's "Come On" backed with "I Want to be Loved." Reaction was good and it would only take another six months for the group to make it big. Continuing their eight-month residence at the Crawdaddy Club in Richmond, they released their version of the Beatles "I Wanna Be Your Man" followed by Buddy Holly's "Not Fade Away," which made it to Number 3 in Great Britain. Their fourth single would climb all the way to the top in their homeland, "It's All Over Now" by Bobby Womack. Their next hit, "Little Red Rooster," likewise reached Number 1 but was banned in the United States.

They already had two albums out in England by the time they broke the U.S. Top 10 with "The Last Time," written by Jagger and Richard. And in the summer of 1965 they had a worldwide Number 1 hit with "Satisfaction." Propelled by Richard's fuzz-tone riff and Jagger's lyrics of a man who couldn't get enough, the song immediately secured a seat in rock history. Oldham had played up the outlaw image of the band to the point where they became his creation, and he was no longer needed.

Allan Klein took over as manager and in 1966, after having relied on other artist's songs, they released their first all-originals LP, *Aftermath*. The band was plagued with drug busts during the psychedelic era and in 1967 recorded their reply to the Beatles' *Sgt. Pepper's Lonely Hearts Club Band,* titled *Their Satanic Majesties Request*. The album paled in comparison to the Beatles masterpiece and is noted mainly as the last album Brian Jones truly worked on, having become too involved in drugs.

Taking on the extra load, Richard met the challenge with 1968's *Beggar's Banquet*. His acoustic guitar work sounded as full as an orchestra on "Street Fighting Man," and one of the most deadly electric solos ever can be found on "Sympathy for the Devil." It was obvious the Stones didn't need Jones dragging them down anymore and he officially quit (or was booted out) on June 9, 1969. Less than one month later he was found drowned in a swimming pool with the official cause listed as "death by misadventure."

Two days later, the Stones had their replacement in former guitarist for John Mayall's Bluesbreakers, Mick Taylor. His first gig was a free concert in memory of Jones at Hyde Park. Taylor's influence would bring the level of musicianship up a few notches until he quit in 1975. Their first album after he joined was still mostly a Richard album however. *Let It Bleed* was released to coincide with an American tour and contained two haunting tunes, "Midnight Rambler" and "Gimme Shelter." The latter became the title of the Stones' movie of their free concert at Altamont, California, that became a disaster when Hell's Angels members (hired as security guards) stabbed a youth to death right in front of the stage.

In 1971 The Stones formed their own label, Rolling Stones Records, and began to expand their musical horizons. *Sticky Fingers* contained jazz with "Can't You Hear Me Knockin" and the country-flavored "Dead Flowers" continued the trend of "Honky Tonk Women." Their next album, *Exile on Main Street,* oddly enough, was passed over by critics when it came out, but over the years has come to be regarded as probably their finest recording. With Richard hanging out with Gram Parsons, the country influence was stronger than ever but the album also contains gospel ("I Just Want To See His Face"), blues ("Shake Your Hips"), and full-tilt rock ("Rip This Joint"). Four sides of vintage Stones at their tightest, and loosest.

Their next two albums, *Goat's Head Soup* and *It's Only Rock and Roll,* contain both outstanding tracks and what some critics considered real dogs. "Time Waits For No One," with a beautiful solo by Taylor, shows just how much the Stones had changed, yet tracks like "Star Star" reveal just the opposite: the bad boys of rock just couldn't grow up. Five years was enough for Taylor and he decided to walk away from one of the most sought-after positions in rock. "The fact is I was becoming stagnant and lazy with the Stones. I really got off on playing with them, but it wasn't enough of a challenge," he told *Rolling Stone.* Many guitarists were rumored to take his place (Roy Buchanan, Jeff Beck, Peter Frampton, and Rory Gallagher among them).

The obvious choice, though, was Rod Stewart's right hand man, Ron Wood. Wood pinch-hit for Taylor on the 1975 tour of America, bounding back and forth with the Faces before finally settling with the Stones. The first full album he contributed to was *Black and Blue* in 1976. Once again the Stones stretched out by dabbling in reggae ("Cherry Oh"), disco ("Hot Stuff"), and a smoky lounge lizard treatment on "Melody." Wood fit the Stones mold perfectly, almost a carbon copy of Richard both physically and musically. The group's future was in doubt in 1977 when Richard was busted in Toronto for heroin dealing, but his sentence did not include any jail time. "Drugs were never a problem," he told Edna Gundersen. "Policemen were a problem." Save for 1978's *Some Girls,* the next four Stones' records seem indistinguishable from each other. The songs are vehicles for Richard's guitar hooks with nothing equaling the emotion of previous hits like "You Can't Always Get What You Want" or "Moonlight Mile."

Jagger has done nothing to dispel constant rumors of a breakup. Richard was reportedly not too happy when Jagger took time off to work on his solo album (even though Wyman and Wood both have records outside the group). Jagger refused to tour to support the Stones' *Dirty Work* LP, instead hitting the road to promote his own *She's The Boss.* Richard had toured with Wood's New Barbarians in 1979, but he was outraged that Jagger would make the Stones a second choice. "I felt like I had failed. I couldn't keep my band together," he told the *Detroit Free Press.* He stated that the Stones will "have to wait for me. They kind of pushed me into this

> *Often billed as "the world's greatest rock and roll band," the Rolling Stones have earned the title; if not for their musical prowess, then certainly for their longevity.*

solo thing, which I really didn't want, and now they're paying a price." Richard released his own album, *Talk Is Cheap,* with plenty of barbs for Jagger. "I'm enjoying myself too much to all of a sudden stop," Richard said.

But rumors of the band's breakup had to be put on hold in 1989, when the Stones announced plans for a new album and a world tour. A favorite with critics, *Steel Wheels* quickly sold over two million copies; the tour, sponsored by Anheuser-Busch, drew barbs from many for being blatantly overcommercialized. Despite the criticism, however, the *Steel Wheels Tour*—which reportedly raked in over $140 million—was a hit with music reviewers and fans. The 1990 *Rolling Stone* readers' and critics' polls selected the Stones as best band and artist of the year, and cited *Steel Wheels* as 1989's best tour.

The group's ability to overcome internal dissention and the toll of more than 25 years in rock and roll's fast lane to put together the industry's success story of the year surprised some observers, but not the Stones themselves. "The Stones, it's a weird thing, it's almost like a soap opera," Richard told *Rolling Stone*. "We needed a break to find out what you can and can't do on your own. I had to find myself a whole new band. . . . But then I realized maybe that's the way to keep the band together: leaving for a bit. . . . I never doubted the band, personally—but I'm an incredible optimist where this band is concerned. It never occured to me that they might not be able to cut it. Absolutely not."

Selected discography

On London Records

England's Newest Hit Makers—The Rolling Stones, 1964.
12 x 5, 1964.
The Rolling Stones Now!, 1965.
Out of Our Heads, 1965.
December's Children, 1965.
Big Hits (High Tide and Green Grass), 1966.
Aftermath, 1966.
Got Live If You Want It!, 1966.
Between the Buttons, 1967.
Flowers, 1967.
Their Satanic Majesties Request, 1967.
Beggar's Banquet, 1968.
Through the Past Darkly, 1969.
Let It Bleed, 1969.
Get Yer Ya Yas Out, 1970.

On Rolling Stone Records, except as noted

Sticky Fingers, 1971.
Hot Rocks: 1964-1971, London Records, 1972.
Exile on Main Street, 1972.
More Hot Rocks (Big Hits & Fazed Cookies), London Records, 1972.
Goat's Head Soup, 1973.
It's Only Rock 'n' Roll, 1974.
Made in the Shade, 1975.
Metamorphosis, ABKCO, 1975.
Black and Blue, 1976.
Love You Live, 1977.
Some Girls, 1978.
Emotional Rescue, 1980.
Sucking in the Seventies, 1981.
Tattoo You, 1981.
Undercover, 1983.

Dirty Work, 1986.
Steel Wheels, 1989.

Sources

Books

Charone, Barbara, *Keith Richards, Life as a Rolling Stone*, Dolphin, 1982.
Christgau, Robert, *Christgau's Record Guide*, Ticknor & Fields, 1981.
Dalton, David, *The Rolling Stones, The First Twenty Years*, Knopf, 1981.
The Guitar, Allan Kozinn, Pete Welding, Dan Forte & Gene Santoro, Quill, 1984.
The Guitar Player Book, by the editors of *Guitar Player*, Grove Press, 1979.
The Illustrated Encyclopedia of Rock, compiled by Nick Logan and Bob Woffinden, Harmony, 1977.
Rock 100, by David Dalton & Lenny Kaye, Grosset & Dunlap, 1977.
Rock Revolution, by the editors of *Creem*, Popular Library, 1976.
The Rolling Stone Illustrated History of Rock & Roll, edited by Jim Miller, Random House/Rolling Stone Press, 1976.
The Rolling Stone Interviews, by the editors of *Rolling Stone*, St. Martin's Press/Rolling Stone Press, 1981.
The Rolling Stone Record Guide, edited by Dave Marsh with John Swenson, Random House/Rolling Stone Press, 1979.
Sanchez, Tony, *Up and Down With the Rolling Stones*, Signet, 1979.
What's That Sound?, edited by Ben Fong-Torres, Anchor, 1976.

Periodicals

Detroit Free Press, December 4, 1988.
Detroit News, September 27, 1988.
Guitar Player, February 1980; April 1983; May 1986; January 1987.
Guitar World, March 1985; March 1986.
Metro Times (Detroit), December 7, 1988.
Oakland Press, December 4, 1988.
Rolling Stone, May 6, 1976; May 20, 1976; May 5, 1977; November 3, 1977; November 17, 1977; June 29, 1978; August 10, 1978; September 7, 1978; March 8, 1990.

—*Calen D. Stone*

Nadja Salerno-Sonnenberg

Violinist

Nadja Salerno-Sonnenberg has attracted the attention of classical music concertgoers for her virtuostic and emotive performances; her highly individual interpretations have been the focus of both negative and positive criticism. Nadja has surprised audiences with her audacious concert attire and endeared herself to them with her warmth and interesting personality.

Salerno-Sonnenberg was born in Rome, Italy, to an Italian pianist and her husband, a Russian singer who deserted the family when his daughter was three months old. Salerno-Sonnenberg's name is a composite of her mother's maiden name and the name of her stepfather, who also left the family.

Nadja's exposure to music began early at the family's Sunday afternoon gatherings, which were attended by friends who would come to hear her mother play the piano and her older brother, Eric, sing. Friends suggested that Nadja might feel left out, hidden in the shadow of her brother's natural musical talent, and suggested that she be given an instrument to play. Thus, at five years old, Nadja found a $40 violin and bow thrust into her hands, and she began lessons with a member of the Italian Radio Orchestra. The young girl's talent was soon evident, and upon the suggestion of her violin teacher, the entire family—mother, stepfather, brother, and grandparents—moved to Cherry Hill, New Jersey, so that Nadja could get better musical training.

At age eight Nadja became the youngest student at the Curtis Institute of Music, one of the most prestigious conservatories in the United States, to which only the best students are admitted and awarded full tuition scholarships. It was a rather overwhelming experience to learn English and study with students often twice her size and age. In the public school, where she went to study academic subjects, Nadja was picked on by the other students until they recognized her athletic ability. Overall, Nadja adapted well and studied at Curtis for six years with Jascha Brodsky. She was, however, reprimanded several times for such practical jokes as dropping water-filled plastic bags from a four-story roof on unsuspecting targets and hiding in the attic-like space enclosing the organ's pipes to read comic books.

Nadja made her solo debut at age ten with the Philadelphia Orchestra, during which she audaciously waved at her friends in the audience. Peter Schoenbach, then dean of the Curtis Pre-College Division, described the young violinist to *Ovation* writer Charles Passy: "Nadja was a real live wire. She kept us busy, but we got a kick out of watching. There were inklings of a major career brewing. She had an intuitive understanding of music. And she had a goal. It was just a question of getting there." Her goals, as stated in a grammar school essay:

to be a space traveler, an athlete, and a famous concert artist. "I want a life no one has ever led before," she told *Life* reporter Rosemarie Robotham.

In 1975 New Jersey instrument maker Sergio Presson gave Nadja a $15,000 violin, paid for by an anonymous donor, and the young prodigy entered the Pre-College Division of the Juilliard School of Music in Manhattan. There she studied with the renowned Dorothy DeLay, who had taught such violin greats as Itzhak Perlman and Shlomo Mintz. DeLay guided Salerno-Sonnenberg's artistic progress, fostering her individuality. Nadja commented on DeLay's training to *Instrumentalist* writer Judith Wyatt: "I always did what I wanted to do, and Miss DeLay knew not to interfere with my ideas. She brought out the best in every one of us and didn't have a set method in the way she taught. She never said 'you do this passage this way because this is the way it's been done before.' She knew I had enough imagination to do it my way and if it didn't work, I would find out on my own. I was a very stubborn student." In 1984, looking back on Nadja's studies with her, DeLay told Barbara Jepson of *Connoisseur:* "Her sound has developed beautifully. . . . She has an independent imagination; her ideas are very individual now."

Unlike some Juilliard students who limit their activities entirely to music, Salerno-Sonnenberg took advantage of the cultural life of New York to attend operas and ballets, to visit museums, and to enjoy sports. Nor does she limit her musical taste to the classical genre. She listens to music from many eras and many styles, including pieces by Ella Fitzgerald, Elvis Presley, Barbra

Streisand, the Beatles, Wynton Marsalis, Benny Goodman, Stevie Wonder, and Oscar Peterson. She also calls herself an "opera freak" and is inspired by the celebrated soprano Maria Callas. Salerno-Sonnenberg believes that everything goes into her musical performances, from her playing softball to listening to rock music, to getting drunk. She asked *Washington Post* writer Joseph McLellan: "How do you know what to say in the music if you spend all your time practicing instead of living?"

While at Juilliard, Nadja's stubbornness turned to rebellion, and for seven months in 1981 she quit playing violin except to earn money for rent. DeLay finally gave her an ultimatum: Work or quit as my student. Salerno-Sonnenberg then committed herself to a life as a musician. She began practicing for the prestigious Walter W. Naumburg International Competition only a few months before the contest was to take place. In what she calls "a sick time" the violinist secluded herself, practicing twelve hours a day, binging on fried sausages, Coke, and Baskin-Robbins peanut butter and chocolate ice cream. She only came out for lessons with DeLay and to do her laundry.

Salerno-Sonnenberg's intense work paid off. She won the coveted Naumburg prize, which includes a $3000 cash award, two recitals at Alice Tully Hall in New York City, a recording with the Musical Heritage Society, and orchestral and recital appearances throughout the United States. "She simply wowed the audience," foundation director Lucy Rowan Mann told Robotham. "There is something electric that happens with only a very few performers. Nadja has it in spades."

Since then Salerno-Sonnenberg, who left Juilliard without graduating, has maintained a busy concert schedule. She has appeared with the Baltimore Symphony, Chicago Symphony, Cincinnati Symphony, Cleveland Orchestra, Detroit Symphony, Houston Symphony, Indianapolis Symphony, Los Angeles Chamber Orchestra, Milwaukee Symphony, Montreal Symphony, New Orleans Philharmonic, Philadelphia Orchestra, and the Pittsburgh Symphony. She has also performed in France, Austria, Germany, Canada, Portugal, and the Philippines.

Salerno-Sonnenberg's performances have stirred controversy. Some critics have praised her virtuostic technique and big silky tone with its highly expressive quality, while others criticize her for immature interpretations and poor stage presence. She has been called a neo-Romantic for her emotive and very individual interpretations, which rarely fail to please audiences— regardless of critics' comments. To play works of Mozart in such a manner horrifies the "purists," but Nadja is a risk-taker according to DeLay, who once commented to Leslie Kandell of the *New York Times:* "Nadja never plays it safe. Nadja very often puts herself in danger, playing as fast as she can move, taking a phrase to a really high point. Or in a slow passage, as she draws the bow across the string, the note gets softer and softer as she sustains the tone longer and longer. You'd think it wouldn't be possible. It's breathtaking—the kind of thing you hear opera singers do.

Reviewers seem to focus unjustly on the violinist's attire and stage presence. They have compared her athletic gait, violin swinging in one hand, to that of Martina Navratilova striding onto a tennis court. They often find her facial expression—grimaces, tears, tightly shut eyes, disheveled hair—distracting. They are also surprised at her choice of attire, which initially included gowns bought at garage sales. Though Nadja has made concessions to the critics' complaints by buying a gown from Saks and having her auburn hair cut short, she continues to wear slacks and unconventional costumes on stage. "The way I am on stage is what they're not used to," she told Wyatt. "Classical music is a business based on tradition. So, for a woman to walk on stage in pants is unheard of. Everybody will just have to

---

"To educate an audience, you need to have the publicity."

---

get used to it. It's not any less glamorous, I can assure you. I think a lot of the problem classical music has financially is that not too many people, especially younger people, are interested in finding out about it. You've got to attract them to the halls."

Nadja has become a darling of the media and a happy spokesperson for the cause of classical music. She has appeared several times on *The Tonight Show*, was the subject of a *60 Minutes* program, and appeared on PBS in a "Mostly Mozart" concert broadcast from Lincoln Center. Though she admits that the attention takes away from her practice time and sometimes invades her privacy, she cooperates with the media in order to promote classical music. As she explained to Passy: "To educate an audience, you need to have the publicity. If I'm going to withstand a summer of pressure because '60 Minutes' is following me everywhere, then I'll do it because it brings classical music to more people. But it's no fun."

Nadja fills her leisure time with a variety of hobbies: playing softball, working with ceramics, cooking gourmet meals, fishing, going to beer parties, and shopping at thrift stores. The trumpet is what Nadja calls her "therapy instrument"—a way to have fun with music. Yet she plays well enough to have once performed "Bugler's Holiday" with Doc Severinsen on *The Tonight Show*.

Salerno-Sonnenberg is constantly searching for balance in her life, between musical and non-musical activities, her needs and the demands of her profession. She admits that she would not have chosen the violin had she had a choice of an instrument to play, but she is happy to be able to contribute her music to the well-being of the world. Though she sometimes has doubts about the role of the musician when faced with the prospect of global tragedies, she told Wyatt: "What would we do without entertainers? That somebody can come to a concert and for thirty minutes not think of anything but feel happy about listening to a piece of music. I think of it now as a lot more important than I had given it credit for."

Selected discography

Sergei Prokofiev, *Violin Sonata No. 1* [and] Gabriel Faure, *Violin Sonata No. 1*, Musicmasters, 1981.
Felix Mendelssohn, *Concerto in E-Minor*; Jules Massenet, *Meditation from "Thais"*; [and] Camille Saint-Saens, *Havanaise* [and] *Rondo capriccioso*, Angel Records, 1988.

Sources

Akron Beacon Journal, March 21, 1988.
Chicago Sun-Times, July 28, 1986.
Cincinnati Enquirer, December 1985.
Cincinnati Post, December 7, 1985.
Connoisseur, February 1984.
Contra Costa Times, April 10, 1986.
Dayton Daily News, December 7, 1985.
Denver Post, October 2, 1987.
Elle, February 1987.
Instrumentalist, January 1987.
Kalamazoo Gazette, January 20, 1988.
Life, October 1984.
Ms., October 1987.
Music Journal, August-September 1981.
New Haven Register, November 26, 1986.
Newsday, June 1, 1987; July 9, 1987.
Newsweek, July 20, 1987.
New Woman, April 1987.
New York Post, July 8, 1987.
New York Times, July 21, 1986; May 11, 1987; May 24, 1987; June 1, 1987.
Ovation, April 1987.

Philadelphia Inquirer, November 12, 1987.
San Francisco Chronicle, April 10, 1986.
San Francisco Examiner, April 9, 1986.
Saturday Evening Post, December 1987.
Seattle Times, June 5, 1986; October 14, 1986.
Spokane Chronicle, January 24, 1986.
Stagebill, February 1987.
Star-Ledger, November 9, 1984.
Stereo Review, February 1988.
Tacoma News Tribune, June 6, 1986.
Time, April 11, 1988.
Wall Street Journal, May 11, 1987.
Washington Post, July 8, 1983; November 24, 1986; June 29, 1987.

—*Jeanne M. Lesinski*

Earl Scruggs

Banjo player, songwriter

The instrumental sound most closely associated with bluegrass music—a banjo picked at furious pace with three fingers—was created by Earl Scruggs, a country picker from rural North Carolina. As a member of Bill Monroe and the Blue Grass Boys, and later as half of Flatt and Scruggs, Scruggs literally sent bluegrass in the direction it has followed to this day. His banjo virtuosity was an amazing novelty in 1945; today it is a requirement for every bluegrass band. In *Country Music U.S.A.,* Bill C. Malone writes that Scruggs "added a new and dynamic ingredient to the Blue Grass Boys sound, and audiences were bowled over by the boy who, with a shower of syncopated notes, had made the banjo a lead instrument capable of playing the fastest of songs. Here was something new under the sun."

Earl Eugene Scruggs was born in Flint Hill, North Carolina, and raised on a farm in the foothills of the Appalachians. He was one of six children. His father died when he was four, but the family kept itself solvent by farming and performing; two of his sisters played banjo, and his mother played the organ. Earl himself picked up the banjo at an early age, and he imitated the three-finger picking style that was common in his region. In Earl's youth the three-finger style was relatively rare, but it offered several advantages. It had a more fluid sound, was closely tied to fiddle music, and used a G tuning that was more compatible with other stringed instruments. Earl could play the banjo before he entered first grade, and by the age of ten he was devising new "licks" of his own.

Before World War II Scruggs worked as a professional musician, first with his brothers and then with several groups, including the Carolina Wildcats and the Morris Brothers. These groups broadcast over radio stations in Gastonia, North Carolina, and Spartanburg, South Carolina. When America entered the war, Scruggs quit performing for work in the textile mills; he often labored seventy-two hours a week for weeks at a time. Music was merely a hobby for him during that period, but after the war he began to perform professionally again. For a time in 1945 he played with "Lost" John Miller on a WSM Radio Saturday broadcast out of Nashville. Then, when Miller quit the business, Scruggs was hired by Bill Monroe.

Bill Monroe and the Blue Grass Boys were a favorite on the Grand Ole Opry, and many musicians dreamed of a chance to play in the group. When Scruggs joined in 1945 he caused an overnight sensation. The banjo was traditionally a supporting instrument in string bands, and most banjo players were comics who clowned onstage. Scruggs was dead serious in the spotlight, and the avalanche of notes that cascaded from his banjo astounded audiences. Neil V. Rosenberg notes in *Stars of Country Music* that Scruggs's version of banjo picking "sounded fresh, new, and exciting, especially at the higher pitch and tempos of the Blue Grass Boys." Monroe was quick to capitalize on the talents of his young protege. Malone writes: "In the three-year period from 1945 to 1948 the banjo assumed a prominence in Monroe's music that it had never enjoyed in any previous band. . . . Throughout the nation, largely unnoticed by the more commercial world of country music, a veritable 'bluegrass revolution' got underway as both fans and musicians became attracted to the music."

In 1948 Scruggs quit the Blue Grass Boys and formed his own band. His partner, Lester Flatt, was also a veteran of Bill Monroe's group, as were band members Jim Shumate, Cedric Rainwater, and Mac Wiseman. Calling themselves Flatt and Scruggs and the Foggy Mountain Boys, the group signed with Mercury Records and began performing in a style very similar to Monroe's. Scruggs quickly transformed his banjo into the lead instrument (Monroe had often led with mandolin), and when he was not picking the banjo he led with equally impressive guitar picking. He also began to write "breakdowns" for the banjo, imitating the furious fiddle music that had been so popular for generations.

His first instrumental release was "Foggy Mountain Breakdown," one of the most famous bluegrass songs ever written. Used as the theme for the 1968 movie *Bonnie and Clyde,* "Foggy Mountain Breakdown" finally made a place for itself on the pop charts after selling well in the country market for nearly two decades. It is still a staple in the repertoire of almost every bluegrass band.

Flatt and Scruggs and the Foggy Mountain Boys toured and recorded at an exhausting pace throughout the 1950s. By 1960 theirs was the best-known bluegrass band in America; the "folk revival" of the early 1960s opened up new audiences on college campuses and in the big cities of the North and West. Their "Ballad of Jed Clampett," the theme for the "Beverly Hillbillies" television show, topped the country charts for a number of weeks, and they were the first bluegrass band ever to play a concert at Carnegie Hall. Rosenberg claims that by 1963 "Flatt and Scruggs were becoming a household name, a synonym for country music. . . . The 'hot' band, the one everybody was listening to, was the Foggy Mountain Boys; a good banjo picker was said to sound 'just like Earl Scruggs.'"

> *The avalanche of notes that cascaded from his banjo astounded audiences.*

Bluegrass purists were therefore dismayed when Scruggs began to lead the group in new directions. Flatt and Scruggs recordings in the later 1960s included snare drums, synthesizers, harmonica, and twelve-string guitar. Scruggs himself often played guitar rather than banjo, and the repertoire began to include works by folk-rock songwriters and Scruggs's three rock-oriented sons. Flatt did not approve of this "progress," so the group disbanded in 1969. Flatt formed his own ensemble, the Nashville Grass, and Scruggs formed the Earl Scruggs Revue, a showcase for his sons Gary, Randy, and Steve.

The Earl Scruggs Revue sported electric guitars, piano, drums, and even a Moog synthesizer—all completely "taboo" at the time for bluegrass bands. Rosenberg notes, however, that many younger fans "liked . . . and approved of Earl's new group. After all, bluegrass music had not been a static form in 1948, it had been an innovation. After twenty-five years, it was time for further innovation." Indeed, adds Rosenberg,

"Earl's band was part of the new country-rock movement which was gathering momentum."

Scruggs still performs occasionally with his Earl Scruggs Revue, a band he calls a "no-cubbyhole, category-free, barrierless approach to music." He told the *Country Music Encyclopedia:* "Music can't stand still. I've always been for progress and keeping up with the times." This should come as no surprise, since Scruggs's signature "progressive" banjo playing helped to create bluegrass music and to make it the dynamic form of entertainment it is today.

Selected discography

With Lester Flatt and the Foggy Mountain Boys

Country Music, Mercury, 1958.
Flatt & Scruggs with the Foggy Mountain Boys, Harmony, 1960.
Songs of Our Land, Columbia, 1962.
Hard Travelin', Columbia, 1963.
Flatt & Scruggs at Carnegie Hall, Columbia, 1963.
Flatt & Scruggs at Vanderbilt University, Columbia, 1964.
The Original Sound of Flatt & Scruggs, Mercury, 1964.
Flatt & Scruggs with the Foggy Mountain Boys, Mercury, 1964.
The Golden Era of Flatt & Scruggs, Rounder.
Foggy Mountain Breakdown, Hilltop.
Flatt & Scruggs' Greatest Hits, Columbia, 1966.
Lester Flatt and Earl Scruggs, Columbia.
20 All-Time Great Recordings of Flatt & Scruggs, Columbia.
The World of Flatt & Scruggs, Columbia.
Foggy Mountain Chimes, Harmony.
Sacred Songs/Great Original Recordings, Harmony.
Bonnie and Clyde, Columbia.
Wabash Cannonball, Harmony.
The Mercury Sessions: Volume 1, 1948-1950, Volume 2, 1950, Rounder, 1985.

You Can Feel It in Your Soul, County, 1988.

With the Earl Scruggs Revue

I Saw the Light with a Little Help from My Friends, Columbia.
The Earl Scruggs Revue Live at Kansas State, Columbia, 1972.
Family and Friends, Columbia.
Rockin' 'cross the Country, Columbia.
The Earl Scruggs Revue, Columbia.

Sources

Books

The Illustrated Encyclopedia of Country Music, Harmony, 1977.
Malone, Bill C., *Country Music U.S.A.,* revised edition, University of Texas Press, 1985.
Malone, Bill C. and Judith McCulloh, *Stars of Country Music,* University of Illinois Press, 1975.
Sandberg, Larry and Dick Weissman, *The Folk Music Sourcebook,* Knopf, 1976.
Scruggs, Earl, *Earl Scruggs and the 5-String Banjo,* Peer International, 1968.
Shestack, Melvin, *The Country Music Encyclopedia,* Crowell, 1974.
Stambler, Irwin and Grelun Landon, *The Encyclopedia of Folk, Country, and Western Music,* St. Martin's, 1969.

Periodicals

Bluegrass Unlimited, February 1971.
Country Music, October 1972.
Esquire, October 1959.
New York Times, July 19, 1959.
New York Times Magazine, September 13, 1970.

—*Anne Janette Johnson*

Seals
&
Crofts

Pop/rock duo

A vocal duo rising out of country and rock backgrounds, Jim Seals and Dash Crofts won a wide audience with music difficult to classify. Blends of jazz, rock, folk, and hints of classical harmonies all have surfaced in melodic combinations over the years since they left the instrumental rock group the Champs.

Fascinated by fiddle playing at a young age, Seals began his musical career with bow in hand, winning the Texas state fiddle championship at the age of nine. He had also begun toying with his father's guitar and eventually learned the mandolin, which resulted in the unique flavor common to many of the duo's later arrangements. Crofts, too, began playing early, picking out tunes on the piano as a small boy and later receiving classical training. After a brief period of waning interest, he was sparked again when he began hearing late-night rhythm and blues broadcasts on the radio. This time he took up drums and soon met Seals in junior high school in the mid-1950s. With rock and roll the music of the day, they merged their talents in a school rock band.

Duo comprised of **Jim Seals** (full name, James Seals; born October 17, 1941, in Sidney, Tex.; began career as saxophonist; vocalist and songwriter; also plays guitar, mandolin, and violin) and **Dash Crofts** (given name, Darrell; born August 14, 1940, in Cisco, Tex.; began career as drummer; vocalist and songwriter; also plays guitar, mandolin, and piano); first performed together in Texas during mid-1950s in group Dean Beard and the Crew Cats; performed together as members of group the Champs, 1958-65; pursued solo careers briefly before performing together in groups the Mushrooms and the Dawnbreakers during the late 1960s; formed duo Seals & Crofts, 1970.

Addresses: *Record company*—Warner Bros., 3300 Warner Blvd., Burbank, CA 91510.

In 1958 Crofts left Texas for California, becoming the drummer of the Champs, who produced the top-ten hit "Tequila." Seals later joined the band and seven years of worldwide travel followed until the group broke up in 1965. After an unsuccessful solo career, Seals rejoined Crofts first in a four-man bean, the Mushrooms, then in the moderately successful seven-member group the Dawnbreakers. The next breakup partly owed to the conversion of most of the band's members to the Baha'i religion. Early in the 1970s, after much prayer and consideration, Seals and Crofts emerged again as a duo, this time becoming well known on the West Coast club circuit, their new soft-rock sound meeting with critical acclaim.

While their first two albums, *Seals & Crofts* and *Down Home,* were marginal sellers, their 1971 album, *Year of Sunday War,* was to make the charts by the end of the year. In 1972, *Summer Breeze* did better, appearing in the top ten and going gold early in 1973, the title track becoming a Seals & Crofts standard. Later that year, while the duo played to capacity audiences in both large and small venues across the country, their album *Diamond Girl* went into the top five in the United States, earning them another gold record and the admiration of soft-rock and folk music fans alike.

Subsequent albums followed the melodic trend, the duo experimenting with jazzy contemporary sounds ("Castles in the Sand") and rich harmonies reminiscent of the folk ballads of the 1960s ("I'll Play For You" and "Ruby Jean and Billie Lee"), many closely akin to the work of Jim Seals's brother, Dan Seals, of England Dan and John Ford Coley fame. Other songs combined their unique vocal flavor with allusions to Baha'i scripture as in the upbeat "Hummingbird" and the delicate, moody "East of Ginger Trees."

As exponents of Baha'i, a world religion having its origin in Muslim beliefs and emphasizing such concepts as "the oneness of the human race, the unity of religion" and the "independent search for truth," Seals and Crofts invite their fans to join in discussing the merits of their religion after concerts. Of the total influence of his faith over his life, Seals comments "Being a Baha'i is like being in love with a girl. You think about it all the time, and the message, sometimes inadvertently, comes out in your music."

Selected discography

Seals and Crofts, Talent Associates, 1970.
Down Home, Bell, 1970.
Year of Sunday War, Warner Bros., 1971.
Summer Breeze, Warner Bros., 1972.
Diamond Girl, Warner Bros., 1973.
Unborn Child, Warner Bros., 1974.
I'll Play For You, Warner Bros., 1975.
Greatest Hits, Warner Bros., 1975.
Get Closer, Warner Bros., 1976.
Sudan Village, Warner Bros., 1976.
One by One, Warner Bros., 1977.
Takin' It Easy, Warner Bros., 1978.
Longest Road, Warner Bros., 1980.

Sources

Anderson, Christopher P., *The Book of People,* Putnam, 1981.
Nite, Norm N., *Rock On,* Volume 2, Harper, 1978.
Stambler, Irwin, *Encyclopedia of Pop, Rock and Soul,* St. Martin's, 1974.

On Baha'i

Encyclopedia of American Religions, Gale Research Company, 1987.

—*Meg Mac Donald*

Sheila E.

Singer, songwriter, drummer

"**S**heila E. . . . is probably the hottest female drummer in the business," asserted Lynn Norment in *Ebony*. First coming to the musical spotlight in the early 1980s as funk/pop superstar Prince's duet partner on the hit single "Erotic City," Sheila E. soon struck solo success with her debut album *Glamorous Life*. The title song proved popular enough to help earn the young drummer-vocalist a gold album, and her second long-playing effort, 1985's *Romance 1600*, also turned gold. As Pamela Bloom pointed out in *High Fidelity*, "Sheila demonstrates on *Romance 1600* how equally at home she is in fusion, funk, pop, and salsa, as well as in the traditional r & b dance mix." The critic concluded: "Hers is an innate musicality that refuses to be waylaid and is propelled by an insatiable physical energy always on the prowl."

Sheila E. was born Sheila Escovedo in the late 1950s in Oakland, California. She arrived in the midst of a musical family—her father, Pete Escovedo, was famed for his drum work with the rock group Santana and, later, the Latin band Azteca. Her brothers also became drummers. By the time Sheila was three, she became devoted to watching Pete Escovedo with his conga drums. She recalled for Bloom: "When my father practiced, I'd sit in front of him and copy him, mirror style. I was just mocking then, but later I'd come back and play by myself." Because of this "mirroring," Sheila developed what Bloom labeled a "left-handed style" on the drums, which allows her to beat them faster and harder than most drummers.

Despite Sheila E.'s early enthusiasm for percussion, her father hoped instead that she would become a symphony performer, and began sending her to violin lessons when she was ten. A competent student, she nevertheless quit five years later because, as she confided to Bloom, "my friends thought it was square and so did I." Meanwhile, Sheila picked up the skills of playing other instruments, including guitar and keyboards, as well as traps and timbales. She also widened her musical tastes, and, as she revealed to Bloom, she and her siblings "used to blast different music from every room in the house. That's probably why I can write [any type of music] I want." Yet she realized from an early age that female drummers were practically unheard of in the professional music business, and in her adolescence she believed she had a greater chance of becoming an Olympic athlete than a successful musician. Thus Sheila focused on sports; playing football with boys, and constantly challenging her peers to foot races.

Sheila continued to stick with drumming, however, and began to land professional gigs while still in her teens. Though her father was grateful for the extra financial

For the Record. . .

Full name Sheila Escovedo; born c. 1958 in Oakland, California; daughter of Pete (a drummer) and Juanita Escovedo.

Drummer, vocalist; played with father, Pete Escovedo, in group Azteca, beginning c. 1973; also did studio work with artists including Herbie Hancock, Lionel Richie, Diana Ross, and Marvin Gaye; began working with Prince, c. 1984; solo recording artist and concert performer, 1985—. Appeared in film, *Krush Groove,* 1985.

Awards: At least two gold albums.

Addresses: 11355 W. Olympic Blvd., #555, Los Angeles, CA 90064.

help her talent brought him, he gently scoffed at her ability, telling her she was too young to be a drummer. But eventually Pete Escovedo let Sheila replace an ailing percussionist in his band. She soloed in her first appearance with her father, and met with an overwhelming response from the audience. Sheila told Bloom: "When I heard that ovation, I had this feeling I had never had in my whole life . . . it felt like the ultimate." Soon after, she quit high school to concentrate on her musical career.

In addition to touring Europe and Asia with her father's band, Azteca, and cutting two albums as part of that group, Sheila E. also got work as a studio musician for artists including Herbie Hancock, Lionel Richie, Diana Ross, and the late Marvin Gaye. In 1978 she was touring the United States with George Duke when she met the man who has perhaps had the biggest impact on her career, Prince. He had just released his first album, and, as Sheila recalled for Bloom, "I heard about this kid who was writing and producing his own stuff, and I was impressed. When I first saw him, I just thought he was this cute guy standing against the wall. But when we met, he was impressed, too, because he had heard about *me.* We've been friends ever since."

But Sheila E. did not work with Prince until 1984, when she sang duet with him on the hit single "Erotic City." As Bloom explained, "Sheila's viscous vocal timbre shadows Prince's pungent baritone—an odd combination that works." Sheila also worked for Prince on Apollonia's album, *Apollonia 6,* and it was during this project that Prince advised her to go solo. He also taught her how to

compose songs faster than she had been doing. The result was Sheila's debut solo album, *The Glamorous Life,* and its title-track hit single. Prince helped her gain even more exposure by having her provide the opening act for his *Purple Rain* tour. But despite rumors that the musical pair were lovers, Sheila told Norment that they were just "very good friends." She further added that she enjoys working with Prince because "he can get the best out of you . . . sometimes he will suggest things and it will be like the icing on the cake."

Sheila E.'s subsequent albums have met with mixed success. Her second album, *Romance 1600,* included another duet with Prince, "Love Bizarre," which shot up the charts. Critical reaction to the tune ranged from that of Bloom, who called it "tedious" and the disc's "most ironic disappointment," to Davitt Sigerson reviewing in *Rolling Stone,* who claimed it made *Romance 1600* "worth purchasing." As for the rest of the album, it led Bloom to acclaim Sheila E.'s "mastery of studio technique, by which she turns everything in sight—including her own barks, snorts, and trills—into a percussion instrument." Both Bloom and Sigerson singled out "Bedtime Story" as being "pretty," and, although Sigerson claimed that the instrumental "Merci for the Speed of a Mad Clown in Summer" was marred by the "interpolation" of "circus music," Bloom hailed it as "a [modern classical composer] Charles Ives delight." On the percussionist's third album, simply titled *Sheila E.,* her father, mother, brothers, and sister sing or play on many of the songs. Though this effort did not yield any hits, "Soul Salsa" was singled out for praise by a *People* magazine reviewer, who concluded that "Sheila is a hot property as a performer."

Selected discography

The Glamorous Life (includes "The Glamorous Life"), 1984.
Romance 1600 (includes "Romance 1600," "Dear Michaelangelo," "Love Bizarre," "Toy Box," "Merci for the Speed of a Mad Clown in Summer," and "Bedtime Story"), 1985.
Sheila E. (includes "Soul Salsa"), 1987.

Sources

Ebony November 1987.
High Fidelity, January 1986.
People, April 13, 1987.
Rolling Stone, November 21, 1985.

—Elizabeth Thomas

Bessie Smith

Singer

They called her the "Empress of the Blues." Born into poverty in Chattanooga, Tennessee, Bessie Smith began singing for coins on street corners and rose to become the largest-selling recording artist of her day. So mesmerizing was her vocal style in person, reinforced as it was by her underacclaimed acting and comedic skills, near-riots frequently broke out when she appeared. Those outside the theaters clamored to get in; those inside refused to leave without hearing more of their Bessie. At two critical points, she was instrumental in helping to save Columbia Records from bankruptcy. While at her peak, in 1925, Smith bought a custom-designed railroad car for herself and her troupe on which they could travel and live. This luxury allowed her to circumvent some of the dispiriting effects of the racism found in both Northern and Southern states as she traveled with her own tent show or with the Theater Owners' Booking Association (TOBA) shows throughout much of the country, commanding a weekly salary that peaked at $2,000.

One of the many myths about Bessie is that she was tutored (some versions claim kidnapped) by Ma Rainey, the prototype blues singer, and forced to tour with Rainey's show. In fact, Rainey didn't have her own show until after 1916, long after Bessie had achieved independent success through her apprenticeships in a variety of minstrel and tent shows. Rainey and Smith worked together and established a friendship as early as 1912, and no doubt Smith absorbed vocal ideas during her early association with the "Mother of the Blues." Originally hired as a dancer, Bessie rapidly polished her skills as a singer and often combined the two, weaving in a natural flair for comedy. From the beginning, communication with her audience was a hallmark of the young singer. Her voice was remarkable. Able to fill the largest hall without amplification, it reached out to each listener with its earthiness and beauty. In *Jazz People,* Dan Morgenstern quotes guitarist Danny Barker: "Bessie Smith was a fabulous deal to watch. She was a large, pretty woman and she dominated the stage. You didn't turn your head when she went on. You just watched Bessie. If you had any church background like people who came from the South as I did, you would recognize a similarity between what she was doing and what those preachers and evangelists from there did, and how they moved people. She could bring about mass hypnotism."

When Mamie Smith (no relation) recorded the first vocal blues in 1920 and sold 100,000 copies in the first month, record executives discovered a new market and the "race record" was born. Shipped only to the South and selected areas of the North where blacks congregated, these recordings of black performers found an eager audience, a surprising segment of

For the Record. . .

Born April 15, 1894, in Chattanooga, Tennessee; died in an automobile accident in Clarksdale, Mississippi, September 26, 1937; daughter of William (a part-time Baptist preacher) and Laura Smith; married Earl Love, c. 1918 (died); married Jack Gee (a night watchman and part-time manager), June 7, 1923; children: Jack Gee, Jr. (adopted 1926). *Religion:* Baptist.

Blues singer, dancer, and comedian in various performing groups and solo, 1912-1937; recording artist for Columbia Records, 1923-1933.

Addresses: *Record company*—Columbia Records, 51 W. 52nd Street, New York, NY 10019.

which was made up of white Southerners to whose ears the sounds of the blues were quite natural. Bessie's first effective recording date, February 16, 1923, produced "Down-Hearted Blues" and "Gulf Coast Blues," with piano accompaniment by Clarence Williams. The public bought an astounding 780,000 copies within six months. Bessie's contract paid her $125 per usable recording, with no provision for royalties. Frank Walker, who supervised all of Bessie's recordings with Columbia through 1931, quickly negotiated new contracts calling first for twelve new recordings at $150 each, then twelve more at $200—and Bessie's fabulous recording career of 160 titles was successfully launched. On the brink of receivership in 1923, Columbia recovered largely through the sale of recordings by Eddie Cantor, Ted Lewis, Bert Williams, and its hottest-selling artist, Bessie Smith.

During her ten-year recording career, the first six of which produced most of her output, Bessie recorded with a variety of accompanists, including some of the most famous names in jazz as well as some of the most obscure. Among the elite were pianists Fred Longshaw, Porter Grainger, and Fletcher Henderson; saxophonists Coleman Hawkins and Sidney Bechet; trombonist Charlie Green; clarinetists Buster Bailey and Don Redman; and cornetist Joe Smith. Perhaps her most empathetic backing came from Green and Smith, as well as from Louis Armstrong and piano giant James P. Johnson. Examples of the support given her by Green and Smith may be found on such songs as "The Yellow Dog Blues," "Empty Bed Blues," "Trombone Cholly," "Lost Your Head Blues," and "Young Woman's Blues." When Bessie and Louis Armstrong first teamed up for 1925's brilliant "St. Louis Blues" and "Cold In Hand Blues" it marked the end of the acoustic recording era,

with Bessie's first electrically recorded sides coming on May 6, 1925. Other standouts with Armstrong include "Careless Love Blues," "Nashville Woman's Blues," and "I Ain't Gonna Play No Second Fiddle." Johnson's accompaniment sparkles on 1927's "Preachin' the Blues" and "Back Water Blues," as well as a number of 1929 efforts, "He's Got Me Goin'," "Worn Out Papa Blues," and "You Don't Understand."

Feeding on the popularity of her records, Bessie's personal-appearance schedule escalated. As she moved from her home base of Philadelphia to Detroit, Chicago, Washington, Atlanta, and New York, adoring crowds greeted her at each stop. Extra police details to control the enthusiasm became the norm. What was the attraction? Critic and promoter John Hammond wrote in 1937: ". . . Bessie Smith was the greatest artist American jazz ever produced; in fact, I'm not sure that her art did not reach beyond the limits of the term 'jazz.' She was one of those rare beings, a completely integrated artist capable of projecting her whole personality into music. She was blessed not only with great emotion but with a tremendous voice that could penetrate the inner recesses of the listener." In *Early Jazz,* Gunther Schuller listed the components of Bessie's vocal style: "a remarkable ear for and control of intonation, in all its subtlest functions; a perfectly centered, naturally produced voice (in her prime); an extreme sensitivity to word meaning and the sensory, almost physical, feeling of a word; and, related to this, superb diction and what singers call projection. She was certainly the first singer on jazz records to value diction, not for itself, but as a vehicle for conveying emotional states. . . . Perhaps even more remarkable was her pitch control. She handled this with such ease and naturalness that one is apt to take it for granted. Bessie's fine microtonal shadings . . . are all part of a personal, masterful technique of great subtlety, despite the frequently boisterous mood or language." Further, Schuller heralds Bessie as "the first complete jazz singer," whose influence on Billie Holiday and a whole generation of jazz singers cannot be overestimated.

In spite of her commercial success, Bessie's personal life never strayed far from the blues theme. Her marriage to Jack Gee was stormy, punctuated by frequent fights and breakups, and, despite the 1926 adoption of Jack Gee, Jr., it ended in a bitter separation in 1929, after which Gee contrived to keep the boy from Bessie for years by moving him from one boarding home to another. Another battle Bessie waged was with the liquor bottle. Though able to abstain from drinking for considerable periods, Bessie often indulged in binges that were infamous among her troupe and family. Equally well known to her intimates was Bessie's bisexual promiscuity.

Bessie rode the crest of recorded popularity until about 1929, when the three-pronged fork of radio, talking pictures, and the Great Depression pitched the entire recording industry onto the critical list. Though her personal-appearance schedule continued at a brisk pace, the prices she could demand dipped, she was forced to sell her beloved railroad car, and the smaller towns she played housed theaters whose general quality and facilities were a burden. Even so, she starred in a 1929 two-reel film, "St. Louis Blues," a near-autobiographical effort that received some exposure until 1932.

Bessie's lean years were coming to an end in the summer of 1937. The recording industry's revival soared on the craziness of the early Swing Era, spearheaded by the success of the Benny Goodman band. Bessie had proved adaptable in her repertoire and could certainly swing with the best of them; even better, blues singing was experiencing a revival in popular taste. Bessie's only appearance on New York's famed Fifty-second Street came on a cold February Sunday afternoon in 1936 at the Famous Door, when she was backed by Bunny Berigan, Joe Bushkin, and other

---

They called her the "Empress of the Blues."

---

regulars of the "Door" band. The impact of her singing that day has remained with those present for more than half a century. Much was made of the fact that Mildred Bailey wisely refused to follow Bessie's performance. Further, that one afternoon's singing gave rise to other possible Smith appearances with popular swing performers: John Hammond claimed a 1937 record date teaming Bessie and members of the Basie band was in the works; Lionel Hampton recalled Goodman's eagerness to record with Bessie. Another film was planned. Even Bessie's personal life was on the upswing in 1937 with the steady and loving influence of companion Richard Morgan.

Early in the morning of September 26, 1937, Bessie and Morgan were driving from a Memphis performance to Darling, Mississippi, for the next day's show. Near Clarksdale, Mississippi, their car was involved in an accident that was fatal to Bessie. One of the persistent myths about Bessie is that she bled to death because a white hospital refused to admit her. This story was given impetus by the unfortunate 1937 down beat story by John Hammond, and was perpetuated by Edward Albee's 1960 play, The Death of Bessie Smith. Author Chris Albertson puts this myth firmly to rest. Albertson

won a Grammy award for his booklet that accompanied the 1970 Columbia reissue of Bessie's complete works (their second major reissue project). He was spurred to deeper investigation, resulting in his acclaimed 1972 biography, Bessie.

Albertson describes Bessie's funeral: "On Monday, October 4, 1937, Philadelphia witnessed one of the most spectacular funerals in its history. Bessie Smith, a black super-star of the previous decade—a 'has been,' fatally injured on a dark Mississippi road eight days earlier—was given a send-off befitting the star she had never really ceased to be. . . . When word of her death reached the black community, the body had to be moved [to another location] which more readily accommodated the estimated ten thousand admirers who filed past her bier on Sunday, October 3. . . . The crowd outside was now seven thousand strong, and policemen were having a hard time holding it back. To those who had known Bessie in her better days, the sight was familiar."

Selected discography

The following Columbia LP reissues represent the entire published output of Bessie Smith. The notes in the accompanying booklet are by Smith biographer Chris Albertson. Many of the records used in this remastering process were borrowed from the Yale University collection donated by Carl Van Vechten and from the private collection of Robert Fertig.

The World's Greatest Blues Singer, Columbia GP 33, 1970.
Any Woman's Blues, Columbia G 30126, 1970.
Empty Bed Blues, Columbia G 30450, 1971.
The Empress, Columbia G 30818, 1971.
Nobody's Blues But Mine, Columbia, G 31093, 1971.

Sources

Books

Albertson, Chris, Bessie, Stein and Day, 1972.
Donaldson, Norman, and Betty Donaldson, How Did They Die?, St. Martin's Press, 1980.
Kinkle, Roger D., The Complete Encyclopedia of Popular Music and Jazz 1900-1950, Volume 3, Arlington House, 1974.
Morgenstern, Dan, Jazz People, Harry N. Abrams, 1976.
Rust, Brian, Jazz Records 1897-1942, 5th Revised and Enlarged Edition, Volume 2, Storyville Publications, 1982.
Schuller, Gunther, Early Jazz, Oxford University Press, 1968.
Schuller, Gunther, The Swing Era, Oxford University Press, 1989.
Shapiro, Nat, and Nat Hentoff, Editors, The Jazz Makers (Bessie Smith chapter by George Hoefer), Rinehart & Co., 1957.

Terkel, Studs, and Millie Hawk Daniel, *Giants of Jazz,* revised
  edition, Thomas Y. Crowell Company, 1975.

Periodicals

Esquire, June 1969.
High Fidelity Magazine, October 1970; May 1975.
National Review, July 1, 1961.
Newsweek, February 1, 1971; January 22, 1973.
Saturday Review, December 29, 1951; February 26, 1972.

—*Robert Dupuis*

The Smiths

Rock group

The Smiths burst onto the British music scene in 1983, just a few months after guitarist Johnny Marr approached a bookish recluse named Steven Morrissey with the idea of forming a band. The marriage of Marr's bright sound and Morrissey's brooding lyrics proved irresistable to British youth, who sent the group's debut album, *The Smiths,* to the number-two position on the charts. With songs about the immorality of beef-eating, the brutality of school headmasters, and the impossibility of finding happiness in love, the group seemed an unlikely candidate for pop stardom, but as Mark Peel noted in *Stereo Review:* "The Smiths' songs are never oppressive or despair-inspiring, thanks to Morrissey's breezy, almost whimsical vocals and Johnny Marr's cheerful acoustic and ringing electric guitars. . . . For those who like music that bites back, I can't think of a more stimulating way to spend an evening than in the company of the Smiths."

Morrissey's dark outlook began in his childhood, which he remembered as "totally morbid," according to *People* contributor Fred Hauptfuhrer. It was full of "undercurrents of violence and hopelessness among the pupils at school" and "dreadful, incredibly uninteresting episodes with girls." The divorce of his parents sent him even deeper into his private world of books and music. Oscar Wilde, Susan Brownmiller, and Molly Haskell were favorite authors; his best-loved band was the New York Dolls, five glitter-rockers from Manhattan. "For me, they were the official end of the Sixties," David Fricke quotes him in *Rolling Stone.* "They were the first sign that there was change, that someone was going to kick through and get rid of all the nonsense. It gave people hope." Fricke commented, "With their homely appearance, Marr's Byrds-abilly jangle and Morrisscy's wistful, introspective lyrics, the Smiths look and sound nothing like the singer's beloved sex-mad Dolls," but Morrissey insists that there is a strong spiritual link between the two groups. "Obviously, it's a different time," he said, "but it's the same, in that you can feel the danger."

For several years after his high school graduation, Morrissey remained holed up in his mother's house. He drew unemployment, read obsessively, and wrote for his own amusement. He might have continued indefinitely in this pattern, had Johnny Marr not knocked on his door in 1982. Morrissey told Fricke: "[Marr] had heard of me, of this strange literary recluse. . . . He was curious." After reading Morrissey's poetry, Marr's curiosity turned to eagerness to work with the eccentric writer, who was several years older than himself. By 1982 the duo had joined forces with bassist Andy Rourke and drummer Mike Joyce to form the Smiths. The name was chosen for its earthy, nondescript quality, as a way of lashing out at the empty glitz that the Smiths felt typified most popular groups. Their aim was to produce music that would be "like consciousness-raising sessions," Morrissey told Fricke. "They're very depressing. 'Why should we sit around and talk about our innermost feelings?' But those little things bring people together. They allow people to open and blossom, to learn things about themselves. That's what the Smiths aim to achieve."

The Smiths were able to start spreading their message without the painful dues-paying most bands must endure. After they'd played just seven gigs together, radio producer John Walters arranged for them to record several sessions for the BBC and also won them a contract with the independent Rough Trade Records label. The radio broadcasts built up an enthusiastic following for the band even before their first album, *The Smiths,* was released. *Encyclopedia of Rock* authors Phil Hardy and Dave Laing called that recording "a superb piece of work by their producer that showcased the florid blend of Marr's fluid, intricate guitar work and Morrissey's plaintive vocal style." By the time *Meat Is Murder* was released in 1985, the Smiths had spawned "a new U.K. generation of bands like James, the Woodentops and Easterhouse that play evocative but distinctively nonphallic rock and roll," according to Fricke. The album entered the British charts in the number-one slot and went gold within a week. It also captured the attention of U.S. listeners who gave the Smiths an enthusiastic welcome at their first U.S. appearances in April 1985.

Newsweek contributor Jim Miller credited the band with forging "one of the most striking neoclassical approaches in contemporary rock. Synthesizers are strictly taboo. . . . Marr uses a 12-string Rickenbacker—the folk-rock instrument made famous by the Byrds—to fashion intricate arabesques of sound with a faintly Moorish aura. The exotic effect is amplified by Morrissey, who looks like a bookish version of James Dean. Onstage he affects the manner of a pallid, swooning manchild and often makes his voice sound like an oriental flute navigating a non-Western scale. . . . His lyrics are laced with images of loneliness, abandonment and sexual langor. But the music, powered by Marr's guitar, has a sharp edge." Frank Rose offered additional praise in *The Nation:* "The sound of the Smiths is a difficult but strangely compelling amalgam of American blues and British folk set to a spinning beat. . . . [Johnny Marr's] off-center compositions serve as a perfect vehicle for Morrissey's ethereal quaverings. Morrissey doesn't sing with the tune, he sings all around it, and the resulting tension is as hypnotic as it is disorienting. . . . His voice and Marr's guitar are capable of being simultaneously forthright and tremulous in a way that captures the essence of vulnerability."

While the Smiths' musical talent was for the most part unquestioned, it was occasionally overshadowed by Morrissey's persona. Convinced of the social relevance of rock music and outspoken in his belief, he supplied journalists with a steady stream of controversial quotes. He told Hauptfuhrer that "many people underestimate [rock] as a force; this is dramatically wrong. . . . It is the last refuge for young people; no other platform has so much exposure." He was quick to criticize those whom he considered less than serious about the social power of their music, observing: "Duran Duran and Wham! are planets from what I feel . . .

Michael Jackson has outlived his usefulness. . . . Prince and Madonna are of no earthly value whatsoever." The music press also speculated at length about Morrissey's sexual orientation, with many writers assuming he was gay because of the lack of specific male-female references in his lyrics. Morrissey brushed such questions aside, saying that he was celibate and had no sexual viewpoint at all. He deliberately wrote ambiguous lyrics, he told Fricke, because "when people and things are entirely revealed in an obvious way,. . .it freezes the imagination of the observer. There is nothing to probe for, nothing to dwell on or try to unravel. With the Smiths, nothing is ever open and shut."

The Smiths are generally considered to have been at their peak when they recorded *The Queen Is Dead.* By the time *Strangeways, Here We Come* was released, the group had broken up. Marr had decided to work as sideman for various rock superstars; Morrissey, after some consideration, elected to disband the Smiths and embark on a solo career. *Stereo Review* was highly critical of *Strangeways.* Its reviewer praised Marr's

---

The Smiths' aim was to produce music that would be "like consciousness-raising sessions."

---

contribution to the album, but declared that Morrissey had "gone off the deep end" and created "a vicious, raging, stream of consciousness tirade" with little to redeem it. "This guy is just plain nuts. . . . I imagine Marr spinning out these wonderful guitar arpeggios and twisting, odd chord progressions—and all the time nervously watching out of the corner of his eye, hoping that the Smiths' tormented singer doesn't come at him with an axe."

Simon Reynolds was kinder to the group's final effort in his *New Statesman* review of *Strangeways,* calling it "a fascinating mess." He also speculated on the defunct group's contribution to popular music: "Morrissey's own idea of why the Smiths were important is rather traditional—he talks of the Smiths as a solitary bastion of Meaning and Human Depth in an age of processed, vapid, dehumanised, plastic pop. In fact, it's more complex and interesting than this. . . . Morrissey *glamorises* failure. And rather than matching our misery to his in a simple process of identification, we're seduced into aspiring to the same heroic pitch of maladjustment and exile. . . . Smiths music is perfectly poised between the vague dream of something more and the sinking realisation that the dream will always remain out of reach."

Selected discography

The Smiths, Rough Trade, 1984.
Hatful of Hollow, Rough Trade, 1984.
Meat Is Murder, Sire, 1985.
The Queen Is Dead, Sire, 1986.
Louder Than Bombs, Sire, 1987.
Strangeways, Here We Come, Sire, 1988.
"Rank," Sire, 1988.

Sources

Books

Hardy, Phil, and Dave Laing, *Encyclopedia of Rock*, McDonald, 1987.

Periodicals

Mademoiselle, July 1984.
Nation, August 3-10, 1985.
New Statesman, September 18, 1987.
People, June 24, 1985.
Rolling Stone, October 9, 1986; December 15, 1988.
Stereo Review, July 1985; October 1986; January 1988.

—Joan Goldsworthy

Mercedes Sosa

Singer

Mercedes Sosa's songs about the pain of exile, the fear of political violence, and the struggle for justice inspire millions of Latin Americans who know that Sosa has lived her words. Born in rural Tucuman, Argentina, she grew up in a culture closer to that of the Incas than to that of their European conquerors. Singing came naturally to her, and by the age of fifteen she had won the amateur hour at a local radio station. Sosa knew then that singing was her life's work, but she also suffered from intense stage fright that made every performance a struggle. Nevertheless, she controlled her fears and became one of the leaders of the "nueva cancion" movement that revitalized Latin American music.

Nueva cancion merged folk rhythms with lyrics that were an artistic response to growing government brutality. Sosa, who grew up in poverty, says that social problems have always been a source of artistic inspiration for her. She dislikes being labeled a protest singer, however; she explained to Larry Rohter in the *New York Times:* "It is like an invitation for someone to put a stamp on the songs that says 'prohibited' or 'interdicted.' The intelligence of the artist needs to be broader in the face of such possible barriers. Besides, artists are not political leaders. The only power they have is to draw people into the theater."

Censorship is something with which Sosa is intimately acquainted. During the height of Argentina's military dictatorship, which was responsible for the deaths and disappearances of more than 9,000 citizens, she was targeted for official harassment and intimidation. Sosa, her band, and her audience were all arrested at one concert because she dared to sing "When They Have the Land," a call for agrarian reform. After her release, she set out to show the military that she could not be intimidated and scheduled several more concerts. They sold out almost immediately, but had to be canceled due to numerous bomb threats. Finally, the military governor forbade her from making anymore live appearances. As her music was already banned from Argentine radio and television, Sosa was forced to leave the country in order to support herself, traveling to Europe in January 1979.

For three years she lived in France and Spain, but the psychic toll of exile proved to be too much for her; she felt she could no longer sing. "It was a mental problem, a problem of morale," she told Rohter. "It wasn't my throat, or anything physical. When you are in exile, you take your suitcase, but there are things that don't fit. There are things in your mind, like colors and smells and childhood attitudes, and there is also the pain and the death you saw. You shouldn't deny those things, because to do so can make you ill."

Sosa returned to her native land in 1982, just in time to see the military leadership crumble and be replaced by civilian rule. Her first public performance in the newly democratic country was recorded and released as *Mercedes Sosa Live in Argentina. Esquire* magazine commented on her performance: "Her voice nearly strikes you dead. It is soft, deep, and compelling. And it moves you as it did the fifty thousand adoring countrymen who could be heard erupting into applause." Rather than being bitter about the years she was unwelcome in her homeland, Sosa is philosophical, reflecting that exile broadened her horizons and allowed her to reach new audiences. Besides folk-based tunes, she now includes jazz, pop, and other forms in her repertoire. *Boston Globe* contributor Fernando Gonzalez praised both her stylistic diversity and her "stunning range of nuance and dynamic. She can turn a song into an anthem or an intimate conversation seemingly at will." "Your Spanish may or may not be good, but Mercedes Sosa requires no translation," concluded *Esquire.* "Hers is the song of all those who have overcome their fear of singing out."

Selected discography

Gracias A La Vida, Philips, 1988.

Sources

Boston Globe, November 3, 1989.
Esquire, May 1989.
New York Times, October 9, 1988.
Variety, October 26, 1988.

—*Joan Goldsworthy*

Cat
Stevens

Singer, songwriter, pianist, and guitarist

Singer-songwriter Cat Stevens has gone through many changes during the course of his career. Beginning as a British teen idol in the late 1960s, he eventually rose to great heights of popular and critical acclaim as a folk artist in the 1970s. Then, while still enjoying a large following of music fans, Stevens converted to Islam and stopped putting out records to devote himself to his new religion. He took the name Yusuf Islam, and eventually rid himself of all vestiges of his secular career, giving away his guitars and the many gold records he had earned.

Stevens was born Steven Georgiou to Greek immigrant parents, July 21, 1948, in London, England. Interested in music from an early age, he preferred the stirring songs of his parents' native country as a child, but in his adolescence became more attracted to the rock and roll music his friends enjoyed. By the time Stevens had graduated from secondary school and was attending the Hammersmith College of Art, he was also performing in small clubs in London. He had gathered a fairly large following, and eventually a professional manager became interested in the young man's talent. Shortly afterwards, Stevens's first demo tape garnered him a recording contract with Decca in England.

Decca saw Stevens as a pop artist, and wanted him to record teen-oriented songs. Perhaps because of his youth, the singer-songwriter at first had no trouble complying. His first album, *Matthew and Son,* was released in 1967, and the title track became a British hit. More successes, including "I Love My Dog" and "The First Cut Is the Deepest," followed, and he toured England, Belgium, and France. But Stevens became dissatisfied with his material, and tried to get Decca to record some more mature tunes that he had written. When they refused, he grew more depressed about his career. He later told Mark F. Zeller in *Rolling Stone* that during this period, "in order to get onstage, I used to have to drink. To get drunk." Stevens also neglected his health in other ways, and in late 1968 had to be hospitalized for three months with tuberculosis.

By the time Stevens was well enough to leave the hospital, he had decided to drop out of the music scene for a while. He reemerged with a more mature, folk-oriented style, his instrumentation was more spare, and his appearance drastically changed—the cleanshaven teen idol now had long hair and a bushy beard. The album he recorded in 1970, *Mona Bone Jakon,* received a great deal of critical acclaim and brought Stevens to the attention of music fans in the United States. The follow-up, 1970's *Tea for the Tillerman,* became his first gold album, and included the classics "Wild World," "Father and Son," and "Miles from Nowhere." His popularity was further increased in that year by a live radio concert in Los Angeles, California, which prompted *Los Angeles Times* critic Robert Hilburn to hail Stevens as "an exceptional singer and artist whose highly distinctive voice has the rare ability to combine the strength, fragility, and sometimes mystery of his highly personal compositions."

Stevens's success continued throughout the 1970s, and he racked up gold album after gold album. *Teaser and the Firecat,* his 1971 effort, had on it three songs that are perhaps his most famous—"Moonshadow," "Morning Has Broken," and "Peace Train." In 1972, *Catch Bull at Four* yielded the hit "Sitting"; 1974's *Buddah and the Chocolate Box* brought forth "Oh, Very Young" and a remake of the Sam Cooke smash, "Another Saturday Night." But the latter album began a period of slight critical disfavor for Stevens—many reviewers felt it and his subsequent albums did not measure up to his earlier work. He was still supported by his fans, however, and his hits during the late 1970s included "Ready," "Two Fine People," and his last big-selling single, "Old School Yard."

But as early as the mid-1970s, forces were at work in Stevens's personal life which foreshadowed a drastic turn-about. According to Zeller, he nearly drowned while swimming at a California beach. Struggling against the undertow, Stevens made a promise to serve God if his life was spared. He told Zeller: "Immediately, a wave came from behind and pushed me forward. All of a sudden, I was swimming back." Then, shortly afterwards, his older brother gave him a copy of the Koran—the holy scriptures of the Islamic faith—to read. By 1977, Stevens went public with his conversion to Islam and his decision to stop recording secular music; however, A&M, his record company, had enough of his material stored up to release a final album, *Back to Earth,* in 1978.

When last heard from, Stevens, or Yusuf Islam, as he now prefers to be called, was running a Muslim school for children in London, England. There, he uses his musical talents to write religious songs and poems for the pupils. Though in 1984 he emphatically denied rumors that he was living in Iran as a follower of the late Ayatollah Khomeini and that he was studying to become an Ayatollah himself, he resurfaced as the object of controversy in 1989 when he came out in support of the late Ayatollah's death threats to author Salman Rushdie, whom he considers to have defamed the Islamic religion with his book, *The Satanic Verses.* Reportedly, Yusuf Islam is still considering recording again, though his albums would most likely be expressions of his faith aimed primarily at children. "He believes his mission is to teach others to accept his religion," explained Zeller.

Selected discography

LPs

Matthew and Son (includes "Matthew and Son"), Decca, 1967.
New Masters, Decca, 1968.
Mona Bone Jakon (includes "Mona Bone Jakon," "I Think I See the Light," "Lady D'Arbaville," "Fill My Eyes," and "Lilywhite"), A&M, 1970.
Tea for the Tillerman (includes "Tea for the Tillerman," "Sad Lisa," "Longer Boats," "Father and Son," "Wild World," and "Miles from Nowhere"), A&M, 1970.
Teaser and the Firecat (includes "Moonshadow," "Morning Has Broken," and "Peace Train"), A&M, 1971.
Catch Bull at Four (includes "Sitting"), A&M, 1972.
Foreigner, A&M, 1973.
Buddah and the Chocolate Box (includes "Oh, Very Young" and "Another Saturday Night"), A&M, 1974.
Greatest Hits (includes "Ready" and "Two Fine People"), A&M, 1975.
Numbers, A&M, 1975.
Izitso (includes "Old School Yard" and "Is a Dog a Doughnut"), A&M, 1977.
Back to Earth, A&M, 1978.

Also released singles, "I Love My Dog" and "The First Cut is the Deepest," Decca, c. 1968.

Sources

Los Angeles Times, June 8, 1971.
Rolling Stone, August 25, 1988.
Variety, March 15, 1989.

—*Elizabeth Thomas*

Andy Summers

Guitarist, songwriter

When the Police gained worldwide fame in the late 1970s, guitar aficionados began talking about Andy Summers. His was an unusual style for a rocker, one that bypassed gratuitous fretboard flash and stressed texture and color instead. Though power-packed, it bordered on lushness; critics rhapsodized about it with words suggesting wetness—liquid phrasing, floating arpeggios, washes of sound. Along with Sting's melodic bass playing and Stewart Copeland's splashy, propulsive drumming, Summers's guitar style sculpted the sound of the Police.

For five consecutive years beginning in 1984, which marked the onset of his post-Police career, Summers was named best pop guitarist in the prestigious *Guitar Player* Readers Poll Awards. The tribute reflects his deservedly high stature, but it's nevertheless odd: At that time, he was moving increasingly away from both rock and pop and into territory more suited to his atmospheric, coloristic bent. With *The Golden Wire,* his 1989 solo release, he arrived at a genre that straddled jazz and new age, one he called "new fusion." "This is it for me now, the way I want to continue," he told *Guitar Player.* "I don't really want to do too much more rock stuff. I had a great shot at all that, but musically I really have a need to move on, and this record sets the path for me. Aping what one has already done is just so dangerous and unrewarding."

Andrew James Somers was born in 1942 in Poulton-Fylde, England. (He later changed his surname to Summers to avoid having to spell it.) Soon afterward his family moved to Bournemouth, a resort town on the south coast, where his father bought a restaurant. From his earliest years he was captivated by music, introducing himself to jazz and blues through his brother's record collection, and later soaking in live sounds from Bournemouth's busy jazz scene. He shrugged off piano lessons as a child, but became serious about music at the age of 14, when he got his first guitar. Less than two years later he landed a steady gig with a hotel band at a local jazz club. There, he caught the interest of George "Zoot" Money, leader of an r&b/jazz ensemble called Big Roll Band. Money convinced him to come up to London and join the band; a live album cut shortly thereafter—*The All Happening Zoot Money's Big Roll Band At Klook's Kleek*—prominently featured the young guitarist. Summers's preliminary career as journeyman had begun.

During the second half of the 1960s Summers played and recorded with a variety of rock bands, including the psychedelic Dantalion's Chariot, the experimental Soft Machine, and one of the seminal English Rock Invasion bands, the Animals, on whose 1968 release *Love Is* he was featured. Around 1969 the Animals broke up, and

For the Record. . .

Full name, Andrew James Summers; surname originally Somers; born December 31, 1942, in Poulton-Fylde (near Blackpool), England; grew up in Bournemouth, England; father was a restaurant owner; married and divorced twice, first time with Kate Unter (attributes both divorces to the stresses of fame and touring with the Police); children: (first marriage) Layla. *Education:* Studied classical composition and guitar at the University of California at Los Angeles, 1969-73.

Took up guitar at the age of 14; less than two years later, was playing professionally at a local jazz club; in mid- and late-1960s, played and recorded with Zoot Money's Big Roll Band, Dantalion's Chariot, the Soft Machine, and the Animals; in 1969 moved to U.S. and enrolled at UCLA to study classical music; after graduating in 1973, returned to England, where he played with bands led by Neil Sedaka, Kevin Coyne, and Kevin Ayers; while playing with Strontium 90 in 1977, met drummer Stewart Copeland and bass player Sting of the Police, and subsequently joined their group; played with the Police until their breakup around 1984, then branched out with film, duo, and solo projects.

Awards: Best pop guitarist in the *Guitar Player* Readers Poll five consecutive years, 1984-89 (as a five-time winner, he is now listed in *Guitar Player*'s Gallery Of The Greats.)

Addresses: *Home*—Los Angeles, CA. *Record company (press/public information)*—Private Music, 220 East 23rd Street, New York, NY 10010.

Summers changed course. Enrolling at the University of California at Los Angeles, he spent the next four years studying classical guitar and composition; to earn spending money he gave guitar lessons. After graduating he returned to both rock and England. Again bouncing from band to band, he spent the next few years backing such musicians as Neil Sedaka, Kevin Coyne, and Kevin Ayers. His last stint as sideman was with a band called Strontium 90.

One night in May 1977 Summers was joined by two London musicians at a Strontium 90 gig. They were drummer Stewart Copeland and bass player Sting, from a new pop-rock trio called the Police, and their playing made a quick and deep impression upon the guitarist. "I thought, 'Jesus Christ, this is what I've been looking for for ages,'" Andy told *Melody Maker*. "I'd always wanted to play in a three-piece band, and at that point I'd just been playing behind people all the time and I was getting pretty frustrated with it. Then I

saw these two and I felt that the three of us together would be very strong." That summer, Summers went to hear the Police in London. After jamming with them as a second guitar player—the group at that time included guitarist Henri Padovani—they asked him to join. For various reasons, Padovani soon left the group, and the Police was again a trio.

Over the next year, the Police cut their style on England's volatile punk-rock scene, playing night after night until a distinctive style began to emerge. "I started playing all these jazz chords, moving into different keys, trying all kinds of things behind Sting's vocals," Summers recalled in the *New York Times*. "Stewart would try different cross-rhythms. And Sting, who had played in jazz-rock bands, took it in stride. That's where our style came from." In 1978 they scored their first hit with their second single, "Roxanne," and the Police sound—a blend of Jamaican reggae, new wave, English pop, and hard rock—hit the airwaves. That concoction was served up on their first two albums, *Outlandos D'Amour* and *Reggatta De Blanc;* on *Zenyatta Mondatta,* their third release, they broadened their sound, lightening up on the reggae feel and mixing in other ethnic hues. By the release of *Ghosts in the Machine* in 1981, the Police were a worldwide phenomenon; Summers, recognized as a premier guitar stylist, appeared on the September 1982 cover of *Guitar Player.* But to many critics, their finest work came in 1983, with their final studio album. On *Synchronicity,* the *New York Times* wrote, "they have brought all the aspects of their singular pop art into focus"; like the Beatles' landmark *Sgt. Pepper's Lonely Hearts Club Band,* the LP has "its finger so firmly on the pulse of the times that it manages to be genuinely avant-garde and genuinely commercial at the same time."

In a sense, Sting's approach to songwriting dictated Summers's instrumental style. With an open, jaunty feel borrowed from reggae, the songs made musical use of space, giving Summers room to indulge in subtleties that would otherwise be obscured. "I wanted to float more, to use extended harmonies and a kind of echo rather than that heavy, bar-chord, power-chord kind of playing," he told the *New York Times.* "There was a desire in the group to avoid rock cliches and avoid sounding like a heavy rock trio." To that end, his guitar style "became very harmonic and orchestral," as he explained in *Guitar Player.* "Instead of the guitar wailing all the time and being supported by drums and bass, we found we had three soloists." (Stretching that concept to the limit, the group would actually reverse the traditional roles of guitar and bass, bringing the latter to the fore. As the *New York Times* noted, "Often the drums and guitar seem to be filling in dabs of color around Sting's stripped-down bass patterns.")

On his own, meanwhile, Summers realized a longtime dream—to collaborate with Robert Fripp, a guitarist who cut his chops on the same Bournemouth jazz-club circuit and went on to fame with King Crimson. In 1982 they recorded *I Advance Masked,* an instrumental album that blends jazz and oriental influences, and followed that up two years later with *Bewitched.* Though still involved with the Police, Summers found a certain liberation in his new stylistic direction. "*I Advance Masked* opened up people's ears somewhat to what else I could do, and I think *Bewitched* really will," he told *Guitar Player* at the time. "With an instrumental album, you can express more abstract kinds of musical feelings and be more elliptical. You're not tied to accompanying a vocal or to necessarily a verse-chorus-bridge format. You can be more experimental and explore different areas altogether."

When the Police began drifting apart in mid-1984, Summers moved to Hollywood to work in film, scoring such movies as *Down And Out in Beverly Hills.* Like his albums with Fripp, the film projects offered him an opportunity to move beyond rock. "I've been offered a lot of stuff, but most of it I turn down because I don't really like the screenplays," he told *Guitar Player.* "[Rock musicians] tend to get offered fairly dumb, rock-type movies, and that's not what I want to do. I'd rather do stuff outside the rock and roll genre." Soon he returned to making records, completing his first solo effort, *XYZ,* in 1987. Critically, it fared poorly; most writers echoed the *New York Post*'s Richard Gehr, who remarked upon the guitarist's "harmonically intricate solos that sound impressive but say little." But Summers saw it as part of a personal artistic progression. "This record is in some ways a synthesis of my involvement with ambient music, the work with Fripp and the film scores," he told the *New York Times,* "all contained in a rock vocal album with little hooky songs."

As suggested by *Mysterious Barricades,* his subsequent solo LP, the strongest element in Andy's post-Police style was not rock but ambience. His greatest success in that style came with his 1989 *The Golden Wire,* a guitar-intensive album that he recorded and co-produced at his own 24-track studio. Part of the record's appeal is its stylistic ambiguity. "It's not absolutely jazz or absolutely new age," the composer observed in the *New York Times.* "If I had to put a new name to it, I would call it a 'new fusion' record." Yet without a ready slot in which to stick the album, record stores and radio programmers had difficulty promoting it, and its commercial success was disappointing. With the critics, on the other hand, the album hit the bull's eye. "By turns spooky, propulsive and spellbinding," wrote *Musician,* "*The Golden Wire* is a guitar-paced cascade of rock, jazz, blues and classically textured world beat that translates into 11 exquisite numbers." *Guitar Player* was more succinct, calling it "instrumental music of exquisite beauty and shifting moods."

One of the album's highlights is its sole vocal track, an Indian song called "Piya Tose" that Summers first heard in a movie. Like his Arabic-influenced "Mother" from *Synchronicity,* "Piya Tose" displays his talent for simulating the idiosyncrasies of an ethnic style. In *Guitar Player,* he explained how he achieved an authentic guitar sound: "Moving the pitch around with the whammy bar facilitates that Indian kind of phrasing—those bends and cries. I learned a lot of the phrasing years ago, when I first started. I used to copy Vilayat Kahn's solos when I was trying to learn Indian sitar solos on the guitar. He was my favorite. For that kind of playing, I keep the bar in my hand the whole time I'm soloing."

Summers is a wizard with electronic modifiers; the ambient, moody sounds he favors are achieved part-

---

Along with Sting's melodic bass playing and Stewart Copeland's splashy, propulsive drumming, Andy Summers's guitar style sculpted the sound of the Police.

---

ly through various effects devices. He's also known for his pioneering work in guitar synthesis, the results of which can be heard on albums as early as the Police's *Ghosts in the Machine.* The basic principle that underlies his approach, he explained in *Guitar Player,* is that guitar synth shouldn't be used to mimic guitar. "They are two different instruments, so why even confuse the two?" (He also revealed a not-surprising preference: "My favorite sounds are the high, spacey ones that are very ambient.") Yet Summers derives more from guitar synths than weird sounds. "For me, the guitar synthesizer is a great writing instrument. I certainly find composition is often inspired purely by sound itself."

In his spare time, Summers often turns to photography. He shot all of the Police's world tours, and his work, featured in several magazines and U.S. exhibitions, has been published in a 1983 book called *Throb.* For him, having passions outside of music is crucial. "The most important thing is to live a full, exciting, rounded-out life," he told *Guitar Player.* "If you get so into playing guitar and living that life, you become a very boring person eventually. There are so many people like that. Develop as a person and try to keep things in perspective."

Selected discography

With the Police

Outlandos D'Amour, A&M, 1978.
Reggatta De Blanc, A&M, 1979.
Zenyatta Mondatta, A&M, 1980.
Ghost in the Machine, A&M, 1981.
Synchronicity, A&M, 1983.

With Robert Fripp

I Advance Masked, A&M, 1982.
Bewitched, A&M, 1984.

Solo LPs

XYZ, MCA, 42007, 1987.
Mysterious Barricades, Private Music, 1988.
The Golden Wire, Private, 1989.

Soundtracks

Down and Out in Beverly Hills, MCA, 1986.
A Weekend at Bernie's, 1989.

Sources

Books

Kamin, Philip, *The Police Chronicles,* New York, c1984.
Quatrochi, Danny, *Police Confidential,* New York, c1986.
St. Michael, Mick, *Accompanying the Police,* New York, 1985, c1984.
Sutcliffe, Phil, *The Police,* London, c1981.

Periodicals

Guitar Player, September 1982; October 1984; June 1986; July 1989.
Life, November, 1983.
Melody Maker (insert), [c.Aug. or Sept.], 1983.
Musician, May, 1989 (review).
New York Times, November 11, 1979; October 10, 1980; June 26, 1983; July 15, 1987; March 22, 1989 (preview); April 2, 1989 (review).
People, January 21, 1980.
Village Voice, January 14, 1989.

—*Kyle Kevorkian*

The Temptations

Vocal group

The Temptations, one of the few groups to survive from the days when the sound of the Motown record company ruled the airwaves, have maintained their popularity through more than two decades of changing styles in popular music. Commenting on the group in the *Rolling Stone Illustrated History of Rock and Roll,* Joe McEwen and Jim Miller wrote: "While the Four Tops covered the frenetic side of the Motown sound and the Miracles monopolized its romantic side, the Temptations quite simply stood as the finest vocal group in Sixties soul: they could outdress, outdance, and outsing any competition in sight." Today, the "Tempts" continue to project this dynamic yet elegant image in both their recordings and their live performances.

The group came together in Detroit in 1961, when Eddie Kendricks and Paul Williams, of the Primes, joined forces with Otis Williams, Al Bryant, and Melvin Franklin of the Distants. Both the Primes and the Distants were popular in Detroit, but neither had had a national hit. The five men originally christened the new group the Elgins, after a high-quality watch. Upon learning that the name was already taken, they settled for calling

For the Record. . .

Originally formed in Detroit, Michigan, in 1961 as the Elgins; name changed to the Temptations, 1961; original group consisted of **Otis Williams** (born October 30, 1949, in Texarkana, Texas), **Melvin Franklin** (born October 12, 1942, in Montgomery, Alabama), **Paul Williams** (born July 1, 1939, in Birmingham, Alabama; died August 17, 1973, in Detroit, Michigan, of a self-inflicted gunshot wound), **Edward James Kendricks** (born December 17, 1939, in Birmingham, Alabama), and **Elbridge Bryant**. Paul Williams was replaced in 1971 by **Richard Street** (born October 5, 1942, in Detroit, Michigan). Eddie Kendricks was replaced in 1971 by **Ricky Owens**; Owens was replaced in 1971 by **Damon Otis Harris** (born July 3, 1950, in Baltimore, Maryland); Harris was replaced in 1974 by **Glenn Leonard**; Leonard was replaced in 1982 by **Ron Tyson**. Elbridge Bryant was replaced in 1964 by **David Ruffin** (born January 18, 1941, in Wyanot, Mississippi); Ruffin was replaced in 1968 by **Dennis Edwards** (born February 3, 1943, in Birmingham, Alabama); Edwards's spot was filled from 1976-79 by **Louis Price** and from 1982-86 by **Ollie Woodson.**

Awards: Grammy Award for best rhythm and blues performance by a group, 1969, for "Cloud Nine," and 1972, for "Papa Was a Rolling Stone"; Grammy Awards for best rhythm and blues song and best rhythm and blues instrumental performance, 1972, for "Papa Was a Rolling Stone" American Music Award for best vocal group, 1974.

Addresses: *Office*—c/o Motown Record Corporation, Hollywood, Calif. 90028.

themselves the Temptations. "You can see today that it was the perfect name," commented Otis Williams in his book *Temptations.* "It was about style and elegance but also suggested romance and, frankly, sex." Williams added that from their earliest days, the group consciously cultivated a sophisticated image: "In our songs and in our moves, we were subtler and more romantic than some other guys, who were always grunting and sweating and carrying on."

After a few months of rehearsing, the Temptations auditioned for Detroit record producer Berry Gordy. Impressed by their intricate harmonizing, Gordy immediately offered them a contract with his fledgling record company, Motown. In their early days, the group played numerous gigs at Detroit clubs (where they had an enthusiastic following), sang backup for many of Motown's established stars, and toured the country with the Motortown Revue in the company of the

Supremes, Dionne Warwick, and others. Despite their obvious talent, however, the Temptations released seven singles without a hit. Gordy briefly renamed the act "the Pirates" in 1962, hoping to change their luck. The group's members were relieved when the Pirates' "Mind Over Matter" and "I'll Love You Till I Die" flopped. Williams explained in *Temptations,* "We'd have died for a hit, but if it meant going through life in pirate uniforms, no thanks!" By 1964, personality conflicts forced Al Bryant to leave the group; he was replaced by David Ruffin, a Detroit singer who had enjoyed some solo success. Ruffin had an athletic stage presence; his spins, cartwheels, and splits added an exciting new dimension to the Tempts' act. Further improvements came through the group's association with Cholly Atkins. This long-time professional dancer, who had served as choreographer for Gladys Knight and the Pips, Frankie Lymon and the Teenagers, the Cadillacs, and other successful groups, developed many of the Temptations' trademark smooth moves.

National success finally came in 1964 with "The Way You Do the Things You Do," a tune written and produced by Smokey Robinson, which peaked at number eleven on the pop charts. Capitalizing on the song's popularity, Motown released *Meet the Temptations,* an album containing "The Way You Do the Things You Do," and its B side, "Just Let Me Know," along with all of the group's previously unsuccessful singles. In 1965 another Smokey Robinson song, "My Girl," became their first number-one hit. Like most of the Tempts' early music, it was a ballad that Robinson had produced as well as written. In 1966 the group worked with producer Norman Whitfield for the first time, cutting one of their most popular songs, "Ain't Too Proud to Beg." It was the beginning of a long and successful collaboration. "Norman Whitfield could and did produce soft, smooth ballads with the best of them but, stylistically speaking, he was headed into another realm," wrote Otis Williams. "His backing tracks crackled with more intricate percussion, wailing, almost rock-style guitars, and arrangements that featured us as five distinct singers instead of one lead singer fronting a homogenized doo-wop chorus. . . .[He] took us in new directions without losing the heart of our sound."

For several years, the Temptations were one of the most popular acts in America. They played the hottest nightclubs, appeared on *The Ed Sullivan Show* and numerous other television programs, and did a series of recordings and television appearances with the Supremes that broadened both groups' appeal. Their stage routine became even more refined after a special four-headed microphone was designed for them. It allowed them to keep their distance so that even when executing complicated moves, they were in no danger of stepping on each other. Their great success brought its own set of problems, however. Some members proved unable to handle the wealth and popularity that had come their way. Ego clashes within the group became common. There were many personnel changes during the late sixties and early seventies: David Ruffin left to pursue a solo career in 1968 and was replaced by Dennis Edwards. Edwards's career with the group was fitful; he was asked to leave in 1974 and replaced by Louis Price; he returned briefly in 1979 but was soon turned out in favor of Ollie Woodson; and he came back to the group a third time in 1986. In 1970, Eddie Kendricks decided to follow Ruffin's lead and go solo; he was replaced by Ricky Owens of the Vibrations, but Owens was almost immediately dismissed in favor of Damon Harris, who stayed with the group until 1974. Harris was then replaced by Glenn Leonard, whose spot was taken by Ron Tyson in 1982. Paul Williams, considered by some as the soul of the Temptations,

---

Today, the "Tempts" continue to project their dynamic yet elegant image in both their recordings and their live performances.

---

was asked to leave the group in 1971 because of his worsening alcoholism and related health problems; his spot was filled by Richard Street. Two years later, Williams committed suicide in Detroit.

In the late 1960s and early 1970s, the Temptations and producer Whitfield pioneered the "psychedelic soul" movement, which was characterized by an electric funk sound and socially conscious lyrics. The trend yielded several big hits for the Tempts, including "Cloud Nine," "Ball of Confusion," and "Papa Was a Rolling Stone." Whitfield stuck with it long after it had been imitated enough to become a cliche, however, and the once-creative relationship between the Temptations and their producer stagnated. Otis Williams reported in *Temptations* that Whitfield began minimizing the singers' contributions to their own albums: "On some tracks our singing seemed to function as ornamentation for Norman's instrumental excursions. When we started reading articles where writers referred to us as 'the Norman Whitfield Choral Singers,' we really got mad." The Temptations' fans were disappointed as well. Record sales fell dramatically. The Temptations sought more artistic control over their recordings, but Berry Gordy was deaf to their requests. Frustrated, the group severed its association with Motown in 1976.

A two-year contract with Atlantic failed to help them out of their slump, however. It was the age of disco, when many Motown acts faded away. The Temptations weathered their share of personnel changes and inactive periods, but remained intact. In 1979 they renegotiated with Motown and returned to their old company. Shortly thereafter, the classic Motown sound came back into vogue and the Temptations were once again in demand. They reunited briefly with Ruffin and Kendricks for a tour, but personality conflicts soon resurfaced, and they quickly returned to a five-man lineup. After their appearance on the *Motown 25* television special, they teamed with the Four Tops for a "T'n'T Tour" that played to enthusiastic audiences around the world for nearly three years.

Selected discography

Singles; for Gordy Records, except as noted

"The Way You Do the Things You Do," 1964.
"My Girl," 1964.
"Since I Lost My Baby," 1965.
"Get Ready," 1966.
"Ain't Too Proud to Beg," 1966.
"Beauty Is Only Skin Deep," 1966.
"(I Know) I'm Losing You," 1966.
"I Wish It Would Rain," 1967.
"Cloud Nine," 1968.
(With the Supremes) "I'll Try Something New," Motown, 1969.
"I Can't Get Next to You," 1969.
"Ball of Confusion (That's What the World Is Today)," 1970.
"Just My Imagination (Running Away with Me)," 1971.
"Papa Was a Rollin' Stone," 1972.
"Keep Holding On," 1975.
"I Just Don't Know How to Let You Go," Atlantic, 1979.
"Sail Away," 1984.
"Treat Her Like a Lady," 1984.
"How Can You say That It's Over," 1985.
"I Wonder Who She's Seeing Now," Motown, 1987.

LPs; for Gordy Records, except as noted

Meet the Temptations, 1964.
The Temptations Sing Smokey, 1965.
Temptin' Temptations, 1965.
The Temptations Greatest Hits, 1966.
Temptations Live!, 1967.
Cloud Nine, 1969.
Temptations Greatest Hits, Volume II, 1970.
All the Million-Sellers, 1981.
The Temptations 25th Anniversary, Motown, 1986.
To Be Continued, 1986.
Together Again, Motown, 1987.

LPs; with Diana Ross and the Supremes; all for Motown

Diana Ross and the Supremes Join the Temptations, 1968.
TCB, 1968.
Together, 1969.
On Broadway, 1969.

Sources

Books

Dalton, David and Lenny Kaye, *Rock l00*, Grosset & Dunlap, 1977.

Hardy, Phil and Dave Laing, *Encyclopedia of Rock*, McDonald, 1987.
Miller, Jim, editor, *The Rolling Stone Illustrated History of Rock and Roll*, Rolling Stone Press, 1976.
Williams, Otis, and Patricia Romanowski, *Temptations*, Putman, 1988.

Periodicals

Billboard, May 3, 1986.
Newsweek, January 27, 1986.
People, August 25, 1986; September 1, 1986.

—Joan Goldsworthy

10,000 Maniacs

Rock group

"**O**ne of the most forceful and innovative young bands in America," according to John Leland in *Vogue,* is 10,000 Maniacs. Composed of lead singer and lyricist Natalie Merchant, bass player Steve Gustafson, drummer Jerry Augustyniak, keyboard player Dennis Drew, and lead guitarist Robert Buck, the Maniacs have been recording since the early 1980s but only began enjoying substantial success with the release of their 1987 album, *In My Tribe*. That disc, and the subsequent *Blind Man's Zoo,* have made popular 10,000 Maniacs' particularly tuneful manner of social protest—their songs take on issues such as child abuse, environmental problems, and unwanted pregnancy. As Ira Robbins of *Rolling Stone* summed, the band's "plain-spoken music is an elegant rock descendant of American and British folk traditions."

The core of the group that became 10,000 Maniacs formed around Gustafson, Drew, and Buck in Jamestown, New York, in 1981. Soon afterwards, the band, which had played under monikers such as Still Life, and the Burn Victims, decided to change its name. The new name evolved from a mistake about the title of a B-grade horror film, *2,000 Maniacs*. Merchant, though younger than the other group members, knew Gustafson

and Drew because they ran the student radio station at Jamestown Community College, where she attended classes. She began showing up where the Maniacs performed, at small clubs and parties, and one night they invited her up to the microphone to sing. They liked her looks, her dancing, and her ability to improvise songs, and she quickly became an official Maniac. But there were problems because of Merchant's age. "Her mother hated us," Gustafson recounted for Anthony DeCurtis of *Rolling Stone.* "She thought we were having all these orgies and selling drugs. . .so [Merchant] used to have to sneak out of the house to come down to the bar at the Hotel Franklin to play. And her mother used to come down and drag her out . . . and yell at her and make her go home."

Despite such obstacles, Merchant and the other Maniacs gained a local following in western New York. They also put out two recordings on their own label—one extended-play disc in 1982 entitled "Human Conflict Number Five," and an album in 1983, *Secrets of the I Ching*. Both came about partially as projects of the sound-engineering program at the State University of New York at Fredonia, and the latter included protest songs like "My Mother the War" and "Grey Victory"—about the World War II atomic bombing of Hiroshima, Japan. The records received airplay on alternative and college radio stations, and drew praise and comparisons with the British folk group Fairport Convention from critics, but were commercial failures.

The band's luck began to change in 1983, when it came under the management of Peter Leak, an Englishman who got them their first British tour, and, in 1985, a contract with Elektra Records. Elektra tried to give the band a more New Wave look—"wanted to make us look like the Human League," guitarist Buck told DeCurtis. The image consultant that was called in wore leather and had "a samurai haircut," but gave up when he took his first look at 10,000 Maniacs. "He was really nice about it," recalled Buck. "He's going, 'I'm sorry. There's obviously nothing I can do for you. You people are hicks. The best thing you can do is accentuate the fact that you're hicks.' "

The Maniacs' first album for Elektra, *The Wishing Chair,* enjoyed little more commercial success than their previous efforts. Like the earlier recordings, however, it received some highly favorable reviews—for instance, Ira Robbins in *Rolling Stone* hailed it as "a thought-provoking, toe-tapping joy." Hoping to make the band's next album more salable, Elektra suggested Peter Asher as producer. Asher had produced records for many popular performers, most notably Linda Ronstadt, and during the 1960s had been half of the popular British duo, Peter and Gordon. The combination proved to be

Band formed in 1981, in Jamestown, N.Y.; original members include **Natalie Merchant** (born c. 1964; daughter of Tony and Ann [a secretary]; home: Jamestown, N.Y.), vocals; **Steve Gustafson** (born c. 1957; married), bass; **Jerry Augustyniak** (born c. 1959; home: Buffalo, N.Y.), drummer; **Dennis Drew** (born c. 1958), keyboardist; **Robert Buck** (born c. 1958; home: Albany, N.Y.), guitarist.

Became 10,000 Maniacs in 1981, after having such names as Still Life, and the Burn Victims; played in small clubs and recorded on their own label during the early 1980s; signed with Elektra in 1985.

Awards: A gold album for *In My Tribe.*

Addresses: *Manager*—Peter Leak. *Record company*—Elektra, 75 Rockefeller Plaza, New York, N.Y. 10019.

winning. The resulting disc, *In My Tribe,* spawned the group's first popular hit, "Like the Weather." But as *Rolling Stone* critic J. D. Considine pointed out in his review of the album, "this [was] no slick sellout." He added that "Asher should be applauded for the fact that he has allowed 10,000 Maniacs to remain themselves." Other songs, like the controversial cut about child abuse "What's the Matter Here," and a remake of Cat Stevens's "Peace Train," received airplay also. However, the group now refuses to play the latter song in concert, due to Stevens's support of the death threats to author Salman Rushdie. The band gained even more exposure when they opened a series of concerts for rock group R.E.M. Merchant explained 10,000 Maniacs' formula for success to *People*'s Steve Dougherty: "A lot of the songs are about really frightening subjects. But we hide them in nice little pop melodies, and it kind of lures people in."

That formula succeeded again with 1989's *Blind Man's*

Zoo. Again using Asher as producer, the Maniacs released an album labeled both "vitriolic" and "charming" by Leland. He and David Browne of *Rolling Stone* agree, however, that it is probably 10,000 Maniacs' best work. *Blind Man's Zoo* has brought the group two more hit singles—"Trouble Me," which Merchant wrote for her father while he was hospitalized, and "Eat for Two," which, in the words of *People* reviewer Andrew Abrahams, concerns "the darker side of deciding to bear a child." Other noteworthy songs from the disc include "Jubilee," a strike at religious fanatics, "The Big Parade," about a veteran of the Vietnam War, and "Hateful Hate," about the colonization of Africa.

Selected discography

Albums

Secrets of the I Ching (includes "My Mother the War" and "Grey Victory"), Christian Burial Music, 1983.
The Wishing Chair (includes "Among the Americans," "Maddox Table," "Can't Ignore the Train," and "Back o' the Moon"), Elektra, 1986.
In My Tribe (includes "Like the Weather," "What's the Matter Here?" "Peace Train," "Don't Talk," "Verdi Cries," and "Cherry Tree"), Elektra, 1987.
Blind Man's Zoo (includes "Trouble Me," "Eat for Two," "Jubilee," "The Big Parade," "Hateful Hate," "Please Forgive Us," "Dust Bowl," and "Poison in the Well"), Elektra, 1989.

Also released extended-play disc, "Human Conflict Number Five," Christian Burial Music, 1982.

Sources

People, May 23, 1988; July 3, 1989.
Rolling Stone, March 27, 1986; October 22, 1987; June 16, 1988; June 15, 1989; August 10, 1989.
Vogue, July 1989.

—*Elizabeth Thomas*

Timbuk 3

Pop/rock duo

Pat and Barbara MacDonald, better known as Timbuk 3, are "keen observers of American culture," according to reviewer Andrew Abrahams in *People* magazine. The couple—and their rhythm-providing boombox—burst on the music scene with their debut album *Greetings from Timbuk 3* in 1986. With a musical style that blends pop, rock, folk, country, and even funk, Timbuk 3 combines lyrics that can be "sarcastic, whimsical and unflinchingly emotional," in the words of *Rolling Stone* reporter Moira McCormick. The mixture won the approval of fans and critics alike, especially as embodied in the hit single, "The Future's So Bright, I Gotta Wear Shades," and the MacDonalds have released two subsequent albums, *Eden Alley* and *Edge of Allegiance*.

Barbara grew up in San Antonio, Texas, and Pat was raised in Green Bay, Wisconsin. They met in 1978 in Madison, Wisconsin, where Barbara was making preparations to attend the university there. Pat was a solo performer at a local club, and Barbara admired what McCormick described as "the intense young man's deft picking and pithy lyrics." They became friends, but the relationship soon deepened into love. In the following year, Barbara gave up bartending to become a solo performer in her own right. She recalled for McCormick:

"I'd play Fond du Lac, Pat'd play Green Bay. We'd meet at the Stretch Truck Stop on Highway 41 at 3:00 A.M., have some coffee and drive back home in tandem." Eventually each became involved in separate musical groups, he with the Essentials, she with Barbara K and the Cat's Away. After they married in 1982, Barbara left her group to join Pat and the Essentials.

But there were problems, and the band broke up, leaving the MacDonalds to their own devices. Actually, the couple saw this turn of events as an opportunity. "For Barbara and me," Pat explained to McCormick, "music was our whole life, but everybody else I've played with has been more casual. So we figured with just the two of us, we could achieve what we were going after." With just the two of them, however, the MacDonalds found it difficult to create the kind of sound they wanted; Pat finally came up with the idea of prerecording a rhythm track and playing it back on a boombox while they played acoustic guitars. Once they bought the proper equipment, they came up with the name Timbuk 3 and headed for New York City to try out their act as street musicians. After a week, they moved to Austin, Texas.

Fortunately, Timbuk 3 went quickly from performing on Austin's streets to performing in its nightclubs, including the Hole in the Wall and the Black Cat Lounge. At about this time they also managed to get a demo tape to Carl Grasso, of I.R.S. Records, who was in charge of finding new talent to feature on the MTV program, "The Cutting Edge." In 1985 the show featured Austin talent, including the MacDonalds, whose performance garnered them a recording contract with I.R.S. By the following year they had released *Greetings from Timbuk 3* and made a splash with what Steve Simels of *Stereo Review* hailed as "the world's first rockabilly ode to an undergraduate physics major"—"The Future's So Bright, I Gotta Wear Shades." Supposedly a song protesting the dangers of nuclear technology, many misinterpreted "Shades" as an upbeat, optimistic ditty. Pat MacDonald complained to a *People* reporter: "I thought my point was clear as a bell. The man in the song is naive and dangerous." Other cuts from *Greetings* included "Hairstyles and Attitudes" and "I Love You in the Strangest Way."

Though Richard C. Walls, reviewing in *High Fidelity,* asserted that Timbuk 3's 1988 second album, *Eden Alley,* "is just as inventive" as was *Greetings,* many critics deemed it something of a disappointment. It didn't yield any hits, but David Browne of *Rolling Stone* singled out the songs "A Sinful Life" and "Little People Make Big Mistakes" for praise, commenting that "husband and wife wrap their voices around each other's, spin off into solo parts and then converge like lovers" on the latter cut. In 1989 the MacDonalds released their third album, *Edge of Allegiance,* to better reviews. Andrew Abrahams of *People* voiced his approval, saying that "musically the duo gets a fuller sound" and lyrically "they've sharpened their satirical knives." *Edge of Allegiance* includes the hit, "National Holiday," which makes fun of patriotic celebrations like Independence Day and Memorial Day, and "B-Side of Life," which "both satirize[s] and lament[s] Joe Everyman who picks up his dinner at 7-Eleven," according to Abrahams.

But despite the often sarcastic bent of Timbuk 3's lyrics, which have tackled everything from television evangelists to homelessness, Walls noted the "essentially sympathetic quality" of the band's work. He claimed that their songs are more detailed than they are judg-

mental, and that their subdued delivery softens the bite of their satire. The MacDonalds' songs, Walls concluded, "can't fail to warm the cockles of any world-weary secular humanist's heart."

Selected discography

LPs

Greetings from Timbuk 3 (includes "The Future's So Bright, I Gotta Wear Shades," "Life Is Hard," "Hairstyles and Attitudes," "Facts about Cats," "I Need You," "Just Another Movie," and "I Love You in the Strangest Way"), I.R.S., 1986.
Eden Alley (includes "Eden Alley," "Easy," "Reverend Jack and His Roamin' Cadillac Church," "Sample the Dog," "Tarzan Was a Bluesman," "A Sinful Life," and "Little People Make Big Mistakes"), I.R.S., 1988.
Edge of Allegiance (includes "National Holiday," "B-Side of Life," "Standard White Jesus," and "Wheel of Fortune"), I.R.S., 1989.

Sources

High Fidelity, August, 1988.
Interview, March, 1987.
People, January 26, 1987; February 16, 1987.
Rolling Stone, November 6, 1986; August 11, 1988.
Stereo Review, January, 1987.
Texas Monthly, November, 1986.

—*Elizabeth Thomas*

Tone-Lōc

Rap artist

The best-selling pop single of all time is "We Are the World," the 1985 charity song that solicits aid for Africa's starving masses. The single that comes closest to matching that success, ironically, is about casual sex—a song that celebrates, in the words of its now-famous refrain, "doin' the wild thing."

"Wild Thing" is intoned by one Tone-Lōc, a young Los Angeles rap singer who has etched his name in pop-music history without really trying. (His name is a story in itself: "Tone-Lōc" is short for his "homeboy handle" Tony Loco, meaning "crazy" in Spanish; his real name is Tony Smith.) "Wild Thing" was recorded on a shoestring budget, on an eight-track tape machine in his coproducer's Hollywood apartment. With a drum machine supplying rap's characteristic boom, and sampled guitar riffs providing instrumentation, all Lōc had to do was lay down a simple rap in his inimitably sexy drawl. Largely through heavy exposure on MTV of the song's video, which was made for a mere $419.77, "Wild Thing" hit the bull's-eye, going multi-platinum within months of its late-1988 release. Suddenly Tone-Lōc was a star. With the subsequent release of his debut album, *Lōc-ed after Dark,* he became the first black rapper to hit the number-one spot on Billboard's pop-album charts—no small feat.

Smith was a preteen when the tuneless, rhyming, and intensely rhythmic music known as rap, or hip-hop, emerged in mid-seventies urban America. Born and raised in West Los Angeles, he was the youngest of three sons in a single-parent household—his father died when he was six—and, not surprisingly, took to hanging out on the streets, where the music was evolving. Too impatient for guitar lessons, he found the do-it-yourself immediacy of rap appealing.

At the age of thirteen he began rapping himself, over instrumental passages on records by the Ohio Players, Funkadelic, and other funk groups he admired. He also formed a rap trio called Triple A, which soon dissolved, but inspired him to continue inventing lyrics. Meanwhile, the L.A. street youth culture was fostering more than musical creativity for Smith: at one point, he began dipping into gang life, prompting his mother to enroll him at the exclusive Hollywood Professional School. After graduating from high school he formed a rap duo with a local record-scratcher named M-Walk. He enrolled in junior college, but soon dropped out to try his hand at real estate, buying houses that had been foreclosed by banks and repairing and reselling them at a good profit. All the while, he continued to rap.

For Tone-Lōc, rapping comes easily. "Some days you get out of bed and things go through your mind," he told *Time.* "Most people don't write these down, but I do." Of course, most people also don't have Smith's distinctive

Full name, Anthony Terrell Smith; born 1966 in Los Angeles, Calif.; father, James Smith, died in 1972, leaving Tony and his three older brothers to be raised by mother, Margaret, a retirement-home manager. *Education:* Hollywood Professional School, an exclusive private high school; attended junior college briefly.

In early teens, began rapping over instrumental passages of records; sang in Triple A, a short-lived rap trio. After high school, teamed up with L.A. scratcher M-Walk to form a local rap duo. Enrolled in junior college, but soon dropped out to work in real estate. Last day job: computer systems programming for Northrup Aerospace.

Musical influences: Parliament/Funkadelic (led by George Clinton), Bootsy's Rubber Band (led by William Collins), Sly and the Family Stone, Dazz, Led Zeppelin, the Bar-Kays, Rick James, early Prince.

Awards: Named "Best Rap Artist of the Year" at the 1989 Black Radio Exclusive convention.

Addresses: *Home*—Los Angeles, Calif. *Record company*—Delicious Vinyl, 7471 Melrose Avenue, Suite 25, Los Angeles, Calif. 90046.

vocal huskiness, a sound he acquired during a bout with strep throat when he was thirteen. His mother gave him hot tea with brandy; instead of soothing his throat, the mixture burned him. "The low-riding rasp Smith was left with gave the teenager a romantic edge and brought him one step closer to becoming Tone-Lōc," commented *Rolling Stone.* Years later, in August of 1987, Smith was heard by Matt Dike and Mike Ross, two entrepreneurs trying to establish a label called Delicious Vinyl. "Once [Ross and Dike] heard *the voice,* it was like, 'Oh, we gotta get that voice on wax,'" Smith related in *Rolling Stone.* "By scorching my throat, Mom gave me a career."

Before his rapping career took off, Smith worked as a computer systems programmer, a job that he recalls with fondness for its generous pay and minimal work. "I used to go in the corners underneath people's desks and go to sleep on the floor and shit," he bragged to *Musician.* "Yeah man. I used to kick it and get paid!" In a sense, this is the attitude he has brought to his latest career: despite the millions he's made so far from his debut album and national tour, he's far from single-minded about music. "Lōc doesn't have the passion, never mind the messianism, that is characteristic of

other rappers," wrote *Rolling Stone.* "He doesn't write his music, and the lyrics to his two best-known raps"—"Wild Thing" and "Funky Cold Medina"—were largely written by someone else."

Yet this is fine for Smith, who is the first to point out his lack of ambition. "I'm having fun," he told *People.* "I'm a natural celebrator. I can celebrate anything any day, any time." Aside from rapping, he's passionate about sports—he had hoped to make a career of soccer, until he injured an ankle—hunting, gun-collecting, and Yesca, his fourth pet pit bull (whose name is L.A. slang for "weed" in Spanish). "I really don't care about too many things," he told *Rolling Stone.* "People ask me, 'Do you have any advice?' Not really. . . . I got to have access to a vehicle and sunshine and women. Hey, that's it. That's life. What's left?"

Upon its release, *Lōc-ed after Dark* was described by *Spin* as being "full of bass whomp that soothingly rumbles the chest at high volumes." The music, though,

> *The subjects of Tone-Lōc's songs—himself and his pursuit of pleasure—appeal as readily to middle-class suburbanites as to inner-city street kids.*

was only part of the rumble. While many of the songs stormed the singles charts, the raciness of the lyrics sent a few waves through the industry and the public. At a time when youths are taught to "Just Say No" to drugs, "Cheeba Cheeba," a paean to marijuana smoking, was almost startling for its blatant pro-drug message. (Notably, there's no other pro-drug song in hip-hop.) "Funky Cold Medina," while less risky, is nevertheless in the same vein—as Smith told *Time,* it's about "a drink that gets you in the mood for the Wild Thing." Tone-Lōc's producers exercised some caution with "Wild Thing," hiring another rapper to write new lyrics after deeming the original set, written by Tone-Lōc, too filthy for airplay. Nevertheless, many radio programmers regarded the song's gleefully recounted sexcapades as inappropriate for an AIDS-ridden America. Some forty stations refused to play it, which prevented the record-selling single from rising above the number-two slot on the charts.

Still, those who find his lyrics offensive are in the minority: rather than alienating listeners, Lōc has broadened the rap audience. His success has helped both to weaken the New York monopoly on rap and to establish the West Coast school, long regarded as inferior, as a force to be reckoned with. "There's a whole other market now other than New York," Lōc told *Music Express*. "Sometimes the audience'll be all black people, and the next night it's all white. The L.A. rap scene is getting a little more respect now with good quality records."

The key to Tone-Lōc's popularity seems to be accessibility. Since its birth, rap has spoken primarily to the black urban lower class, often drumming up nationalist pride or venting frustration over racial injustices. Lōc's fare, on the other hand, bypasses social commentary. Laid-back and downright funny, his raps are pure entertainment, and the subjects of his songs—himself and his pursuit of pleasure—appeal as readily to middle-class suburbanites as to inner-city street kids. In addition, the music itself—a catchy blend of rap, pop, and metal—strikes a more accessible chord than the stark, hard-hitting groove of straight rap, which tends to alienate mainstream listeners. As *Rolling Stone* commented, Tone-Lōc has gone far in "making rap safe for pop radio." The only damper on his widespread appeal has come from critics and rap purists, who generally regard him as a sellout.

Detractors notwithstanding, Tone-Lōc's rise to the top has been a smooth one. Of course, smoothness is what he's mostly about. "I feel like I'm in a car full of gas, he told *USA Today*. "I'll just ride it through until it runs out. Then maybe I'll fill it up." Perhaps, he told *Musician*, he'll cut another album. "Then that's it. Tone'll go kick it somewhere, be in the house . . . I'll probably just get back into my real estate, buying foreclosures, fixin' 'em

up and selling 'em for an enormous profit." (According to *Rolling Stone*, there's only one concern that's pressing for him: "to star in a movie about his life, currently being planned, which he hopes will turn out like *Scarface* or *The Godfather*, his two favorite flicks.") Still, a continued career in music may be in the cards for Tone-Lōc after all. As the singer elusively remarked to the people at Delicious Vinyl, "I see the future as holding a lot of promises, all of which I will fulfill."

Selected discography

Lōc-ed after Dark (includes "On Fire," "Wild Thing," "Lōc'ed after Dark," "I Got It Goin' On," "Cutting Rhythms," "Funky Cold Medina," "Next Episode," "Cheeba Cheeba," "Don't Get Close," "Lōc'in on the Shaw," and "The Homies," Delicious Vinyl, 1989.)

Sources

BAM, April 21, 1989.
Details, May, 1989.
Music Express, March, 1989.
Musician, June, 1989.
New York Times, June 11, 1989; August 27, 1989.
People, March 20, 1989; May 8, 1989.
Rolling Stone, June 1, 1989.
Spin, June, 1989.
Time, March 27, 1989.
USA Today, February 13, 1989.
Yo!, August, 1989.

—Kyle Kevorkian

Peter Tosh

Singer, songwriter, guitarist

Jamaican-born singer-songwriter Peter Tosh was a "god of reggae," in the words of Harrison Tazwell Cook in *Seventeen*. He first came to the attention of music fans during the 1960s in tandem with other reggae greats, Bob Marley and Bunny Wailer; the three men were collectively billed as the Wailers. Tosh became better known on an international scale after launching a solo career in the mid-1970s. He will be remembered for the controversial political nature of his compositions which brought him into conflict with Jamaican authorities many times during the course of his career. Nevertheless, after he was killed in 1987, "the Jamaican government sought to give Tosh an official funeral," according to a reporter for *Jet,* in recognition of his contribution to his country's musical culture.

Tosh, who was born Winston Hubert MacIntosh, on October 19, 1944, formed the Wailers with Marley and Neville Livingston—a.k.a. Bunny Wailer—in 1963. Though the late Marley was then and probably is still better known than Tosh, as Cook explained, the latter "soon earned a title as the aggressor, the juvenile delinquent of reggae. This was due in part to his witty anti-government songs and his sharp, sarcastic voice. He soon became a name in his own right." Bill Beuttler in *down beat* confirmed that "Tosh wrote some of the Wailers' most political material, including "400 Years," "Stop That Train," and the anthemic "Get Up, Stand Up."

Apparently, Tosh's music became even more controversial after he broke with the Wailers in 1974. Even before the release of his first solo album, he was seized by police in Jamaica and severely beaten. The reason for the incident remains a mystery, but it inspired Tosh to record his first single, "Mark of the Beast," as a protest. The song was promptly banned from Jamaican radio. Also quickly banned was Tosh's "Legalize It," from his 1976 debut album of the same title. In this song Tosh promoted the legalization of marijuana; as a follower of the Rastafarian religion, according to Cook, he believed the substance brought a user closer to God. Despite the ban, "Legalize It" became a big seller for Tosh.

Though eventually the Jamaican government stopped banning his creations, Tosh continued getting into trouble. He smoked marijuana publicly during a 1978 concert in Kingston, Jamaica, and criticized Jamaican Prime Minister Michael Manley, a member of the audience, for not legalizing the drug. Later that year, possibly as a result of this incident, Tosh was arrested again and nearly beaten to death before being allowed to leave the police station.

At about the same time, Tosh became the second musical act after the Rolling Stones themselves to sign with the newly formed Rolling Stones Records. His association with the famed rock group increased his exposure—he opened for the Stones' U.S. concerts during the summer of 1978, and recorded a duet with lead singer Mick Jagger, a remake of the Temptations' hit "Don't Look Back." Tosh also appeared with Jagger on the television show "Saturday Night Live." Despite his growing popularity, however, Tosh did not waver from his commitment to political and social commentary in song. In 1981, he released what Cook termed his "greatest" album, *Wanted Dread and Alive,* a scathing criticism of political corruption and the condition of poor people. Just a month before his death, Tosh's peace-promoting *No Nuclear War* was released.

On the evening of September 11, 1987, Tosh was shot and killed in his home in St. Andrew, Jamaica, under mysterious circumstances. Apparently he and his girlfriend, who was wounded in the attack, knew at least one of their assailants personally. At first it appeared that robbery was the motive, but there has since been speculation that Tosh's death was a revenge killing, or that his murderer was involved in drug trafficking.

Selected discography

LPs

Legalize It, Virgin Records, 1976.
Equal Rights, Virgin Records, 1978.
Bush Doctor (includes "Don't Look Back"), Rolling Stones Records, 1978.
Mystic Man, Rolling Stones Records, 1979.
Wanted Dread and Alive, Rolling Stones Records, 1981.
No Nuclear War, EMI America, 1987.
The Toughest, Capitol, 1988.

Also recorded album *Mama Africa,* and the song "Mark of the Beast."

Sources

down beat, December 1987.
Jet, October 26, 1987.
Rolling Stone, October 22, 1987.
Seventeen, March 1988.

—*Elizabeth Thomas*

Tanya Tucker

Singer

Tanya Tucker, described as "the wildest filly in country and western music" by David Hutchings in *People,* began making an impact in her singing career when she was only thirteen years old. Her first single, "Delta Dawn," reached the top ten of the country charts soon after its release in 1972. Tucker has since proved that she was in no way a fluke or a short-lived child star with a long string of successful albums, several nominations for awards from the Country Music Association, and a list of hit songs that includes 1973's "What's Your Mama's Name?" and "Blood Red and Going Down," 1975's "Lizzie and the Rainman," and 1988's "Strong Enough to Bend." As Ralph Novak put it in his *People* review of the latter, "Somebody make some room on that list of good ole gals."

Tucker was born on October 10, 1958, in Seminole, Texas, the youngest of three children. Her father, Jesse "Bo" Tucker, was a heavy-equipment operator, and the family moved often as he sought better work. Tanya's early childhood was spent primarily in Wilcox, Arizona, where the only radio station in town played nothing but country music. The Tuckers also went to the concerts of country stars such as Ernest Tubb and Mel Tillis, and Tanya's older sister LaCosta was praised in the family for her vocal abilities. At the age of eight, Tanya told her father that she, too, wanted to be a country singer when she grew up.

Bo Tucker took his youngest daughter's ambition very seriously after she began to sing songs for him and, by the time she was ten, Tanya had begun to sing in talent shows in Phoenix, Arizona, where the family had recently moved. Though she didn't win anything, the experience helped her learn how to perform before live audiences. Even as early as this, Tucker cut demo tapes which her father took to Nashville, Tennessee, in hopes of impressing record producers, but when they learned that the singer Bo was trying to promote was his own daughter, most wrote Tanya off as just another child whose naturally biased parents thought she had talent.

Meanwhile, the Tuckers moved again, this time to Saint George, Utah, and there Tanya's mother, Juanita, took her daughter to audition for the film, *Jeremiah Johnson.* Tanya did not win the bigger role she tried out for, but she was hired as a bit player. At about this time she also got one of her first big musical breaks, due to the dedication of her father. He drove Tanya and the rest of the family all the way back to Phoenix for the Arizona State Fair, on the chance that the featured performer, country singer Judy Lynn, could use Tanya in her show. Tanya sang for the fair's entertainment people, and she went on to sing at the fair itself.

After the Arizona State Fair, the Tuckers were unsure of

For the Record. . .

Born October 10, 1958, in Seminole, Texas; daughter of Jesse "Bo" (a heavy equipment operator and music manager) and Juanita Tucker.

Solo recording artist and concert performer, 1972—; bit player in film *Jeremiah Johnson*, c. 1970.

Awards: Several nominations for awards from the Country Music Association; several gold and platinum albums.

Addresses: *Home*—Nashville, Tenn. *Record company*—Capitol Records, Inc., 1750 Vine, Hollywood, Calif. 90028.

the next step in the pursuit of Tanya's career. When Tanya was about twelve years old, the family decided to move to Las Vegas, Nevada, figuring that it was a good city for an entertainer to get started. There the young girl made more demo tapes, and Bo took them to music agent Dolores Fuller, who had been influential in the career of pop singer/songwriter Johnny Rivers. Fuller liked what she heard, and brought the tapes to the attention of Billy Sherrill, executive producer of Columbia Records in Nashville, who flew out to talk to the Tuckers in Las Vegas. After Tanya sang for Sherrill in person, he signed her to a contract.

Before Tanya Tucker had turned fourteen, she had become a major country sensation. "Delta Dawn," her first single—about a middle-aged woman who cannot forget the lover who abandoned her in her youth and wanders around Brownsville, Texas, looking for him—made critics rave over her surprisingly mature "throaty style," as Novak described it. Though Australian singer Helen Reddy's version of "Delta Dawn" dominated the pop charts, Tucker's version beat out others by country artists Kitty Wells, Waylon Jennings, and Bobby Bare to become by far the most popular with country audiences. Two other songs on *Delta Dawn* scored hits for the fledgling country crooner; "Jamestown Ferry" and "Love Is the Answer" also did well on the country charts. Tucker quickly followed these successes with her second album, *What's Your Mama's Name?* The title song describes the sad life of a man trying to find his illegitimate daughter, and another hit, "Blood Red and Going Down," portrays a husband hunting down his unfaithful wife and her lover and killing them. Reviewers noted the adult nature of the young singer's records; the title of her third hot-selling album

speaks for itself: *Would You Lay with Me (in a Field of Stone)*.

Though she continued to release hits, such as "San Antonio Stroll," "You've Got Me to Hold Onto," "Texas (When I Die)," and "Pecos Promenade," Tucker began to acquire a wild reputation as she grew up. She had begun drinking in her late teens, and she told Hutchings how it started: "You send your ass out on the road doing two gigs a night and after all that adoration go back to empty hotel rooms. Loneliness got me into it." In 1978, Tucker moved to Los Angeles, California, to try, unsuccessfully, to broaden her appeal to pop audiences, and was quickly captivated by the city's nightlife. She confessed to Hutchings that she "was the wildest thing out there. I could stay up longer, drink more and kick the biggest ass in town. I was on the ragged edge." The young woman also made gossip columns buzz with a series of romantic involvements. Her famous *amours* included country singer Merle Haggard, actor Don Johnson, the late pop-singer Andy Gibb, and—most

> *"I was the wildest thing out there. I could stay up longer, drink more and kick the biggest ass in town. I was on the ragged edge."*

notably—country and western star Glen Campbell, with whom she had a very stormy relationship and a hit duet, "Dream Lover."

Though she moved to Nashville after her breakup with Campbell in 1982 and began to lead a more secluded life, Tucker continued to drink and use cocaine. Finally, in 1988, her family confronted her and persuaded her to enter former First Lady Betty Ford's alcohol and drug addiction clinic. At first, Tucker admitted to Hutchings, she rebelled against her treatments, but after private counseling sessions she began to improve: "Yeah, I got help . . . I learned about the addictions. But mainly I saw a lot of people were worse off than I am, which made me feel lucky." Another lucky thing for Tucker in 1988 was her hit album, *Strong Enough to Bend*. The title track rose high on the country charts and earned her a nomination for Best Female Vocalist of the Year by the Country Music Association. Critics raved, including Novak, who praised the album as "resonant." "All I wanted was to make good music," Tucker summed for Hutchings.

Selected discography

LPs

Delta Dawn (includes "Delta Dawn," "Jamestown Ferry," and "Love Is the Answer"), Columbia, 1972.

What's Your Mama's Name? (includes "What's Your Mama's Name" and "Blood Red and Going Down"), Columbia, 1973.

Would You Lay with Me (in a Field of Stone?) (includes "Would You Lay with Me" and "The Man Who Turned My Mama On"), Columbia, 1974.

Tanya Tucker, MCA, 1974.

Lizzie and the Rainman (includes "Lizzie and the Rainman" and "San Antonio Stroll"), MCA, 1975.

Lovin' and Learnin' (includes "You've Got Me to Hold Onto"), MCA, 1976.

Ridin' Rainbows (includes "It's a Cowboy Lovin' Night"), 1977.

TNT (includes "Texas"), MCA, 1978.

Tear Me Apart, MCA, 1979.

Dreamlovers (includes "Dream Lover" and "Pecos Promenade"), MCA, 1980.

Girls Like Me (includes "I'll Come Back"), Capitol, 1986.

Love Me Like You Used to (includes "Love Me Like You Used to"), Capitol, 1987.

Strong Enough to Bend (includes "Strong Enough to Bend," "Back on My Feet," and "Daddy and Home"), Capitol, 1988.

Sources

Country Music, November/December 1986.

People, October 31, 1988; November 14, 1988.

—Elizabeth Thomas

Suzanne Vega

Singer, songwriter, guitarist

On ABC-TV's *Good Morning America,* Suzanne Vega marvelled that she could be a folk singer and still be successful. The singer-songwriter acoustic guitarist has been called neo-folk, new waif, and even unclassifiable. But Vega described her own style as a blend of jazz, rock and roll, and minimalism. "Like a journalist," Vega explained, she looks for a unique angle on life. The lyrics and music follow.

Vega was born in Santa Monica, California, but grew up in New York's Spanish Harlem. Her work was influenced by her Puerto Rican stepfather, who is a novelist, short-story writer, and teacher. Her mother, a computer analyst, was also musical. As the oldest of four children, Vega found herself entertaining her younger siblings with Woody Guthrie and Simon and Garfunkel-style tunes that she learned to play on her acoustic guitar on her own. "I missed the whole punk movement in New York because I babysat on Saturday Nights," she said in the *Los Angeles Times.*

But Vega didn't miss out on rock and roll, even though she didn't attend her first rock concert until she was twenty: a Lou Reed performance that made a profound mark on Vega's musical life. "Suddenly it hit me that I could write about things I had experienced without softening up the edges or apologizing for it or putting it in a nice package necessarily," recalled Vega in the *Los Angeles Times.* In 1986 she met Reed, who was aware of her progress. "Suzanne is one of the more articulate new songwriters," he stated in the *Village Voice.*

Vega began performing in Greenwich Village coffeehouses when she was sixteen. She'd already been songwriting for two years. Then, while working as a receptionist with a temporary agency, Vega met lawyer Ron Fierstein and musician Steve Addabbo, who were just putting together a partnership in music promotion. This led to a contract with the A&M label and to two hit albums.

Addabbo described Vega's musical style as "unbelievably simple, and yet it comes out sounding very complex," in *Guitar Player.* Vega calls her self-contained way of playing guitar "circular." She pares down to three or four chords she likes and sticks with them. She generally uses glue-on nails for stronger plucking.

Vega's talents don't stop with songwriting and performing. She has also studied dance since the age of nine. Vega studied ballet at New York's High School for the Performing Arts, the school in *Fame.* "I just had this feeling that I would never have the drive to make it out of the chorus," she confessed in *Rolling Stone.* But now that Vega is in the spotlight, she seems interested in reviving the part of herself that's a dancer. She's noted that ten years of her life were devoted to dance, then she became verbally oriented. "The dancer character is much more powerful, more eloquent in a way," she told *Rolling Stone.* Yet Vega does not move much on stage. Instead, she stands still and magnetizes the audience's attention. She has said she'd like to move around like Lou Reed but is too nervous when performing.

There's yet another intriguing side to Vega as well. Audiences "expect me to be like Joan Baez, to take on a political slant," she stated in the *Chicago Tribune,* "when I actually think the answers are more spiritual than political." And perhaps this spiritual base comes from the twice-daily chanting Vega does as a Nichiren Shoshu Buddhist.

Perhaps surprisingly, Vega appeals to a diverse range of listeners. Counted among her fans are New Age yuppies, folk singer aficionados in their thirties and forties, and young men "who look sincere and earnest with their notebooks and their Camus and their Sartre," reflected Vega in the *Los Angeles Times.* She concluded that her followers are made up of people who feel isolated and who come together at her concerts. She made it clear, however, that she doesn't see isolation, or solitude, as a negative state at all. This view, which is reflected in Vega's songs, particularly those on her second album, *Solitude Standing* (which sold over half a million copies within three months of its release in 1987), has generated a great deal of critical interest in her lyrics on the part of reviewers"

To promote *Solitude Standing* Vega toured the United States, Canada, Europe, and the Far East. The American tour included performances at Carnegie Hall and the Shubert Theater. She has been rewarded with a ranking in the *Billboard* Top 30 for the album. Vega's first album also met with surprising success. Called simply *Suzanne Vega,* the LP sold 200,000 copes in the United States and 500,000 abroad, where it reached double gold status. Her record company, A&M, had conservatively estimated sales of 30,000 albums. But Vega had become something of a cult figure. Her songs were played on campus radio stations. "She emerged as the strongest, most decisively shaped songwriting personality to come along in years," wrote John Rockwell in the *New York Times.*

Selected discography

Suzanne Vega (includes "Marlene on the Wall," "The Queen and the Soldier," "Small Blue Thing, " "Undertow," "Straight Lines," "Freeze Tag," "Some Journey," "Knight Moves," and "Neighborhood Girls"), A&M, 1985.
Solitude Standing (includes "Tom's Diner," "Luka," "Ironbound/ Fancy Poultry," "In the Eye," "Night Vision," "Solitude Standing," "Calypso," "Gypsy," "Language," "Wooden Horse [Caspar Hauser's Song]," and "Tom's Diner [Reprise]"), A&M, 1987.
Days of Open Hand (includes "Book of Dreams"), 1990.

Also contributor of song "Left of Center" to *Pretty in Pink* soundtrack album, 1986.

Sources

Chicago Tribune, July 12, 1987.
Guitar Player, October 1987.
Los Angeles Times, July 26, 1987.
Mademoiselle, August 1985.
Ms., April 1986.
New York, April 27, 1987.
Newsweek, August 3, 1987.
People, June 8, 1987.
Rolling Stone, July 4, 1985; June 4, 1987; June 18, 1987; March 22, 1990.
Washington Post, May 10, 1987.

—*Victoria France Charabati*

Jennifer Warnes

Singer

The career of vocalist Jennifer Warnes can be viewed in two distinct stages. She first came to public attention as a folksinger in the late 1960s, gaining important exposure as a regular feature of the television series "The Smothers Brothers Comedy Hour." After dropping out of music during the mid-1970s, however, Warnes resurfaced later in that decade as a country artist, scoring a huge success with the 1977 single, "The Right Time of the Night." She has since garnered a wider audience with her duet performances of popular film themes, such as those from *An Officer and a Gentleman* and *Dirty Dancing*. Warnes also won much critical acclaim by returning to her folk roots and recording an album of songs composed by Leonard Cohen, *Famous Blue Raincoat*.

Warnes was born in Orange County, California, in about 1947. She developed an interest in music early in life, and first sang in front of an audience when she was five years old. She also enjoyed acting, but she was so committed to Catholicism that she entered a convent when she graduated from high school. Apparently, however, Warnes discovered that she did not have a religious vocation; by the late 1960s she had landed an important part in a local production of the rock musical "Hair."

From there Warnes joined the cast of "The Smothers Brothers Comedy Hour" on the Columbian Broadcasting System's (CBS) television network; she was known to the viewers by her first name only. In addition to singing folk songs, she put her acting talent to use in some of the show's comedy skits. Because of her popularity with the television audience, Warnes was signed to a recording contract with Warner Brothers, and she put out several albums, including *See Me* and *Jennifer*. She also worked as a back-up singer for other artists, including Cohen.

While touring Europe with Cohen in 1972, Warnes's career began to deteriorate. She had angered Warner Brothers by turning down an opportunity to serve as pop star Neil Diamond's opening act in order to make Cohen's European tour, and the company dropped her from its roster of recording artists as a result. She returned to California to find that she had little money left from her previous work. Warnes had a further setback in 1974 when a longtime boyfriend, a cabdriver, was killed during a robbery. Following that personal tragedy, she retreated to a cabin in a quiet area near Carmel to sort out her feelings. Finally, as she told reporter Dennis Hunt in the *Los Angeles Times,* she "got bored," and "moved back to [Los Angeles] and put a band together and started putting my career back together again."

By 1977 Warnes had released a comeback album on the Arista label, titled simply *Jennifer Warnes*. Her music now had a flavor that was something of a cross between country and pop, and the formula worked well for her. She had a top-ten hit with the smash love ballad, "The Right Time of the Night," and scored with a follow-up from the same album, "I'm Dreaming." She toured the United States that year, and found that she was much more popular than she had ever been in the first stage of her career. Nevertheless, Warnes continued working as a back-up singer, working on the *Excitable Boy* album for rock artist Warren Zevon. She also did vocal arrangements for a 1979 Cohen album, and performed duets with him on some of its tracks.

Around the same period, Warnes began exploring a career avenue that would eventually yield some of her greatest hits—she recorded a theme song for the film *Norma Rae*. Though that particular theme did not attract much attention, her later romantic duet with rock star Joe Cocker, "Up Where We Belong," from the motion picture *An Officer and a Gentleman* received a great deal of radio airplay. Even more successful was her 1987 theme from the film *Dirty Dancing,* "The Time of My Life," which she performed with former Righteous

Brother Bill Medley. Warnes also sang one of the songs for the motion picture *Ragtime.*

Meanwhile, Warnes continued to release country-oriented albums. Her 1979 effort, *Shot Through the Heart,* pleased country fans and included a remake of "Don't Make Me Over" which became a hit in 1980. But her finest hour in the eyes of music critics came in 1986 when she recorded some of Cohen's songs. Having maintained a deep friendship with Cohen throughout her career, Warnes also held onto her desire to make an album of his work. The various companies with which she has recorded long discouraged the idea because they did not think it would be profitable, but finally Cypress, a smaller record label, provided her with the opportunity to fulfill her dream. The result, *Famous Blue Raincoat,* was heralded by Steve Pond of *Rolling Stone* as "a collection of some of the finest versions ever of Cohen's songs," and labeled "one of the year's most stirring recordings" by critic Alanna Nash in *Stereo Review.* Especially praised was Warnes's African-style rendition of Cohen's classic "Bird on a Wire," influenced by her interest in the South African folk group Ladysmith Black Mambazo. Cohen himself told Pond, "I always thought it was a country song, and when I heard the track without her vocal, I couldn't see it at all. But she was right: it is really, I think, a stunning treatment of the song." Nash also expressed appreciation for "Warnes's remarkable vocal ability," and her "intelligently sexy readings" of Cohen's work. Pond concluded that *Famous Blue Raincoat* was an excellent example of "resonant and often stirring adult pop music."

Selected discography

LPs

See Me, Warner Bros., 1970.
Jennifer, Warner Bros., c. 1971.
Jennifer Warnes (includes "The Right Time of the Night," "Love Hurts," "Daddy Don't Go," and "I'm Dreaming"), Arista, 1977.
Shot Through the Heart (includes "Don't Make Me Over"), Arista, 1979.
Famous Blue Raincoat (includes "Bird on a Wire," "Joan of Arc," "Song of Bernadette," and "First We Take Manhattan"), Cypress, 1986.

Also recorded singles "Up Where We Belong," with Joe Cocker, and "The Time of My Life," with Bill Medley.

Sources

Los Angeles Times, May 22, 1977.
People, November 24, 1986.
Rolling Stone, March 12, 1987.
Stereo Review, May 1987.

—Elizabeth Thomas

The Who

Rock group

The Who, with songwriter, guitarist, and keyboard player Pete Townshend, vocalist Roger Daltrey, bass player John Entwistle, and drummer Keith Moon, became one of the most enduring parts of the British invasion of the 1960s. With hits like "I Can't Explain" and "My Generation," the band became a symbol of the era's youth movement. They helped define and popularize the concept of the rock opera with the critically acclaimed "Tommy" and "Quadrophenia." Despite setbacks, such as the death of Moon and long dry spells during which the group was considered disbanded, the Who has managed to maintain its following, which has been augmented by the ranks of fans who were babies when the band first burst upon the music scene. As David Gates reported in *Newsweek*, "after the Beatles and the Stones, they're *it*."

The roots of the band that would become the Who grew early. Townshend, Daltrey, and Entwistle were school acquaintances during their adolescence in London, England. Particularly close were Townshend and Entwistle, who played together in a Dixieland band

Group became the Who in 1964; members included **Pete Townshend** (full name, Peter Dennis Blandford Townshend; born May 19, 1945, in London, England; son of Clifford [a musician] and Betty [a singer] Townshend, mother's maiden name: Dennis; married Karen Astley, 1968; children: Emma and Aminta), songwriter, guitarist, keyboard player; **Roger Daltrey** (born March 1, 1944, in London, England) vocalist; **John Entwistle** (born September 10, 1944 [one source says October 9, 1946] in London, England) bass player; **Keith Moon** (born August 23, 1946, in London, England; died September 7, 1978, in London, England) drummer; **Kenny Jones** (born September 16, 1949, in England) replaced Moon as drummer.

Entwistle, Daltrey, and Townshend performed in a group called the Detours, 1962; added Keith Moon and changed their name to the High Numbers, 1963; changed group name to the Who, 1964; drummer Keith Moon died, 1978; added Kenny Jones as drummer, 1979; group disbanded, c. 1983; reformed to appear at Live Aid, 1985; reformed with Simon Phillips replacing Jones, and Steve Bolton, for a reunion tour, 1989. Appeared in films, including *Tommy, Quadrophenia,* and *The Kids Are Alright.*

Awards: Many gold and platinum albums.

Addresses: *Home*—(Townshend) The Boathouse, Ranelagh Dr., Twickenham, TW1 1QZ, England. *Office*—(Townshend) c/o Entertainment Corporation of America, 99 Park Ave., 16th Floor, New York, N.Y. 10016-1502. *Record company*—Warner Brothers Records, Inc., 3300 Warner Blvd., Burbank, Calif. 91505.

when they were thirteen. Eventually they lost interest in that type of music and both became enamored of rock and roll, but while Townshend went to an art college, Entwistle joined a group called the Detours with Daltrey. When the Detours concluded that their guitarist was inadequate, Townshend was recruited. By 1962, they were one of the most popular attractions in London's small clubs.

In 1963, the Detours came under the management of Pete Meaden and Helmut Gordon, who changed the group's name to the High Numbers in hopes of appealing to England's new "Mod" youth culture—Mods valued psychedelic drugs, and it was hoped that "High" would be interpreted as a reference to intoxication. Also in keeping with the image, Meaden and Helmut decided that the band's thirty-five-year-old drummer

was too old to attract young fans and should be replaced. While in the throes of these changes, the High Numbers recorded an unsuccessful single, "I'm the Face." With the drumming question unresolved, they were playing at the Oldfield Hotel in Greenford when a drummer from a surf band asked if he could sit in with them for a few sets. The High Numbers and their managers liked what they heard, and Keith Moon joined the group.

Shortly afterwards, the High Numbers again came under new management, film directors Kit Lambert and Chris Stamp. Lambert and Stamp suggested yet another name change, and this one stuck. As the Who, the band attracted even more attention, gaining a reputation in London's clubs for violent stage antics like Townshend's now famous guitar-smashing and Daltrey's equally renowned twirling his microphone cord like a lariat. As for Moon, countless critics have described his manner with the drums as "attacking" or "destroying." Entwistle, perhaps for contrast, stood relatively still while playing his bass. By the end of the same year, 1964, the Who had also landed a recording contract

> *As David Gates reported in Newsweek, "after the Beatles and the Stones, they're it."*

with Decca Records (later MCA). Their first major single, "I Can't Explain," was released early in 1965. Though the disc was only moderately successful in the United States, it made the top ten of the British charts. A string of English hits followed, including 1965's "Anyway, Anyhow, Anywhere," and "My Generation," 1966's "The Kids Are Alright," and "Happy Jack," 1967's "I Can See for Miles," and 1968's "Magic Bus."

The Who gained important U.S. exposure with their appearances at the Monterey Pop Festival in 1967 and at Woodstock in 1969, and their following in the United States had been growing steadily since the release of "My Generation"; but their star did not really rise there until the advent of their rock opera, "Tommy." Townshend's story of "Tommy," a deaf, dumb, and blind boy who becomes both a phenomenal pinball player and a sort of messiah, changed the way rock music was perceived. The Who performed "Tommy" in serious opera houses all over the world, including the Royal Theatre of Copenhagen in Denmark, the Cologne Opera House in Germany, and the Champs Elysees Theatre in Paris, France. Their presentation of "Tommy" at the Metropolitan Opera House in New York City was judged one of the greatest rock concerts of all time by *Rolling Stone.* As the magazine concluded, the rock opera "directly challenged the cultural establishment's dismissal of rock as three-minute segments of cacophony."

In addition to gold albums, such as 1971's *Who's Next* and *Meaty Beaty Big and Bouncy,* the Who also created a second rock opera, which they released on the 1973 album, *Quadrophenia.* Like "Tommy," "Quadrophenia" was primarily written by Townshend and also eventually became a successful film; the latter creation centers on a member of the Mod culture named Jimmy, whose diverse character aspects reflect those of the Who's members. But the band was beginning to age—in fact, the theme behind 1975's *The Who by Numbers* was the question of whether older rock musicians could retain their relevancy.

The Who suffered its first major setback in 1978 when Keith Moon died of an overdose of an anti-alcoholism drug. Though Kenny Jones was enlisted to take over drumming duties, the band continued to have problems, including some close calls with drugs on Townshend's part. A 1979 concert in Cincinnati, Ohio, further lowered the Who's morale when eleven people were trampled to death in the crowd's rush to get to the seats. The group changed to Warner Brothers Records to release *Face Dances* in 1981 and *It's Hard* in 1982, but despite hits like "You Better You Bet," "Athena," and "Eminence Front," most of the Who's members felt these albums were not of consistent quality with their previous work. Townshend told *Rolling Stone* reporter Steve Pond: "I think the Who stopped two albums too late." Also, the group was never completely at ease with Jones's style of drumming, and missed Moon. As Townshend confided to Pond, "the fact of the matter is, there *is* a ghost. . . . There's the ghost of the void which is left when the person is gone." After a farewell tour that ended early in 1983, the Who disbanded.

The band reunited in 1985, however, to perform for Live Aid, the concert effort for Ethiopian famine relief. The Who came together again in 1989 for a reunion tour, despite the problems created by Townshend's debilitating tinnitus, a hearing problem probably caused by his many years of exposure to the high decibel levels of the group's music. For the 1989 tour, Townshend, Daltrey, and Entwistle were joined by drummer Simon

Phillips—who is said to recall Moon's energetic style—and guitarist Steve Bolton. Fred Goodman reported that "for most of [the tour's] shows . . . the Who rumbled and thundered with the authority of a freight train. . .the group brought an urge and verve to many of its warhorse anthems." The proceeds from two performances of "Tommy" benefited charities for autistic and abused children; the proceeds from another two concerts featuring the Who's hits over the years went to Special Olympics.

Selected discography

LPs

My Generation, Decca, 1966.
Happy Jack, MCA, 1966.
The Who Sell Out, Decca, 1967.
Magic Bus, Decca, 1968.
Tommy, Decca, 1969.
Live at Leeds, Decca, 1970.
Who's Next, Decca, 1971.
Meaty Beaty Big and Bouncy, Decca, 1971.
Quadrophenia, MCA, 1973.
Odds and Sods, MCA, 1974.
The Who by Numbers, MCA, 1975.
Who Are You, MCA, 1978.
The Kids Are Alright, Polydor, 1979.
Hooligans, MCA, 1981.
Face Dances, Warner Brothers, 1981.
It's Hard, Warner Brothers, 1982.

Sources

Books

Marsh, Dave, *Before I Get Old: The Story of the Who,* St. Martin's, 1983.

Periodicals

Newsweek, July 3, 1989.
Rolling Stone, June 4, 1987; July 13, 1989; August 10, 1989.

—*Elizabeth Thomas*

Jackie
Wilson

Singer

The late Jackie Wilson combined top quality vocals and a riveting stage presence to become one of the best known rhythm and blues performers of the 1950s and 1960s. A contributor to the *Rolling Stone Record Guide* notes that although many of Wilson's recordings suffer from "over-orchestrated arrangements, heavy-handed choral accompaniment and dubious song selection," still "the sheer power and virtuosity of Wilson's voice overcame many of the obstacles." With hits such as "Reet Petite," "Lonely Teardrops," "Whispers," and "(Your Love Keeps Lifting Me) Higher and Higher," Wilson assured his own success while he helped launch the pioneering Motown music corporation. Sadly, few of his live performances remain on tape, to the disappointment of r&b aficionados.

Jackie Wilson was born and raised in the same Detroit ghetto that produced Motown founder Berry Gordy, Jr. Like Gordy, Wilson donned boxing gloves at an early age and sought glory in the Golden Gloves championships. At sixteen he lied about his age and competed as an eighteen-year-old, winning his division. His mother, who feared for his health, forced him to quit boxing despite his success in the sport. He decided to seek a singing career instead, and after graduating from Highland Park High School, he went to work in local night clubs.

Soon Wilson was entertaining as a solo act and as part of Hank Ballard and the Midnighters. In 1953 he won a coveted position as lead singer with the Dominoes, an r&b group that had already recorded a string of hits. Wilson sang lead tenor for the Dominoes until 1957. That year he signed with the Brunswick label and began a solo career that would last almost two decades. Wilson's years with the Dominoes prepared him well for live performances, but he suffered from a lack of recordable material. He turned to his old friend Berry Gordy for advice and was provided with some songs Gordy had written himself.

Wilson's first solo hit was "Reet Petite," a Gordy tune. In 1958 he had his first number one r&b hit with another Gordy number, "Lonely Teardrops." By 1960 Wilson was a major star with a number of r&b and crossover chart-toppers, including "Doggin' Around" and "A Woman, A Lover, A Friend." Gordy used the royalties for his Wilson songs to found Motown, and Wilson used the songs to propel himself to fame. A handsome and frankly sexual performer onstage—music fans called him "Mr. Excitement"—Wilson quickly became a favorite among female fans. His appearance could whip crowds into hysteria, and he even received a serious gunshot wound from an unbalanced admirer.

Wilson was a regular on the charts through the mid-1960s, with songs such as "All My Love," "My Empty

Arms," "Baby Workout," and "You Better Know It." In 1966 he was matched with veteran producer Carl Davis, who engineered two of his biggest hits, "Whispers" and "(Your Love Keeps Lifting Me) Higher and Higher." Thereafter Wilson's career began to decline, and by 1972 he was playing the oldies circuit in casino lounges and dance clubs. Some critics have maintained that the Brunswick label did little to enhance Wilson's talents over the years, suggesting that he might have fared better if he had recorded elsewhere.

On the night of September 25, 1975, Wilson was headlining a Dick Clark Revue at the Latin Casino in Cherry Hill, New Jersey, a suburb of Philadelphia. Midway through his act he suffered a severe heart attack and collapsed. Although he lived another eight years he was a bedridden invalid, often semi-comatose and completely unable to care for himself. He died January 19, 1984, at a hospital in Mount Holly, New Jersey. Since his death, a number of his hits have been re-released by Epic, Columbia, and Rhino Records. *The Rolling Stone Record Guide* lists Wilson as a "performing genius" who "may have been the best pure vocalist of his generation."

Selected discography

Singles; released on Brunswick

"Reet Petite," 1957.
"To Be Loved," 1958.
"We Have Love," 1958.
"Lonely Teardrops," 1958.
"That's Why," 1959.
"I'll Be Satisfied," 1959.
"You Better Know It," 1959.
"Talk That Talk," 1959.

"Night," 1960.
"Doggin' Around," 1960.
"All My Love," 1960.
"A Woman, A Lover, A Friend," 1960.
"Alone At Last," 1960.
"Am I the Man?" 1960.
"My Empty Arms," 1961.
"Please Tell Me Why," 1961.
"I'm Comin' On Back to You," 1961.
"Years from Now," 1961.
"The Way I Am," 1961.
"The Greatest Hurt," 1961.
"Hearts," 1962.
"I Just Can't Help It," 1962.
"Baby Workout," 1963.
"Shake, Shake, Shake," 1963.
"Baby Get It," 1963.
"Squeeze Her-Tease Her," 1964.
"Danny Boy," 1965.
"No Pity (In the Naked City)," 1965.
"Whispers," 1966.
"I Don't Want To Lose You," 1967.

> *"Jackie Wilson was a performing genius who may have been the best pure vocalist of his time."*

"(Your Love Keeps Lifting Me) Higher and Higher," 1967.
"Since You Showed Me How To Be Happy," 1967.
"I Get the Sweetest Feeling," 1968.
"For Once in My Life," 1968.
"Let This Be a Letter (To My Baby)," 1970.
"This Love Is Real," 1970.
"Love Is Funny That Way," 1971.

LPs

Lonely Teardrops, Brunswick, 1958.
Doggin' Around, Brunswick, 1959.
So Much, Brunswick, 1960.
Jackie Wilson Sings the Blues, Brunswick, 1960.
My Golden Favorites, Brunswick, 1960.
A Woman, A Lover, A Friend, Brunswick, 1960.
You Ain't Heard Nothin' Yet, Brunswick, 1961.
By Special Request, Brunswick, 1961.
Body & Soul, Brunswick, 1962.
Baby Work Out, Brunswick, 1962.
Shake a Hand, Brunswick, 1962.
Something Else, Brunswick, 1964.

Spotlight, Brunswick, 1965.
Soul Galore, Brunswick, 1966.
Whispers, Brunswick, 1966.
Higher and Higher, Brunswick, 1967.
I Get the Sweetest Feeling, Brunswick, 1968.
It's All a Part of Love, Brunswick, 1971.
You Got Me Walking, Brunswick, 1973.
Jackie Wilson's Greatest Hits, Brunswick, 1973.
This Love Is Real, Brunswick, 1973.
Nobody But You, Brunswick, 1977.
The Jackie Wilson Story, Epic, 1984.
The Jackie Wilson Story, Volume 2, Epic, 1985.
Reet Petite—The Best of Jackie Wilson, Columbia, 1987.
Through the Years: A Collection of Rare Album Tracks and Single Sides, Rhino, 1987.
The Very Best of Jackie Wilson, Ace, 1987.

Sources

Books

Nite, Norm N., *Rock On,* Crowell, 1974.
The Rolling Stone Encyclopedia of Rock & Roll, Summit, 1983.
The Rolling Stone Record Guide, Random House, 1979.
Stambler, Irwin, *The Encyclopedia of Pop, Rock, and Soul,* revised edition, St. Martin's, 1989.

Periodicals

New York Times, January 21, 1984.

—*Anne Janette Johnson*

Subject Index

Volume numbers appear in **bold**.

Jones, John Paul
  See Led Zeppelin **1**
Kitaro **1**
Lamm, Robert
  See Chicago **3**
Lawry, John
  See Petra **3**
McDonald, Michael
  See The Doobie Brothers **3**
Metheny, Pat **2**
O'Donnell, Roger
  See The Cure **3**
Osmond, Donny **3**
Thompson, Porl
  See The Cure **3**
Tolhurst, Laurence
  See The Cure **3**
Wilson, Brian
  See The Beach Boys **1**
Winwood, Steve **2**
Wonder, Stevie **2**
Wood, Danny
  See New Kids on the Block **3**
Wright, Rick
  See Pink Floyd **2**

Latin Music
Blades, Ruben **2**
Estefan, Gloria **2**
Iglesias, Julio **2**
Los Lobos **2**
Ronstadt, Linda **2**
Santana, Carlos **1**

Mandolin
Crofts, Dash
  See Seals & Crofts **3**
Hartford, John **1**
Lindley, David **2**
Monroe, Bill **1**
Rosas, Cesar **2**
Seals, Jim
  See Seals & Crofts **3**

Minimalism
Glass, Philip **1**

Musical comedy
Pearl, Minnie **3**

Musicals
Bacharach, Burt **1**
Buckley, Betty **1**
Curry, Tim **3**
Hamlisch, Marvin **1**
Patinkin, Mandy **3**

Music Publishers
Acuff, Roy **2**

New Age
Ackerman, Will **3**
Hedges, Michael **3**
Jarre, Jean-Michel **2**
Kitaro **1**
Story, Liz **2**
Summers, Andy **3**

New Wave
Talking Heads **1**
Costello, Elvis **2**

Nortena
Los Lobos **2**

Opera
Cotrubas, Ileana **1**
Curry, Tim **3**
Domingo, Placido **1**
Pavarotti, Luciano **1**
Te Kanawa, Kiri **2**

von Karajan, Herbert **1**

Percussion
Adler, Steven
  See Guns n' Roses **2**
Allen, Rick
  See Def Leppard **3**
Augustyniak, Jerry
  See 10,000 Maniacs **3**
Beard, Frank
  See ZZ Top **2**
Best, Pete
  See The Beatles **2**
Bonham, John
  See Led Zeppelin **1**
Buck, Mike
  See The Fabulous Thunderbirds **1**
Christina, Fran
  See The Fabulous Thunderbirds **1**
Collins, Phil **2**
Crofts, Dash
  See Seals & Crofts **3**
De Oliveria, Laudir
  See Chicago **3**
Derosier, Michael
  See Heart **1**
Farriss, Jon
  See INXS **2**
Frantz, Chris
  See Talking Heads **1**
Gallup, Simon
  See The Cure **3**
Hartman, John
  See The Doobie Brothers **3**
Henley, Don **3**
Herndon, Mark
  See Alabama **1**
Hoffman, Guy
  See BoDeans **3**
Hossack, Michael
  See The Doobie Brothers **3**
Jones, Kenny
  See The Who **3**
Joyce, Mike
  See The Smiths **3**
Knudsen, Keith
  See The Doobie Brothers **3**
Kramer, Joey
  See Aerosmith **3**
Lee, Tommy
  See Mötley Crüe **1**
Lewis, Otis
  See The Fabulous Thunderbirds **1**
Mason, Nick
  See Pink Floyd **2**
McCracken, Chet
  See The Doobie Brothers **3**
Moon, Keith
  See The Who **3**
Mullen, Larry
  See U2 **2**
Perez, Louie
  See Los Lobos **2**
Seraphine, Daniel
  See Chicago **3**
Sheila E. **3**
Silva, Kenny Jo
  See The Beaver Brown Band **3**
Starr, Ringo
  See The Beatles **2**
Sweet, Robert
  See Stryper **2**
Watts, Charlie
  See The Rolling Stones **3**
Weaver, Louie
  See Petra **3**
Williams, Boris
  See The Cure **3**

Wilson, Dennis
  See The Beach Boys **1**

Performance Art
Anderson, Laurie **1**

Piano
Arrau, Claudio **1**
Bacharach, Burt **1**
Basie, Count **2**
Browne, Jackson **3**
Charles, Ray **1**
Clayderman, Richard **1**
Cleveland, James **1**
Cole, Nat King **3**
Cotoia, Robert
  See The Beaver Brown Band **3**
Crofts, Dash
  See Seals & Crofts **3**
Domino, Fats **1**
Drew, Dennis
  See 10,000 Maniacs **3**
Ellington, Duke **2**
Frey, Glenn **3**
Gibb, Maurice
  See The Bee Gees **3**
Glass, Philip **1**
Guaraldi, Vince **3**
Hamlisch, Marvin **1**
Hornsby, Bruce **3**
Horowitz, Vladimir **1**
Jarrett, Keith **1**
Joel, Billy **2**
John, Elton **3**
Lamm, Robert
  See Chicago **3**
Lennon, John
  See The Beatles **2**
Lewis, Jerry Lee **2**
Little Richard **1**
Manilow, Barry **2**
McCartney, Paul
  See The Beatles **2**
McDonald, Michael
  See The Doobie Brothers **3**
Milsap, Ronnie **2**
Mitchell, Joni **2**
Rich, Charlie **3**
Stevens, Cat **3**
Stewart, Ian
  See The Rolling Stones **3**
Story, Liz **2**
Waits, Tom **1**
Winwood, Steve **2**
Wonder, Stevie **2**
Wright, Rick
  See Pink Floyd **2**

Piccolo
Galway, James **3**

Pop
Abdul, Paula **3**
Adams, Bryan **2**
Aerosmith **3**
Bacharach, Burt **1**
The Beach Boys **1**
The Beatles **2**
The Beaver Brown Band **3**
The Bee Gees **3**
Bennett, Tony **2**
Berry, Chuck **1**
The Blues Brothers **3**
BoDeans **3**
Bowie, David **1**
Branigan, Laura **2**
Brickell, Edie **3**
Browne, Jackson **3**
Campbell, Glen **2**

Ferry, Bryan **1**
Fogerty, John **2**
Fox, Samantha **3**
Frampton, Peter **3**
Frey, Glenn **3**
  Also see The Eagles **3**
Gabriel, Peter **2**
Gift, Roland **3**
Grebenshikov, Boris **3**
Guns n' Roses **2**
Harrison, George **2**
  Also see The Beatles **2**
Hendrix, Jimi **2**
Henley, Don **3**
  Also see The Eagles **3**
Holly, Buddy **1**
Idol, Billy **3**
INXS **2**
James, Rick **2**
Jett, Joan **3**
Joel, Billy **2**
John, Elton **3**
Joplin, Janis **3**
Knopfler, Mark **3**
Led Zeppelin **1**
Lennon, Julian **2**
Lewis, Jerry Lee **2**
Lindley, Dave **2**
Little Richard **1**
Loggins, Kenny **3**
Los Lobos **2**
Marx, Richard **3**
Mellencamp, John "Cougar" **2**
Miller, Steve **2**
Morrison, Jim **3**
Morrison, Van **3**
Mötley Crüe **1**
Nelson, Rick **2**
Nicks, Stevie **2**
Nugent, Ted **2**
O'Connor, Sinead **3**
Orbison, Roy **2**
Osbourne, Ozzy **3**
Palmer, Robert **2**
Paul, Les **2**
Pink Floyd **2**
Plant, Robert **2**
  Also see Led Zeppelin **1**
Pop, Iggy **1**
Presley, Elvis **1**
Prince **1**
Raitt, Bonnie **3**
Reed, Lou **1**
Reid, Vernon **2**
Rich, Charlie **3**
Robertson, Robbie **2**
Rogers, Kenny **1**
The Rolling Stones **3**
Roth, David Lee **1**
Sheila E. **3**
Simon, Paul **1**
Smith, Patti **1**
The Smiths **3**
Stevens, Cat **3**
Stewart, Rod **2**
Sting **2**
Stryper **2**
Summers, Andy **3**
10,000 Maniacs **3**
Timbuk 3 **3**
Tosh, Peter **3**
Townshend, Pete **1**
  Also see The Who **3**
Turner, Tina **1**
U2 **2**
Vaughan, Stevie Ray **1**
The Who **3**
Wilson, Jackie **3**
Winwood, Steve **2**

Young, Neil **2**
Zappa, Frank **1**
ZZ Top **2**

Rockabilly
Holly, Buddy **1**
Nelson, Rick **2**
Presley, Elvis **1**
Robillard, Duke **2**
Watson, Doc **2**

Salsa
Blades, Ruben **2**

Saxophone
Antunes, Michael
  See The Beaver Brown Band **3**
Berlin, Steve
  See Los Lobos **2**
Carter, Benny **3**
Love, Mike
  See The Beach Boys **1**
Parazaider, Walter
  See Chicago **3**
Pengilly, Kirk
  See INXS **2**
Sanborn, David **1**

Songwriters
Ackerman, Will **3**
Acuff, Roy **2**
Adams, Bryan **2**
Anka, Paul **2**
Augustyniak, Jerry
  See 10,000 Maniacs **3**
Bacharach, Burt **1**
Baez, Joan **1**
Barrett, (Roger) Syd
  See Pink Floyd **2**
Basie, Count **2**
Beard, Frank
  See ZZ Top **2**
Berry, Chuck **1**
Blades, Ruben **2**
Bono
  See U2 **2**
Brickell, Edie **3**
Brown, James **2**
Browne, Jackson **3**
Buck, Robert **3**
Buckley, Betty **1**
Cafferty, John
  See The Beaver Brown Band **3**
Cash, Johnny **1**
Cash, Rosanne **2**
Cetera, Peter
  See Chicago **3**
Charles, Ray **1**
Childs, Toni **2**
Clapton, Eric **1**
Clark, Steve
  Def Leppard **3**
Clayton, Adam
  See U2 **2**
Cleveland, James **1**
Cohen, Leonard **3**
Cole, Nat King **3**
Collins, Phil **2**
Cooder, Ry **2**
Cooke, Sam **1**
Costello, Elvis **2**
Cougar, John(ny)
  See Mellencamp, John "Cougar" **2**
Croce, Jim **3**
Crofts, Dash
  See Seals & Crofts **3**
Crosby, David **3**
Denver, John **1**
Diamond, Neil **1**

Diddley, Bo **3**
Domino, Fats **2**
Drew, Dennis
  See 10,000 Maniacs **3**
Dylan, Bob **3**
The Edge
  See U2 **2**
Ellington, Duke **2**
Elliot, Joe
  See Def Leppard **3**
Everly, Don
  See The Everly Brothers **2**
Everly, Phil
  See The Everly Brothers **2**
Farriss, Andrew
  See INXS **2**
Felder, Don
  See The Eagles **3**
Ferry, Bryan **1**
Flatt, Lester **3**
Fogerty, John **2**
Frampton, Peter **3**
Franklin, Aretha **2**
Frey, Glenn **3**
  Also see The Eagles **3**
Gabriel, Peter **2**
Gibb, Barry
  See The Bee Gees **3**
Gibb, Maurice
  See The Bee Gees **3**
Gibb, Robin
  See The Bee Gees **3**
Gibbons, Billy
  See ZZ Top **2**
Gibson, Debbie **1**
Gift, Roland **3**
Gilmour, David
  See Pink Floyd **2**
Grebenshikov, Boris **3**
Griffith, Nanci **3**
Guthrie, Woodie **2**
Haggard, Merle **2**
Hamlisch, Marvin **1**
Harrison, George **2**
  Also see The Beatles **2**
Hartford, John **1**
Hartman, Bob
  See Petra **3**
Hedges, Michael **3**
Hendrix, Jimi **2**
Henley, Don **3**
  Also see The Eagles **3**
Hidalgo, David
  See Los Lobos **2**
Hill, Dusty
  See ZZ Top **2**
Holly, Buddy **1**
Hornsby, Bruce **3**
Hutchence, Michael
  See INXS **2**
Idol, Billy **3**
Iglesias, Julio **2**
Jackson, Freddie **3**
Jackson, Michael **1**
Jagger, Mick
  See The Rolling Stones **3**
James, Rick **2**
Jarreau, Al **1**
Jett, Joan **3**
Joel, Billy **2**
John, Elton **3**
Johnston, Tom
  See The Doobie Brothers **3**
Jones, Brian
  See The Rolling Stones **3**
Jones, Quincy **2**
Joplin, Janis **3**
Judd, Naomi
  See The Judds **2**

King, Albert **2**
King, B.B. **1**
Knopfler, Mark **3**
Lamm, Robert
   See Chicago **3**
Leadon, Bernie
   See The Eagles **3**
Lennon, John
   See The Beatles **2**
Lennon, Julian **2**
Lightfoot, Gordon **3**
Little Richard **1**
Llanas, Sammy
   See BoDeans **3**
Loggins, Kenny **3**
Loughnane, Lee
   See Chicago **3**
Lynn, Loretta **2**
MacDonald, Barbara
   See Timbuk 3 **3**
MacDonald, Pat
   See Timbuk 3 **3**
Manilow, Barry **2**
Marley, Bob **3**
Marley, Ziggy **3**
Marx, Richard **3**
McCartney, Paul
   See The Beatles **2**
McDonald, Michael
   See The Doobie Brothers **3**
Medley, Bill **3**
Meisner, Randy
   See The Eagles **3**
Mellencamp, John "Cougar" **2**
Merchant, Natalie
   See 10,000 Maniacs **3**
Miller, Steve **2**
Milsap, Ronnie **2**
Mitchell, Joni **2**
Morrison, Jim **3**
Morrison, Van **3**
Mullen, Larry
   See U2 **2**
Near, Holly **1**
Nelson, Rick **2**
Nelson, Willie **1**
Newmann, Kurt
   See BoDeans **3**
Nicks, Stevie **2**
Nugent, Ted **2**
O'Connor, Sinead **3**
Orbison, Roy **2**
Osbourne, Ozzy **3**
Oslin, K.T. **3**
Owens, Buck **2**
Palmer, Robert **2**
Pankow, James
   See Chicago **3**
Parton, Dolly **2**
Paul, Les **2**
Perez, Louie
   See Los Lobos **2**
Perry, Joe
   See Aerosmith **3**

Plant, Robert **2**
   Also see Led Zeppelin **1**
Pop, Iggy **1**
Presley, Elvis **1**
Prince **1**
Raitt, Bonnie **3**
Ray, Amy
   See Indigo Girls **3**
Reed, Lou **1**
Reid, Vernon **2**
Rich, Charlie **3**
Richard, Keith
   See The Rolling Stones **3**
Richie, Lionel **2**
Robertson, Robbie **2**
Robillard, Duke **2**
Robinson, Smokey **1**
Rodgers, Jimmie **3**
Roth, David Lee **1**
Sade **2**
Saliers, Emily
   See Indigo Girls **3**
Schmit, Timothy B.
   See The Eagles **3**
Scruggs, Earl **3**
Seals, Jim
   See Seals & Crofts **3**
Seraphine, Daniel
   See Chicago **3**
Sheila E. **3**
Simmons, Patrick
   See The Doobie Brothers **3**
Simon, Paul **1**
Smith, Patti **1**
Smith, Robert
   See The Cure **3**
Starr, Ringo
   See The Beatles **2**
Stevens, Cat **3**
Stewart, Rod **2**
Sting **2**
Streisand, Barbra **2**
Summers, Andy **3**
Taylor, Mick
   See The Rolling Stones **3**
Taylor, James **2**
Tone-Lōc **3**
Tosh, Peter **3**
Townshend, Pete **1**
   Also see The Who **3**
Tyler, Steve
   See Aerosmith **3**
Vandross, Luther **2**
Vega, Suzanne **3**
Vox, Bono
   See U2 **2**
Waits, Tom **1**
Walsh, Joe
   See The Eagles **3**
Waters, Roger
   See Pink Floyd **2**
Watts, Charlie
   See The Rolling Stones **3**
Williams, Deniece **1**
Williams, Hank Jr. **1**

Willis, Pete
   See Def Leppard **3**
Wilson, Brian
   See The Beach Boys **1**
Winwood, Steve **2**
Wonder, Stevie **2**
Wood, Ron
   See The Rolling Stones **3**
Wyman, Bill
   See The Rolling Stones **3**
Wynette, Tammy **2**
Yoakam, Dwight **1**
Young, Neil **2**
Zappa, Frank **1**

Soul
The Blues Brothers **3**
Brown, James **2**
Charles, Ray **1**
Cooke, Sam **1**
Franklin, Aretha **2**
Jackson, Freddie **3**
Knight, Gladys **1**
Little Richard **1**
Medley, Bill **3**
Morrison, Van **3**
Pendergrass, Teddy **3**
Reid, Vernon **2**
Robinson, Smokey **1**
Ross, Diana **1**
The Temptations **3**
Vandross, Luther **2**
Wilson, Jackie **3**
Wonder, Stevie **2**

Trombone
Pankow, James
   See Chicago **3**

Trumpet
Berigan, Bunny **2**
Bumpus, Cornelius
   See Chicago **3**
Davis, Miles **1**
Jones, Quincy **2**
Loughnane, Lee **3**
Severinsen, Doc **1**

Tuba
Phillips, Harvey **3**

Violin
Acuff, Roy **2**
Anderson, Laurie **1**
Hartford, John **1**
Hidalgo, David
   See Los Lobos **2**
Lindley, David **2**
McFee, John
   See The Doobie Brothers **3**
O'Connor, Mark **1**
Perlman, Itzhak **2**
Salerno-Sonnenberg, Nadja **3**
Seals, Jim
   See Seals & Crofts **3**

Musicians Index

Volume numbers appear in **bold.**

Abdul, Paula **3**
Ackerman, Will **3**
Acuff, Roy **2**
Adams, Bryan **2**
Adler, Steven
  See Guns n' Roses
Aerosmith **3**
Alabama **1**
Allen, Rick
  See Def Leppard
Anderson, Laurie **1**
Anka, Paul **2**
Antunes, Michael
  See The Beaver Brown Band
Arrau, Claudio **1**
Augustyniak, Jerry
  See 10,000 Maniacs
Aykroyd, Dan
  See The Blues Brothers
Bacharach, Burt **1**
Baez, Joan **1**
Barnwell, Ysaye Maria
  See Sweet Honey in the Rock
Barrett, (Roger) Syd
  See Pink Floyd
Barton, Lou Ann
  See The Fabulous Thunderbirds
Basie, Count **2**
Baxter, Jeff
  See The Doobie Brothers
The Beach Boys **1**
Beard, Frank
  See ZZ Top
The Beatles **2**
  Also see Harrison, George
The Beaver Brown Band **3**
The Bee Gees **3**
Beers, Garry Gary
  See INXS
Belushi, John
  See The Blues Brothers
Bennett, Tony **2**
Berigan, Bunny **2**
Berlin, Steve
  See Los Lobos
Bernstein, Leonard **2**
Berry, Chuck **1**
Best, Pete
  See The Beatles
Blades, Ruben **2**
The Blues Brothers **3**
Blues, Elwood
  See The Blues Brothers
Blues, "Joliet" Jake
  See The Blues Brothers
BoDeans **3**
Bolade, Nitanju
  See Sweet Honey in the Rock
Bonham, John
  See Led Zeppelin
Bono
  See U2
Bowie, David **1**
Branigan, Laura **2**
Brickell, Edie **3**
Brown, James **2**
Browne, Jackson **3**
Bryant, Elbridge
  See The Temptations
Buck, Mike

  See The Fabulous Thunderbirds
Buck, Robert
  See 10,000 Maniacs
Buckley, Betty **1**
Bumpus, Cornelius
  See The Doobie Brothers
Byrne, David
  See Talking Heads
Cafferty, John
  See The Beaver Brown Band
Campbell, Glen **2**
Carter, Anita
  See The Carter Family
Carter, A.P.
  See The Carter Family
Carter, Benny **3**
The Carter Family **3**
Carter, Helen
  See The Carter Family
Carter, Janette
  See The Carter Family
Carter, Joe
  See The Carter Family
Carter, June
  See The Carter Family
Carter, Maybell
  See The Carter Family
Carter, Sara
  See The Carter Family
Cash, Johnny **1**
Cash, Rosanne **2**
Cates, Ronny
  See Petra
Cetera, Peter
  See Chicago
Chapman, Tony
  See The Rolling Stones
Charles, Ray **1**
Cher **1**
Chicago **3**
Childs, Toni **2**
Christina, Fran
  See The Fabulous Thunderbirds
Clapton, Eric **1**
Clark, Dick **2**
Clark, Roy **1**
Clark, Steve
  See Def Leppard
Clarke, Stanley **3**
Clayderman, Richard **1**
Clayton, Adam
  See U2
Cleveland, James **1**
Cohen, Leonard **3**
Cole, Nat King **3**
Cole, Natalie **1**
Collin, Phil
  See Def Leppard
Collins, Phil **2**
Cooder, Ry **2**
Cook, Jeff
  See Alabama
Cooke, Sam **1**
Copland, Aaron **2**
Costello, Elvis **2**
Cotoia, Robert
  See The Beaver Brown Band
Cotrubas, Ileana **1**
Cougar, John(ny)
  See Mellencamp, John "Cougar"

Croce, Jim **3**
Crofts, Dash
  See Seals & Crofts
Crosby, David **3**
The Cure **3**
Curry, Tim **3**
Dacus, Donnie
  See Chicago
Daltrey, Roger **3**
  Also see The Who
D'Arby, Terence Trent **3**
Davis, Miles **1**
Def Leppard **3**
de Lucia, Paco **1**
Dempsey, Michael
  See The Cure
Denver, John **1**
De Oliveria, Laudir
  See Chicago
Derosier, Michael
  See Heart
Diamond, Neil **1**
Diddley, Bo **3**
Domingo, Placido **1**
Domino, Fats **2**
The Doobie Brothers **3**
Drew, Dennis
  See 10,000 Maniacs
Dylan, Bob **3**
E., Sheila
  See Sheila E.
The Eagles **3**
  Also see Frey, Glenn
  Also see Henley, Don
Easton, Sheena **2**
Eckstine, Billy **1**
The Edge
  See U2
Edwards, Dennis
  See The Temptations
Ellington, Duke **2**
Elliot, Joe
  See Def Leppard
Entwistle, John
  See The Who
Estefan, Gloria **2**
Evans, Dave
  See U2
The Everly Brothers **2**
Everly, Don
  See The Everly Brothers
Everly, Phil
  See The Everly Brothers
The Fabulous Thunderbirds **1**
Farriss, Andrew
  See INXS
Farriss, Jon
  See INXS
Farriss, Tim
  See INXS
Felder, Don
  See The Eagles
Ferguson, Keith
  See The Fabulous Thunderbirds
Ferry, Bryan **1**
Fisher, Roger
  See Heart
Fitzgerald, Ella **1**
Flatt, Lester **3**
Fogerty, John **2**

Mitchell, Joni **2**
Monk, Meredith **1**
Monroe, Bill **1**
Montgomery, Wes **3**
Moon, Keith
  See The Who
Morrison, Jim **3**
Morrison, Van **3**
Morrissey, Patrick
  See The Smiths
Mötley Crüe **1**
Mullen, Larry
  See U2
Mwelase, Jabulane
  See Ladysmith Black Mambazo
Near, Holly **1**
Neil, Vince
  See Mötley Crüe
Nelson, Rick **2**
Nelson, Willie **1**
New Kids on the Block **3**
Newmann, Kurt
  See BoDeans
Newton, Wayne **2**
Nicks, Stevie **2**
Nugent, Ted **2**
O'Connor, Mark **1**
O'Connor, Sinead **3**
O'Donnell, Roger
  See The Cure
Orbison, Roy **2**
Osbourne, Ozzy **3**
Oslin, K.T. **3**
Osmond, Donny **3**
Ott, David **2**
Owen, Randy
  See Alabama
Owens, Buck **2**
Owens, Ricky
  See The Temptations
Page, Jimmy
  See Led Zeppelin
Palmer, Robert **2**
Pankow, James
  See Chicago
Parazaider, Walter
  See Chicago
Parton, Dolly **2**
Patinkin, Mandy **3**
Paul, Les **2**
Pavarotti, Luciano **1**
Pearl, Minnie **3**
Pendergrass, Teddy **3**
Pengilly, Kirk
  See INXS
Perez, Louie
  See Los Lobos
Perlman, Itzhak **2**
Petra **3**
Phillips, Harvey **3**
Phungula, Inos
  See Ladysmith Black Mambazo
Pink Floyd **2**
Perry, Joe
  See Aerosmith
Plant, Robert **2**
    Also see Led Zeppelin
Pop, Iggy **1**
Porter, Tiran
  See The Doobie Brothers
Presley, Elvis **1**
Price, Louis
  See The Temptations
Prince **1**
Raitt, Bonnie **3**
Ray, Amy
  See Indigo Girls
Reagon, Bernice Johnson
  See Sweet Honey in the Rock

Redpath, Jean **1**
Reed, Lou **1**
Reid, Vernon **2**
Rich, Charlie **3**
Richard, Keith
  See The Rolling Stones
Richie, Lionel **2**
Robertson, Robbie **2**
Robillard, Duke **2**
Robinson, Smokey **1**
Rodgers, Jimmie **3**
Rogers, Kenny **1**
The Rolling Stones **3**
Ronstadt, Linda **2**
Rosas, Cesar
  See Los Lobos
Rose, Axl
  See Guns n' Roses
Ross, Diana **1**
Roth, David Lee **1**
Rourke, Andy
  See The Smiths
Ruffin, David
  See The Temptations
Sade **2**
Salerno-Sonnenberg, Nadja **3**
Saliers, Emily
  See Indigo Girls
Sanborn, David **1**
Santana, Carlos **1**
Savage, Rick
  See Def Leppard
Schlitt, John
  See Petra
Schmit, Timothy B.
  See The Eagles
Scruggs, Earl **3**
Seals & Crofts **3**
Seals, Jim
  See Seals & Crofts
Seraphine, Daniel
  See Chicago
Severinsen, Doc **1**
Shabalala, Ben
  See Ladysmith Black Mambazo
Shabalala, Headman
  See Ladysmith Black Mambazo
Shabalala, Jockey
  See Ladysmith Black Mambazo
Shabalala, Joseph
  See Ladysmith Black Mambazo
Sheila E. **3**
Shogren, Dave
  See The Doobie Brothers
Silva, Kenny Jo
  See The Beaver Brown Band
Simmons, Patrick
  See The Doobie Brothers
Simon, Paul **1**
Sinatra, Frank **1**
Sixx, Nikki
  See Mötley Crüe
Slash
  See Guns n' Roses
Smith, Bessie **3**
Smith, Patti **1**
Smith, Robert
  See The Cure
The Smiths **3**
Sonnenberg, Nadja Salerno
  See Salerno-Sonnenberg, Nadja
Sosa, Mercedes **3**
Starr, Ringo
  See The Beatles
Stevens, Cat **3**
Stewart, Ian
  See The Rolling Stones
Stewart, Rod **2**
Sting **2**

Story, Liz **2**
Stradlin, Izzy
  See Guns n' Roses
Street, Richard
  See The Temptations
Streisand, Barbra **2**
Stryper **2**
Summers, Andy **3**
Sutcliffe, Stu
  See The Beatles
Sweet, Michael
  See Stryper
Sweet, Robert
  See Stryper
Sweet Honey in the Rock **1**
Talking Heads **1**
Taylor, Dick
  See The Rolling Stones
Taylor, James **2**
Taylor, Mick
  See The Rolling Stones
Te Kanawa, Kiri **2**
The Temptations **3**
10,000 Maniacs **3**
Thompson, Porl
  Scc The Cure
Timbuk 3 **3**
Tolhurst, Laurence
  See The Cure
Tone-Lōc **3**
Tosh, Peter **3**
Townshend, Pete **1**
    Also see The Who
Tucker, Tanya **3**
Turner, Tina **1**
Tyler, Steve
  See Aerosmith
Tyson, Ron
  See The Temptations
U2 **2**
Vandross, Luther **2**
Vaughan, Jimmie
  See The Fabulous Thunderbirds
Vaughan, Sarah **2**
Vaughan, Stevie Ray **1**
Vega, Suzanne **3**
Volz, Greg
  See Petra
von Karajan, Herbert **1**
Vox, Bono
  See U2
Wahlberg, Donnie
  See New Kids on the Block
Waits, Tom **1**
Walsh, Joe
  See The Eagles
Warnes, Jennifer **3**
Warwick, Dionne **2**
Waters, Roger
  See Pink Floyd
Watson, Doc **2**
Watts, Charlie
  See The Rolling Stones
Weaver, Louie
  See Petra
Weymouth, Tina
  See Talking Heads
Whitford, Brad
  See Aerosmith
The Who **3**
  Also see Daltrey, Roger
  Also see Townshend, Pete
Williams, Andy **2**
Williams, Boris
  See The Cure
Williams, Deniece **1**
Williams, Hank Jr. **1**
Williams, Otis
  See The Temptations